Leicester–Nottingham Studies in Ancient Society
Volume 6

HUMAN LANDSCAPES IN CLASSICAL ANTIQUITY

HUMAN LANDSCAPES IN CLASSICAL ANTIQUITY

Environment and Culture

Edited by

GRAHAM SHIPLEY and JOHN SALMON

London and New York

First published 1996
by Routledge
11 New Fetter Lane, London EC4P 4EE

Simultaneously published in the USA and Canada
by Routledge
29 West 35th Street, New York, NY 10001

Routledge is an International Thomson Publishing company

Typeset in Times by
Florencetype Ltd, Stoodleigh, Devon

Printed and bound in Great Britain by
Biddles Ltd, Guildford and King's Lynn

British Library Cataloguing in Publication Data
A catalogue record for this book is available
from the British Library

Library of Congress Cataloguing in Publication Data
Human landscapes in classical antiquity: environment and culture/
    edited by John Salmon and Graham Shipley.
        p.   cm – (Leicester–Nottingham studies in ancient society: v. 6)
        Includes bibliographical references and index.
        ISBN 0–415–10755–5
        1. Greece – Civilization.   2. Rome – Civilization   3. Ecology –
    Greece – History.   4. Ecology – Rome – History.   5. Human
    ecology – Greece – History.   6. Human ecology – Rome – History.
    7. Landscape – Greece – History.   8. Landscape – Rome – History.
    I. Salmon, J. B.   II. Shipley, Graham.   III. Series.
    DE61.E25H85   1996
    304.2′0938 – dc20   95–35216
                                                                      CIP

Contents

Figures

Contributors

Mary Beagon is Lecturer in Ancient History at the University of Manchester.

Neil Christie is Lecturer in Medieval Archaeology at the University of Leicester.

Gillian Clark is Senior Lecturer in Classics at the University of Liverpool.

Catherine Delano Smith was formerly Reader in Historical Geography at the University of Nottingham, and is now a Research Fellow of the Institute of Historical Research, University of London.

Hamish Forbes is Lecturer in Archaeology at the University of Nottingham.

Lin Foxhall is Lecturer in Ancient History at the University of Leicester.

Robin Lane Fox is Fellow and Tutor in Ancient History at New College, Oxford, and a University Lecturer in Ancient History.

David J. Mattingly is Reader in Roman Archaeology at the University of Leicester.

Nicholas Purcell is Fellow and Tutor in Ancient History at St John's College, Oxford, and a University Lecturer in Ancient History.

Oliver Rackham is a Fellow of Corpus Christi College, Cambridge.

Jim Roy is Senior Lecturer in Ancient History at the University of Nottingham.

John Salmon is Senior Lecturer in Ancient History at the University of Nottingham.

Graham Shipley is Lecturer in Ancient History and Head of the Ancient History Division at the University of Leicester.

Preface

Like the earlier volumes in this series, the chapters of this book are revised versions of papers originally presented at the Leicester–Nottingham Ancient History Seminar. 'Nature Matters: Approaches to the Ecology of Antiquity' was the theme of a two-year series of meetings held in Leicester and Nottingham between October 1991 and May 1993.

We are once again grateful to all participants in the seminars, both colleagues old and new in Leicester and Nottingham and those who joined the audience, often travelling from long distances; many of them came from non-classical departments, and their contribution was especially valued. We particularly thank all those who presented papers; regrettably, considerations of space prevented us from publishing all those we would have liked to. Once again we thank those present and former colleagues who read and commented extensively on earlier drafts of the published papers.

We are grateful as always to Adrienne Edwards (Nottingham) and Janet Bradford (Leicester) for invaluable secretarial assistance, to the catering and library staff of both universities, and to the Audio-Visual Service at Leicester. Mary Harlow gave generously of her time to assist the practical organization of the Leicester meetings. The editorial staff at Routledge, particularly Richard Stoneman and Victoria Peters, deserve our thanks for initial encouragement to proceed, and have awaited delivery of the volume with their customary blend of firmness and forbearance. Thanks are also due to the copy-editor, Janet Tyrrell.

The success of the Leicester–Nottingham series owes much to the continuing support of the Research and Publications Committee of the School of Archaeological Studies at Leicester, and of the staff and successive heads of the Department of Classical and Archaeological Studies (now constituted as the Departments of Classics and Archaeology) at Nottingham.

The series is now recognized as an established forum for the concentrated exploration of new and important themes in the study of ancient societies, particularly issues involving a collaboration between ancient history and archaeology, and we are proud to be associated with it.

May 1995   *Graham Shipley*
                                                        John Salmon

It was with great sadness that we learned that our Routledge desk-editor, Joanne Snooks, who oversaw the volume in the later stages of its production, died shortly before it went to press. We are grateful for her efforts and trust that the book may be in some measure a fitting tribute to her memory.

Note on transliteration of Greek

Where there is a well-established English form of an ancient name (e.g. Athens, Corinth), it is generally used. For other names, Greek-like forms are used (e.g. Theophrastos, Pindos, Elektra, Hippolytos), except for some well-established names of literary works (e.g. *Oedipus Rex*, *Bacchae*). In transliterated Greek, eta is sometimes represented by $\hat{e}$ and omega by $\hat{o}$.

Abbreviations

The names of ancient authors and their works are generally abbreviated using the forms used in *The Oxford Classical Dictionary*, 2nd edn (ed. N. G. L. Hammond and H. H. Scullard; Oxford, 1970). Exceptions:

Cato, *RR*	Cato, *De re rustica* (*De agri cultura*)
Columella, *RR*	Columella, *De re rustica*
Varro, *RR*	Varro, *De re rustica*
Xen. *Kyn.*	Xenophon, *Kynegetikos* (*The Hunting Man* or *The Huntsman*)
Xen. *Lak. pol.*	Xenophon, *Lakedaimonion politeia* (*Constitution of the Spartans* or *Spartan Society*)

For modern works the following standard abbreviations are used:

AE	*L'Année épigraphique*
AJP	*American Journal of Philology*
Annales ESC	*Annales: économies, sociétés, cultures*
Ant. Afr.	*Antiquités africaines*
BMC	*British Museum Catalogue of Coins*
BSA	*Annual of the British School at Athens*
CCL	*Corpus Christianorum, series Latina*
CIL	*Corpus inscriptionum Latinarum*
CQ	*Classical Quarterly*
CSEL	*Corpus scriptorum ecclesiasticorum Latinorum*
FGH	F. Jacoby (1923–58), *Die Fragmente der griechischen Historiker* (Berlin)
GCS	*Griechische christliche Schriftsteller*
IG	*Inscriptiones Graecae*
JFA	*Journal of Field Archaeology*
JHS	*Journal of Hellenic Studies*
JRA	*Journal of Roman Archaeology*

JRS	*Journal of Roman Studies*
Lib. Stud.	*Libyan Studies*
OJA	*Oxford Journal of Archaeology*
OLD	*Oxford Latin Dictionary*
P. Oxy.	*Oxyrhynchus Papyri*
Page, *GLP*	D. L. Page (1942), *Greek Literary Papyri*, i (Loeb Classical Library)
PBSR	*Papers of the British School at Rome*
PG	J.-P. Migne (ed.), *Patrologiae cursus completus: series Graeca*, i–clxi (Paris, 1857–66)
SC	*Sources chrétiennes*
SIG[3]	W. Dittenberger (1915–24), *Sylloge inscriptionum Graecarum*, 3rd edn (Leipzig)
SVF	H. von Arnim (1903–24), *Stoicorum veterum fragmenta*, i–iv (Leipzig)
Tod, *GHI* ii	M. N. Tod (1948), *A Selection of Greek Historical Inscriptions*, ii: *From 403 to 323* BC (Oxford)

1

Ancient history and landscape histories

Graham Shipley

A natural concern?

A larger proportion of the world's population now lives in cities than at any time in history; yet interest in the 'natural world' is greater than ever.

A consciousness that society is inextricably situated within, and dependent upon, its non-constructed environment is far from new. In Eurocentric culture it goes back most directly to the Romantic movement (witness the writings of Goethe, Wordsworth, and many others) and beyond. In the nineteenth century the politics of reform and revolution emphasized bad living conditions in industrial towns, while before long people learned to make excursions back into a countryside they had left when it no longer offered them a livelihood, but which was now seen as healthy and a public good. In the late nineteenth century steps were taken to improve public access to the countryside, such as by the foundation of the National Trust in England and Wales, precisely one hundred years ago at the time of writing (1995).

More recently, environmental issues have been in the forefront of politics for different reasons. Since the early 1970s, pressure groups have campaigned to curb the environmental pollution caused by industry and the internal combustion engine; and politics at the 'grass roots' (telling phrase!) is increasingly informed by a 'green' consciousness that transcends party loyalties. The public has probably never been so well informed about 'nature', thanks to a rich diet of programmes about wild life and news items about environmental issues in the media.

Since the 1970s there has been increasingly wide concern at the effects of industrial development on the 'third world', motivated by compassion for human suffering, anxiety at the destruction of other species or their habitats, and fear of permanent damage to the global environment. In the later Cold War years anti-nuclear campaigners found common ground with the environmental movement, stressing the global catastrophe a nuclear war might bring and, more controversially, pointing to nuclear power stations as a menace to the health of humans and other species. The fall of the Soviet bloc brought new knowledge of environmentally destructive industries in some eastern countries. In Britain, 'green' consciousness is widely believed to have peaked in 1989 with a 19 per cent vote for the Green Party at the European Parliamentary elections, at a time when the media were constantly featuring environmental issues. In the late 1980s and 1990s, recycling facilities sprang up all over Europe, some industrialists declared themselves environmentally friendly, and for a time non-destructive household goods were prominent on supermarket shelves. A prime concern of British environmentalists in recent years has been to urge governments to slow down road-building and promote public transport and less environmentally damaging forms of transport, particularly the bicycle. Appropriately for one of the hosts of this seminar series, Leicester is now dubbed 'Britain's First Environment City'.

During the space missions of the late 1960s and early 1970s we first saw the image of the Earth from afar, floating, as it were, in the black sea of empty space – a cultural icon often credited with having promoted the rise of the 'green' movement (though, for example, the role of motor traffic in London smogs and the effect of dangerous pesticides on the land had been appreciated many years earlier). Our environment is commonly seen as fragile; for some, including those influenced by the Gaia theory (Lovelock 1979; 1988), the human species even represents a threat to all life on earth (cf. Collard 1988, arguably taking an extreme position).

This environmental awareness is not the same as the Romantics' love of nature. Rather than stressing the spiritual benefit to humankind of awareness of, and contact with, nature (though that view is also widely put forward), it proclaims the mutuality inherent in any ecological system and the responsibility we have to keep our surroundings fit for ourselves, our descendants, and other creatures. Just as the Romantic movement reflected the social and economic situation of the writers of the day, so present-day concern for 'the environment' reflects the unprecedented conditions of industrialized society (the fashionable term 'post-industrial' seems premature), with increasing public access to sources of information, much of it based on current scientific understanding; a society in which for many people, by choice or through force of circumstance, the periods defined as 'leisure' are getting longer; and a society in which great importance is placed on individuals cultivating their own path through life and expressing their personality. Democratic politics seems to operate more at the level of individual voices than ever before, and with ever more sophisticated telecommunications (notably the InterNet, the global computer network of the 1990s) it is possible for individuals to make themselves heard.

I enumerate these aspects of modern environmental concern in order to emphasize that the points of contact with a pre-industrial, largely agricultural society such as the ancient Mediterranean are close to zero. We should be wary of assuming, simplistically, that in the ancient world there were, even *mutatis mutandis* or allowing for differences of scale, any comparable threats to the environment, or any similar awareness of human responsibilities, unless we find evidence to support such a claim. For ancient Greece, Oliver Rackham, in the second chapter in this volume, seeks to correct a number of myths and misconceptions about both the modern landscape and what it can tell us about the ancient one. While landscape change is evident today, he argues, 'the big changes took place long before there were writers to put them on record', and human activity in the classical period made little long-term difference to the Greek countryside. Thus 'there was no particular need for them [the Greeks] to be explicitly ecologically minded'.

Ancient history: old and new

Living in an industrial society we tend to see the primary landscape division as between country and town. This is one stimulus for the current volume: in what ways did political societies that saw themselves as town-based (the Greek *politês*, citizen, is a 'polis man'), but were inextricably linked to rural production, control and modify their rural surroundings?

The new environmental concerns of modern society, too, legitimately raise provocative questions about Greek and Roman antiquity that could scarcely have been formulated a generation ago. People are keen to know whether the Greeks and Romans were in any sense 'environmentally conscious': for example, have we anything to learn from them about how to live in a productive landscape without damaging it? Did ancient society (as is all too often claimed) accelerate, or even initiate, detrimental changes in Mediterranean landscapes that we are still coping with? Were ancient farmers more empathetic to the landscape, and to other living species, and did they take better care of their surroundings? Several of the authors in this volume give carefully nuanced answers to these questions.

A generation ago it was rare for British scholars writing about ancient history to bring the landscape into play alongside political accounts of antiquity. Greek and Roman history, for mid-twentieth-century scholars, seems to have been political history – 'the Long March to democracy and the Roman road back from it', as Robin Lane Fox puts it below (ch. 6) – not surprisingly, perhaps, in view of the experience of those generations, many of whose lives were shaped by war in Europe and the struggles of democracy, communism, and fascism. Reading some textbooks of that era, one can sometimes almost forget that Spartans and Athenians depended almost entirely for their survival upon a farming economy, while Roman political history, even of the Gracchi, seems at times curiously lacking in any roots in the real Italian landscape.

The potential for a different approach was always there: earlier generations of scholars had not separated the study of ancient history so completely from the Mediterranean landscapes. To cite a few examples at random: the fundamental work on ancient population geography, still cited today, was by a late nineteenth-century German scholar, K. J. Beloch (1886); early twentieth-century British scholars had explored the Peloponnese for rural forts and settlements;[1] and authors like Alfred Zimmern (1911) were sensitive to the importance of the landscape in early Greek society and, in some cases, to the reality of the Greek country-side. Max Cary, himself the author of many pages of political history, wrote a book on the geography of the Mediterranean (Cary 1949); and classical teachers and scholars contributed extensively to the geographical handbooks on Greece, Italy, the Dodecanese, and other lands produced by the British Admiralty during the two world wars, whose second series, produced in the 1940s, is continually referred to by scholars even today.[2] There were exceptions after the war, too, including historians and archae-ologists who had seen wartime service in the Mediterranean (A. R. Burn, Antony Andrewes) or who spent time in Greece or Italy before or after the war (L. F. Fitzhardinge, W. G. Forrest, J. B. Ward-Perkins).[3]

Meanwhile, archaeology was a growing discipline. After the second world war, Roman historians were perhaps quicker to realize the implications of new techniques – not surprisingly, given the long tradition of excavating Roman sites in Britain and western Europe, and the higher frequency with which organic remains were found. K. D. White's work on Roman farming was, however, largely based on literary evidence (White 1977). At the same time, classical scholars studied representations of nature from literary or artistic vantage-points (e.g. Toynbee 1973).

More innovatively still, with the rise of a distinctively French 'school' of ancient history that emphasized religion and myth, initially under the influence of the anthropologists Gernet and Lévi-Strauss, nature once more began to be seen as one of the sites of meaning that could help us penetrate the ancient psyche (one thinks of works by Vidal-Naquet, Vernant, and Detienne). Technical studies of particular aspects of society's relation to the natural world were being produced in English; but reading Meiggs

[1] e.g. Forster 1903–4; 1906–7; Wace and Hasluck 1907–8; 1908–9; Ormerod 1909–10.
[2] Admiralty 1941; 1944–5a; 1944–5b, and related volumes; cf. the work of A. N. Sherwin-White in Algeria.
[3] e.g. Andrewes 1967; Burn 1962; Fitzhardinge 1980; Forrest 1968; Ward-Perkins 1974.

(1982) on trees or Scullard (1974) on elephants one feels they laboured under a certain unease and were not ready to claim that the interaction of ancient society with the natural world could be talked of in the same breath as explanations in terms of imperialism, trade, or political systems (despite Meiggs's articulate and persuasive claims for the historical importance of timber in antiquity).

We all know that classics has 'declined' for a hundred years, at least if measured by the number of those learning Greek and Latin; so it may seem perverse to claim that its trajectory has in fact been an upward one for several decades. Yet public interest in ancient civilizations is probably keener than ever; and in terms of the sympathetic understanding of ancient society (one might almost say *wie es eigentlich gewesen*), scholars have come a long way from the narrowly political chapters (in general) of the first edition of the *Cambridge Ancient History* or the drily narrative textbooks of the mid-century. One reason may be the fundamental changes in the society from which scholars themselves are drawn; another may be that, once classics lost its pre-eminent position in the education of the élite and became a specialist subject, it was forced (partly stimulated by seeing how the subject was taught in North America) to seek a wider audience: first, by offering classics and ancient history in translation; second – and most importantly for the present discussion – by reaching out in research to engage with other, more modern disciplines such as anthropology, sociology, literary theory, gender studies, and above all archaeology. Anthropology, for example, shows its influence in studies by Forbes and others.[1] The real effects of the changes in Roman élite land ownership in the middle Republican period became apparent with the sociologically grounded work of Hopkins and others.

With the increasing availability of air travel, the growth of higher education in the UK and other countries, and the rise of archaeological departments, there were opportunities for students and scholars to visit Greek and Roman lands more often and in greater numbers. It can be no coincidence that there was a resurgence of historical writings that sought to illuminate the political and

---

[1] e.g. Forbes 1982, and works cited by Forbes and Foxhall in this volume; cf. also Shaw 1981 on Roman markets.

economic history through an awareness of the geographical setting.[1] These were part of a movement towards regional studies linking landscapes with history more integrally.[2] Aspects of the ancient economy were increasingly studied through a combination of literary, documentary, and archaeological evidence.[3]

This being the period, too, when the environmental movement became clearly defined, it is perhaps unsurprising that archaeology seems to have been preoccupied for a time with how the geology, geography, and productive capacities of a territory may have influenced, or even determined, the development of a society.[4] Thiessen polygons, central place theory, and environmental carrying capacities were all the rage, and archaeologists were keen to move outside traditional focuses of classical archaeology, such as vase-painting, sculpture, and civic architecture, in order to understand the whole of a society – in particular, those groups in society not normally reached through studying those kinds of remains, such as smallholders, craft producers, and pastoralists.

In both Greek and Roman lands, archaeological field survey had already begun to raise new areas of enquiry. Early surveys included the Minnesota Messenia Expedition and the South Etruria Survey, both carried out over many years, or smaller operations like the exploration of prehistoric Laconia in the 1950s (Waterhouse and Hope Simpson 1960; 1961); the Minnesota Messenia Expedition's volume is specifically subtitled 'Reconstructing a Bronze Age Regional Environment' (McDonald and Rapp 1972). By the late 1970s archaeologists, in collaboration with historians and geographers, were starting to carry out field surveys in many areas of the Greco-Roman world. Sometimes it was a case of small groups or single individuals searching for standing monuments and visible structures in areas not previously surveyed – continuing the tradition of lone topographic research embodied,

[1] Among a host of works, the following are cited simply as examples: on the Argolid, Tomlinson 1972; on Lakonia, Forrest 1968, Cartledge 1979, and Fitzhardinge 1980; for the Roman world, Finley 1968 on Sicily, Potter 1987 on Roman Italy, Richardson 1986 and Keay 1988 on Spain, or Drinkwater 1983 on Gaul.
[2] e.g. for Greece, Salmon 1984; Osborne 1985; 1987; Shipley 1987; Spencer 1995; for Italy, Spurr 1986; Dyson 1992.
[3] See e.g. Forbes and Foxhall 1978; Rathbone 1981; 1991; Garnsey 1988; Foxhall 1995; Gallant 1985; 1991.
[4] An observation I owe to Dr S. Karpyuk.

for Greece, in the work of Richard Hope Simpson, Eugene Vanderpool, and W. K. Pritchett.[1] Alternatively, and more in keeping with developments in archaeological theory and scientific methods of data analysis, systematic 'intensive' surveys were conducted by larger teams, many of whose results are beginning to see the light of day.[2]

Realities and meanings

The study of ancient history has therefore changed in the way it deals with landscapes. The means by which Greeks and Romans manipulated their physical environment are increasingly well understood, and this understanding can be fed back, so to speak, into the cultural legacy of ancient society to illuminate the ways in which the environment was thought about. These two axes of investigation – put more simply, how the ancient environment worked and how it was regarded – were the two main questions posed at the outset of the seminar series from which these papers derive. Many of the papers in this volume, however, touch on both aspects.

A commonplace observation is that in studying the history of the Greeks and Romans we cannot divorce the town from the country. The typical Greek city-state, or polis, was a totality embracing both a built-up area (*asty*) and a rural territory (*chora*). Yet, as Osborne (1987) points out, after the archaic period the countryside seems under-represented in art and literature. In the hellenistic period the cultural distancing of the élite from rural realities seems to go one step further with the re-imagining of the natural environment through art and literature, such as the bucolic poems of Theokritos.

There is, therefore, a problem at the outset when trying to reconstruct how the Greek landscape worked: there is very little written evidence. One cannot hope, for example, to write a classical equivalent of Keith Thomas's *Man and the Natural World*, for we lack

[1] See, most impressively, Pritchett 1965–92.
[2] cf. e.g. Bintliff and Snodgrass 1985; Cherry *et al.* eds 1991; Mee and Forbes eds 1995; Cavanagh *et al.* 1996. Work on Roman Greece is reviewed by Alcock 1993; for a survey of work in the Roman world, including Greece, see Barker and Lloyd eds 1991.

the quantity of 'private' writings necessary for such a treatment. Besides, as Gillian Clark notes in chapter 12, the new perceptions of the natural world in the early modern period reflected increased scientific knowledge and a different outlook. Conversely, much of what ancient written evidence we have was not written to give us information but had a rhetorical purpose for its own times. A case in point is the philosophical or forensic evidence for land use, one aspect of which, the use of terraces in Greek and Roman agriculture, is studied in Lin Foxhall's chapter. Only by using written sources in combination with archaeological data, interpreted without prior assumptions, can we arrive at a reasonable picture of the management of soil retention on cultivated slopes, which was probably achieved more often through trenching than through terracing. Landscape management techniques, Foxhall observes, 'were chosen because they answered economic and social needs rather than environmental or ecological ones' – a point made elsewhere in this volume. We can also understand the manipulation of the natural environment by studying particular cultivated species. David Mattingly's study (ch. 9) of the olive in the Roman world shows just how fundamental this tree and its varied products were in antiquity. The scale of its cultivation at the height of the Roman empire well illustrates how we cannot comprehend the relations of power, wealth, and status within ancient society without understanding how the landscape was controlled, managed, and modified. In North Africa the extent of specialized cultivation in areas often considered marginal, and of capital-intensive estate agriculture, may surprise many readers. In this instance economic exploitation may well have had deleterious effects on a region, though further work is needed to test this.

Several authors in this volume examine the role played in ancient society, or the economy, by so-called wild places. In the sources and works of art the best-attested use of the 'wilderness' is hunting, examined here by Robin Lane Fox (ch. 6). Organized hunting was an élite pastime, but much more than that: recreation and politics were bound up with one another. Hunting was not merely a means of pest control or a way of varying the diet, but a fundamental expression of élite identity, particularly for aristocrats and kings. Like any social activity, however, it changed as society and the location of power changed. Hamish Forbes (ch. 4), using anthropology and archaeology, shows how in ancient and modern Greece the 'wilderness' – a term with no simple referent – has not been unproductive land. The active management of uncultivated land illustrates how modern notions of ownership are not always applicable: different people may have had different use-rights over the same land. These areas are a reservoir of plants to be transplanted and cultivated; they yield wood for purposes from house-building to basket-making and for fuel; and provide herbs, greens, wild game, and honey. The 'wastes' or marginal areas are not like the fearsome forests of northern European folk-tales, conceived as wholly alien to the community, nor a simple reserve of spare arable: they play a special role within the complex Mediterranean societies.

Catherine Delano Smith (ch. 7) considers the idea of the wilderness with reference to Roman Italy. Stressing, like Rackham, the episodic nature of landscape change in the Mediterranean, illustrated by Roman and later silting up of some coastal harbours, she shows that the major alterations, including the disappearance of most primeval wildwood, took place before the historical period under the impact of early human cultivators, resulting from the effects of nucleated settlement and the environmental impact of forest industries like charcoal-burning. The 'wilderness' of historical Italy was probably, in fact, like the modern maquis and garrigue of Mediterranean lands. For the late Roman period Neil Christie (ch. 10) shows that Italy did not succumb to rural abandonment in the face of barbarian onslaughts, as some have thought. The pattern of change was not uniform: towns suffered as well as the country, and there were times of revival. As time went on, particularly in the era of warfare with Byzantium, settlement locations were more strongly determined by natural features such as defensible heights, though there were exceptions; and human control of environmental threats such as floods became less effective owing to lack of resources. Control of the natural landscape weakened until from the eighth century onwards the church, through monastery estates, began to re-harness water resources, clear forests, and promote village formation.

Turning to the more conceptual line of investigation, J. Roy (ch. 5) examines the representation of landscape in Attic drama. Generally landscapes are reinvented by tragedians and comic poets to suit their dramatic purposes, even to the extent that

Euripides omits completely the fertile plain of Thebes in the *Bacchae*. Similarly in the *Elektra*, though there are points of contact with the real Argive landscape, it is 'ruthlessly rearranged'. However, like Menander's adaptation of the real landscape of Phyle in the *Dyskolos*, which is made less remote than it is in reality, Euripides in the *Elektra* is careful to make the Peasant's isolated farmstead seem real to his Athenian audience.

Roman civic ideology was, perhaps, more bound with ideas of nature and the countryside, and the control thereof, than were Greek notions of citizenship. Nicholas Purcell (ch. 8) examines an aspect of Roman control that has been insufficiently stressed: the management of water resources and wet places generally. Rome's riverine situation was something Romans were keenly aware of; and both in reality and in their minds, Rome's fortunes were bound up with the control of watery landscapes and the resources they offered. Even place-names within Rome itself reflect a consciousness of the ambivalent role of abundant water within a city, at once a benefit and a hazard. This was in tune with Romans' accurate realization that theirs was a landscape heavily affected by human actions. It was at the height of Roman power, too, that universal histories and compendia of knowledge began to be written, of which one of the most famous is Pliny the Elder's *Historia naturalis*. Mary Beagon (ch. 11) shows that for Pliny as for other Romans the landscape was full of meaning. He is at pains to describe certain parts of the world as pleasant, but for him aesthetic delight is closely linked to the value and usefulness of a landscape to mankind. Generally it is man's role to improve nature. The hostility nature sometimes displays to man reflects the strife inherent in the world, through which balance and order are often attained; and nature is a source of instructive curiosities and paradoxes. Yet man is weak and his situation precarious, and 'it is Pliny's careful evaluation of what man's needs really are, both material and moral, that often leads him to place restrictions on man's activities in nature'. There is no sense here of our owing a duty to preserve the natural world for its own sake; but to mistreat nature is to incur danger and divine wrath. From a man-centred perspective Pliny thus reaches a position not far distant from a modern concern for the environment – which is, after all, sometimes justified by self-interest, as when we are told to preserve the Amazon because its flora may contain useful drugs.

Gillian Clark (ch. 12) here examines the philosophical and religious debates of late antiquity, when it was commonly held by Neoplatonist and Christian thinkers that the world around us is merely an appearance, not reality. They make frequent allusions to nature in their writings, but often in order to make moral and symbolic points, and these allusions are often based on an understanding of nature borrowed from earlier authors, rather than on any new empirical understanding. Rationality was what distinguished humans from animals, and following through the logic that humans should not behave like animals could lead to arguments for vegetarianism; but this was not the same as a concern for other creatures in their own right or an interest in the natural world and its workings. Occasions on which a surprisingly accurate understanding of nature is evinced by writers of this period can be matched by other cases, probably more numerous, where the symbolic meaning, for writer and audience, was far more important than biological accuracy. However, given the technology and pathology of ancient societies, the instability of the food supply, the prevalence of war at certain periods, and the real dangers that nature presented (albeit perhaps magnified in the perception of them), it would have been surprising had the Greeks and Romans *not* been so anthropocentric in their outlook.

Landscapes exist differently for different cultures and for different groups within a society; and landscape is always given meaning, which may not equate to its practical significance. There is, of course, a caution to make: élite writings are not necessarily evidence of ordinary people's outlook. Enough examples have been cited here to show the 'non-fit' between what was stated or believed about the landscape by writers and what the likely reality was, at least as it can be retrieved through archaeology and other techniques and as it was, presumably, lived by real farmers and pastoralists and by their families. But élite writers themselves are shaped by society, and both in antiquity and at other times they have frequently exercised leadership by debating, trying to steer, and partly reflecting the values of those they have influence over. There is, in any case, precious little sign of an 'environmental consciousness' among non-literate ancient people.

Still, this is not to attribute to them any other particular attitude to nature, whether compassionate or negligent. One important message of the studies presented here is that before we blithely retroject modern ecological concerns onto ancient societies, whether seeking to find fault or to praise, we need to try to understand those societies – both their material workings and their culture – in their own terms. If they did not spoil the landscapes of the Mediterranean as we do, but as it is sometimes (wrongly) claimed they also did, it was neither because they were especially 'in tune with' the landscape, nor merely because their technological limitations protected it against their (alleged) ignorance of how it 'really worked'. Having said that, of course, at least on the local scale their future often depended on taking the long view – as does ours, but now on a global scale.

Bibliography

Admiralty Naval Intelligence Division (1941), *Dodecanese* (Geographical Handbooks, BR 500 [London]).

—— (1944–5a), *Greece*, i–iii (Geographical Handbooks, BR 516, 516 a–b; [London]).

—— (1944–5b), *Italy*, i–iv (Geographical Handbooks, BR 517, 517 a–c; [London]).

Alcock, S. E. (1993), *Graecia Capta: The Landscapes of Roman Greece* (Cambridge).

Andrewes, A. (1967), *The Greeks* (London; reissued as *Greek Society*, Harmondsworth, 1971).

Barker, G., and Lloyd, J. (eds 1991), *Roman Landscapes: Archaeological Survey in the Mediterranean Region* (British School at Rome Archaeological Monographs, 2; London).

Beloch, K. J. (1886), *Die Bevölkerung der griechisch-römischen Welt* (Leipzig).

Bintliff, J. L., and Snodgrass, A. M. (1985), 'The Cambridge–Bradford Boeotian expedition: the first four years', *JFA* 12: 123–61.

Burn, A. R. (1962), *Persia and the Greeks: The Defence of the West, c.546–478 BC* (London; 2nd edn, London and Stanford, Calif., 1984).

Cartledge, P. (1979), *Sparta and Lakonia: A Regional History 1300–362 BC* (London).

Cary, M. (1949), *The Geographic Background of Greek and Roman History* (Oxford).

Cavanagh, W., Crouwel, J., Catling, R.W.V., and Shipley, G. (1996), *Continuity and Change in a Greek Rural Landscape: The Laconia Survey* (BSA supp. vols 26–7; London).

Cherry, J. F., Davis, J. L., and Mantzourani, E. (eds 1991), *Landscape Archaeology as Long-term History: Northern Keos in the Cycladic Islands* (Monumenta Archaeologica, 16; Los Angeles).

Collard, A., with Contrucci, J. (1988), *Rape of the Wild: Man's Violence against Animals and the Earth* (London).

Drinkwater, J. F. (1983), *Roman Gaul: The Three Provinces, 58 BC–AD 260* (London).

Dyson, S. L. (1992), *Community and Society in Roman Italy* (Ancient Society and History; Baltimore, Md., and London).

Finley, M. I. (1968), *Ancient Sicily* (London).

Fitzhardinge, L. F. (1980), *The Spartans* (Ancient Peoples and Places, 95; London).

Forbes, H. A. (1982), *Strategies and Soils: Technology, Production and Environment in the Peninsula of Methana, Greece* (Ph.D. thesis, University of Pennsylvania; Ann Arbor, Mich.).

—— and Foxhall, L. (1978), '"The queen of all trees": preliminary notes on the archaeology of the olive', *Expedition*, 21 (1): 37–47.

Forrest, W. G. (1968), *A History of Sparta 950–192 BC* (London; 2nd edn, London, 1981).

Forster, E. S. (1903–4), 'South-western Laconia', *BSA* 10: 158–89.

—— (1906–7), 'Laconia, II: topography. §1: Gythium and the north-west coast of the Laconian gulf', *BSA* 13: 219–37.

Foxhall, L. (1995), *Olive Cultivation in Ancient Greece: The Ancient Economy Revisited* (Bulletin of the Institute of Classical Studies, supp.; London).

Gallant, T. W. (1985), *A Fisherman's Tale: An Analysis of the Potential Productivity of Fishing in the Ancient Mediterranean* (Miscellanea Graeca; Brussels).

—— (1991), *Risk and Survival in Ancient Greece: Reconstructing the Rural Domestic Economy* (Cambridge).

Garnsey, P. (1988), *Famine and Food Supply in the Graeco-Roman World: Responses to Risk and Crisis* (Cambridge).

Keay, S. J. (1988), *Roman Spain* (Exploring the Roman World; London).

Lovelock, J. E. (1979), *Gaia: A New Look at Life on Earth* (Oxford and New York).

—— (1988), *The Ages of Gaia: A Biography of Our Living Earth* (Commonwealth Fund Book Program; Oxford and New York).

McDonald, W. A., and Rapp, G. R., jun. (eds 1972), *The Minnesota Messenia Expedition: Reconstructing a Bronze Age Regional Environment* (Minneapolis).

Mee, C. B., and Forbes, H. A. (eds 1995), *Settlement and Land Use in the Peninsula of Methana, Greece* (Liverpool).

Meiggs, R. (1982), *Trees and Timber in the Ancient Mediterranean World* (Oxford).

Ormerod, H. A. (1909–10), 'Laconia, II: topography. Bardoúnia and north-eastern Maina', *BSA* 16: 62–71.

Osborne, R. (1985), *Demos: The Discovery of Classical Attika* (Cambridge).

—— (1987), *Classical Landscape with Figures: The Ancient Greek City and its Countryside* (London).

Potter, T. W. (1987), *Roman Italy* (London).

Pritchett, W. K. (1965–92), *Studies in Ancient Greek Topography*, i–viii (i–vi: California Studies in Classical Antiquity; Berkeley, Los Angeles, and London; vii–viii: Amsterdam).

Rathbone, D. (1981), 'The development of agriculture in the "ager Cosanus" during the Roman republic: problems of evidence and interpretation', *JRS* 71: 10–23.

—— (1991), *Economic Rationalism and Rural Society in Third-century AD Egypt: The Heroninos Archive and the Appianus Estate* (Cambridge Classical Studies; Cambridge).

Richardson, J. S. (1986), *Hispaniae: Spain and the Development of Roman Imperialism, 218–82 BC* (Cambridge).

Salmon, J. B. (1984), *Wealthy Corinth* (Oxford).

Scullard, H. H. (1974), *The Elephant in the Greek and Roman World* (London).

Shaw, B. D. (1981), 'Rural markets in North Africa and the political economy of the Roman empire', *Antiquités africaines*, 17: 37–83.

Shipley, G. (1987), *A History of Samos 800–188 BC* (Oxford).

Spencer, N. (1995), 'Early Lesbos between east and west: a "grey area" of Aegean archaeology', *BSA* 90: 269–306.

Spurr, M. S. (1986), *Arable Cultivation in Roman Italy: c.200 BC–c.AD 100* (*JRS* Monographs, 3; London).

Tomlinson, R. A. (1972), *Argos and the Argolid* (London).

Toynbee, J. M. C. (1973), *Animals in Roman Life and Art* (London).

Wace, A. J. B., and Hasluck, F. W. (1907–8), 'Laconia, II: topography. South-eastern Laconia', *BSA* 14: 161–82 (pp. 161–6 by Wace, pp. 167–82 by Hasluck).

—— and —— (1908–9), 'Laconia, II: topography. East-central Laconia', *BSA* 15: 158–76.

Ward-Perkins, J. B. (1974), *Cities of Ancient Greece and Italy* (London).

Waterhouse, H., and Hope Simpson, R. (1960), 'Prehistoric Laconia: part I', *BSA* 55: 67–107.

—— and —— (1961), 'Prehistoric Laconia: part II', *BSA* 56: 114–75.

White, K. D. (1977), *Country Life in Classical Times* (London).

Zimmern, A. (1911), *The Greek Commonwealth: Politics and Economics in Fifth-century Athens* (London; 5th edn, London, 1931).

2

Ecology and pseudo-ecology: the example of ancient Greece

Oliver Rackham

The classical authors noted deforestation that they believed to be wide-spread and severe.

(Hughes 1983, 437)

The only complaint known to me is a mild protest in the late Roman Empire against overcutting in the Apennine forests. There is certainly no evidence of any general alarm at the depletion of the forests and there is no evidence of any attempts to redress the balance.

(Meiggs 1982, 377)

Ecology is the science of plants and animals in relation to each other, to their environment, and to human activities. It is the most complex and difficult of the biological sciences, and therefore of all sciences.

Ecology, rightly, is thought of as having political consequences. Politically minded people find the complications of real ecology too difficult, and try to argue from a reduced version. Some of the simplifications and generalizations are legitimate, but others take the form of 'factoids'. A factoid is a statement that looks like a fact, makes sense like a fact, commands the respect due to a fact, and has all the properties of a fact except that it is not true. An example is the belief that trees die when cut down and disappear for ever. Stories grow taller in the telling, and eventually the tissue of factoids forms a 'pseudo-ecology': a coherent, logical, reasonable, and widely accepted system of belief having no connection with the real world. There is something about land-scape history peculiarly productive of factoids (Rackham 1987, 13–17; 1991, 102–5; 1992a).

The first step on the road to pseudo-ecology is to confuse ecology with environment: to treat living creatures as part of the scenery of the theatre, rather than as actors in the play. Plants and animals are not a generalized nature, not the passive recipi-ents of whatever mankind chooses to inflict on them: they are thousands of individual species, each with its own behaviour which has to be understood. An ash tree differs from a pine to much the same degree that a cat differs from a codfish. Cutting down the pine kills it, but the ash sprouts and recovers. Knowledge of these matters is being added to, especially as a result of rare events such as the 1987 storm in England.

There are four opportunities for creating a pseudo-ecology of the ancient world.

(1) Not understanding the nature of evidence. Scholars easily suppose that written sources provide the only, or best, infor-mation about their periods. This cuts them off from ever knowing what was happening at times when people were not writing. Ecologists tend to be credulous and uncritical when dealing with ancient texts, and fail to understand their limi-tations.

(2) Projecting modern ecological fallacies on to the ancients. It is all too easy to seek in ancient philosophers confirmation of the fashionable misperceptions of the present.

(3) Being preoccupied (as many scholars are) with ancient *atti-tudes* to nature, regardless of what nature consisted of at the time or what it was the ancients were attitudinizing about. For example, Professor J. D. Hughes (1983) writes on 'How the ancients viewed deforestation', expressly disclaiming any discussion of what deforestation there was in ancient times. The history of nature is not the same as the history of the things that people have *said* about nature.

(4) Geographical over-generalization. Scholars assemble frag-ments of information – a scrap from Italy, a phrase in Homer, a snippet from Cyprus, a verse or two from the Bible – as if these added up to a history of Mediterranean ecology. This would not pass muster in any other branch of archaeology.

The fact is that even so small an area as Crete has its jungles and its deserts, its snow-mountains and its stifling gorges, its primrose woods and its palm-groves, its waterfalls and its sun-baked screes – a range of habitats not unlike the difference between Wales and Morocco. There is also the tendency for different groups of people to create different cultural landscapes out of what looks like much the same physical environment. It is useless to generalize even about the landscape history of Crete.

The ecology of modern Greece

One has to begin by understanding how the modern Greek landscape functions, and what factors maintain it (Rackham 1983; 1990b; Rackham and Moody 1995). Greek trees and plants have been exposed to woodcutting for thousands of years, and to browsing and burning for much longer. These influences affect each of the principal trees and other plants separately. For

Figure 2.1   Ebenus cretica on a cliff (Akrotíri peninsula, Crete, July, 1981).

Figure 2.2 An apparently barren hillside which may be as full of shrubs and undershrubs as the root-room will hold (Anógeia, Crete, July 1987).

example, prickly oak, *Quercus coccifera*, is highly adapted to all three and immediately sprouts from the base if cut or burnt. Holm-oak, *Q. ilex*, is also well adapted to woodcutting and burning, but not to browsing; in most parts of Greece it tends to grow on cliffs where animals cannot reach it. Two common and disagreeable undershrubs, Jerusalem sage (*Phlomis fruticosa*) and spiny broom (*Calicotome spinosa*) are discouraged by fires, which is one reason why shepherds burn the vegetation. Another undershrub, *Ebenus cretica*, one of the most beautiful of the many **endemic** plants confined to Crete, does not mind burning but is very sensitive to browsing. A sign that browsing has ceased in an area is that *Ebenus* moves from cliffs (its usual habitat: fig. 2.1) into accessible places.

In lands where water is short, as in much of Greece, roots are just as important as above-ground parts in determining what grows where. As can be seen in road cuttings, the roots of plants can easily occupy more space than the tops. Many an apparently 'barren' hillside (fig. 2.2) is really a closed plant community below ground; roots completely fill the space available.

In Mediterranean countries, trees do not necessarily occur in the form of forests: they can constitute **maquis** (trees reduced to the form of shrubs) or **savanna** (grassland or undershrubs with scattered trees).

In the last hundred years there has been an unusually large amount of change: notably the decline of cattle, decline of cultivation on the more difficult (especially terraced) soils, increased olive-growing, intensification of agriculture on the easier soils, and depopulation, especially of small or remote settlements. It is easier to understand classical Greece if we compare it, not with Greece today, but with the country as it was before these changes: what Anthony Snodgrass calls Greece Yesterday.

A consistent change from Greece Yesterday to Greece today is the increase in wild vegetation, especially trees (fig. 2.3). Early photographs and pictures, and the age distribution of the trees themselves, leave no doubt of it. I have found such an increase in every part of Greece – indeed of the European Mediterranean – where I have looked. Yet very few people are aware of the

Figure 2.3 New wood of cypress and pine springing up on former pasture (Samariá, Crete, July 1987).

Figure 2.4 Burnt pinewood (Soúgia, Crete, July 1988). The cultivation terraces prove that the woodland was recent.

change: Greeks and foreigners alike are under the delusion that trees are in decline.

Increasing vegetation has consequences, such as an increase in fires. This is not just because there is more vegetation to burn. The ability to burn is itself an adaptation, which some plants have but not others. The most rapidly spreading trees happen to be pines, the most fire-promoting and fire-adapted of trees. Much of Greece is exchanging a browsing-dominated for a fire-dominated landscape (fig. 2.4). Discussions of this change tend to concentrate on the source of ignition, rather than on what makes a landscape combustible. The British government in Cyprus went to great lengths to promote the growing of pines, against the opposition of the shepherds, and were surprised and hurt when this led to a great increase in wildfires (Thirgood 1987). As A. T. Grove and I have noticed, exactly the same policy has been repeated, and with exactly the same result, more recently by the foresters of Spain.

Another feature of Greece that ecologists find difficult to come to terms with is that many processes are episodic rather than continuous. Greece is affected by the periodicities in natural events and in human affairs – for example, by the combination of war and high rainfall in the 1940s. The landscape is not slowly worn away by the gradual dripping of ordinary rains, but is changed overnight by a sudden immense storm. Many trees do not arise every year, but only at long intervals when circumstances happen to be favourable. Prickly oak is one of the commonest trees, yet in many years of looking I have only once or twice seen a seedling.

The real ecology of ancient Greece[1]

Ancient Greek authors tell us comparatively little about what Greece looked like: they assume their readers will know. Written evidence needs to be handled critically. We need to verify each piece of information: to consider whether an author was interested in describing accurately what a place looked like, and whether he was in a position to know (Rackham 1992a). Plato (*Laws*, 1. 625 b) throws out a few remarks about roadside cypresses in Crete in the context of three aged philosophers strolling one afternoon from Knossos to the Idaean cave. In reality this is one of the most arduous journeys in all this arduous island. All we can infer is that Plato liked to give a pleasant setting to a dry philosophical discourse, but knew nothing about the topography or vegetation of Crete.

Written evidence, where it can be relied upon, is uneven in its distribution: it is copious for Boiotia, scanty for Crete. Pausanias gives an apparently accurate description of Greece (but, alas, not Crete) in the Roman period, which can be compared, place by place, with what was there a century ago (Frazer 1898) and what is there now (his extreme accuracy has most recently been vindicated by Habicht 1985). It is unfortunate that almost nothing relevant should survive from late Roman and the succeeding early

[1] The following is a summary of the methods and conclusions I have presented in detail elsewhere: see Rackham 1983; 1990b; Rackham and Moody 1996.

Figure 2.5 Wood of holm-oak and arbutus (Sphakoúriac gorge, Amári, Crete, April 1982). Homer's heroes might have stuck wild boar in such a place, had there been any boar in Crete.

Byzantine times, which, as archaeological surveys show, would have been one of the formative periods in the development of the Greek landscape.

I illustrate the problems of interpretation from Homer. I am unable to endorse the fulsome praise some scholars have heaped on the *Odyssey* for its supposed insights into vegetation (e.g. Regenbogen, in Rubner 1985). Homer, it is true, was not blind to the beauties of gardens and cultivation, and once sang of a pig-sticking in terms which are genuinely evocative of wild landscape:

> It was in this spot that a mighty boar had his lair, in a thicket so dense that when the winds blew moist not a breath could penetrate, the Sun's rays never entered, the rain never soaked right through, and the ground was deep in dead leaves.
>
> (*Od.* 19.439–43, trans. Rieu 1991)

This vividly evokes dense heather–arbutus–ilex maquis, with its dark, dry interior crackling with dead leaves (fig. 2.5). It is in such maquis (the typical vegetation of damp schist rocks) rather than in noble forests that wild swine lurked in Greece before the coming of guns, as they still do in Sardinia and the south of France. However, this is a nearly unique passage; it is not for his landscapes that Homer is read.

What are we to make of Homer's epithets? Some scholars have treated them as one-word descriptions. When he sings of 'woody Zakynthos' in the same breath as Ithakê, Samê (Kephallenia), and Doulichion (*Od.* 9.24 and several other places), does he mean that it was what a modern German, or a modern Englishman, would call 'wooded'? Or that it was more wooded than the other three places? Zakynthos is probably more wooded today than the other islands near it. Homer uses the same epithet 'woody' (ὑλήεσσα) for Samothrake ('Thracian Samos', *Il.* 13.12), which today is one of the most wooded islands in the Aegean; a few lines later he calls it 'craggy' (παιπαλόεσσα), which it also is in places. Homeric epithets thus make some sense, but I hesitate to use them as evidence that Homer's Greece was very like, or very unlike, Greece now. We do not even know whether Homer meant them for contemporary Greece, or for a vaguely remembered heroic past. They may have been mere platitudes and not necessarily true, just as the modern platitude that Cambridge is in the Fens is not true.

Archaeology has much to reveal about ancient landscapes and land uses. Every archaeological survey now includes an 'environmentalist'; the term may be unfortunate (since much more than environment is involved), but such a specialist is rightly regarded as an essential member of the team. Allied to archaeology is the study of ancient living trees, which contain their own chronology in the form of annual rings. These can reveal, for example, whether soil has been eroded or accumulated around their bases in their lifetimes.

Pollen analysis is generally difficult in Greece, except in the north, because suitable deposits do not easily form in this climate, and many of them have been lost in the nineteenth-century mania for destroying wetlands. But without this method we would know no details of the aboriginal landscape before civilization.

All that is revealed by these methods needs to be interpreted in the light of studies of the modern vegetation. Relics of earlier periods in landscape history survive, especially on cliffs which have escaped browsing, burning, and woodcutting.

Conclusions for the classical to Roman periods

A modern Greek, transported back to classical times, would find the *environment* very similar. The climate may not have been identical: passages of Xenophon (*Kynegetikos* (*The Hunting Man*), 4. 9) and Theophrastos (*On Winds*, 13) imply that snow was then a more ordinary occurrence in inhabited areas than it is now.[1] The *landscape* in general would not be very different from that of Greece Yesterday: the proportions of cultivation, roughland, and woodland would have been roughly the same in classical times as in 1900. There have, however, been two, possibly three, big changes.

(1) *Changes in the relative levels of land and sea*, brought about by tectonic action and other causes. This can be seen in the form of 'wave-notches' marking former higher levels of the sea on the Cretan coast. A famous example is Thermopylai,

---

[1] The Little Ice Age (*c*.AD 1550–1750) certainly had considerable effects on Greece: see Grove 1992.

where a retreat of the sea makes it difficult to understand the ancient battles.

(2) *Disappearance of fens and marshes*. In ancient Greece these were often extensive (such as the Kopaïs basin), and are part of the solution to the problem of how the ancients kept so many cattle in a seemingly unsuitable climate.

(3) *Terraces*. As far as I can discover there is no unambiguous allusion anywhere in ancient Greek writing to terraces (cf. Foxhall, Chapter 3, this volume). Yet Greeks lived in places where cultivation seems inconceivable without terracing. Were they too commonplace to be worth describing? If so, why are there not incidental allusions to terraced ground deciding the issue of battles or hunts? (Rackham and Moody 1992; see also Baladié 1974.) Most battles were fought in plains, and most plains have terraces in their corners: why did the infantry never take advantage of terraced ground where the cavalry could not get at them?

These changes apart, it is remarkably difficult to detect differences between the landscapes of ancient and modern Greece. Woodland seems to have been rather less extensive then than in Greece today, but more extensive than in Greece Yesterday. Most of the big wooded areas known in ancient Greece still exist; a few have probably disappeared, but there are also wooded areas (such as Mt Taÿgetos in Laconia) that seem not to have been wooded in classical times.

Prehistory

The bronze age may have been a little different. From a first look at some of the charcoal found at Knossós, I find a change from predominantly evergreen oak in the Middle Minoan to cypress or juniper in the Late Minoan. There is no oak at Knossós now.[1]

In **aboriginal** times, before the coming of civilization, mainland Greece had been very different. Pollen evidence shows that it was

[1] This work was done at the invitation of Mr Sinclair Hood, and is mentioned by permission of the Managing Committee of the British School at Athens.

much more wooded, with more deciduous trees (especially on lands later to be cultivated) and with northern European trees such as lime and alder. The latter were consistently present throughout the area for which pollen evidence is available, including Crete. The change to something like the present landscape took place mainly in the neolithic and the bronze age – far too early to be described in writing. Partly it was brought about by human activities: the introduction of cultivation and of domestic livestock, and the extermination of native mammals. But there can be little doubt that the climate also has changed. In the pre-neolithic, the climate was less arid and less strongly 'Mediterranean' than it is today.

Aboriginal Crete is known to have had a peculiar native fauna: elephants, hippopotamuses, and deer, but no effective flesh-eater and no human population. There can be little doubt that in Crete (unlike mainland Greece) the normal state of the vegetation would have been what today would be called 'excessively browsed'. The native mammals were probably exterminated either by the explorers who first discovered the island or by those who first settled it (Rackham and Moody 1996, ch. 5). This may well have caused the island to be less browsed, and more wooded, than ever before or since.

Modern fallacies about ancient Greece

The Abbé Barthélemy, writing in the 1780s, placed the heroic events of ancient Greece in a land of noble forests and crystal fountains, like Marie-Antoinette's France (Barthélemy 1788). Thus began the traditional theory that Greece has gone to the bad since classical times. The forests, we are told, have been felled and burnt, and the remains grazed to create the present 'scrub'. The soil, no longer under the magic protection of the trees, has washed away, and the fountains have dried up. Even, some say, the very climate has changed. These changes are supposed to be irreversible and cumulative: mischief done in the age of Greeks, Romans, Byzantines, Venetians, Turks, and railways all adds up to the present arid, 'degraded' modern landscape.

Barthélemy was popularizing the theories of the contemporary scientist Sonnini (1801). If it were true, the theory ought to have been filled out with detail by all the research done on Greece since the 1780s. Specialist books ought to have been written on each aspect of it. This has not happened. The Sonnini theory is very much alive, and has been the subject in the last ten years of many books and articles and of the television programme *The First Eden*; but it is still based on the few ancient texts that were all the evidence that Sonnini had.

Scholars are tempted to exaggerate the extent of woodland in antiquity, and to play down its extent today. They seldom ask whether noble forests and crystal fountains still exist. The fact is that Athens had roughly as much forest in classical times as in the 1920s, and less than it has now (Rackham 1983). In the classical period there were regular arrangements for carrying wood, and perhaps timber, to the city for ordinary purposes. Demosthenes describes a farm that had six donkeys working all the time taking *hylê* to market. As Russell Meiggs points out, the low price implies that it was wood rather than timber that was taken, but there is hardly enough information to work out the quantity. For serious construction Athens had to bring timber from Macedonia or Sicily. Control of these sources was one of the main objectives of Athenian foreign policy (Meiggs 1982, ch. 7). Timber supply was much more of a problem for Athens than for Rome.

Scholars too often assume that ancient accounts of trees imply *tall* trees[1] and forests; they forget about maquis and savanna. In reality, ancient authors may not have made the same distinction between 'forest' and 'scrub' that modern English, and especially American, writers make. Tree pollen can as easily come from maquis or savanna as from forest.

Hughes (1983) collects all that ancient historians, poets, and philosophers said about cutting down trees – even sacred trees, olive groves, and orchards – and claims that this added up to deforestation. This is unwarranted. Deforestation is tree-felling *not balanced by regrowth*. Human nature is such that people, especially literary writers, take notice of sudden changes such as felling but are most unlikely to notice the gradual regrowth. The only exception that I know in all antiquity is the statement by Eratosthenes that charcoal-burning and shipbuilding could not keep up

---

[1]   An assertion often expressly made by McNeill 1992.

with the growth of trees in Cyprus (quoted in Strabo, 14. 6. 5 (684)). The lack of any direct mention of formation of new woodland is no evidence that it did not happen.

Authors such as Hughes relentlessly enumerate every mention of timber or firewood or their products, as if they all implied deforestation. Polemic language like 'a felony against the Greek heritage of nature' comes easily to the pen on such occasions. But even if all the ancient authors were stating the literal truth, it would still have been perfectly possible for the classical period to have been a time of net increase of trees.

Nonsense multiplies. Once it has become the accepted wisdom that trees were becoming scarce in antiquity, every change in human activity is attributed to this cause, no matter how far-fetched. If the guess fits your theory, you print it. Sir Arthur Evans solemnly stated that the men of Knossós took to using gypsum for door- and window-frames because they had run out of timber (Evans 1921–35, ii. 565). We may smile at such naïvety, but within the last ten years scholars have glibly attributed everything – erosion, the recycling of bronze, the orientation of houses, moving the sites of potteries – to a shortage of trees (e.g. Perlin 1989), without demonstrating either that trees *were* diminishing or that there is no alternative explanation. If an ancient author writes disapprovingly of goats, this is taken as an illustration of how the ancients appreciated their destructive character (Hughes 1983) – even if the original author says he disliked goats for some quite different reason. It is all too easy to interpret what a modern scholar would like the ancients to have said, rather than what they did say. Theophrastos' fascinating passage about climatic change in Crete (*On Winds*, 13) is interpreted as showing that the ancients were already 'aware' that felling forests changes the climate (Hughes 1994), even though this passage mentions neither forests nor felling.

Theodore Wertime (1983) claims that fuel-using industries were the prime factor in the deforestation of Mediterranean lands during antiquity. He works out that all the silver produced by the Laureion mines would have called for one million tons of charcoal, implying that this is an unreasonably large amount and proves deforestation. But the figure is of no value without knowing how long it took the wood to grow; it does not, in itself, prove deforestation. Wertime does not ask whether 'industrial' Attica was more deforested than non-industrial Boiotia. In reality, a million tons of charcoal over 500 years implies about 14,000 tons of wood a year. Even if one hectare of maquis produced only a ton of wood a year, Laureion could have kept going for ever on 14,000 hectares of land. Maybe we should double this area, to allow for most of the smelting being done over a shorter period (*c*.480–300 BC).[1] Even so, was it really unreasonable for the Athenians to use one-seventh of their land area as a fuel supply for what was by far their biggest industry and the sole means of keeping Athens solvent?[2]

Wertime is shocked at the size of the kiln needed to fire 144 tiles for the temple of Nemea; but the tiles were huge, and the whole temple could have been roofed with only fifteen firings of the kiln. Was this unreasonable for what was by far the grandest building between Corinth and Argos? He interprets changes in metallurgical technology as 'evasive energy strategies' determined by shortage of trees, disregarding the many possible alternatives (such as a shortage of labour). This is a curious fallacy from one of the first scholars to point out the corresponding error in the history of wood-burning industries in England (Wertime 1961, 110 ff.).

Sense is restored to this debate by the work of Russell Meiggs (1982). As he points out, evidence for deforestation in classical writings is unexpectedly meagre. Rarely is it explicitly stated that a wood existed in early classical times but not in late classical times; even then, the source may not be first-hand but may be a report or a tradition, sources which (as English parallel experience shows) are most untrustworthy in such matters.

A recent specialized symposium on Roman deforestation (Frenzel ed. 1994), which includes also the evidence of archaeological surveys and pollen analysis, has produced very little evidence for a decrease in trees that can definitely be dated to

---

[1] Dates accompanied by AD or BC in small capitals are historical dates, not radiocarbon dates of any kind.

[2] Many authors have similarly argued that the even bigger iron age and Roman silver and lead mines of Rio Tinto 'must have deforested' wide tracts of SW Spain – as though such a large, long-lived industry, highly organized in other respects, was somehow incapable of organizing a secure fuel supply. Whether the amount of forest around Rio Tinto did in fact decrease we do not know.

Figure 2.6 Badlands of the N. Peloponnese (Stimánga, Korinthía, May 1989). The soft marl rocks are being heaved up by the movement of the great Corinth fault; in consequence floods eat them away every time there is a great storm, despite the dense vegetation.

the Roman period. Such evidence as there is mainly relates to the fringes of the Mediterranean – northern Spain, the southern Alps, some northern parts of modern Greece, Bulgaria; there is virtually none for ancient Greece. Whether or not trees decreased in the Mediterranean proper is still an open question.

Do trees, and only trees, protect soils from erosion? This is one of those 'facts that are too well known to need demonstration'. The theory is usually stated as a mere generality, without, for example, going into the soil-retaining merits of different trees. It may well be true in other parts of the world, with different combinations of soil, climate, and trees. In Greece I can find little evidence that it is true. Most of Greece is not very erodible, compared with south-eastern Spain, Italy, or Cyprus. Erodible areas are determined less by vegetation than by geology, climate, and tectonics. The most actively eroding areas I have seen in Greece are the Pindos mountains and the island of Rhodes, both of which are very wooded. The huge 'badland' gullies which make

Figure 2.7 Effects of a deluge (eleven months previously) on a bulldozed hillside (Istron, Merabéllo, Crete, August 1987). In recent years it has become the fashion in Crete to dig hill-slopes into steps on which to grow olives, subsidized by the European Community. Unlike proper terraces, the steps are not supported by walls and melt away in storms.

the surrealist scenery of the northern Peloponnese – determined by the very active Corinth geological fault – are also well wooded (fig. 2.6).

No vegetation can withstand the upheaving of the earth's crustal plates; nor can it make much difference to erosion when steep, young mountains of unconsolidated rocks, as in Pindos, Rhodes, and the northern Peloponnese, are subject to occasional tremendous storms. But vegetation can have some effect, in the form not of trees but of low-growing crusts of mosses and lichens which hold the surface together against the assaults of running water and even rolling stones. In most of Greece trees have, at best, only a slight influence. The only effective agent of erosion in modern Crete is road-making and the bulldozing of terraces (fig. 2.7).

Did the ancient Greeks have an attitude to ecology?

I do not know. Few ancient authors expressly state their attitudes; attitudes to nature have been read (with greater or less probability) into the words of many others. Even these are only the surviving fraction of all the authors who ever set down thoughts on the subject; there is nothing to suggest that the authors whose works survive were the most significant (cf. Lewis 1950). All authors together were only a small fraction, maybe not a very influential fraction, of the population; the thoughts of those who actually did things to Nature will probably forever remain hidden. The medieval English had a strong tradition of woodland conservation, which they took for granted: we know of it from the earthworks constructed round the boundaries of woods, which seem not to exist in Greece, and from implications in workaday texts of a kind that do not survive from classical times (Rackham 1990a). But conservation was normally beneath the notice of English poets, historians, and philosophers.

The ancient Greeks were responsible for a number of ecological factoids that still persist, such as the notion that ivy destroys the tree it grows up (Theophr. *History of Plants*, 3. 18. 9) and probably the belief (which I have been unable to trace to its source) that destroying forests diminishes the local rainfall.[1]

There is an almost irresistible temptation to read modern theories into the words of ancient authors. An example is the much-abused passage of Plato which every modern author repeats as evidence that the ancients were aware of the evils of deforestation:

> It all lies as a promontory, projecting far from the rest of the continent into the sea. The basin of the sea around it happens to be deep and steep-to. Since many and great deluges (*kataklysmoi*) occurred in the nine thousand years (which years elapsed from that time until now), in the said times and calamities the soil of the earth from the heights did not run down, as in other places, into a noteworthy outpouring, but always flowed round in a circle and disappeared into the deep. There is left from then to now, just as in small islands, only the bones of a sick body, all the fat and soft of the earth having fallen away, only the bare body of the place. But then it was intact and the

---

[1]   R. Grove tells me that this was a widespread assumption among the learned in the eighteenth century.

mountains were high earth-hills, and the plains now called Phelleos were full of fat earth, and there was much woodland in the mountains, of which even now there are visible signs. For some of the mountains now have only food for bees, but not very much time ago trees, from whence roofs were cut for the greatest buildings. And besides, there were many tame trees, and it bore boundless pasturage for herds. And also it garnered the yearly water from Zeus, which was not as now lost by flow from the bareness of the land into the sea; but holding much and receiving it back, and storing it up in the rooftile-producing earth, and drinking down from the heights the water absorbed in the hollows, it provided all the places with plentiful streams of springs and rivers. And even now, on the spots where there formerly were springs, there remain shrines, which are signs that what is now said about this is true.

... The Acropolis was then not as it is now. For now it happened one night waters, carrying away the earth, melted it away and made it bare, when earthquakes happened at the same time as the third extraordinary disaster of water before Deukalion's ...

(*Kritias*, 111; my translation)

The Greek of this passage is difficult, and commentators tend to work from smooth-tongued translations (written under the influence of modern thought on erosion) rather than the crabbed original. There can be no doubt that Plato meant deluges to be the cause of loss of soil, and the loss of soil to be the cause of the loss of trees, not vice versa. (He did not appreciate that some trees grow perfectly well on fissured bare rock.) To read this piece as a denunciation of the evils of deforestation is to stand Plato on his head.

Plato was not writing about the geographical Attica, but about a fictional Attica which went to war with a fictional Atlantis, and we are not obliged to take literally anything which he says in this book.[1] In so far as he may have been inspired by actual observation, he has three important insights. He apparently had in mind the great erosions of the Pleistocene, and made a surprisingly good guess ('nine thousand years') at the date. He appreciated that erosion is a catastrophic rather than a gradual process, and understood the great importance of deluges. And he raises the possibility of a yet

---

[1] Zangger 1992 has a bold reinterpretation of the *Kritias* as history – including an eloquent defence of the traditional interpretation of this passage – without, however, convincingly explaining away the discrepancies.

greater catastrophe if an earthquake happens to coincide with a deluge, the vibration turning to liquid soils already soaked by rain – a rare combination which no modern European eye has seen.

A few ancient Greek writers had the beginnings of 'ecological awareness'. Theophrastos, the father of botany, was at his best as a meteorologist, with his accounts of frost and frost hollows (e.g. *Causes of Plants*, 5. 12–14). Plants are more difficult to understand. He had a keen interest in plant physiology, especially the germination and death of trees, but he tells us something about their habitats too (Rubner 1985). He has a few ecological descriptions of remarkable places like Lake Kopaïs (*Hist. Pl.* 4. 10–11). It is from such beginnings of discernment that an interest in ecology must grow, but I find no evidence that the Greeks got very far. Too often they were bogged down in the ancient Greek vices of philosophizing from not enough data, and of not verifying such data as they did have.

Real evidence is contaminated by misunderstanding, tall stories, and taproom gossip. Even such a relatively near place as Crete was a little-known land about which nonsense could be believed. It was repeatedly stated that there were no snakes and no owls in Crete, and that any brought to the island died (e.g. Aelian, *On the Nature of Animals*, 5. 2). Even Theophrastos mentions a 'black poplar' (*aigeiros*) which grew at the Idaean cave (*Hist. Pl.* 3. 3. 4); pharmacological writings refer to 'berries of Cretan black poplar' (Hippocrates, Littré edition, 7. 350. 2; 8. 182. 2). Black poplar has nothing like a berry and no longer grows in Crete; it could have grown there in antiquity, but not at the Idaean cave, which is much too high. I suspect a confusion with the Cretan name for some special Cretan mountain plant, such as the elm-like tree *Zelkova cretica*.

Aristotle wrote much about animals, especially their anatomy, physiology, and reproduction, but his surviving works have only scraps of ecological information. Most of the latter is in book 8 (also numbered 9) of the *History of Animals*, which shows little discrimination between true and false data and may not be a genuine work of Aristotle. I hope the great man was not responsible for the Aristotelian treatise *On Plants*, a work full of inaccurate trivia (such as 'some plants live in wet places and others in dry, others in either, like the willow') which reads like a sleepy student's lecture notes.

The limitation of ancient ecology: identifying the plants

One cannot do real ecology without knowing the plants. We all know how difficult it is to recognize a plant from a description by a non-botanist. To select the diagnostic features that make a workable description was a craft not well advanced in ancient times. Pictures would have helped, but botanical illustration is also not a straightforward craft, and illustrations are corrupted by copyists much more quickly than text. Without descriptions and pictures the aspiring ancient botanist would have been reduced to being taken to the localities and having the plants pointed out. He would have found it difficult to verify doubtful identifications and avoid perpetuating mistakes, and impossible to compare his own observations with those of his predecessors or with plants of regions he had not visited. It is hardly surprising that ancient botanists, as far as we know, were acquainted with only a small fraction of the 6,000 or more species that grow within the modern limits of Greece, and did not know even these accurately.

The ancients knew their plants for various purposes. Wild plants interested them as food, in art and mythology, and for sacred and ceremonial reasons; these are reviewed at length by Baumann and the Stearns (Baumann 1993), who, however, understate the difficulties of identification. The chief reason for knowing plants systematically was to identify *materia medica*. The only surviving representative of the ancient Floras is the work of Dioskorides in the first century AD, incorporating – it appears – illustrations by Krateuas some 200 years earlier. Text and illustrations are known from a sixth-century manuscript (Gunther 1933). Out of 411 descriptions of plants I find that 14 per cent are good or excellent (in the sense that they specify a recognizable species of plant), 36 per cent poor, doubtful, or generic, and 50 per cent useless. Out of 380 illustrations, 27 per cent are good or excellent, 33 per cent borderline, and 43 per cent useless. These statistics include 270 plants which have both a description and an illustration; out of these, 27 per cent are good or excellent (in that I can identify the plant from the text and illustration combined), 42 per cent intermediate, and 28 per cent useless (i.e. text and illustration together fail to identify the plant), while in 4 per cent the text is at variance with the illustration. Even so well-known a drug plant

Figure 2.8 Origanum dictamnus (ancient *diktamnon*), endemic to Crete (Akrotíri peninsula, July 1981).

as *diktamnon* (which to modern eyes is unmistakeable: fig. 2.8) is given a useless description and a useless illustration, accompanied by a number of accounts of other plants which were evidently passed off for it. Not the least of the difficulties under which the ancient doctor laboured was that of not knowing for certain what it was that he was prescribing for his patients. In a similar manner, Theophrastos again and again gives the impression of not knowing exactly what plants he was writing about, of having to depend on the vague descriptions and unreliable memories of his informants: φασὶ δὲ καί ... ('and they say that ...').

Plant identification had to wait until the medieval invention of woodblock printing made it possible to produce exact copies of illustrations. Without accurate identification – or rather, without means of putting identifications on record and conveying them from the originator to another botanist in a different country or at a later date – I doubt if there could have been much ecological investigation.

The Romans and Hebrews

As far as written evidence goes, the Greeks were less ecologically minded than other ancients. Roman writings, though much less copious, contain rather more ecology. For example, Columella writes about coppice-woods and deer parks (*De re rustica*, 9. 1), Palladius Rutilius (1. 34) gives an elaborate technique for establishing hedges, and Siculus Flaccus (*De condicionibus agrorum*) describes the natural features to be encountered by a surveyor. (See also Bender 1994.)

As one walks the mountains of Crete, it is not the words of Theophrastos or Plato, or even Siculus Flaccus, that run through one's head, but those of the Bible. This is not just because biblical writers had more sympathy with sheep, goats, and shepherds than most Greeks and Romans. For the ancient Hebrews, plants and animals were not part of the environment, but independent beings in God's creation and fellow-citizens with the human species. They were second-class citizens, maybe, and some of them disagreeable; but they were citizens none the less. Indeed, the environment itself could be personified (or animalified) as a set of independent beings:

Praise the Lord upon earth: ye dragons,[1] and all deeps;
Fire and hail, snow and vapours: wind and storm, fulfilling his word;
Mountains and all hills: fruitful trees and all cedars;
Beasts and all cattle: worms and feathered fowls;
Kings of the earth and all people: princes and all judges of the
world . . .

(Psalm 148: 7–10)

Considering that it is much smaller in bulk than Greek and Roman
literature, and that none of it expressly sets out to do so, the Bible
tells us a remarkable amount about plants and animals. They are
not (except sometimes in the Song of Songs) mere decorative
names, like the pretty names of plants which embellish the verses
of Theokritos and Sappho. The writers knew something about
them, where they lived and how they behaved. The Hebrews were
not interested merely in useful creatures, but had a sense of
wonder and delight in the extraordinary, remote and dangerous.

The book of Job has accounts of the ostrich, wild ass, and crocodile. Each has a personality that is understood by the author:

Who hath sent out the wild ass free: or who hath loosed the bands of
the wild ass:
Whose house I have made the wilderness, and the salt places his
dwellings.
He scorneth the multitude of the city, neither regardeth he the
crying of the driver.
The range of the mountains is his pasture, and he searcheth after
every green thing.

(Job 39: 5–8)

Feral donkeys still do just this in the jagged, spray-soaked mountains of the north-western prong of Crete.

Biblical writers are forever likening the short lives of the wicked,
or the righteous, to annual grasses – evidently to species of *Vulpia*,
Aira, and *Bromus* which germinate in autumn on wall-tops and
on the flat earthen roofs of houses, and which last (in Crete) until
late April: 'Let them be even as the grass growing upon the house-
tops: which withereth afore it be plucked up; Whereof the mower
filleth not his hand: neither he that bindeth up the sheaves his
bosom' (Psalm 129: 6–7).

---

[1] 'Dragon' here denotes a large marine animal.

Isaiah (11. 1–2) expresses the most cherished hopes of his nation under the allegory of the regrowth of a coppiced tree, a subject mentioned only two or three times in the vastly more extensive Greek and Roman literature: 'And there shall come forth a rod out of the stem of Jesse, and a Branch shall grow out of his roots: and the spirit of the Lord shall rest upon him.' The structure of vegetation is vividly evoked by the horrid fate of a son of King David:

> And Absalom rode upon a mule, and the mule went under the thick boughs of a great oak, and his head caught hold of the oak, and he was taken up between the heaven and the earth; and the mule that was under him went away. And a certain man saw it, and went and told Joab, and said, Behold I saw Absalom hanged in an oak. . . . And Joab took three darts in his hand, and thrust them through the heart of Absalom, while he was yet alive in the midst of the oak.
>
> (II Samuel 18: 9–14)

Figure 2.9 Wood-pasture of prickly oak with a clear space under the trees (Kritsá, Crete, September 1986).

A similar accident could happen to anyone hurrying through the mountain savannas of East Crete today. The widely set prickly oak trees have dense, tangled crowns on short boles, rather like the oaks in an English park (fig. 2.9). Generations of browsing animals have eaten away all the foliage within reach, leaving a clear space above the ground which tends to be not quite as high as it looks, tempting the passer-by to take unwise short cuts.

An understanding of nature extends into the Gospels and a little way into early Christian literature. The most extensive account of the vegetation of any part of ancient Greece is in the early Christian book called the *Shepherd of Hermas*. His vision is built around the twelve contrasted mountains of Arkadia and the trees, plants, and animals growing and living on each of them. It is remarkably like Arkadia – the wild interior province of the Peloponnese – today. (The literary Arcadia is a Renaissance invention.)

Conclusions

The Greek landscape is quite robust. As our grandfathers knew it, it was at least 3,000 years old. It was very different from aboriginal Greece, but the big changes took place long before there were writers to put them on record. Some of those changes, such as the extermination of the Cretan mammals, may have been anthropogenic, but there were climatic changes as well.

The classical Greeks appear to have lived well within the limitations of their environment. The landscape was not rapidly changing, nor were there technical innovations having unforeseen consequences; there was no particular need for the Greeks to be explicitly ecologically minded. They apparently had less of an attitude to ecology than the Romans, though this appearance could be an accident of survival of the documents. It is much more likely that the ancient Hebrews were more appreciative of nature than either Greeks or Romans.

At certain periods in its history, such as the nineteenth century, Greece was being overworked by over-population. Virtually every scrap of possible land, and much that would seem impossible, was being cultivated; terraces extended on to all but the steepest slopes (cf. Foxhall, this volume), and far into the mountains on any slope that had soil; browsing animals devoured all the palatable plants they could reach. As Gerola's Cretan photographs (1905–32) show, the walls of cities towered above a desert-like landscape. In most places virtually every tree that was not a fruit-tree, even trees on cliffs, was felled every ten years or so. But as the last hundred years show, the landscape has resilience from such treatment. Terraces have decayed back to the former slope and have reverted to pasture-land or woodland; felled trees have sprouted and grown up again; palatable plants are beginning to come down from their cliff refugia. Only the fens, still arable land, have not recovered.

Such processes may well have occurred in the past whenever, for one reason or another, a high human population declined. In antiquity it was not easy, in most of Greece, to do permanent damage to the landscape. The critical step in the degradation of the Greek environment was the invention of the bulldozer.

Bibliography

Baladié, R. (1974), 'Sur le sens géographique du mot grec "ophrys", de ses dérivés et de son équivalent latin', *Journal des savants*, 153–91.

Barthélémy, J. J. (1788), *Voyage du jeune Anacharsis en Grèce* (Paris).

Baumann, H. (1993), *Greek Wild Flowers and Plant Lore in Ancient Greece*, trans. and augmented by W. T. Stearn and E. R. Stearn (London).

Bender, H. (1994), 'Historical environmental research from the viewpoint of provincial Roman archaeology', in Frenzel (ed.), 145–55.

Evans, A. (1921–35), *The Palace of Minos*, 4 vols (New York).

Frazer, J. G. (1898), *Pausanias' Description of Greece*, i–vi (London).

Frenzel, B. (ed. 1994), *Evaluation of Land Surfaces Cleared from Forests in the Mediterranean Region during the Time of the Roman Empire* (Paläoklimaforschung, 10, special issue: ESF Project 'European Palaeoclimate and Man', 5; Mainz, Strasburg, Stuttgart, Jena, and New York).

Gerola, G. (1905–32), *Monumenti veneti dell'isola di Creta*, i–iv (Venice).

Grove, J. M. (1992), 'Climatic reconstruction in the eastern Mediterranean with particular reference to Crete', in Grove *et al.* (eds), 16–20.

——, Moody, J. A., and Rackham, O. (eds 1992), *Stability and Change in the Cretan Landscape* (Petromarula, no. 1).

Gunther, R. T. (1933), *The Greek Herbal of Dioscorides: Illustrated by a Byzantine AD 512, Englished by J. Goodyer AD 1655* (Oxford).

Habicht, C. (1985), *Pausanias' Guide to Ancient Greece* (Berkeley).

Hughes, J. D. (1983), 'How the ancients viewed deforestation', *JFA* 10: 436–45.

—— (1994), 'Forestry and forest economy in the Mediterranean region in the time of the Roman empire in the light of historical sources', in Frenzel (ed.), 1–14.

Lewis, C. S. (1950), 'Historicism', *The Month*, 4.

McNeill, J. R. (1992), *The Mountains of the Mediterranean World: An Environmental History* (Cambridge).

Meiggs, R. (1982), *Trees and Timber in the Ancient Mediterranean World* (Oxford).

Perlin, J. (1989), *A Forest Journey* (New York).

Rackham, O. (1983), 'Observations on the historical ecology of Boeotia', *BSA* 78: 291–351.

—— (1987), 'The countryside: history and pseudo-history', *The Historian*, 14: 13–17.

—— (1990a), *Trees and Woodland in the British Landscape*, 2nd edn (London).

—— (1990b), 'Ancient landscapes', in O. Murray and S. Price (eds), *The Greek City: From Homer to Alexander* (Oxford), 85–111.

—— (1991), 'On teaching ecological fallacy', *Bulletin of the British Ecological Society*, 22: 102–5.

—— (1992a), 'Vegetation history of Crete', in Grove *et al.* (eds), 29–39.

—— (1992b), 'Ecology and pseudo-ecology: the triumph of unreason', *Tern* (Norfolk Naturalists' Trust), 4: 19.

—— and Moody, J. A. (1992), 'Terraces', in B. Wells (ed.), *Agriculture in Ancient Greece (Proceedings of the 7th International Symposium at the Swedish Institute at Athens)* (Skrifter utgivna av Svenska Institutet i Athen, series in 4to, 42; Stockholm), 123–33.

—— and —— (1996), *The Making of the Cretan Landscape* (Manchester).

Rubner, H. (1985), 'Greek thought and forest science', *Environmental Review*, 9: 277–96.

Sonnini, C. S. (1801), *Voyage en Grèce et en Turquie fait par ordre de Louis XVI* (Paris).

Thirgood, J. V. (1987), *Cyprus: A Chronicle of its Forests, Land and People* (Vancouver).

Wertime, T. A. (1961), *The Coming of the Age of Steel* (Leiden).

—— (1983), 'The furnace versus the goat', *JFA* 10: 445–52.

Zangger, E. (1992), *The Flood from Heaven: Deciphering the Atlantis Legend* (London).

3

Feeling the earth move: cultivation techniques on steep slopes in classical antiquity

Lin Foxhall

Introduction

Terrace systems are one of the most characteristic features of the modern landscape of southern Greece. The question of whether this seductive lattice-work of dry-stone walls can be projected back into antiquity has intrigued scholars for some time, and in recent years discussion has become particularly lively.[1] Here I shall argue that the terrace systems now visible are modern (i.e. probably post-medieval) for the most part. The ancient systems of cultivation in Greece (and Italy) for which we have a reasonable amount of information largely used other means of keeping soil on hillsides. For farming, as for most other aspects of Greek and Roman life, our sources emerge from the wealthiest sector of society. It is virtually impossible to ascertain securely how peasants attempted to solve the problems of soil movement and erosion, even if we can sometimes make plausible guesses. This is not to say that terracing was not practised in antiquity; on the contrary, I am sure it was. What I am suggesting is that we cannot now 'see' ancient agricultural terraces, for two reasons: (1) terracing is virtually invisible in the documentary sources; more importantly,

---

[1] Bradford 1956; Lohmann 1993, 166–73; 196–219 and *passim*; Lohmann 1992, 51–6; Rackham and Moody 1992; Isager and Skydsgaard 1992, 81–2; cf. Leveau 1991.

(2) the landscape itself has been constantly worked and reworked since antiquity, so that any ancient terracing systems have been either obliterated or incorporated into modern terracing in such a way as to render them undatable. I remain unconvinced by any claimed finds of agricultural terraces dating back to classical antiquity or beyond.

I shall begin by outlining the techniques of farming on slopes documented from antiquity. I shall confine the discussion to Greek material as much as possible, but occasional forays into the Roman agricultural writers will be necessary. I shall then describe the process of constructing terraces[1] and compare the process and labour requirements of trenching for a vineyard or other crop-trees. Finally, I shall examine some of the archaeological examples of what have recently been claimed as ancient agricultural terraces and field systems, suggesting that these are of dubious antiquity: indeed, none can be proven to date to any particular period.

Terraces: the ancient references and non-references

There is extraordinarily little evidence for the use of agricultural terracing in classical antiquity. This does not, of course, mean that it did not exist. Rather, it suggests that (for the various reasons to be discussed below) terracing was not much used by the farmers at the wealthy end of the socio-economic scale to whom most of the ancient evidence refers.

The earliest probable reference to genuine agricultural terracing comes in Homer's *Odyssey*:

> Stranger, would you wish to work, if I were to take you on, on the marginal fields (*agrou ep' eschatiês*) – there will be a sufficient wage for you – assembling walls (*haimasias*) and planting tall trees?
>
> (*Od.* 18. 357–9)

I will not even attempt to consider the problems of the socio-economic context (if any) of 'Homeric' farming, let alone its relation to later farming systems; and this passage is not unambiguous and need not necessarily represent agricultural

---

[1] The material presented in that section I owe to Hamish Forbes.

terracing, though I am not the first to interpret it in this way.[1] But if this interpretation is correct, the circumstances of the proposed work are significant. Terracing is meant to be constructed (1) on marginal land (the most likely meaning of *eschatiê*); (2) it is done in connection with tree cultivation on this marginal land; and (3) the work is done for a wage for someone else. This is not a peasant farmer making his own terraces for cereal cultivation, but a larger project in agricultural development organized by someone who is wealthy. The passage also gives no indication of the kind of terrace:[2] these could just as easily be small 'pocket' terraces, around individual trees, as long cultivation terraces.

I use the phrase 'genuine terracing' because the most prominent difficulty with identifying terrace walls in historical sources is penetrating the language. The words used for agricultural terracing in ancient Greek are those used generally for 'wall': *teichos* and *haimasia*. Frequently it is impossible to determine from the context whether an agricultural terrace or some other kind of wall is meant. Hence Strabo says that the inhabitants of the peninsula of Methana, because they would not go and fight in the Trojan war, were cursed by Agamemnon 'to build walls forever' (8. 6. 15 (575)). Given the rocky, volcanic landscape and ubiquitous terracing of the present day on Methana's steep slopes, it is tempting to interpret the story as an aetiological account of the honeycombed human landscape of antiquity.

Similarly, in Menander's comedy *Dyskolos* (lines 375–7) a wealthy young man goes out into the fields to try his hand at manual labour. His slave companion sets him to digging, and then says, 'Meanwhile I shall build up the wall, since that's a job that needs doing.' Again, this could very well refer to a terrace wall, but could just as easily refer to a wall along a road, or a boundary wall.

A more explicit literary example of this problem comes in a speech by Demosthenes, in which it might be expected that terrace walls would be mentioned:[3]

[1]   Jameson 1977–8, n. 32; Isager and Skydsgaard 1992, 81.
[2]   cf. Rackham and Moody 1992; Rackham (this volume), p. 26 above.
[3]   I quote the passage in full, with the Greek text in an appendix (pp. 65–6 below), since the most accessible translation (the 1939 Loeb by Murray) is so incorrect as to be positively misleading.

(10) In the middle between my field and theirs is a road, and hills surround the fields in a circle, so some of the run-off water is carried on the road and some on the fields. The water which falls on the road, as long as the way is clear, is carried on down the road. But should there be something in the way, then it is forced to rise up onto the fields. (11) So of course water hurtled on down this field, men of the jury, when it rained. However, this field was neglected when my father did *not* own it; but when it belonged to a person who loathed the area and preferred town life, two or three times water made its way on, and both damaged the fields and increasingly was making itself a path. For this reason, when my father saw what was happening (as I hear from those knowing the circumstances), and because at the same time the neighbours were grazing their animals on the field and traipsing through it, my father built this wall around it. (12) ... Kallikles says I am damaging him having built a wall blocking the *réma* [seasonal watercourse].[1] But I shall show that this is a field, not a *réma*. (13) If it were not conceded to be our private property, then perhaps we might have done damage, for example if we had walled off a piece of public land; but in this case they do not dispute this, and there are trees planted on the field, vines and figs. And yet who would think it worthwhile to plant them in a *réma*? Absolutely no one! And again, who would bury his forefathers there? Nobody, I think. (14) Well now, both these things have happened, O men of the jury. For the trees were planted earlier than my father built the wall around, and the tomb memorials are old and were there from before we possessed the field.

(Dem. 55. 10–14)

The dispute in this speech centres on damage caused by run-off water, allegedly because the defendant (the speaker) had built a wall impinging on the main outlet for the water, a *réma* or seasonal watercourse. Careful reading of the text (especially §§10–11) suggests that the disputants had plots on either side of a large gully (cf. Isager and Skydsgaard 1992, 118), which for most of its course coincided with a road. The speaker claims that in the past the field had been neglected. The implication of his description of this neglect in §11 is that during this time the *réma* had begun to change its course and the speaker's father had built a field boundary wall, which also served to encourage the seasonal river to go back into its old bed. Both vines and figs were planted on the plot belonging to the speaker (§13). Though the speaker

---

[1] The modern Greek word *réma* (ρέμα) is here used as a suitable term to convey the sense of Demosthenes' χαράδρα; *charadra* would have connoted the modern Greek χαράδρα, which has a different meaning.

tries to imply they are old, they may have been planted by his father. There were old grave memorials on the land as well. The speaker's trees may have been planted along the road, like those he alleges his opponent to have; that is, planted along the road/*réma* and then walled in when the trees were quite large:

> Because he himself is at fault: first, having made the road narrower, for, extending the wall outward, he made it so that the trees by the road were inside it. And then he threw the rubbish out into the road, as a result of which the road came to be made higher as well as narrower.
>
> (Dem. 55. 22)[1]

The description of run-off on the fields, the regular problems with flooding, the presence of tombs, and the fact that there is no mention of a system of terrace walls all suggest that on these plots tree cultivation was carried on without terracing. However, none of these criteria is definitive, and we cannot be sure there were no terraces here either. The walls under dispute include walls along the road, and field boundary walls (perhaps both simultaneously, in the case of the speaker's wall); they are not necessarily agricultural terrace walls.

An epigraphic example containing similar problems of ambiguity can be found in the well-known lease from Arkesine on Amorgos, which is full of references to walls which may or may not be terraces.[2] The discussion of this inscription also anticipates some of the points about alternative cultivation systems I shall make later.

> (1) The lessee . . . will pay the rent in the month Thargelion[3] (2) every year, (3–4) free of all taxes. If he fails to pay there shall be exacted from the lessee and his sureties a fine equivalent to half the rent. He is to *cultivate* half the land each year, (5) and not all the land in a

---

[1] ὃν ὅτι μὲν αὐτὸς ἐξημάρτηκε, πρῶτον μὲν τὴν ὁδὸν στενοτέραν ποιήσας, ἐξαγαγὼν ἔξω τὴν αἱμασιάν, ἵνα τὰ δένδρα τῆς ὁδοῦ ποιήσειεν εἴσω, ἔπειτα δὲ τὸν χλῆδον ἐκβαλὼν εἰς τὴν ὁδόν, ἐξ ὧν ὑψηλοτέραν τὴν αὐτὴν καὶ στενοτέραν πεποιῆσθαι συμβέβηκεν.

[2] Most of the inscription is translated by Osborne 1987, 37, whose translation I largely reproduce here, with some amendments; sections where my translation differs are italicized. Numbers in parentheses indicate approximate line divisions.

[3] May.

single year. (6) *If he ploughs fallow land he is to do three ploughings.* (7) He is to dig round the vines twice, first in Anthesterion[1] and again before the 20th of Taureion,[2] and round the figs once. If he fails to do this (8) according to the contract he must pay a fine of an obol for each vine or fig-tree round which he fails to dig, and three drachmas for each zygon[3] (9). *The sureties are to secure the payment for all additional work* (10) *that is required of the lessee, if someone wants to hold the lease. If not, the magistrates are to put it out to tender.* He is to build up again all walls that collapse, (11) on pain of a fine of a drachma for each fathom of collapsed wall. He must '*fence*'[4] all the walls along the road and (12) leave them *with fencing material in place* at the end of the lease. He is to apply 150 loads of dung a year (13) with a basket holding one medimnos and four hemihektea,[5] (14) or pay a fine of half a drachma for each basket shortfall. He must swear (15) to the temple magistrates that he has indeed applied this manure in accordance with the agreement. He must keep (16) the roofs watertight, and hand them over (17) in this condition. *The vine prunings* the temple magistrates (18) will sell. The lessee will dig trenches (19) in the month Eiraphorion[6] (20) where the magistrate will mark them out, four-foot ones and three-foot ones, and will put in the plants in the presence of the temple magistrates, planting each year twenty vines (21) at the spacing ordered by the magistrates, and ten fig-trees; and he must build a wall *on the upper part of* the land. (22) The storage jars (23) shall be considered security for the building of this wall, and the lessee will make a pledge to the magistrates. For failure to do this the fine shall be one drachma per plant ...

(SIG[3] 963. 1–23)

Lines 10–11 specify that the leaseholder must rebuild all walls that have fallen down, and a penalty of one drachma per fathom (*orguia*) of wall is charged for all walls not rebuilt. These could be boundary walls, or terrace walls, or both. Though agricultural terrace walls may well be included here, it is impossible to be certain from the context.

Lines 11–12 refer to an operation to be performed on the walls along the road: *phraxei*. Osborne translates this as 'repair', which I think is incorrect. The previous lines are concerned with repairs to walls, using the verb *anorthoô*; this seems to be something

---

[1] February.
[2] April.
[3] A measure of land, of uncertain area.
[4] i.e. put brushwood on top and make beast-proof.
[5] *c.*70 litres.
[6] December.

different. In fact, the verb φράσσω means 'to fence, enclose, hedge', and often seems to imply the use of perishable, or at least less durable, materials. When used in a military sense, it more often refers to blockades and palisades than to 'proper' fortifications.[1] On the road walls in this inscription, I think it means to put fencing material (e.g. juniper, spiny broom, etc.) on top of them, as it does in some of the military examples (see Forbes, this volume, ch. 4). The reason why this was done on the (probably) free-standing walls bordering the road was presumably to keep out athletic two- and four-legged intruders, to whom low dry-stone walls would prove to be no barrier. Because the materials are perishable and the barriers impermanent, they would need regular renewing, hence the provision that the walls be left fenced when the leaseholder gives up the lease (this also, of course, prohibits the leaseholder from taking the fencing material with him). So these lines should probably be translated 'he shall fence all the walls along the road, and when he goes he will leave them behind fenced'. This is interesting in terms of ancient security, but it is not a terrace wall.

The final reference to walls comes in the section where provisions for new plantings of vines and figs are specified (lines 19–23). The correct interpretation of this passage is not at all clear. The *traphai* (τράφαι = τάφραι) could be either drainage ditches or planting-trenches;[2] the specifications about planting here indicate that they are almost certainly planting-trenches. But it is not clear what the dimensions 'four-foot' and 'three-foot' mean. Are there two lots of trenches, or are these the dimensions (width × depth, or vice versa) of one trench? Comparative recommendations from other ancient sources suggest that one, if not both, of these

---

[1] e.g. Hdt. 7. 142, the fence made of thorny brushwood which allegedly surrounded the Acropolis in olden days; *not* 'a thorn hedge' as de Sélincourt (1954, 489), with most others, translates; 8. 51, the makeshift barricade of the Acropolis in the face of the Persian attack; 9. 70, the temporary wooden palisade erected by the fleeing Persians near the temple of Demeter at Thebes; Thuc. 8. 35, temporary defences rapidly put up by the Knidians after being attacked by the Peloponnesian fleet.
[2] Theophrastos, *Causes of Plants*, 3. 4. 4, and *passim*; 3. 6. 3–4, though usually he uses *gyros* to mean a planting-hole and *taphra* to mean a drainage ditch, as at 3. 12. 1; however, the distinction is not so clear at 3. 6. 4.

dimensions refers to the depth to which the planting-trenches should be dug.[1] The lease provides that the lessee must plant out twenty vines and ten figs annually, and that the temple magistrates will specify the locations for the plantings and inspect them. A wall is to be built up (the verb used is ἐποικοδομέω) *hyper gês* (ὑπὲϱ γῆς: the meaning of this phrase is not clear: 'at the top of the plot'?). The wall was obviously considered important because the pithoi were to be held as security against the wall being built. But is this wall-building an annual event? The passage suggests that the temple magistrates were trying to develop an area of uncultivated hillside with plantings of figs and vines, by getting their lessees to cultivate another section every year (this is why they specify where plantings should be, and that they are to be inspected so carefully). It could be that the area was gradually being terraced, and that a new retaining wall was built annually. Or the wall could be a 'one-off'. One difficulty with the former alternative is that the wall is specified as being built *hyper gês*, apparently meaning on the upper part of the plot. Normally when terraces are made the wall is built at the lower end of the terrace under construction (see below). But in either case, *if* the arrangements prescribed in the lease were carried out as planned for any length of time, a lot of earth was moved around in the development of this land for arboriculture.

These are all the references to terracing in classical Greek sources of which I am aware. It is striking how few there are, even in circumstances where they might be expected. Theophrastos does discuss measures for cultivating stony ground (*Causes of Plants*, 3. 6. 5) and sloping plots (ibid., 3. 7. 2; *History of Plants*, 2. 4. 8), but terrace walling is never mentioned as one of the alternatives. The Roman agricultural writers are equally silent on the subject of terraces. Columella implies that he knows about terracing, and that although the fiddly, time-consuming business of constructing terrace walls was an expensive and inefficient use of slave labour, other means of disposing of stones might be even more expensive:

> It is easy to prepare a stony field by gathering up the stones. If there is a great abundance of them, either parts of the field are taken up

---

[1] Columella, *De re rustica*, 3. 13. 8; *On Trees*, 4. 2–3; Xenophon, *Oikonomikos*, 19. 1–12.

with supporting terrace walls that the rest may be thoroughly cleared, or the stones are buried to some depth in a sunken trench, which should be done if the cheapness of the labour recommends it.

(*RR* 2. 2. 12)[1]

Substructio elsewhere means a supporting embankment or foundation wall.[2] Here it must mean a supporting field wall – that is, a terrace wall. Columella also seems to feel that terracing wastes space, which was probably true for the agrarian regimes he favoured since terracing a hillside leaves less area available for tree-planting than does planting directly on the un-terraced slope.

Leveau also notes that one of the *agrimensores* mentions building walls on land, referring to 'whoever would make his own walls on his land for supporting and protecting his own fields'.[3] Leveau is convinced that *servandosque* in this passage refers to protecting fields from the dangers of erosion. I think it more likely refers to protecting crops from livestock, but perhaps *sustinendos* could refer to holding soil in place. This is not a very enlightening reference.

Building a terrace

So why and how are terraces built, and what alternatives might have been used in antiquity? The main aims of terracing are: (1) to do something with the big rocks in the soil (similar to Columella, quoted above), and (2) to slow down run-off, which means (a) that water stays in the same place longer, and thus penetrates to deeper levels where it will benefit both trees and (to a lesser extent) arable crops and is less likely to be lost through evaporation, and (b) that soil erosion is reduced.

---

[1] 'ac saxosum facile est expedire lectione lapidum, quorum si magna est abundantia, velut quibusdam substructionibus partes agri sunt occupandae, ut reliquae emundentur, vel in altitudinem sulco depresso lapides obruendi; quod tamen ita faciendum erit, si suadebit operarum vilitas.'

[2] *OLD* s.v. *substructio*, also *substructum, substruo*.

[3] Siculus Flaccus (gromatist), *De condicionibus agrorum*, 148–50, discussed by Leveau 1991, 19: 'proprias [macerias] quis faciat in terris suis ad sustinendos servandosque agros suos'.

In the modern period agricultural terraces have been constructed for growing both trees and arable crops, often simultaneously. They are built by individual households, frequently those with an abundance of adult male labour (not surprisingly, terrace-building is considered men's work). Normally the work is done in the summer, the agricultural slack season in the present (and past) peasant farming regime. Although the soil is dry and hard at this time of year, it is lighter in weight. A line of rocks is placed along the hillside at what will be the front of the finished terrace, normally following the contour of the hill. The earth is then dug out behind, and ramped up behind, the line of stones. Obviously any unwanted trees and bushes are also removed, and sizeable ones may be made into charcoal as the work goes along (thus slowing down the work of terrace-building, but producing charcoal for cash sale). When the ramp has reached the top of the first line of stones, another course is added on top of the first course and the digging and ramp-building operations continue further back into the hill, creating an increasingly greater area of level space behind the growing terrace wall. The process continues until the desired (or maximum feasible) width is reached. At this point a line of stones is laid out for a new terrace wall, behind and above the first one, and the whole process is repeated.

How long this takes is best summed up by the modern Greek term *analóghos* (ἀναλόγως): 'it depends'. Ground cover, soil type and depth, the number of large rocks that need blasting, and so on all vary from place to place and make normative estimations very difficult. Generally, we would estimate that a family could not construct more than one small *skála* (terrace system) in a summer, perhaps 0.1 hectares in size (equal to 1 *stremma* or half a day's ploughing). If these newly made terraces were to be used for cereals or other annual crops, they would produce returns relatively quickly, within one or two years. But if they were planted in trees or vines it would be several years, at best, before even a small return was realized.

Trenching: the alternative to terracing

This last point, I believe, provides a key to answering the question why alternative techniques seem to have been used for planting on slopes in classical antiquity. The farming techniques most clearly documented in our sources are those used by wealthier households. These households owned the most land, and perhaps often the best-quality land.[1] Their main source of labour was slaves (despite Wood 1983; 1988). Certainly they grew cereals, and in large quantities to judge from the stored produce of the wealthy households whose property was auctioned off in the Attic Stelai (*IG* i³ 421–30) and other inscriptions of the *pôleitai*. But they almost certainly grew the major proportion of these cereals on some of their better lands: generally in the valley bottoms or on gentle slopes, not on the steeper slopes.

When such households acquired land on relatively steep slopes, the evidence suggests they did not usually develop it for arable cultivation. In the first instance, it may have been exploited for firewood and charcoal (as in the famous case of at least part of Phainippos' *eschatia*: Dem. 42. 2. 5–7). This may have been a temporary expedient until the proprietor got round to developing it further. Such land might also be exploited for timber plantations: Adeimantos, son of Leukolophides, is recorded on the Attic Stelai as owning an 'oakery' and a 'pinery' (*IG* i³ 430a. 1–4; cf. Forbes, this volume, ch. 4). Or land that was not too steeply sloping could have been cultivated without terracing, with appropriate drainage provisions for run-off (Theophr. *Caus. Pl.* 3. 6. 3–4). A considerable amount of the modern Greek landscape is in fact farmed in this way.

When areas of steep sloping land were developed by large landowners it was most often for arboriculture. Generally the intercropping of cereals and arable was not practised on these estates (though this is not to say it was not done by small-scale farmers). If the land was of good enough quality (with a good enough depth of moisture-retentive soil) and well-watered, tree species might be intercropped with each other.[2]

The normal cultivation regimes for tree crops obviated the need for the kinds of terraces most commonly seen in the modern Greek

---

[1]   I have elsewhere estimated (Foxhall 1992) that in classical Attica about 9 per cent of the citizen body owned nearly half of the cultivable land.

[2]   e.g. vines with almonds (Theophr. *Caus. Pl.* 3. 10. 6–7); myrtle (for garlands) trained up olives (3. 10. 4) or vines up fruit-tree or timber-tree species (3. 10. 8; Dem. 53. 15).

landscape, intended for cereal cultivation. On very steep slopes, pocket terraces may have been built around individual trees and used in conjunction with a system of trenching,[1] but the ancient descriptions of desirable techniques for establishing trees and vines on 'virgin' hill-slopes and for the cultivation of established tree crops indicate that terracing was not involved, at least for wealthy farmers.

The main purpose of cultivating the land on which any tree crop is growing is to ensure that the plants receive adequate water and soil nutrients, in part by killing weed growth. The primary limiting variable for tree growth under Mediterranean Greek conditions is normally the availability of water. Hence the primary aim of the cultivation practices used by wealthy farmers who could afford the requisite inputs of labour was to maximize the amount of water (mostly from winter rainfall) available to the roots of the trees. To the same end, repeated digging destroyed roots close to the surface, encouraging the development of roots at lower levels where more moisture was available and where they were less likely to suffer from sun-scorch or exposure; this allowed trees to utilize available water more efficiently (Theophr. *Caus. Pl.* 5. 9. 8). This was particularly important for olives, which mostly have wide-spreading roots close to the surface (Theophr. *Hist. Pl.* 1. 6. 4; Pansiot and Rebour 1961, 14–16), and for vines, which also produce surface roots and for which the conservation of maximum soil moisture is essential to the production of an abundance of high-quality grapes. Basically this means a great deal of digging (Theophr. *Hist. Pl.* 2. 7. 5; *Caus. Pl.* 3. 10. 1; 3. 12. 1; 3. 20. 7).

It is clear that digging was the most laborious and time-consuming part of tree cultivation for olives, figs, and especially vines. Trees were planted in basins or trenches, which served to catch and hold water close to the base of the tree where it would be available to the roots.[2] This increased both the quantity and the quality of the yield. Considerable digging preparatory to

[1] As may be the case in Dem. 55: see above, p. 47.
[2] cf. Pansiot and Rebour 1961, 176–8. In southern Greece total precipitation is quite low, but individual storms may be torrential: the entire winter's rain may sometimes fall in only three or four occurrences. Unless some kind of anti-erosion measures are taken, considerable amounts of soil may well end up at the bottom of the hill. The extent to which the technique of trenching to retain winter rainfall in the soil was specifically

planting was recommended, to a depth of between one and a half and three Greek feet (*c*.0.44–0.89 m) by Xenophon (*Oikonomikos*, 19. 1–12), probably deeper in the case of *SIG*³ 963, discussed earlier. Theophrastos suggests that in dry areas it is advisable to dig as deeply as possible (*Caus. Pl.* 3. 12. 1).

Repeated digging also reduces the weed growth, which would otherwise compete with trees or vines for moisture and soil nutrients (cf. Theophr. *Caus. Pl.* 3. 20. 9). How many times trees were dug depended on the micro-environmental conditions of the plot on which they were growing, the importance of the crop to the owner, and most importantly the amount of labour available. The outline of digging times which I present here, synthesized from the ancient sources, probably represents a maximum labour input.[1] The soil around each tree was dug several times a year to shape it appropriately for the season, to loosen it, and to kill weeds. (1) During the autumn, at or just before the time of the winter rains, a basin-like trench was dug out all round the tree. Soil was loosened and banked around the outer edges of the trench, to hold water around the base and to allow the winter rains to penetrate to the roots. This also, of course, had the effect of slowing down run-off, and thus reducing erosion, as well as keeping run-off water in the places where it would benefit the crop most. (2) In the late winter and early spring, trees were dug again to break up the soil which had become packed down during the winter and to kill the flush of weeds that would have developed. While it was still the rainy period, this further increased the moisture available to the roots and also allowed the sun to warm the soil (by increasing the surface area exposed to the sun), thus bringing on budding more rapidly (cf. Theophr. *Caus. Pl.* 3. 12. 2). Manure or other organic fertilizer was dug into the soil during either the autumn or the spring digging, while there was still sufficient rainfall for the tree to make use of it (ibid. 3. 9. 5; Pansiot and Rebour 1961, 111). Bulky organic fertilizers, in addition to

adapted for Mediterranean environmental conditions is revealed by Theophrastos's comments on how it does *not* work well in regions with cold, wet winters: trees are killed by water standing in the basins and freezing (*Caus. Pl.* 5. 13. 1). This strengthens the suggestion that the technique was normal in the Mediterranean regions of Greece.

[1] cf. Theophr. *Caus. Pl.* 3. 16. 2, suggesting that vines should be dug three times annually.

supplying soil nutrients (especially nitrogen), could also increase the moisture retentiveness of the soil. (3) Later in the spring the top layer of the soil was broken up very finely, trenches were filled in, and the soil was heaped up around the bases of the trees. The loose top layer of soil rapidly became completely desiccated by the hot sun. Because soil particles were separated by air pockets, this layer acted as a dust mulch, preventing evaporation of water via capillary action from the damp soil levels below.[1] (4) In the middle of the summer the soil was broken up yet again, to renew and increase the efficacy of the dust mulch.

It is clear from Theophrastos and other sources (see Foxhall 1995b) that the trenches around trees were only one component in the soil-management systems practised by wealthy farmers.[2] Individual trenches around trees were often connected to each other, ideally across the contour (to further slow run-off and prevent the formation of erosion gullies; see Dem. 55. 10–11, 22, and 26–7). In areas of particularly damp soil, on steeper slopes, or where run-off was especially heavy and/or violent, these small ditches between trees could be connected to larger ditches to drain away run-off without incurring sheet or gully erosion. If there were large stones about that had been removed from the soil during cultivation, these could profitably be placed at the bottoms of ditches, or even occasionally used in the construction of soak-aways (Theophr. *Caus. Pl.* 3. 6. 3–5).

The labour requirements of establishing a vineyard (or orchard) to be worked by a similar system of trenching on hill-slopes in Italy are discussed at length by Columella. This comes from a completely different economic and ecological context and cannot be transplanted directly to classical Greece; none the less it provides a useful comparison for comprehending the large scale of the labour investment entailed in undertaking such a project.

From the wording of his instructions for making vineyards it is clear that Columella had in mind the large-scale development of

---

[1] Theophr. *Hist. Pl.* 2. 7. 5; at *Caus. Pl.* 3. 16. 3, he actually calls the creation and maintenance of a dust mulch 'the dusting'. For the modern use of dust mulching see Forbes 1982, 436–45.

[2] A failure to carry out proper cultivation and soil management seems to be part of the cause of the troubles between the disputants in Dem. 55.

previously unoccupied land (*On Trees*, 1. 4).[1] He suggests that to trench one *iugerum* of flat land to a depth of 1.5–2 Roman feet (0.444–0.592 m) took fifty workers one day (198 man-days per hectare). To trench a hill or sloping ground to a depth of 2 Roman feet (0.592 m) took sixty workers per *iugerum* per day (237 man-days per hectare).

Trenching for a nursery took even longer (perhaps partly explaining the classical Greek reluctance to go in for the nursery rearing of trees). Columella (*On Trees*, 4. 2–3) suggests that land for a nursery, or for setting out unrooted cuttings in permanent locations, be trenched on flat land to a depth of 3 Roman feet (0.888 m), which takes eighty men one day per *iugerum* (316 man-days per hectare). This figure is for land without rocks and other obstructions: on rocky ground the operation took longer. Elsewhere (*RR* 3. 13. 8) he recommends that sloping land to be used for these purposes be trenched to a depth of 4 Roman feet (1.18 m). The added depth needed, and the difficulty of working on hillsides, would have significantly increased the amount of labour necessary. It is extremely likely that for such special operations the normal slave staff of even a large and well-manned villa estate would not have been sufficient, and that additional labour of some kind would have been brought in.

All of the aims of terracing listed above, except the first – finding something to do with the rocks – are fulfilled by continual and intensive digging and trenching on all but very steep slopes (cf. Pansiot and Rebour 1961, 99, 176–8). Hence, in many areas under the tree-cultivation regime of trenches and ditches, which was apparently commonly used by large landowners in classical antiquity, there was generally no need for large-scale terrace systems. Given the substantial proportion of the land in the hands of large landowners (Foxhall 1992), it is likely that this at least partially explains the rarity of terrace walls, in either the archaeological or the documentary record, that can be securely dated to classical antiquity.

It must be stressed that this whole system of cultivation, as it is documented in the ancient sources, needed a tremendous

---

[1] 'If you are going to fill up hills with vineyards or *arbusta*', i.e. trees with vines climbing up them ('nam si colles vineis vel arbustis occupaturus es').

amount of continuous labour throughout the year. In classical Greek economies this was most obviously and effectively provided by slaves.[1] Hence such cultivation regimes for tree crops are the prerogative of the rich. Indeed, the development of sloping land for arboriculture, based on a trenching and ditching system, was probably advantageous for wealthy households aiming more at the generation of income rather than subsistence. These intensive arboricultural regimes were relevant to households where, although they were farming to supply their own food needs, subsistence could be taken for granted and was not the main consideration. Hence the intercropping of annuals was also not a priority in these regimes, allowing the constant digging which obviated the need for terrace construction.[2]

In conclusion – and this must be arguing on a gross level of crude social divisions – any terracing systems like those of modern Greece that were built in classical antiquity were probably mostly constructed by smaller-scale farmers. Wealthier farmers using slave labour to develop sloping land probably most often planted it with trees or vines, using a system of trenches and ditches which demanded more constant maintenance than terraces. These trenching systems probably ensured high returns and fully-occupied slaves, but would have demanded too much labour for small-scale farmers. Terraces, on the other hand, can be constructed in 'spare time', and once planted with trees and/or arable crops they demand much less regular labour input than a system of digging and trenching: trees and vines planted on terraces will crop adequately even if they are cultivated much less energetically than by the methods described above. More importantly, for small-scale farmers, the level ground provided by terraces allowed the

[1] It is interesting that Greek and Roman writers on agrarian matters are less concerned with labour crises and bottlenecks than with keeping the farm workers constantly occupied. To some extent this may be part of the moral agenda of these works, though it may be partly the socio-political setting of slave labour. Though there is some concern with the efficient use of labour, it seems to have been more important to keep slaves busy than to use them efficiently. Constant digging may not have enhanced productivity a great deal, beyond a certain point.

[2] cf., for the modern estate-based cultivation of olives, Pansiot and Rebour 1961, 102: 'The basic argument in favor of it [polycropping] is the spreading of risks; however a better income will be derived from crops grown separately.'

intercropping of cereals or other annuals with the trees. But returns from the trees will not have been as great (or perhaps of such high quality) as from tree crops planted on their own.

The archaeological evidence (?) for ancient terracing

Claims to have discovered ancient terracing systems in Greece have a long ancestry. Bradford's work (1956; 1957) is now very old, and though it is frequently cited as 'fact' by more recent studies (e.g. Isager and Skydsgaard 1992, 81), the areas photographed were not subjected at the time (and have not been since) to intensive archaeological survey, so there is no way of eliminating the possibility that they date to some period other than the classical. Ideas about how to explore ancient landscapes, both in Greece and in Britain, have changed considerably since Bradford's pioneering work. We also have a much better understanding of the human, climatic, ecological, and geomorphological processes involved in the creation and deterioration of landscapes than scholars working in the 1940s and 1950s. However, even at the time of Bradford's work it was clear that many of the ancient villages in the area of south-west Attica that he studied were occupied both earlier and later than the classical period, to which he dated the remains of terraces he saw (1956, 173 nn. 5–6). His basic assumption, that the area had not been cultivated 'for very many centuries' (ibid., 177), is at best unprovable, at worst demonstrably incorrect.[1] The speed with which Greek landscapes can deteriorate, regenerate vegetation, and be again re-sculpted eluded him.[2]

---

[1] Bradford's Attic terrace systems could date to any period; indeed, to many periods. As usual, none of the masonry styles is diagnostic, judging from the published photographs, and at least one terrace identified as ancient seems to have been rebuilt, perhaps more than once, in relatively modern times. Though it incorporates some apparently ancient cut blocks, other stones include large unworked boulders and some small, roughly worked blocks which do not look ancient (Bradford 1956, pl. 10d). His plate 10b could be an eroded terrace of any date. The same is true of plate 10a, which shows not, as he thought, a 'line of stones showing the top of a terrace' (1956, 176), but almost certainly the foundations of an ex-terrace, undatable in the present state of our knowledge.

[2] These processes and the speed at which they occur depend on a number of human, climatic, geological, and ecological variables, which may be

Doukellis is now attempting to trace ancient terracing and land measurement systems in modern field boundaries. Although his results are interesting (Doukellis 1994), there is no secure means of pinpointing the date. The argument that the landscape was unused or uninhabited in later times is unviable, and in fact there are other colonizing powers to whom such cadastration may be attributable, notably the Venetians.

Neither of these studies is very convincing, since there is no definitive means of dating to within a millennium or so the past landscapes discovered by such remote sensing methods. Unfortunately this appears to be true of all Greek terrace systems. The only ones on Methana that we can precisely date are those built by inhabitants to whom we have spoken, or whose parents or grandparents built them. This, in fact, amounts to quite a few terraces and terrace systems. It is clear from the recent history of Methana, as preserved in the documentary record, that the peninsula was largely uninhabited and uncultivated in 1805. By the 1850s the population had risen dramatically because of changing political circumstances in the region. Much of the terracing, including some abandoned terrace systems, demonstrably dates from the later nineteenth century (Forbes 1996; Forbes *et al.* 1996). The Greek landscape has been constantly inhabited and reinhabited since antiquity. At present there is no reliable means of dating agricultural terraces by the presence or absence of artefactual material, though there may be some future possibility with the development of geomorphological and geochemical methodologies such as soil magnetism studies.[1] The relationship of the 'background scatter' found by intensive survey to the landscape is highly problematic, and has recently been the subject of much debate (see Alcock *et al.* 1994 for a summary of the arguments). What is clear is that such inter-site finds emanate from all periods

highly localized. See Forbes and Koster 1976; Rackham and Moody 1992; Rackham, this volume, ch. 2.

[1] James *et al.* 1994. Although James's work is enlightening in relation to the processes that result in the movement of artefactual material on steep slopes, and suggests interesting possibilities for further study, it has still not satisfactorily related artefactual material to the building dates of terraces. The very processes of constant cultivation and terrace construction and reconstruction, as described above, could result in the occasional sherd of early date appearing in the topsoil levels supported by terrace walls but not in the clay subsoil levels beneath them, as James found.

and cannot be used to date agricultural terracing systems now visible.

Recently several archaeological surveys, including Lohmann's project in southern Attica (Lohmann 1985; 1992; 1993) and the work of Wells and Runnels in the Berbati–Limnes region (Wells *et al.* 1990), have claimed to have discovered ancient agricultural terraces. I am not convinced by either, though I have seen both.

Lohmann claims that the now abandoned terrace system he has located in southern Attica was for the cultivation of olives as a cash crop, on the grounds that only classical material was found in the area and that the region would only be suitable for growing olives (Lohmann 1985, 81–4; 1992, 42–56; 1993, 196–219). In fact, there seems to be very little sherd material of *any* period in the area, though diagnostic sherds cover all the periods for which diagnostic pottery most often survives in survey contexts all over Greece: notably classical, late Roman, and medieval (Lohmann 1993, ii, LE16–18). Moreover, all the farmsteads he pinpoints as 'olive-growing' farms (notably sites LE16 and CH31) in fact have either no surviving pressing equipment or pressing equipment belonging to the late Roman period, which presumably goes with the sherd assemblages of that date which he himself documents on these sites. There is no classical pressing equipment at all represented in the published survey (Foxhall 1996b). The amount of surviving pressing equipment, even of late Roman date, is very low in contrast to, for example, Methana, where it is clear that olives really were grown for the market at that time (Foxhall 1996a). None the less, the number of 'farmstead' sites documented by Lohmann that have both a classical and a late Roman component suggests that these conform to the pattern also found across the Saronic gulf on Methana (ibid.).

Lohmann claims that the terraces he found are aligned to the classical farm buildings. However, it is clear from his own drawings and models that in fact several of the terraces incorporate sections of ancient walling, suggesting that whatever the date of the terraces, they postdate the structures.[1] Moreover, terraces

---

[1] See e.g. Lohmann 1992, 53, fig. 27, where the terrace walls on approximately the 44 m and 42 m contours probably joined up with the classical structure (PH33); p. 54, fig. 28, where the terrace walls just above and just below the classical structure probably originally incorporated it. In

genuinely dating from the classical period, over 2,000 years ago, on land claimed not to have been cultivated since then, ought to have fallen down a lot more than these have. Terraces demand moderately low maintenance compared to other cultivation systems on slopes, but they are still not maintenance-free. If they are abandoned, walls fall down and vegetative regrowth takes place, even in remarkably inhospitable-looking areas.[1] Walls eventually disappear, sometimes allowing considerable erosion to take place before the maquis re-establishes itself (Forbes and Koster 1976). The area where Lohmann's terraces are located looks as if it has been abandoned relatively recently, judging from the lack of vegetative regrowth and the lichen build-up on the stones of the terrace walls. The walls themselves are in moderately good condition, which would not be expectable if they are 2,000 or more years old. Indeed, many of the exposed faces of the limestone boulders used in the construction of these terraces are still quite angular. If they were truly ancient, more weathered surfaces might be expected (E. Zangger, pers. comm.). And given the arguments presented above, there is every reason to think they were not made in classical antiquity for the cultivation of olives.

Similar arguments can be brought forward to counter the claims of the antiquity of the Berbati–Limnes terraces. These are alleged to be bronze age terraces, again because of the artefact finds (though there is a considerable amount of modern sherd material in the area) and because they are constructed of particularly large rocks. At present these are cultivated with luxuriant olive trees. Again, although a bronze age date cannot be eliminated, neither can it be vigorously sustained on present evidence. The size of the rocks is not conclusive for dating: farmers make terraces using the rocks at hand, and if there were large rocks on the plot they would have been used in any period. Since earth is heaped up behind the terrace walls in the process of construction, it is not difficult to roll big rocks up the ramp to the upper courses. Terraces can, of course, be rebuilt, and once a terrace system is

our experience, terraces in the vicinity of ancient structures frequently include ancient cut blocks, but this does not certify them as ancient agricultural terraces.

[1] This is, after all, exactly what the speaker claimed had happened to the wall of his field in Dem. 55, discussed above.

in place it is likely to be kept up and repaired as long as it is in use. Once it goes out of use, though, depending on the local environment, all traces of it may disappear within a century or less. It is a very hopeful archaeologist who claims continuous occupation of a field system for 3,000 or more years, though stranger things have happened.

All the archaeological evidence so far cited has proven to be negative. Remarkably often it appears that the period that most interests the archaeologists on a particular project coincides with the dating assigned to the terraces they find. But there is one positive analysis. The only systematic study so far that has attempted to correlate the occupation of rural sites with angle of slope (Whitelaw forthcoming) in fact suggests that ancient farmers preferred to avoid slopes that needed extensive terracing. Whitelaw has clearly shown that on Keos most of the small 'farmstead' sites of the classical period are situated on slopes of less than 15 degrees, which would probably not need terracing under the systems of cultivation outlined above.

Conclusions

Systems of cultivation in the classical past of Greece were often (though not always) remarkably different from those in use today. There are many ways to skin that particular cat, and probably most of them have been tried over the last 8,000 years of cultivation of Mediterranean environments. In particular, the Greek landscape has been constantly re-sculpted between the fifth century BC and the present. It is unrealistic to expect that the present system of land management can be projected back infinitely into the past on a substantial scale.

In classical antiquity, systems of trenched trees grown on even quite steep slopes without terracing seem to have been widespread. This technique allowed wealthy farmers to develop hill-slopes efficiently and profitably (in both the social and the economic sense) utilizing slave and/or dependent labour. One hesitates to make too much of a Homeric reference, but the one mention of terracing in the *Odyssey* may suggest that such agrarian development strategies were used by wealthy farmers from very early times. This must cast much doubt on the extent to which movement on to sloping lands can be considered to be a measure of desperation, or a result of over-population. It would seem more likely that, at least when done by the rich, such schemes of land development made use of available surplus labour for generating income. Tree-trenching was probably not such a useful technique for small-scale subsistence farmers, who probably did indeed use agricultural terraces on any steep bits of the landscape they cultivated.

The implications for gully and sheet erosion of the abandonment of the tree-trenching systems widely in use in antiquity are also important. Abandoned terraces can allow substantial erosion after cultivation has ceased, before vegetative regrowth takes hold (Forbes and Koster 1976), though I take Rackham's point (ch. 2 in this volume) that vegetation does regrow, often quite rapidly. None the less the scale of erosion may have been considerable in some situations when a trenched vineyard was deserted. Untended vines would die within a few years in many locations, and there would be little else, not even walls, to hold soil on the hillsides. Vineyards would perhaps be more problematic in this regard than land with other crop trees, which will survive even if neglected.

Agricultural systems and cultivation techniques exist in conjunction with human social systems. The examples of alternative forms of soil retention and cultivation on slopes in Greece show the extent to which techniques were chosen because they answered economic and social needs rather than environmental or ecological ones. There are many means by which the Greek landscape can be encouraged to bear fruit. Which ones were chosen in antiquity depended on the aims of the farmer (e.g. cash versus subsistence), the labour his household had available, his political pretensions and the kind of lifestyle he was under pressure to keep up, and many similar factors. Nature and culture must walk hand in hand.

Appendix: Demosthenes, 55. 10–14

(10) τοῦ γὰρ χωρίου τοῦ τ' ἐμοῦ καὶ τοῦ τούτων τὸ μέσον ὁδός ἐστιν, ὅρους δὲ περιέχοντος κύκλῳ τοῖς χωρίοις, τὸ καταρρέον ὕδωρ τῇ μὲν εἰς τὴν ὁδόν, τῇ δ' εἰς τὰ χωρία συμβαίνει φέρεσθαι. καὶ δὴ καὶ τοῦτο τὸ εἰσπῖπτον εἰς τὴν ὁδόν, ᾗ μὲν ἂν εὐοδῇ, φέρεται κάτω κατὰ τὴν ὁδόν, ᾗ δ' ἂν ἐνστῇ τι, τηνικαῦτα τοῦτ'

εἰς τὰ χωρί᾽ ὑπεραίρειν ἀναγκαῖον ἤδη. (11) καὶ δὴ καὶ κατὰ τοῦτο τὸ χωρίον, ὦ ἄνδρες δικασταί, γενομένης ἐπομβρίας συνέβη τὸ ὕδωρ ἐμβαλεῖν· ἀμεληθὲν δ᾽ οὔπω τοῦ πατρὸς ἔχοντος αὐτό, ἀλλ᾽ ἀνθρώπου δυσχεραίνοντος ὅλως τοῖς τόποις καὶ μᾶλλον ἀστικοῦ, δὶς καὶ τρὶς ἐμβαλὸν τὸ ὕδωρ τά τε χωρί᾽ ἐλυμήνατο καὶ μᾶλλον ὡδοποίει. διὸ δὴ ταῦθ᾽ ὁ πατὴρ ὁρῶν, ὡς ἐγὼ τῶν εἰδότων ἀκούω, καὶ τῶν γειτόνων ἐπινεμόντων ἅμα καὶ βαδιζόντων διὰ τοῦ χωρίου, τὴν αἱμασιὰν περιῳκοδόμησε ταύτην. (12) ... Καλλικλῆς μὲν γάρ φησι τὴν χαράδραν ἀποικοδομήσαντα βλάπτειν μ᾽ αὐτόν· ἐγὼ δ᾽ ἀποδείξω χωρίον ὂν τοῦτ᾽, ἀλλ᾽ οὐ χαράδραν. (13) εἰ μὲν οὖν μὴ συνεχωρεῖθ᾽ ἡμέτερον ἴδιον εἶναι, τάχ᾽ ἂν τοῦτ᾽ ἠδικοῦμεν, εἴ τι τῶν δημοσίων ᾠκοδομοῦμεν· νῦν δ᾽ οὔτε τοῦτ᾽ ἀμφισβητοῦσιν, ἔστι τ᾽ ἐν τῷ χωρίῳ δένδρα πεφυτευμένα, ἄμπελοι καὶ συκαῖ. καίτοι τίς ἂν ἐν χαράδρᾳ ταῦτα φυτεύειν ἀξιώσειεν; οὐδείς γε. τίς δὲ πάλιν τοὺς αὑτοῦ προγόνους θάπτειν; οὐδὲ τοῦτ᾽, οἶμαι. (14) ταῦτα τοίνυν ἀμφότερ᾽, ὦ ἄνδρες δικασταί, συμβέβηκεν· καὶ γὰρ τὰ δένδρα πεφύτευται πρότερον ἢ τὸν πατέρα περιοικοδομῆσαι τὴν αἱμασιάν, καὶ τὰ μνήματα παλαιὰ καὶ πρὶν ἡμᾶς κτήσασθαι τὸ χωρίον γεγενημέν᾽ ἐστίν.

Bibliography

Alcock, S. E., Cherry, J. F., and Davis, J. L. (1994), 'Intensive survey, agricultural practice and the classical landscape of Greece', in I. Morris (ed.), *Classical Greece: Ancient Histories and Modern Archaeologies* (New Directions in Archaeology; Cambridge), ch. 8 (pp. 137–70).

Bradford, J. (1956), 'Fieldwork on aerial discoveries in Attica and Rhodes, II', *Antiquaries' Journal*, 36: 172–80.

—— (1957), *Ancient Landscapes: Studies in Field Archaeology* (London).

de Sélincourt, A. (trans. 1954), *Herodotus: The Histories* (Harmondsworth).

Doukellis, P. N. (1994), 'Le territoire de la colonie romaine de Corinthe', in P. N. Doukellis and L. G. Mendoni (eds), *Structures rurales et sociétés antiques* (Centre de Recherches d'Histoire Ancienne, Besançon, 126; Paris), 359–96.

Forbes, H. A. (1982), *Strategies and Soils: Technology, Production and Environment in the Peninsula of Methana, Greece* (Ph.D. thesis, University of Pennsylvania; Ann Arbor, Mich.).

—— (1996), 'Turkish and modern Methana', in Mee and Forbes (eds).

——, Foxhall, L., and Mee, C. B. (forthcoming), 'Methana from the mediaeval to the modern periods: population and settlement', in *Dialogos*.

—— and Koster, H. A. (1976), 'Fire, axe and plow: human influence on local plant communities in the southern Argolid', in M. Dimen and E. Friedl (eds), *Regional Variation in Modern Greece and Cyprus: Toward a Perspective on the Ethnography of Greece* (Annals of the New York Academy of Sciences, 268; New York), 109–26.

Foxhall, L. (1992), 'The control of the Attic landscape', in Wells (ed.), 155–60.

—— (1996a), 'Ancient farmsteads, other agricultural sites and equipment', in Mee and Forbes (eds).

—— (1996b), *Olive Cultivation in Ancient Greece: The Ancient Economy Revisited* (Bulletin of the Institute of Classical Studies, supp.; London).

Isager, S., and Skydsgaard, J. E. (1992), *Ancient Greek Agriculture: An Introduction* (London and New York).

James, P. A., Mee, C. B., and Taylor, G. J. (1994), 'Soil erosion and the archaeological landscape of Methana, Greece', *JFA* 21: 395–416.

Jameson, M. H. (1977–8), 'Agriculture and slavery in classical Athens', *Classical Journal*, 73 (2): 122–45.

Leveau, P. (1991), 'L'occupation du sol dans les montagnes méditer-ranéennes pendant l'antiquité', in *Montagnes méditerranéennes dans l'antiquité*, 1–28.

Lohmann, H. (1985), 'Landleben in klassischen Attika', *Jahrbuch der Ruhr-Universität Bochum*, 71–96.

—— (1992), 'Agriculture and country life in classical Attica', in Wells (ed.), 29–57.

—— (1993), *Atene: Forschungen zu Siedlungs- und Wirtschaftsstruktur des klassischen Attika* (Cologne, Weimar, and Vienna).

Mee, C. B., and Forbes, H. A. (eds 1996), *A Rough and Rocky Place: The Landscape and Settlement History of the Methana Peninsula, Greece* (Liverpool).

Murray, A. T. (ed. and trans. 1939), *Demosthenes*, vi: *Private Orations* (Loeb Classical Library; Cambridge, Mass., and London).

Osborne, R. (1987), *Classical Landscape with Figures: The Ancient Greek City and its Countryside* (London).

Pansiot, F. P., and Rebour, H. (1961), *Improvement in Olive Cultivation* (Rome).

Rackham, O., and Moody, J. A. (1992), 'Terraces', in Wells (ed.), 123–33.

Wells, B. (ed. 1992), *Agriculture in Ancient Greece (Proceedings of the 7th International Symposium at the Swedish Institute at Athens)* (Skrifter utgivna av Svenska Institutet i Athen, series in 4to, 42; Stockholm).

——, Runnels, C., and Zangger, E. (1990), 'The Berbati–Limnes archaeo-logical survey: the 1988 season', *Opuscula Atheniensia*, 18: 207–38.

Whitelaw, T. (forthcoming), 'Colonisation and competition in the polis of Koressos: the development of settlement in north-west Keos from the archaic to the late Roman periods', in L. Mendoni, P. Doukellis, and A. Mazarakis-Ainian (eds), *Proceedings of the International Scien-tific Symposium: Kea–Kythnos History and Archaeology* (Provence).

Wood, E. M. (1983), 'Agricultural slavery in classical Athens', *American Journal of Ancient History*, 8: 1–47.

—— (1988), *Peasant-citizen and Slave: The Foundations of Athenian Democracy* (London and New York).

4

The uses of the uncultivated landscape in modern Greece: a pointer to the value of the wilderness in antiquity?[1]

Hamish Forbes

Waer lebt fun fische und jage muss f'rrissne gleder drage.

(Who lives by fishing and hunting must wear torn clothes.)

(Pennsylvania German saying)

An introduction by way of contradictions

In any consideration of the wilderness in Greece today and in the recent past, a major feature is the apparent contradictions which one constantly finds in many aspects of its exploitation. This was epitomized by a continual background feature during my earliest fieldwork in Greece. It was the theme music for the National Programme, a major propaganda radio channel of the highly nationalistic military junta of the time: goat bells on a mountainside, with a goatherd's flute plaintively trilling in the foreground.

[1] I would like to thank John Salmon and Graham Shipley for inviting me to present an earlier version of this contribution as a paper in the seminar series. John Salmon, Jim Roy, Oliver Rackham, and Lin Foxhall all read an earlier draft and all made important suggestions for improving it. Likewise I wish to thank Graham Shipley for his helpful suggestions and editorial expertise. I also acknowledge my debt to A. A. Milne. Lin Foxhall, as usual, has helped to steer me through the pitfalls of a territory in which I am at best only an honorary citizen. Any infelicities in this contribution, however, are entirely my responsibility.

In this simple radio vignette, lasting just ten to fifteen seconds, were intertwined several different strands of the complex, overlapping meanings and uses that are derived from the uncultivated, supposedly unproductive, wild places of the Greek landscape.

The goats represent, at one level, an important economic resource; but are also, in the local ideology, a threat to agriculture. And the work of tending them all day in empty wild places, far from human fellowship, has traditionally been considered an especially low-status occupation. Yet at the same time this solitary existence was here being taken to represent the well-springs of Greek ethnicity itself, untrammelled by the corruption of the city, which in other guises represents civilization and sociability.

The uncultivated landscape of traditional and modern Greece presents a series of contradictions which makes it almost impossible to encompass. It has been the home of Christian hermits, of nineteenth-century revolutionary heroes and rapacious brigands, and of World War II partisans over whose historical status Greeks are still bitterly divided. It is an apparently unproductive wasteland, whose existence is nevertheless essential to the working of rural economies; a place where those who work in it have very low status, but the urban hunter can show off his high status to advantage; a place where free access may be afforded to all, yet where no-go areas may be jealously guarded against all comers.

Behind all the contradictions, however, it is very clear that uncultivated land is not at all *unproductive* land. In many ways the scrub-covered hillsides, marshes, and other uncultivated lands of modern Greece serve much the same function as what was called 'the waste' in the England of the Domesday Book. The uncultivated lands of the forest, marshes, and abandoned arable lands – 'the waste' in the parlance of Domesday geography – were an essential feature of rural communities in medieval England and beyond. They provided grazing, food, fuel, stocks for fruit trees, and so on (see, for example, Darby 1936, 166–89; Bloch 1966, 6–8, 17–20), in much the same way as the uncultivated landscape still does in modern Greece (cf. Rackham 1983, 347). For this reason I shall on occasions use the term 'the waste' as a shorthand for this uncultivated but nevertheless productive part of the Greek landscape.

One thing I will not be attempting is to paint a detailed picture of what the wilderness or waste of ancient Greece looked like. Even those who have travelled only a little in Greece will probably have been struck by the variety of non-cultivated habitats that can be seen from the road, or from ancient sites. These differ, too, between different parts of Greece (see, for instance, the comparisons of Crete with Boiotia contained in Rackham 1983). In the lowland parts of Greece today, non-cultivated vegetational communities range from Mediterranean evergreen forests to low-growing garrigue (*phrýgana*) or even a stony pseudo-steppe, while in the mountains they range from deciduous or coniferous forests to scrubland, alpine meadows, or scree slopes (Polunin 1980, 28–47).

In these circumstances it can be readily understood that there is no single 'typical' modern or ancient Greek wilderness. Rather, there is a wide range of plant communities. These are the result of an interplay between the tolerances of particular plant species and a variety of environmental factors, particularly soils, climate, and above all human interference. Thus areas supporting forests can be reduced to low-growing scrub communities by heavy woodcutting and grazing, while abandoned fields may support a changing sequence of plant communities leading to genuine forests if humans and their animals do not intervene. (Rackham 1983, 290–327, is essential reading on this subject.)

It is readily apparent that some parts of ancient Greece were very different from others. Not only did they have very different ecologies, but also very different human population densities. The greatest concentration of evidence concerning ancient Greece comes from Athens and its surrounding countryside; yet, plainly, Athens' very high population and the relatively arid climate of the region make it distinctive rather than typical of ancient Greece. The kinds of plant communities typical of Attica in antiquity will have been very different from those in, say, Arkadia. Furthermore, given the changes that occurred in Greece within the time-span from the archaic period to early Byzantine times, it is perhaps prudent to assume, unless it is documented to the contrary, that no particular part of the landscape of Greece had exactly the same plant community, or the same pressures of human exploitation, throughout antiquity.

In recent discussions of the ancient Greek landscape the subject of this contribution has, as far as I know, received very little systematic attention.[1] Thus, for example, although some scholars (such as Skydsgaard 1988) argue that ancient Greek herdsmen were largely or exclusively transhumant pastoralists, no attempt seems to have been made to identify, or even speculate on, their grazing resources. Similarly, Sallares' recent *magnum opus* (1991), while claiming to encompass the whole ecology of the ancient Greek world, leaves the uncultivated landscape – probably more than half of the total area of ancient Greece – out of the argument.

The reason for this silence is not far to seek: our ancient sources are largely silent on the subject, and where they speak their utterances are mostly sibylline. It is especially for this reason that I have chosen to tackle this problem primarily from a point of view other than that of the ancient sources. As an academic whose expertise is based in the world of the modern Greek countryside and its recent history, I shall concentrate on the modern end of my title. Although I will present some thoughts on the use of the uncultivated landscape in antiquity, my main aim is to suggest to scholars of the ancient world ways in which the waste places of ancient Greece might be studied. I hope primarily to stimulate, if not infuriate, readers better versed in understanding the ancient world than I am into bringing their own thoughts to bear on this topic. At this juncture I will simply note Hesiod, who, in describing the fundamental benefits of a just society (*Works and Days*, 225–37), gives as much weight to the productivity of the hillsides (*ourea*) as to that of cultivated land (*gaia*) and of humans.

The data on modern Greece presented in this paper are derived primarily from two years of ethnographic fieldwork on the peninsula of Methana (Forbes 1982), further informed by a brief ethnographic foray to Crete and several summers' fieldwork in the southern Argolid. Although they are an unrepresentative sample, these data have the benefit of being placeable within a context of extant, functioning social and economic systems. It will be readily apparent that the same cannot be said of the ancient sources, which too often represent gobbets of information divorced from the wider contexts in which they were originally located.[2]

[1] Obvious exceptions are Rackham 1983; Rackham, ch. 2 above; and other papers of his.
[2] For other aspects of problems in using the ancient sources concerning the non-cultivated landscape, see Rackham, pp. 22–5, 33–5 above.

This is particularly the case with the works of Theophrastos. Although he discusses both domestic and wild plants, his agenda is essentially philosophical: his aim is to attempt to organize botanical knowledge systematically. No real picture emerges of how the waste was exploited as an economic or social resource.

Uncultivated land: a definition?

It might be thought that no definition of the terms 'cultivated' and 'uncultivated' would be necessary. The Mediterranean and Near Eastern regions have a long history of sharp conceptual oppositions along these lines: the desert versus the sown; *agrios* (ἄγριος, wild) versus *hêmeros* (ἥμερος, tamed); Jacob versus Esau; the plains versus the mountains (cf. Sallares 1991, 382–3). Reality is more complex. Land not actually under standing crops – for example, in stubble or fallow – is technically uncultivated, and may provide in some seasons short-term resources, especially grazing, comparable in importance to those provided by the scrub-covered hillsides.

Some land may lie fallow for several years at a time yet still be considered agricultural. Indeed, some highly fertile low-lying plains seem to have had little or no cultivation in the last few centuries. The plain of Troizen, famed for its fertility in antiquity, is a good example: in the seventeenth century Pier Antonio Pacifico (1686, 124) calls it 'una dishabitata Terra' (cf. Forbes 1982, 54), and in the 1880s it was noted that 'most of the plain of Troizen is uncultivated, full of chaste-tree plants[1] and wild bushes' (Miliarakis 1886, 195). It was only in the twentieth century, and often only after World War II, that many of Greece's fertile plains, including that of Troizen, became intensively cultivated. A considerable number, though by no means all, have been malarial areas, and it has often been argued that the presence of endemic malaria made permanent occupation by farmers (as opposed to seasonal visits by transhumant pastoralists) difficult or impossible. I do not wish to investigate this argument here, but it should be noted

---

[1] The word used (λύγον) does not indicate willows (*Salix* spp.), although the word λυγαριά is generally translated in standard Greek dictionaries as 'osier' or 'withy'. *Lyghariá* is the Greek word for the chaste-tree (*Vitex agnus-castus*), which is common in places with damp soils.

that in its simplest form it presupposes that malaria was not a problem in these areas in antiquity.

These lands in flat, fertile areas, even when, as in the past, technically uncultivated, are fundamentally different from the thin-soiled, scrub-covered mountainsides, and have been so conceptually categorized. They are different, too, from salt-marshes, the edges of which often support the tall reed, *Arundo donax* (see p. 82).

Conversely, notionally uncultivated landscapes have been heavily modified, both intentionally and unintentionally, by human intervention. High mountain forests have probably been cleared in recent centuries by the economic activities of woodcutters and shepherds (Halstead 1987, 80), and by military action through the deliberate setting of forest fires as a way of denying cover to enemies, as is said by informants to have happened in parts of Crete during the Turkish occupation, and as certainly happened in parts of Greece during the civil war of the late 1940s (e.g. Chatzigeorgiou 1984).

Much of the scrub and tree vegetation, of lowland southern Greece at least, is both fire-adapted and readily combustible in the summer heat. Periodic scrub and forest fires can therefore be assumed to have a history that long predates agriculture in Greece. We must likewise assume that fires have frequently maintained wild vegetational communities in a state well short of full forest growth for millennia, irrespective of the effects of other forms of human exploitation. In the recent past, however, it is quite clear that most fires have had a human origin. Some have been accidental, others deliberate, but all have acted as a selective pressure on the make-up of scrub and forest communities.[1]

Grazing by animals, too, will inevitably have affected the supposedly 'natural' landscape of Greece, though less than the pessimists claim (Rackham 1983, 322–5). Although careful management of numbers of grazing animals can be demonstrated in at least one area over some centuries (Forbes n.d. a), over the long term of millennia the effects on the environment of grazing cannot be discounted. Even uncultivated scrub plants in the waste may be carefully tended, pruned, and trained, as I shall indicate

---

[1] The relationships of grazing and fires to different plant communities are discussed in more detail by Rackham, pp. 18–22 above.

in due course. Thus, far from being in some way 'natural' and untouched, the uncultivated portion of the landscape is subject to a variety of modifying pressures, most of which stem ultimately from human activities. Even more surprising, part of the 'uncultivated landscape' is found on cultivated land.

The ownership of uncultivated land: a common or garden issue?

Ownership of uncultivated land is also varied and multifaceted. In most mainland Greek rural communities today, as in the recent past, cultivated land is owned by individuals, while uncultivated land is essentially common land, owned by the community as a whole, and is managed by the village council via the mayor and the community secretary. This system is generally accepted as being derived from the period of Turkish occupation. However, whereas this is the formal, legal position, individuals – especially shepherds, but also charcoal-burners and others – have traditionally laid claim to use specific sections of uncultivated hillsides for specific purposes, such as grazing or woodcutting. The boundaries of these territories are widely known to other users, and any infringement can expect very physical retaliation (Koster and Forbes n.d.). Thus, for example, in the southern Argolid, successful shepherds tend to be those with large kinship networks which provide the necessary muscle in disputes with other shepherds over the scrub-grazing of the waste (Koster 1977, 183–4).

The uncultivated hillsides are not inalienable, however. Village councils can sell off sections of community-owned land to individuals who wish to convert them into agricultural land, the proceeds going to the communities' coffers (see p. 77).

Although community ownership of uncultivated hillsides is the norm, in some parts of Greece – of which Methana, not far from the southern Argolid, is one and Crete another – even uncultivated hillsides may be individually owned. However, at least on Methana, individual ownership goes hand in hand with rights of common access to exploit certain aspects of the mountain environment. Animals may be grazed in these areas by all, and scrub may be cut for firewood, as long as the owner has not made it clear that these areas are reserved.

Thus the contradictions multiply. Where common ownership of uncultivated mountainsides is technically the law, in practice individuals claim exclusive rights to exploit certain products. On the other hand, in an area where uncultivated land is privately owned, all community members are normally allowed free access to exploit certain products. On Methana this tradition of free access to individually owned, uncultivated land is extended to cultivated land where there are no standing crops, in certain well-defined situations. Thus, at particular times of year, large blocks of fallow terraces owned by many different farmers are open to all in the community for the grazing of their sheep and goats.

What has been normal for thin-soiled uncultivated hillsides, however, has never, in recent centuries, held good for the uncultivated but potentially highly fertile plains that used to be a feature of the lowlands of Greece. These have always been owned: by individuals, by institutions such as monasteries, or further back in time by the Turkish state as *çiftlik* estates. In the nineteenth and earlier twentieth centuries their owners frequently made an income from the rents paid by shepherds for the right to graze their animals during the winter months, before returning them to the upland mountain pastures for the summer.

From the foregoing, it is plain that the concept of 'ownership', whether by individuals or the community, is not straightforward. It is a complex bundle of use-rights which does not coincide neatly with our normal views of 'ownership'. Moreover, the official, 'legal' position is overlain by local, extra-legal usages, and even by personal preferences which may be defended by threats of recourse either to the official law or to the extra-legal use of main force.

Such an interplay of the legal, the local, and the individual, if it existed in ancient Greece – as it probably did – is by its very nature unlikely to show up in ancient documents. The most likely sources to be of any relevance here are forensic speeches, though theoretically inscriptions might also touch on such matters. But forensic speeches are most likely to be concerned only with the formal, *de jure* situation. Modifications caused by *de facto* local practices are less likely to appear.

In this context we may briefly consider the implications of grants of *epinomia* (the right to graze animals) and *epixylia* (the right to cut wood) by poleis to non-citizens in honorary decrees (such as

SEG xi. 470 and *IG* iv. 853). Grants of these rights are found in many different poleis: it is perhaps unwise to assume that the same thing is meant in all cases, particularly given the likely diversity of both the type and the extent of the waste from state to state. We certainly cannot be sure that such grants automatically indicate the presence of community-owned, uncultivated land. *Epinomia* is mentioned more frequently than *epixylia*; in some states it may well have allowed grazing on community-owned land (as may be the case in *IG* iv. 853). It is not impossible that in some circumstances it meant the right to graze animals on privately owned fallow land, opened up as common grazing for part of the year, as occurs currently on Methana. We should also not exclude the possibility, though it may be remote, that the usage of the term in some states may have meant the right to own grazing-land, differentiated from the right to own cultivated land.

The rights of *epinomia* and *epixylia* were plainly important. Their significance, however, may frequently have been in the sphere of status at least as much as that of economics. It may indicate that the person mentioned had the same rights as citizens in all respects; it is not clear whether the rights were regularly exploited. Nevertheless, specific mention of these rights probably does give at least a hint of the importance of the uncultivated landscape in many states. On occasions, contested rights to grazing-land, woodcutting, and stone-quarrying might be a cause for disputes between poleis (as is indicated, for example, in *SEG* xi. 405 and *IG* iv. 76).

A 'waste of resources': the many uses of the uncultivated landscape

The discussion so far has made unsystematic reference to some of the uses of the waste. In this section I wish to examine more systematically what a number of those uses are. In so doing I wish to emphasize, first, that it is not an exhaustive list, and, second, that in a functioning rural community the uncultivated landscape is indissolubly linked to the cultivated landscape in the organic whole that is the local economy. Third, not all of the uses listed here may be found in any one community.

Agricultural land

One use of the waste is for conversion to cultivated land. The terraced hillsides that give so much of rural Greece its distinctive character seem completely ageless; yet they were all originally carved out of uncultivated hillsides. Large numbers of those visible today probably owe their present form to nineteenth-century activities, although attempts to date their construction have so far met with little success (see Foxhall in this volume, ch. 3). Such land clearance occasionally continues, though nowadays terraces are mostly constructed by bulldozers rather than by the toil of hands, backs, and levers. Villagers may buy an area of hillside from the community by paying a sum to the council, and thereby ownership is theirs alone.

That uncultivated mountain grazing was recognized in antiquity as potential arable land can be seen in Diocletian's tax reforms. Mountain territory in a particular area described as 'pasture land for cattle' was assessed on a local scale by other locals in terms of its potential productivity in *modii* of wheat and barley (Cameron 1993, 36). Furthermore, although the evidence of the passage cited by Cameron is not conclusive, the likelihood is that at least some of the substantial tracts of uncultivated land referred to were privately owned.

Olives and other trees

A common element of the wild vegetation of southern Greece is the wild olive tree (the oleaster). A well-known traditional method of establishing an olive grove has been to buy an area of scrub-covered hillside and clear all the vegetation except for the wild olive bushes growing there. These are used as naturally growing stocks on to which domesticated olives are in due course grafted (cf. Isager and Skydsgaard 1992, 38). On Methana, where this system was widespread in former years, transplanting would be undertaken only if some plants were too close together while there were large gaps between others. Terraces, often of the 'pocket' type (Rackham and Moody 1992, 123–4), were built round such trees on hillsides only once the graft had taken and the tree was successfully established. Isager and Skydsgaard (1992, 38) stress the relative ease with which large olive plantations could have been set up in antiquity by this method, but they say nothing about what it presupposes in terms of ownership of the previously uncultivated land.

On Methana in the later nineteenth century, large numbers of domesticated pear trees were also established by the simple expedient of grafting domesticated pear scions onto naturally growing wild pear stocks (Miliarakis 1886, 207). Undoubtedly there are other tree species which would respond well in this way under certain circumstances.

Besides this means of establishing cultivated trees, the waste in many parts of Greece also provides all the olive-tree stocks planted in pre-existing fields (cf. Isager and Skydsgaard 1992, 36). In this case a farmer seeks out a suitable wild olive bush on a hillside, and first starts to prune it so that it will grow with a single sturdy trunk, rather than a large number of trunks all springing from the base. Trained trees growing on the hillsides are treated as private property, and fuel-cutters and herders are expected to leave them undamaged. Once the stocks have been transplanted and are well established, they are grafted with a domesticated olive scion. Wild pear trees can also be treated as transplantable stocks in much the same way. Once a single substantial trunk has developed, the tree is dug up and moved to its new location.

The system of grafting on stocks growing *in situ* has the major advantage of not demanding the laborious work of transplanting stocks, with the attendant work of watering them regularly for several years during the summer. Such work usually entails carrying water on pack animals, sometimes over several kilometres, and is very time-consuming.

Where these methods are standard, arboriculture in the cultivated landscape is totally dependent on the 'waste' for wild root-stocks. But this is not the only possible way of establishing olive trees, at least. In some parts of Greece there is a tradition of establishing new olives by taking cuttings from domesticated olives, without the need for grafting – a system already known in antiquity (Isager and Skydsgaard 1992, 35–6). This system, however, either depends on specialized nursery beds for raising new plants or else, if unrooted cuttings are placed directly in position, entails quite a high failure rate. Furthermore, greater amounts of water are needed in establishing trees derived from cuttings than those from wild trees (Foxhall 1990, 87–90).

It is also possible to establish new stocks by removing ovules – large growths weighing several kilograms at the very base of the trunk – and planting these. Today this method is primarily used in North Africa (Pansiot and Rebour 1961, 74–5), but there is evidence that it was in common use in classical Attica (Foxhall 1990, 92–7). A major drawback of this method is that only large olive trees produce such ovules, and then usually only two or three. Its advantage is that it is a more reliable way of establishing a root-stock, which entails less watering (Pansiot and Rebour 1961, 74–5; Foxhall 1990, 92).

Construction materials

The practice of training naturally growing bushes in the waste is not confined to fruit trees. Although probably never very common, the same practice has been used in places like Methana to produce construction timber where there is a shortage of naturally growing tall trees. Scrubland bushes, especially junipers, would be pruned to a single trunk, the lower branches being trimmed away to produce as tall and knot-free a piece of timber as possible. Once again, such trees were considered the private property of whoever was working them; the tell-tale signs of cut branches around the tree and the obviously trimmed trunk indicate to others that this tree is not to be tampered with. On Methana, at least, juniper was preferred as a construction timber over the locally growing Aleppo pine (*Pinus halepensis*), despite the additional effort needed to make the bushes grow into more than the 'small short and crooked' trees noted in Boiotia (Rackham 1983, 339). Although the pines tend to grow naturally taller, they are said to be much less resistant to decay and to attack by wood-boring insects.

Theophrastos' comment (*History of Plants*, 5. 4. 6) concerning the timing of bark-stripping the silver fir, to ensure that it did not decay in water, might be thought to represent a comparable tradition of manipulating woodland in antiquity. But this is probably to misinterpret the passage. Elsewhere (5. 1. 1–2) he indicates that bark-stripping was carried out immediately *after* felling, and was largely restricted to the silver fir and the pine. This suggests that the ancients, too, were well aware that pine and fir were particularly prone to rapid decay.

Juniper timber was traditionally used on Methana (along with other types of timber) for the main structural components of roofs: either pitched and supporting tiles, or flat and supporting mud. Juniper timber was also traditionally used for door- and window-frames and for lintels, as well as for floor supports. In Boiotia it is also sometimes used for the timber lacing commonly incorporated into rubble walls in that area (Rackham 1983, 339).

Of course, in twentieth-century Greece, with the possible exception of cypresses and dead fruit trees, all construction timber must be extracted from the uncultivated landscape. However, in much of lowland Greece today there is little suitable timber left, so it must either be imported from other areas which still have timber trees growing in the waste, or produced in a way similar to that just noted (cf. ibid. 347).

Timber for agricultural uses

In the recent past a wide range of items of agricultural equipment was made from local timber: for example, ploughs, plank-harrows, tool-handles, and even carts. Nowadays demand from this quarter is lower, but Hesiod (*Works and Days*, 415–36) reminds us of the importance of this resource in antiquity. Ancient olive presses, likewise, depended on long, stout timbers to provide leverage (Forbes and Foxhall 1978). Similarly, wooden swipes (also known as shadoufs) – simple devices involving a long, stout pole for easing the lifting of water from wells – have traditionally been important in parts of Greece for drawing water for domestic purposes and simple irrigation. In antiquity they were considered significant enough to appear in the Attic Stelai as items of saleable agricultural equipment (*IG* i³ 422. 187–90). They also appear in vase-paintings (e.g. Pfuhl 1923, fig. 276). Vase-paintings and pottery models also indicate the wide range of wooden parts, small and large, needed for simple agricultural equipment: ploughs, ox-yokes, parts of pack-saddles, implement handles, carts, and shoulder-yokes for humans (Isager and Skydsgaard 1992, 48, 50–1, 94). Press-beds are also illustrated, which seem to be made of wood and standing on wooden legs (Boardman 1974, fig. 89;

Christou n.d. 64). Even such relatively small but essential items as long poles for knocking down fruit from trees (Isager and Skydsgaard 1992, 40) would mostly come from the waste: on Methana they tend to be either long reeds (see below) or thin juniper poles.

Timber for industrial uses

In antiquity, large quantities of stout timber would have been needed for non-agricultural purposes as well. Scaffolding was needed for the construction of larger buildings where ladders (themselves built of wood) could not reach. Presses similar to those used for olive-pressing would have been needed for fulling and for dyeing cloth. In mining, wooden pit-props are known to have been used; a substantial mine would have used large quantities (Shepherd 1993, 24–6).

Thin timber and brushwood

The construction of agricultural and domestic structures in traditional Greek communities also demands a range of other products which can be more readily met from the scrub plant communities of the hillside and elsewhere. Poles and stakes are needed for enclosures, for keeping livestock both in and out. In agriculture, stout poles are frequently needed as supports for branches of fruit trees. Smaller stakes are needed in large numbers as vine-props, a situation paralleled in antiquity, as indicated in the Attic Stelai, where in one instance 10,200 of them occur in a single entry (Pritchett 1956, 305–6).

Brushwood (twiggy branches) has also been an extremely important commodity in traditional construction techniques (ibid. 305). Perhaps its most obvious use is in the construction of sheep and goat folds: post and brushwood structures which may involve the use of several tonnes of brush and must be renewed every few years. Herders will frequently exploit several of these during the year, depending on particular circumstances (Koster 1977, 176–8).

Brushwood also has many other uses. In the past, it has been used over thicker timbers to support the layer of mud employed in the traditional mud roofs of houses, and on Methana, at least, for the mud upper floors of two-storey buildings. Brushwood, in combination with poles, has been used as fencing to exclude animals from gardens: placed on field boundary walls (see Foxhall above, p. 50) it may discourage sheep and goats from invading agricultural land. It is also sometimes tied round the trunks of fruit trees, to discourage goats either from eating off the tops of saplings or from climbing into mature trees with sloping trunks. Tied to bare trunks, especially of young trees, it reduces sun-scald; tied round the tops of newly transplanted saplings it helps to shade young shoots as well as protect them from marauding caprines.

A variety of scrub species also supplies withies for the wide range of basketry items essential in the traditional agricultural economy.[1] For example, panniers are needed for transporting on pack animals everything from fresh fruit to manure; and harrows may be made from hurdles (Geroulanou *et al.* 1978, 17). For antiquity the best evidence for such items comes from vase-paintings. For instance, a vintage scene suggests the use of wicker baskets, very similar in shape and design to the modern Greek *zembíli*, for treading grapes (Boardman 1974, fig. 89). Even the frails in which olive pulp was pressed may have been made of basketry (Foxhall 1990, 135), although more recently the traditional material was goat-hair – itself produced by way of exploiting the waste through animal husbandry (Geroulanou *et al.* 1978, 53).

Finally, the giant reed, *Arundo donax*, which grows in marshy places and makes a fine substitute for bamboo, has a wide range of uses. Its length makes it highly suited for fishing-rods and for extra-long (though not very durable) olive-, almond-, and fig-tree beaters. Its ability to split easily lengthwise makes the reed highly suited to basket-weaving. Even certain types of sieves – essential in a wide range of sorting tasks associated with agriculture – are made of reed.

---

[1]   The plants supplying withies are generally not managed in the way that osiers are in northern Europe. It seems unlikely that the 'withy basket-work' mentioned by Wheler in the seventeenth century (Wheler 1682) was actually from osiers, or from pollarded willows as Rackham (1983, 333) suggests. The chaste-tree (*Vitex agnus-castus*), like the willow a plant of damp soils, is commonly used to provide withies in southern Greece (see n. 1, p. 72).

Reeds are also widely used in construction, both for the lighter elements of house roofs and as the main element in the wide array of temporary shelters traditionally employed in the countryside. Aschenbrenner (1972, 57) comments on the high demand in Messenia for reeds, which may be sold to provide a useful income. An agricultural census taken by the Venetians in the southern Argolid in about 1690 refers to several houses that seem to have been built largely of reeds.[1] Imprints of reeds in archaeological finds of burnt daub indicate that in the past it has been used in wattle-and-daub construction.

From the foregoing, it is plain that much of what could broadly be termed the capital equipment on which traditional Greek agriculture has depended would not exist without these inputs from the waste. These resources provide much of the backbone of traditional Greek agriculture, specifically its structures and equipment. It should also be noted that although the waste in much of lowland Greece consists of what are often considered 'degraded' vegetational communities (maquis and garrigue), it is precisely the scrubby vegetation that is used in the greatest quantity: even a small rural community may use on average several tonnes annually for construction purposes, quite apart from fuel (see below). Whether the extensive use of brush is because there is often nothing better available, or whether this is what is fundamentally most useful anyway, is a moot point (Rackham 1983, 347, has an important discussion of this issue).

Our sources of information on the situation in antiquity are more often iconographic than literary. Although it is plain that the countryside (*sensu lato*) was not particularly popular as a source of scenes on Greek pottery, it is evident that there are many more depictions of aspects of rural life than are illustrated in 'standard' works on Greek vase-painting (such as Boardman 1974 and 1975). Detailed research will doubtless provide more examples of illustrations of wooden agricultural equipment. However, it will not indicate the provenance of the raw material used in its manufacture. Likewise, literary sources rarely, if ever,

[1] The census notes houses built *con paglia*, literally 'with straw'; but this is likely to be a mistranslation of με καλάμια, *kalámi* being both a strand of straw and a reed. Presumably these were relatively substantial structures, like their modern counterparts, or they would have been ignored by the census-takers as being of negligible value (Forbes n.d. b).

sink to a concern with such minutiae. Yet it is hard to believe that in the days before mass or bulk transportation most of the scrub material so essential for rural life did not come from quite localized sources, especially in areas away from the coast.

Fuel

The use of timber and brushwood from the waste is not restricted to construction: a far more widespread use of the scrub vegetation of the waste is as fuel. And although simple cooking may be the use that first enters the mind, it is far from the only one. Even before the advent of fossil fuel to rural communities, some of their fuel supplies did *not* derive from the waste. Prunings from olives and other fruit trees provided a certain amount of cooking fuel as well as some heating fuel. Vine-prunings also provided a source of heat, being a preferred fuel source for traditional pottery kilns (Matson 1972, 213, 219). The press-cake remaining at the end of the olive-pressing process likewise provides a usable fuel (ibid., 219), though nowadays it is usually sold for further chemical extraction of the remaining oil. But these sources from the cultivated landscape are a minor proportion of the total fuel used in large numbers of traditional rural communities: the bulk is derived from the uncultivated environment.

Even a rough attempt at quantifying a household's fuel use is a dangerous undertaking, but informants on Methana and the southern Argolid give some partial answers (cf. Forbes and Koster 1976). For instance, approximately 100 kg of brushwood is needed to fire a traditional bread oven, which, given the small families that exist nowadays, will provide bread for three or four weeks at a time. Hence each family will consume approximately 1.5 tonnes of brush annually just for baking bread. In the past, when much larger families were the norm, 2.0–2.5 tonnes may have been needed. For heating, a further 2 tonnes of thicker wood may be needed during the winter months. These estimates are exclusive of the thin wood needed to cook daily meals, at a rough guess at least 2 tonnes annually. A total of close to 6 tonnes of fuel may therefore be suggested as a single traditional Methana family's annual needs, the bulk of which (say 5 tonnes) must come from the waste.

Applying these highly hypothetical figures to a small village of fifty households gives a figure of 250 tonnes of fuel alone derived from the surrounding uncultivated countryside. In areas that are particularly short of fuel, consumption would doubtless be reduced to levels below this figure, and there might be a greater reliance on prunings and the like from agricultural land. Nevertheless, even in areas where there is substantial scrubland, the combination of the thin soils and prolonged drought periods of the lowland Greek environment means that scrub regeneration rates are inherently low.[1]

The amount of uncultivated scrubland necessary to supply even the domestic fuel needed by a small rural community in antiquity must have been very substantial indeed. Yet nowhere, to my knowledge, is there any evidence of what rights to cut fuel ordinary people had, or how their fuel needs were supplied. The much-quoted passage of Demosthenes (62. 5–8) does not help us. Phainippos is here described as owning an *eschatia* producing six donkey-loads of *hylê* (wood), possibly daily, which would make an income of over 12 drachmas a day. The context makes it plain that Phainippos is extremely wealthy; whether the wood he derives from his land is sold to ordinary Athenians as fuel is not made clear. It is equally possible that it was sold for industrial purposes (see below).[2]

Thus far I have only considered the subsistence fuel needs provided to rural communities by the waste. But rural communities have also traditionally supplied urban communities, and even some large villages, with domestic fuel. Some households in the smaller urban communities, at least, cooked on brushwood supplied from the surrounding areas. But much cooking by urbanites was done on charcoal. This was clean-burning, and above all light to transport; hence it could be produced in distant rural communities and transported to urban centres relatively easily by ship, pack animal, or cart. Equally significantly, in recent times these activities have provided a

[1] Rackham (1983, 326) has suggested that 1 ton of wood per hectare per year cut from the uncultivated landscape 'is not prima facie out of balance with what macchia might be expected to produce'. At that rate, a community of fifty households would need around 2.5 sq km of maquis simply to support its own fuel needs.
[2] de Ste Croix 1966; Osborne 1987, 37–8; Burford 1993, 112.

necessary cash element for the economies of numerous poorer rural households (Forbes n.d. a).

Charcoal-burning tends to make use of relatively thick timber and large root systems of bushes and trees extracted from the waste. Smaller, scrubby bushes and shrubs from degraded garrigue (*phrýgana*) plant communities have traditionally provided fuel for lime-burning. In particular, lime-burning has often been heavily dependent on species that have little or no value as a grazing resource, for instance thorny burnet (*Sarcopoterium spinosum*) from garrigue areas and juniper (*Juniperus* species) from garrigue and maquis areas (Huxley and Taylor 1984, 68, 89). Thus these activities (pastoralism, charcoal-burning, and lime-burning), though all dependent on the wilderness, are not in direct competition with each other. Again, they have been activities engaged in by rural populations to generate cash via the sale of the product, largely to urban centres (Forbes n.d. a). They are not primarily occupations producing materials for the local community.

Records of the Greek Forest Service (Dasikí Ypiresía) in the southern Argolid allow us to quantify, however roughly, the cash value of items for sale which were derived from the vegetation of the waste in one small region of modern Greece. This does not include pastoral exploitation: the main products listed are charcoal and lime. The recorded figures suggest that during the 1930s the value of these products was greater than that of the total amount of wheat needed to feed the region's population (Forbes n.d. a).

In social terms, it should be borne in mind that lime- and charcoal-burning have been very low-status occupations; generally lower than that of the goatherd, for instance. They have been engaged in by the rural poor, who have little land or little opportunity to exploit the waste for grazing.

Unfortunately for us, Aristophanes was not an ethnographer. Had he been, he would have presented much more than a mere caricature of the charcoal-burning Acharnians, who must have provided a vital resource – cooking fuel – to the Athenians. He does not indicate whether lime-burning was also an important activity; how Acharnian pyrotechnological activities fitted in with agriculture; how the sale and distribution of their product were organized; and above all what their arrangements were for gaining access to the scrub- or forest-covered hillsides that provided their livelihood. Nevertheless, detailed reading between the lines of his comedy may give us some further clues as to the exploitation of the 'waste' during the Peloponnesian war. One distinct possibility is that the Acharnians would be expected to support the war because of the increased demand for the charcoal they supplied. On the other hand, as vine-growers they may have needed the increased income from charcoal to offset the lack of income from their devastated vines. What does seem clear is that the system of providing fuel for the city of Athens seems to have been different from that found in the outlying villages. In the *Acharnians* Dikaiopolis contrasts the need in Athens to buy charcoal from others with the situation in his own village (Hopper 1979, 67–8, referring to lines 33–6). Again, however, we do not know whether most people in villages owned, or had free access to, scrub-covered hillsides for obtaining their fuel, or whether they mostly had to pay a few wealthy private owners for the privilege of cutting fuel (Hopper 1979, 68).

Possibly significant in this context is the observation that Methana has not been a traditional charcoal-burning area. Yet charcoal-burning was important during the occupation of Greece by the Axis powers during World War II. At that time supplies of charcoal to Athens from distant parts of Greece were cut off: hence the need to provide fuel from places closer to the capital. Methana, in the Saronic gulf, was ideally placed to fill that role, at least in the short term. This recent example raises the question of whether the Acharnians had a long tradition of charcoal-burning, or whether their activities were partly or entirely a direct result of wartime conditions. It also raises the further question of how Athenians – and other ancient Greeks – ensured fuel supplies in peacetime.

Another aspect of fuel on which I can say very little is its use in ceramic and metallurgical pyrotechnology. Nevertheless, in the ancient world it must have been very important. The quantities of pottery and roof-tile produced in antiquity seem to have been prodigious, judging by the small proportion of the total production that turns up in regional surveys. The silver production operations at the Laureion mines must also have demanded exceptionally large amounts of fuel. The initial smelting of the lead–silver ore was followed by further, separate pyrotechnological stages involved in the separation of the silver from the lead in the cupellation process (Hodges 1976, 91–4). The production of lead from the residue of the silver-separation process demanded yet more pyrotechnological treatment. All these smelting and puri-fying operations would have depended on charcoal. The production of iron from its original ore, and its manufacture into tools and weapons (ibid., 80–9), likewise demand considerable quantities of charcoal.

Fire-setting may not have been used to extract the lead–silver ore from the mines at Laureion,[1] but it is well known as a method of mining from other contexts (Healy 1978, 84–5; Davies 1979, 21–2; Shepherd 1993, 19–24, 85). This use of fuel to break up the rock at the mine face would have demanded great quantities of brush, and probably heavier fuel as well (Davies 1979, 21–2; Shepherd 1993, 22).

Resin and other industrial products

Another source of income traditionally provided from the waste on Methana has been resin, which is extracted during the summer months from the Aleppo pine (well illustrated by Baumann 1993, 33). This tree is a common constituent of the lowland Greek land-scape, and like so much of the vegetation of the Greek hillside it is fire-adapted (Rackham, this volume, ch. 2). For antiquity, Theophrastos (*Hist. Pl.* 9. 2–3) devotes considerable space to discussion of the extraction of resin and pitch from a variety of coniferous trees in different parts of the eastern Mediterranean area, including types of fir, pine, and cedar. Characteristically, however, the work in question being a treatise on the properties of plants, we are told nothing of the uses to which the products are put. Whether the intentional use of resin in wine to produce retsina is an inheritance from ancient Greece is still debated (see Baumann 1993, 33, 151), but there are hints that certain resins were used as flavourings. Theophrastos (*Hist. Pl.* 9. 2. 2; 9. 2. 5) evaluates different resins in terms of their fragrance and delicacy of smell. Significantly, the resin of the terebinth (*Pistacia*

---

[1] Hopper 1979, 185, noting laws against filling the Laureion mine-work-ings with smoke, states that fire was used for breaking down the rock; Healy 1978, 84–5, argues that fire-setting was not used.

terebinthus) is considered the best; it is a close relative of the mastic tree (*Pistacia lentiscus*), whose resin has traditionally been used as a breath-sweetener (Baumann 1993, 159) and is used today in some places (notably the island of Chios, where the trees are grown in large numbers) to flavour a sweet confection and the powerful alcoholic drink *mastíkha*.[1] Next best are considered the resins of the silver fir and the Aleppo pine; the latter is used today to flavour Greek *retsina*. However, a more important use of resin was probably as a sealant in various guises: in traditional Greek communities it has been widely used for sealing the mouths of storage jars and the like. This may explain Theophrastos' concern with the consistency of the product (*Hist. Pl.* 9. 2. 2; 9. 2. 5). In antiquity the main use of resin and pitch may have been for sealing cracks between timbers on ships; the sheer quantity of production hinted at in this section of Theophrastos would point in this direction. It is perhaps salutary to ponder whether, without this product of the eastern Mediterranean hillsides, there would have been a Persian defeat at Salamis, or even a Persian force to be defeated at Marathon.

Many of the plants of the uncultivated Greek landscape are highly aromatic. In antiquity a considerable number of these (whether growing wild or cultivated is often unclear) were used to make unguents, cosmetics, and so on. It is clear from Theophrastos' treatise *On Odours* that the manufacture of a wide range of aromatic products based on these plants was a major industry.

The acorn cups of the Valonia oak (*Quercus macrolepis*) were traditionally a major source of income in parts of Greece, because of their use in tanning. At one period the demand for this product was such that Valonia oaks were widely planted (Cherry *et al.* eds 1991, 361–2),[2] as well as being exploited in the wild (Randolph 1689, 17). This is just one more instance of the linking of the wild and cultivated landscapes. The acorns were also traditionally consumed by humans in times of famine (cf. Huxley and Taylor 1984, 71), these being the least bitter of all the eastern

[1] As Graham Shipley informs me. The cultivation of this essentially wild species is another example of the overlap of the wild and cultivated landscapes.
[2] cf. Bennet and Voutsaki 1991, 375–7; Sutton 1991, 387–402.

Mediterranean species of oak – a fact known to Theophrastos (*Hist. Pl.* 3. 8. 2). In antiquity, tanning was also done using the galls of the gall-oak (ἡμερίς, *Quercus infectoria*), while the gall of another oak was used for dyeing wool (ibid. 3. 8. 6). A product of the kermes oak, known in modern Greek as *prinokókki*, was also much prized in the recent past as the source of a vermilion dye (cf. ibid. 3. 16. 1; Baumann 1993, 156, 158; Huxley and Taylor 1984, 71). In previous centuries it provided a major export product from Greece (cf. Randolph 1689, 17).

Food

Traditionally the waste in Greece has been a direct supplier of certain foods. In line with the findings of ethnographic studies in other parts of the world, only a limited number of the total of potentially edible foods are regularly exploited (see Scudder 1971). This is especially true of plant foods. The most regularly exploited wild plant species in the traditional Greek diet are those that add flavour and piquancy to the rather bland staples of bread and olive oil. Thus bitter greens, mushrooms, and a range of culinary herbs are all collected on the hillsides as well as in fallow and cultivated fields. Some of these plants are considered to be useful merely for food, but others are believed to have both medicinal and culinary uses, while others again are used almost exclusively as folk medicines. Wild plants growing on uncultivated hillsides and in cultivated land are widely exploited under normal conditions; but it should be noted that during periods of scarcity more varieties are consumed, and in greater amounts to make up for the lack of cultivated food (Clark Forbes 1976a–c). Wild plants thus provide not only a means of enlivening the diet but also a hedge against hunger.

Modern Greeks have contradictory attitudes to wild greens. Villagers greatly prize them as a major element in the diet, while many urbanites make expeditions to the countryside to collect them. The fact that the cost to urbanites of transport to the countryside may make these greens unreasonably expensive, especially when they can be bought cheaply in urban markets, seems to be irrelevant (Clark Forbes 1976c, 12). Yet although collecting greens for oneself gives status to the urbanite, the sale of such greens is considered a sign of great poverty, and is usually only engaged in by poor widows.[1]

Although plants from the waste contribute to rural subsistence, they also sometimes provide an important source of cash. Apart from the wild greens sold by the poor, the pungent herbs of the mountainside are also sold by villagers for consumption by urbanites. The use of the sap of the mastic tree as a flavouring has already been mentioned. As in the case of the Valonia oak, these 'wild' trees are sometimes tended on cultivated land.

The hunting of the fauna of the waste similarly involves conflicting attitudes (see Lane Fox, ch. 6 in this volume, for other aspects of this activity). The waste is home to hares, partridges, blackbirds, thrushes, and smaller birds, virtually all of which are eaten, even down to robin and blue tit size. By and large, however, the larger the prey the more highly it is prized: on Methana the catching of small birds – sparrows and the like – is normally left to small boys. Of course there are many other animal species in the waste; but predators, carrion-eaters, reptiles, and insects are considered inedible for civilized people. Snails, on the other hand, are collected and eaten as a delicacy, and their sale provides a cash income in some parts of Greece.

The larger prey, particularly hares and partridges, are caught by shooting. For villagers the ownership of a gun is something of a luxury: as well as the high cost of the gun there is the cost of ammunition and a licence. The amount of game caught is also small: quite apart from the limited time available for hunting in the agricultural year, there are not large numbers of game animals or birds in most parts of the Greek countryside. For the urbanite, hunting is an opportunity to flaunt his status in the rural setting. Car ownership, until quite recently, has been restricted to the wealthy minority: so simply arriving in the countryside in one's own car has been a status act. The urban hunter also often dresses the part: expensive high leather boots, and frequently a full American-style 'hunting outfit', along with an expensive shotgun. Given that the size of the bag is usually paltry, the urban hunter seems to be aiming primarily to impress neighbours at home and villagers in the countryside.

---

[1] In ancient Greece wild vegetables are known to have been consumed by the wealthy, though much transformed by expensive ingredients (Foxhall, forthcoming).

The countryside of antiquity seems to have been home to rather larger game than survives today. Boar and deer, at least, seem to have roamed in parts of ancient Greece where none would be expected today. Nevertheless, much the same hunting principle probably held in antiquity: it is doubtful whether the hunting dogs and related paraphernalia owned by the wealthy were ever intended to be much more than an element in conspicuous consumption and social competition. Given the high population estimates currently favoured by scholars, particularly for the classical and late Roman periods, it seems likely that, unless certain parts of the landscape were set aside for them or suitable habitats were at least preserved for other reasons, the numbers of deer and boar would have been small. The chances of successful hunting under such conditions would have been correspondingly low.

Grazing and beekeeping

So far I have largely avoided discussion of the use of the uncultivated landscape as a grazing resource. My main reason is that it is the one aspect of the exploitation of the waste that has already caught the attention of ancient historians. The result of this interest is that there is considerable discussion about the extent to which modern grazing usage in Greece can be used as a pointer to ancient pastoralism (cf. Hodkinson 1988; Skydsgaard 1988).

I do not wish to enter the fray at this juncture. I have tackled the issue in a slightly different way elsewhere (Forbes 1994), although it is necessary to emphasize that modern Greek pastoralism (i) depends on a mix of the cultivated and uncultivated landscapes comparable to that noted for other economic activities, and (ii) is an activity aimed primarily at generating a cash income rather than subsistence (Forbes n.d. a). I shall leave the field (or rather the mountain pastures) to the present protagonists, and briefly turn my attention to bees, before proceeding to some rather hesitant conclusions.

Recent discussion of the use of the uncultivated hillsides as pasture for domesticated ungulates has rather averted our attention from its use as bee pasture. In antiquity, honey was probably the main source of sweetening, and certainly the most highly prized. For Hesiod (*Works and Days*, 232–4) bees feature alongside sheep as the most important features of the hillsides (or perhaps they were simply the easiest to fit into the metre).

Nevertheless, if the analogy with modern Greece is anything to go by, other sources of sweet substances were probably available. One possibility is a concentrate made by boiling down grape juice to about one-third of its original volume, as traditionally made in Greek villages today and in the recent past. Dried figs are also extremely sweet, and various decoctions of them would have been possible, though the laxative effects of 'syrup of figs' (that stand-by of the traditional British nursery medicine cabinet) may suggest why they may have been less sought after. These sources of sweetening, however, come from the cultivated and not the 'wild' landscape. The possibility should be considered, therefore, that one reason for honey's high status in antiquity was not merely because of its inherently superior sweetness, but because, like game, it was derived largely from the 'wild' landscape. However, the suggestion that in antiquity beekeeping may on occasions have been closely linked to the exploitation of agricultural land (Osborne 1987, 78) – a situation also found in Greece today – should be borne in mind.

The honey of Hymettos was well known in antiquity. Its importance has been reified in the later twentieth century AD by the excavation of the Vari house, with its remains of numerous beehives (Jones *et al.* 1973). The high value of Hymettos honey can be expected to have put a premium on maintaining the wild mountain vegetation in such a state as to provide good supplies of wild flowering plants for the honey. Nowadays it is the 'degraded' garrigue plant communities of the Greek hillside which seem to be most prized for this purpose (Rackham 1983, 347): beekeepers often move their hives to different parts of the mountains to take advantage of different plant communities over the course of the year. Yet we never hear in our ancient sources anything about possible conflicts over the use of the mountainsides, which would have affected what seems, from the evidence of the Vari house, to have been an important rural activity.

Conclusion: in which we leave the issue of the waste in antiquity unresolved

At the outset of this paper I emphasized the paucity of readily identifiable ancient evidence on the use of the uncultivated landscape. As a way of approaching the issue I have presented a picture of the uses of this landscape in traditional and modern Greece, with only unsystematic references to ancient Greece. My aim has been to show that this apparently unproductive sector is an essential ingredient, not only in the rural Greek economy, but also in the urban economy, especially before the introduction of fossil fuels. Beyond that, even, the waste is an ingredient in the modern Greek status system, although the way it functions in detail is full of contradictions as far as the outside observer is concerned.

In conclusion, I wish to emphasize four major points.

First, that in both agriculture and stock management the exploitation of the cultivated landscape is completely integrated with that of the uncultivated landscape. Both are essential to the proper functioning of the agrarian economy, and it is impossible fully to understand the one without understanding the other. Of course, there is no guarantee that in antiquity there was the same interdigitation of the cultivated and uncultivated landscapes into a single agrarian system. However, it must be remembered that the same phenomenon has been found in studies of other times and other places,[1] suggesting that it is a normal feature of small-scale agrarian economies.

Second, although the waste is essential for the products that rural households use directly, a great many of its products are exploited primarily for sale outside the community.[2] However, those whose income – as opposed to their recreation – is derived from the waste tend to have a very low status.

Third, a number of scholars of the ancient landscape assume that agricultural land could be greatly expanded on to marginal hillsides in times of extreme population pressure. This is to assume that the waste was of little economic importance. While a great diminution of the waste is theoretically possible, it would have had important knock-on effects in other areas, involving, for

[1]   e.g. Bloch 1966, 6–8, 17–20; Madge 1993.
[2]   cf. Madge 1993, 15–27, for a sub-Saharan African example.

instance, the search for other sources of fuel, probably at greater distances.

Fourth, little is known of the system of use-rights which would have governed access to crucial economic resources provided by the waste. Our understanding of the economic organization of the countryside is seriously hampered by such a gap in our knowledge.

Bibliography

Aschenbrenner, S. (1972), 'A contemporary community', in McDonald and Rapp (eds), 47–63.

Baumann, H. (1993), *Greek Wild Flowers and Plant Lore in Ancient Greece*, trans. and augmented by W. T. Stearn and E. R. Stearn (London).

Bennet, J., and Voutsaki, S. (1991), 'A synopsis and analysis of travelers' accounts of Keos (to 1821)', in Cherry *et al.* (eds), 365–83.

Bloch, M. (1966), *French Rural History: An Essay on its Basic Characteristics*, trans. J. Sonderheimer (London).

Boardman, J. (1974), *Athenian Black Figure Vases: A Handbook* (London).

—— (1975), *Athenian Red Figure Vases: The Archaic Period. A Handbook* (London).

Burford, A. (1993), *Land and Labour in the Greek World* (Baltimore and London).

Cameron, A. (1993), *The Mediterranean World in Late Antiquity* AD 395–600 (London).

Chatzigeorgiou, S. (1984), *Αντάρτικο στη Σάμο 1945-1949: κατάσταση μετά τη Βάρκιζα* (Nikaia).

Cherry, J. F., Davis, J. L., and Mantzourani, E. (1991), 'Introduction to the archaeology of post-Roman Keos', in Cherry *et al.* (eds), 351–64.

—— , —— , and —— (eds 1991), *Landscape Archaeology as Long-term History: Northern Keos in the Cycladic Islands* (Monumenta Archaeologica, 16; Los Angeles).

Christou, Ch. (n.d.), *Η αγροτική ζωή στην τέχνη* (Athens).

Clark Forbes, M. H. (1976a), 'Farming and foraging in prehistoric Greece: a cultural ecological perspective', in Dimen and Friedl (eds), 127–42.

—— (1976b), 'Gathering in the Argolid: a subsistence system in a Greek agricultural community', in Dimen and Friedl (eds), 251–64.

—— (1976c), 'The pursuit of wild edibles, present and past', *Expedition* 19 (1): 12–18.

Darby, H. C. (1936), 'The economic geography of England, AD 1000–1250', in H. C. Darby (ed.), *An Historical Geography of England before 1800: Fourteen Studies* (Cambridge), 165–229.

Davies, O. (1979), *Roman Mines in Europe* (New York).

de Ste Croix, G. E. M. (1966), 'The estate of Phainippos', in E. Badian (ed.), *Ancient Society and Institutions: Studies Presented to V. Ehrenberg* (Oxford), 109–14.

Dimen, M., and Friedl, E. (eds 1976), *Regional Variation in Modern Greece and Cyprus: Toward a Perspective on the Ethnography of Greece* (Annals of the New York Academy of Sciences, 268; New York).

Forbes, H. A. (1982), *Strategies and Soils: Technology, Production and Environment in the Peninsula of Methana, Greece* (Ph.D. thesis, University of Pennsylvania; Ann Arbor, Mich.).

—— (1994), 'Pastoralism and settlement structures in ancient Greece', in P. N. Doukellis and L. G. Mendoni (eds), *Structures rurales et sociétés antiques* (Centre de Recherches d'Histoire Ancienne, Besançon, 126; Paris), 187–96.

—— (n.d. a), 'The struggle for cash: the integrated exploitation of the cultivated and uncultivated landscapes in the southern Argolid, Peloponnesus, Greece', unpublished paper.

—— (n.d. b), 'Aspects of the agrarian economy of Ermionis in the late seventeenth and early eighteenth centuries: an attempt at an ethnohistorical reconstruction', unpublished paper.

—— and Foxhall, L. (1978), '"The queen of all trees": preliminary notes on the archaeology of the olive', *Expedition* 21 (1): 37–47.

—— and Koster, H. A. (1976), 'Fire, axe and plow: human influence on local plant communities in the southern Argolid', in Dimen and Friedl (eds), 109–26.

Foxhall, L. (1990), *Olive Cultivation within Greek and Roman Agriculture: The Ancient Economy Revisited* (Ph.D. thesis, University of Liverpool).

—— (forthcoming), 'Οι ανάγκες κατανάλωσης ελαιολάδου στα σπίτια των πλούσιων της αρχαίας Ελλάδας', in S. Papadopoulos (ed.), *Ελιά και λάδι* (Athens).

Geroulanou, A., Belesioti, N., and Georgiadi, E. (1978), *Παραδοσιακὲς καλλιέργιες* (Athens).

Halstead, P. L. J. (1987), 'Traditional and ancient rural economy in Mediterranean Europe: plus ça change?', *JHS* 107: 77–87.

Healy, J. F. (1978), *Mining and Metallurgy in the Greek and Roman World* (London).

Hodges, H. (1976), *Artifacts: An Introduction to Early Materials and Technology* (London).

Hodkinson, S. (1988), 'Animal husbandry in the Greek polis', in Whittaker (ed.), 35–74.

Hopper, R. J. (1979), *Trade and Industry in Classical Greece* (London).

Huxley, A., and Taylor, W. (1984), *Flowers of Greece and the Aegean* (London).

Isager, S., and Skydsgaard, J. E. (1992), *Ancient Greek Agriculture: An Introduction* (London and New York).

Jones, J. E., Graham, A. J., and Sackett, L. H. (1973), 'An Attic country house below the cave of Pan at Vari', *BSA* 68: 355–452.

Koster, H. A. (1977), *The Ecology of Pastoralism in Relation to Changing*

Patterns of Land Use in the Northeast Peloponnese (Ann Arbor, Mich.).
—— and Forbes, H. A. (n.d.), 'The "commons" and the market: ecological effects of communal land tenure and market integration on local resources in the Mediterranean', unpublished paper.
McDonald, W. A., and Rapp, G. R., jun. (eds 1972), *The Minnesota Messenia Expedition: Reconstructing a Bronze Age Regional Environment* (Minneapolis).
Madge, C. (1993), *Medicine, Money and Masquerades: Gender, Collecting and 'Development' in the Gambia* (Leicester University Discussion Papers in Geography G93/1; Leicester).
Matson, F. R. (1972), 'Ceramic studies', in McDonald and Rapp (eds), 200–24.
Miliarakis, A. (1886), Γεωγραφία πολιτική νέα καὶ ἀρχαία τοῦ νομοῦ Ἀργολίδος καὶ Κορινθίας (Athens).
Osborne, R. (1987), *Classical Landscape with Figures: The Ancient Greek City and its Countryside* (London).
Pacifico, P. A. (1686), *Descrittione delle provincie che formano la tanto decantata peninsola della Morea, nella quale si contiene l'origine d'essa, la citta, il sito, i costumi di quei populi, et altro . . .* (Milan).
Pansiot, F. P., and Rebour, H. (1961), *Improvement in Olive Cultivation* (Rome).
Pfuhl, E. (1923), *Malerei und Zeichnung der Griechen* (Munich).
Polunin, O. (1980), *Flowers of Greece and the Balkans: A Field Guide* (Oxford).
Pritchett, W. K. (1956), 'The Attic Stelai, part 2', *Hesperia*, 25: 178–328.
Rackham, O. (1983), 'Observations on the historical ecology of Boeotia', *BSA* 78: 291–351.
—— and Moody, J. (1992), 'Terraces', in B. Wells (ed.), *Agriculture in Ancient Greece (Proceedings of the 7th International Symposium at the Swedish Institute at Athens)* (Skrifter utgivna av Svenska Institutet i Athen, series in 4to, 42; Stockholm), 123–33.
Randolph, B. (1689), *The Present State of the Morea, Called Anciently Peloponnesus* (London).
Sallares, R. (1991), *The Ecology of the Ancient Greek World* (London).
Scudder, T. (1971), *Gathering among African Woodland Savannah Cultivators* (Zambian Papers, 5; Manchester).
Shepherd, R. (1993), *Ancient Mining* (London and New York).
Skydsgaard, J. E. (1988), 'Transhumance in ancient Greece', in Whittaker (ed.), 75–86.
Sutton, S. B. (1991), 'Population, economy, and settlement in post-revolutionary Keos: a cultural anthropological study', in Cherry *et al.* (eds), 383–402.
Wheler, G. (1682), *A Journey into Greece* (London).
Whittaker, C. R. (ed. 1988), *Pastoral Economies in Classical Antiquity* (Proceedings of the Cambridge Philological Society, supplement 14).

5

The countryside in classical Greek drama, and isolated farms in dramatic landscapes

Jim Roy

Landscape in tragedy and comedy

Considerable efforts are currently being made to invent the ancient Greek countryside. In an ecologically aware volume any such effort should recycle earlier inventions, and this paper will be as ecologically aware as possible: it will recycle not only thoughts which I have offered for consideration before[1] and ideas of modern scholars, but above all the invented countrysides found in the works of the classical Athenian dramatists.

It is the purpose of this paper to consider how landscape is presented in classical Greek drama, in the hope of recovering any worthwhile evidence of what classical Greek landscapes were actually like. This purpose is somewhat different from the general aim of the growing body of work on physical space and geographical locations in classical drama: such work, while increasingly productive in revealing the literary significance of dramatic references to places, is not essentially concerned with

[1] An earlier version of this paper was given to a meeting of the Classics Departments of the University of Wales, and a revised version to the Leicester–Nottingham Ancient History Seminar. I am grateful for suggestions for improvement made on both occasions, and subsequently by colleagues and referees for this publication, and am particularly grateful to Drs J. B. Salmon and R. I. Winton; but remain wholly responsible for any surviving imperfections.

reconstructing the ancient physical environment.[1]

Among the large audiences who watched Athenian drama were, presumably, many men and women who knew the Attic landscape directly from working the land, and it seems safe to suppose that most adult Athenian males had some acquaintance with the Attic countryside.[2] That in itself means that the dramatists had the opportunity to manipulate their audience's knowledge of the countryside, by evoking it directly for its own sake, by using it for other dramatic ends, or by contradicting it.

It is easy enough to illustrate the shared knowledge of the countryside taken for granted by poet and audience. For instance, Whitehead, in a chapter on the deme in comedy, has ten pages concerning Old Comedy (Whitehead 1986, 328–38): drawing not only on Aristophanes but also on the fragments of other writers, he shows easily that Old Comedy made frequent references to the demes as such and to, for example, their produce – nuts from Pithos, red mullet from Aixone, figs from Teithras, and so on. The audience of Old Comedy was clearly familiar with the various communities of rural Attica and their specialities. Equally, however, the passages on which Whitehead draws are for the most part very slight, and the Attic countryside seems to be so familiar that it is virtually taken for granted. Tragedy also draws on knowledge of Attic localities, as Krummen (1993) shows. Tragedy also takes for granted a familiarity with rural life, as can be seen (to choose one minor instance out of many) in an episode of the *Trachiniae* (180–99), when a messenger reports to Deianeira how Lichas is announcing that Herakles will soon be home. While Lichas is speaking to a gathering of some size and must be in a reasonably large open space, for the purposes of the play it is of no consequence where that space might be; but the messenger specifies that Lichas is speaking in the pasture where the cattle feed. The pasturing of the cattle is taken for granted and passed

[1] Among such work may be mentioned – the list is not complete – Bernand 1985; Chalkia 1986; Padel 1990; Zeitlin 1990; Buxton 1992; Saïd 1993; Krummen 1993.

[2] A similar conclusion might be drawn from, for example, the fact that in Xenophon, *Oikonomikos*, 16. 1–7, Sokrates and Ischomachos rapidly agree that many Athenians know how to assess land for agriculture and judge the skill with which it is exploited, or can readily find out how to do so.

over in a moment. Such references to the countryside are trivial, but their very triviality helps to suggest that author and audience knew the rural landscape.

The simplicity with which classical drama was staged did not lend itself readily to representing physically any striking natural or man-shaped landscape, but terrain could readily be described if desired. Thus in the earlier part of the *Hippolytos* Euripides three times sketches in natural settings: first (73–81) Hippolytos describes the unpastured meadow, watered by stream-water and rich in bees, from which the pure may gather garlands, and where he has himself picked flowers to make a circlet for Artemis; then (121–30) the chorus tell how they first heard of Phaidra's troubles by the rock-face where spring-water runs down to the pool below; finally (208–31) Phaidra longs to enjoy the hunt in the open air, by springs, long grass and woods. Such references to the countryside are brief and generalized; any meadow, any spring, any wood would correspond to the poet's brief words. And it must be recognized that dramatists frequently chose to dispense even with description so brief and bland. For instance, in the long scene in *Oedipus Rex* (1015–181) in which the discovery of the baby Oedipus on Mt Kithairon is revealed, we learn almost nothing about the physical appearance of Kithairon save that the child was found 'in folded woods of Kithairon' (1026). It is true that Sophokles does use – with minimal explanation (1133–9), and so as something evidently familiar – the pastoral practice of transhumance to explain the contact between the Theban and Corinthian shepherds on the mountain,[1] but he is here not interested in the mountain landscape itself. While the audience's familiarity with the countryside could be taken for granted and manipulated, it could also be ignored.

Aristophanes is particularly prone to take the countryside for granted. He is obviously familiar with Attica, like other poets of Old Comedy, but seldom describes a rural setting in specific terms. Instead he ruthlessly combines rural and urban settings in comic fantasy to produce a dramatic landscape in which the audience must re-map its social geography. A prime example is the *Acharnians*. The leading character Dikaiopolis is an Athenian peasant,

---

[1] This reference to transhumance is well discussed, in relation to others, by Hodkinson 1988, 54.

who in the opening scene (32–3) expresses his dislike for the town
and his longing for his deme (in fact Cholleidai, north of Athens:
line 406). He does soon go home, and from line 174 on the action
of the play takes place at his house. Here he is able, once equipped
with his own personal peace, to isolate space round his house and
set up his personal free market (719); but this space round his
house is no more real than the lack of space between his house
in Cholleidai on one side of the stage and on the other side the
house of Euripides (393–5). In the *Clouds* the old man, Strepsi-
ades, is heavily characterized early in the play (43–52) as a farmer
of decidedly rustic temperament and habits (though with a wife
with different pretensions), in lines which play on the stereotype
of the *agroikos*; but next door to his house on the stage is the
Phrontisterion where Socrates and his students operate. We are
again in a landscape ruthlessly reinvented by Aristophanes.

Tragedy's use of the countryside is different. In 1957 Parry could
write:

> To sum up in perhaps overly formulaic terms: In the *Iliad*, in Sappho,
> in Pindar, and in most of Greek tragedy (though this is not true of,
> for example, the *Philoctetes*), landscape, as a distinct element, does
> not play a part; and natural description is used, sparingly and briefly,
> as a direct metaphor for things human.
> (quoted from Parry 1989, 35)

Later, however, John Jones (1962, 219–20) argued for an interdependence of man and place in the plays of Sophokles, making
a distinction between the early plays (*Antigone, Trachiniae,
Oedipus Rex*, and to some extent *Ajax*) in which the sense of
locality is weak and vague, and the later plays (*Elektra, Philoktetes*, and *Oedipus at Colonus*) in which this sense of locality is
strong. Taplin agrees strongly with Jones's view, though adding
Ajax to the list of plays in which the sense of locality is strong
(Taplin 1978, 186 n. 19).[1] The arguments of Jones and Taplin are
persuasive; but it must also be recognized that, even in those plays
of Sophokles in which the physical setting is important, that setting
is sketched in very economically: the poet does not choose to
spend many words on describing scenery. Thus the *Philoktetes*

---

[1] cf. Taplin's comments on the importance of landscape in the *Philoktetes* (49–51) and *Ajax* (87–8).

closes with words which stress the place where Philoktetes has spent his years of exile:

> Come now, I call upon this land in valediction.
> Farewell, dwelling which shared my watches,
> you nymphs of the water meadows,
> you broken-voiced booming of the sea and headland,
> where even in the inmost chamber my head
> was often drenched by the south wind's gusty spray,
> and Mount Hermaion returned an echoing groan
> as I hollered in the storm.
> And now, you springs of the Lykian stream, I leave you,
> leave you, as I never dared imagine.
> Farewell, O sea-surrounded land of Lemnos,
> and give me a calm and prosperous voyage,
> where I am sent by mighty fate, the wisdom of my friends,
> and the all-subduing god who brought these things about.
>
> (lines 1452–68, trans. Taplin)

The lines are dramatically important, but the description is sparing; it would offer no precise idea of the island's physical appearance to someone who did not know Lemnos. (A wholly uninhabited Lemnos – *Philoktetes*, lines 1–2 – is of course a landscape invented by Sophokles.) Even in the *Oedipus at Colonus*, in which Sophokles clearly seeks to recall to his audience a real location in Attica – Kolonos, not far from the city itself – he offers little more than the names of significant features at Kolonos.[1] The messenger reports:

> when he [Oedipus] reached the precipitous road rooted by bronze steps in the earth he stood on one of the branching ways, near the hollow basin, where lies the agreement, ever sure, of Theseus and Perithoös; then, standing between the Thorican rock and the hollow pear-tree under the stone tomb, he sat down; then he took off his squalid garments . . .
>
> (lines 1590–7; cf. 16–19, 54–61)

In such plays the unreconstructed countryside is made to work very fast to earn its place, but it is a very modest place.

---

[1] To stress how little Sophokles says about the appearance and physical layout of the location at Kolonos is not, of course, to deny the importance and multiple resonances of the setting, well brought out by Krummen 1993.

Euripides' *Bacchae* shows a quite different way to reinvent the countryside. The *Bacchae* is notoriously the play in which Euripides is most obviously under the influence of the French structuralist school. It is constructed from a series of interlocking oppositions – notably man and god, male and female, order and disorder, and town and country – and the oppositions are then undermined. The action of the play is divided between the city of Thebes where the play is set, and the slopes of Mt Kithairon from which come two long reports (677–774; 1024–67). On the mountainside are the women of Thebes, driven there by Dionysos (32–8), living outside the law of men and outside social bonds; some have even abandoned their babies in Thebes (699–702). The town–country opposition is linked to the opposition between order and disorder, but in a complex way; for while King Pentheus fails to keep order in the city, the women on the mountain live in an antinomian but happy and peaceful state until attacked by the herdsmen tending flocks on the mountain (677–713, followed by the violence of 714–74). Finally, of course, city and country come together when Pentheus climbs the mountainside and perishes at the hands of the now frenzied women (1024–52). It is a commonplace to observe that Euripides' version of the countryside in this play serves to focus all that is the antithesis of the carefully structured polis (though it must be remembered that Euripides ultimately undermines that antithesis).[1] It is less often observed, however, that he reinvents the countryside in order to achieve this antithesis. He does it simply by ignoring much of the Theban landscape. Between the city of Thebes and Mt Kithairon – as any Athenian hoplite surely knew – lay the broad agricultural plain of Thebes, but this arable land barely appears in the play. When the attack by the herdsmen drives the Theban women into a destructive rage and they sweep not only across the mountainside but also down on to the arable land, in two brief lines (749–50) we hear of 'the plains ... which by the streams of Asopos send forth the Thebans' fertile corn crop'. Otherwise these plains are ignored in the play, though they must be crossed by the several characters who commute between the dramatic poles of the city and the mountain. Euripides has invented a countryside which can be presented in the starkest contrast to the man-made city, and

---

[1] See the recent, perceptive observations of Buxton 1992, 12–13.

he has done it by ruthlessly omitting the humanly contrived arable landscape.

The examples so far discussed suggest that classical Greek dramatists, while familiar with the countryside, generally ignore it or, when they do give it some dramatic importance, describe it in very summary fashion. Moreover, when they do refer to landscape they are ready to adapt it ruthlessly to their purposes. We may therefore expect that when, exceptionally, a rural setting is more fully described in a play, the description is equally adapted to some dramatic purpose; and we thus face the question of whether the description corresponds to an actual landscape of the period, or is simply invented to suit the play. The question is particularly important for what is arguably the most difficult Euripidean landscape for us to evaluate, that of the *Elektra*.

Euripides' *Elektra*

In this play, as the prologue explains, Elektra has been married off to a poor peasant farmer and lives with him as his (still virgin) wife. Whatever reality his farm may have, this peasant is a patent contrivance, and he disappears from the play from line 431, leaving no after-effects;[1] since he has virtuously refrained from consummating his marriage to Elektra (as he himself says in his first speech), she is available at the end of the play to marry her brother's friend Pylades (1340–1). Although the Peasant is thus discarded, he and his farm are clearly introduced by Euripides for dramatic purposes. For one thing, the playwright thus moves the action of the play away from the palace at Argos, achieving a contrast with the previous plays on the same theme; and for another he is able to contrast the princess Elektra and her peasant husband. This is, therefore, a play in which location matters, and a good deal of information about the setting gradually emerges.

In the opening words of the play the setting is located in Argive territory, and the immediate invocation of the river Inachos

---

[1] At lines 1286–7 Kastor says that Pylades is to take the peasant to Phokis and give him riches; nothing is said of the peasant's view of this development.

suggests that the location is in the valley of that river.[1] More information on the setting, and on the circumstances in which Elektra
lives with her peasant husband, is given in the course of the play,
but it is of course presented by different characters who take
different views of the setting, and it must be remembered that
their comments on it are coloured accordingly. Characters originally from the palace or the town (including Elektra) see the
setting as wilder, poorer, and more sordid. To take a minor
example, it is notable that Elektra and her husband differ over
how well their house's resources can cater for the obviously distinguished (though still unrecognized) Orestes and Pylades and their
servants: she sees the resources as quite inadequate, while her
husband, though freely admitting his poverty, believes that there
is an adequate supply of simple food for a day at least (404–31).
Thus, when Elektra calls the site remote (251), we may surmise
that her description is due at least as much to her resentment of
her situation as to the physical setting. Again, when she tells
Clytemnestra a made-up tale about having given birth to a child
all alone, Clytemnestra asks whether the house is so 'neighbour-
less of friends', and Elektra replies that no one wants poor people
as friends (1129–31). Even in Elektra's thinking the implication
seems to be, not that the house is utterly remote from other homes,
but that it is cut off by its poverty.

The house lies near enough the Argive frontier for Orestes to
be able to flee from it across the border (95–7); since the upper
Inachos formed the border between Mantineia and Argos, the
setting near the frontier might suggest that the farm lay in the
upper Inachos valley (Cropp 1988, 98). Other considerations,
however, suggest a less precise position within the valley. Elektra
stresses the mountainous surroundings (207–10), and the Old Man
complains of the steep climb up to the farm (489–90); but it is
clear that the farm had arable fields fit for cultivation by a team
of oxen, for the Peasant goes off to work the land with oxen.
(At lines 78–9 he says, 'At dawn I'll put the oxen to the fields
and sow the furrows'; this accurately reflects ancient agricultural
practice, in which sowing and ploughing were closely linked and

---

[1] In the first line of the Greek text the word 'Argos' may be corrupt
(see Cropp 1988 *ad loc.*), but the reference to the Inachos is clear, and
another reference to Argos rapidly follows (line 6).

apparently took place at the same time.)[1] In addition, Orestes, on arriving, supposes that the area is the sort of place where one might meet a ploughman (104–5), so that some reasonably level fields are supposed not far away. There is a path running past the house, on which Orestes and Pylades guess there may be passers-by (103–5, cf. 216–17), and in the direction of Argos it develops into what is called 'a two-tracked wagon-path' (775),[2] along which Clytemnestra eventually arrives in a carriage (998–9). Not far from the farm along that road lie Aigisthos' horse-pastures (621–3, 636) and the well-watered gardens where he gathers myrtle for a sacri-fice (777–8), offering glimpses of a richer rural economy.

Euripides has no reason to preserve realistic distances, or times of travel, from mountain to farm to lowland pasture; and if the farm is indeed to be situated in the Inachos valley that valley has, like other landscapes in classical drama, been ruthlessly rearranged. The actual Inachos valley extends for a considerable distance from Mt Artemision, on the Mantineia–Argos border, roughly eastwards towards Argos itself, and covers a range of terrain from mountain slopes to more level and fertile ground where the valley is wider (Pritchett 1980, 1–53, with map (p. 3), photographs, and references to ancient and modern literature). It formed an important route between Mantineia and Argos, used on occasion by armies; and there was significant classical settle-ment in it, including a town which was probably Orneai, located by Pritchett (ibid., 17–32) on the north side of the valley.[3] Orneai

---

[1] See Isager and Skydsgaard 1992, 47–9, with pl. 3. 3. i–ii; also Amouretti 1986, pls 8 *a–b*, 29 *a*). Hamish Forbes tells me that sowing and ploughing are frequently carried out in rapid succession in the modern Argolid: one technique is to sow on unploughed soil and then plough. Euripides evidently wrote the line from an accurate knowledge of farming practice.

[2] A track with two wheel-ruts is probably meant (Cropp 1988 *ad loc.*). On Greek roads and tracks see Pritchett 1980, ch. 5, esp. pp. 151–8 on the rudimentary nature of Greek roads and pp. 167–96 on wheel-ruts; see also Crouwel 1992, 21–6, on roads and draught animals. See also Pikoulas 1989 on roads and sites in this area, esp. on wheel-ruts found on the route Argos–Oinoë–Mantineia.

[3] Even if the site in question is not Orneai, Pritchett (1980, 24–7) regards it as the remains of a classical town. He also records classical sites near modern Kastro and Chelmes, one of which may be classical Lyrkeion (ibid., 12–17). For military use of the route along the valley and over Mt Artemi-sion, see ibid., 51–2. Pritchett's plates 23 and 27 show something of the terrain of the upper valley; plates 12–13 offer views of the middle valley.

was prominent in Greek affairs in winter 417/6 BC (how long trouble may have been brewing we cannot tell): first the Spartans settled Argive exiles there, arranging a truce between Orneai and Argos, then Argos, helped by Athenians, captured and destroyed it (Thucydides, 6. 7). Whether Euripides' *Elektra* was already written is uncertain.[1] If it was written after the winter of 417/6, when many Athenians will have carried home word of Orneai and made available in Athens detailed information on the Inachos valley, one may speculate about why Euripides chose a setting in the valley but did not mention Orneai; if he wrote the play earlier, it is not clear how good his information would have been.

Since the setting telescopes features that could be found along a number of Greek river valleys, it is difficult to say whether Euripides is trying to represent the actual Inachos valley. If he is, he appears to have telescoped its features, ignoring any town but describing a farm with at least partly arable land, in the hills and near the mountainous border-land but also not far from richer terrain and connected to it by a road fit for carriages.

It is no surprise that the distance between the farm and the home of the Old Man is also subjected to dramatic convenience. He lives far from the farm: Euripides says (410–12) that he lives beside the river Tanaos in the Argive–Spartan border area, which would put his home near the region of the Thyreatis. No precise distance can be calculated from such vague indications; but Cropp estimates that, if the Peasant's farm is in the upper Inachos valley, the Old Man's journey from the farm to his home and back will have been some 35 km each way. Yet the Peasant leaves to fetch him at line 431, and the Old Man appears himself on stage at line 487![2] The farm thus appears to sit, not in the real upper valley of the Inachos, but in a composite, invented landscape.

---

[1] Cropp (1988, l–li) reviews the arguments for its date, setting out the period to be seriously considered as 422–413 BC, the likeliest years being 422–417, particularly 420/19.

[2] See Cropp 1988 on line 410. Another example of loose geography (however well justified in terms of mythical associations) is that Euripides is apparently happy to refer to Mycenae as a synonym of Argos when speaking of the seat of royal power in Argos: see line 963 with the comments of Cropp 1988, 99, on line 6.

The house itself is clearly modest. Elektra describes it as smoke-blackened (1139–40); the words are addressed with deliberate irony to Clytemnestra who is about to enter, recalling her fine clothes, her necessary freedom from physical blemish as a sacrifice about to be offered to the gods, and her moral impurity, but need not be any the less literally true of a simple house with no chimney. Whether Elektra meant any more when she complained to Orestes of being weighed down with squalor (305) is not clear. When Orestes sees the Peasant's house, he describes it as worthy of a digger (*skapheus*, presumably a poor peasant)[1] or a cowherd (252). When Clytemnestra arrives she orders her servants to take her chariot and team to the manger (1135–6), presumably in some farm building; and a stall will have been needed for the oxen. All in all the information suggests a modest farmstead.

Our interpretation of the setting, and particularly of the farm, depends in part on the social setting of the Peasant's household.[2] Early in the play the Peasant describes himself as descended from Mycenaean forebears who were distinguished but poor: he thus establishes his freeborn status, while admitting his poverty (34–8).[3] He is, however, clearly not destitute, despite Elektra's complaints. The word *penês* (πένης), used by the Peasant to describe his ancestors and also used of the Peasant himself (e.g. 253), denotes

---

[1] The word σκαφεύς is rare, but suggests a man performing physical work of fairly low status. On the usage of the word see Archippos fr. 46, with notes in Kassel and Austin 1991; Archippos mentions gardening σκαφεῖς alongside donkey-drivers and women who weed or cut grass.

[2] Donzelli (1978, 227–69) devotes a chapter to a full and detailed analysis of Elektra's peasant husband, and finds him close to the economic and social reality (including, notably, Attic reality) of the end of the fifth century.

[3] He refers to himself in the plural ('us'), to his ancestors in the plural, then to himself in the singular in a verb form; there then follows, in the plural, the phrase 'distinguished [λαμπροί, *lamproi*] in descent but poor in money'. Given that the phrase with the singular verb is grammatically parallel to the phrase quoted with λαμπροί, and indeed that the verb immediately precedes the word λαμπροί, it is difficult to take the plural λαμπροί as referring to the subject of the singular verb, and so it seems more natural to take the phrase quoted as referring to the Peasant's ancestors than to him himself. If that is right, the Peasant is not implying that he himself has sunk to poverty though his family had previously been rich (though the word λαμπροί would normally suggest a fairly elevated social status including wealth).

someone who is not destitute but has to work for a living (Finley 1985, 41). Hammond (1984, 377–8) has observed that we are never told whether the Peasant owns his farm, but there is no suggestion in the play that he is in another man's service, and it is natural to see him as a free peasant farmer rather than a dependant such as is found in Homeric epic. In this respect he is unlike, for instance, Sophokles' herdsmen in the *Oedipus Rex*, of whom the Theban is one of Laios' men (1117–18) while the Corinthian is in *theteia* to an unnamed master (1029). Whether or not the household had a servant is disputed by modern commentators,[1] but the farm with a team of oxen would have belonged, in fifth-century terms, clearly above the poorest rural classes. The clash of status between the princess Elektra and her husband is readily understood if he was to be perceived by the audience as, in effect, a fifth-century Attic peasant of a type familiar to them, a product of the anachronism not uncommon in classical tragedy (Easterling 1985).

If, however, the Peasant was a fifth-century peasant, the question arises of whether his farm could be a realistic fifth-century farm – in fact, an isolated fifth century farmstead – or whether it belonged purely to Euripides' imagination. There has been considerable recent work, largely provoked by the results of field survey, on whether isolated farmsteads existed in classical Greece, and powerful arguments have been deployed to suggest that they did not exist to any significant extent. In this debate isolated farmsteads are contrasted with nucleated settlement, and this vocabulary is retained here. It may therefore be worthwhile to explain that the term 'isolated' is meant simply to convey 'not part of a nucleated settlement', and not necessarily to suggest any extreme isolation in a very remote or wild situation; any farmstead standing alone, even if it has neighbours a few fields away, is in this sense isolated. While the farmstead standing alone ('isolated') can readily be contrasted with the village ('nucleated'), settlement could be less clear-cut: two houses standing together in the countryside would constitute isolated rather than nucleated settlement, but clearly a cluster of houses in a group smaller than a village might pose problems of definition. There is no

---

[1] See Cropp 1988 on line 140. The arguments of Hammond 1984, 378–9, against the presence of a servant are strong.

indication that any other homestead stood beside the Peasant's farm in Euripides' *Elektra*,[1] but the traditional stage setting with three doors could readily suggest adjacent houses which might be either part of a larger nucleated settlement or neighbouring, but still 'isolated', rural dwellings. Robin Osborne (1985, 17) claims that, for Attica, 'there is no clear evidence in the literature for anyone who lives and farms out on his own in the country'. I argued elsewhere (Roy 1988) that this claim sweeps aside too readily Demosthenes' fifty-fifth speech,[2] but before considering whether it also sweeps aside too readily Elektra's Euripidean home I should like to look at Menander.

Menander

In what survives of Menander it is clear that his settings and his characters are, more often than not, urban. None the less the countryside is not alien to their way of life, and Menander uses it freely, whether as an adjunct to a plot or as an actual setting. It is, moreover, the productive farmland that he draws on in this way, not the wilder and more remote mountainside. The *Epitrepontes*, for instance, is set somewhere in Attica: not too far from Athens, since the slave Syriskos can commute to and from the city fairly easily (Gomme and Sandbach 1973, 290). In the play the shepherd Daos explains that he found an abandoned baby while herding sheep in a copse or wood (*dasos*) near some farms, and gave the baby to a charcoal-burner working nearby (242–7). From what survives of the play it is difficult, however, to see how much the countryside really matters to its dramatic development: the major characters could have behaved in much the same way in town. It is therefore possible that Menander occasionally chose a rural setting for no compelling dramatic reason.

In the *Georgos* farming is central to the plot, though the play itself is set in town. The play concerns the fate of a widow's

[1] Hammond 1984, 376–7, reconstructs the setting as having a central gateway leading to the farm's inner courtyard, and a side door into the farmhouse; but there is no need to suppose an inner courtyard (see Cropp 1988 on line 342).
[2] Langdon 1991 independently draws the same conclusions from Demosthenes, 55.

daughter who has had an affair with a rich neighbour's son and is pregnant by him. The widow's son is working on the farm of Kleainetos, and Kleainetos is portrayed as an active farmer, reasonably prosperous but still determinedly working on his land himself. He then suffers a serious accident when working in his vineyard, is helped by the widow's son, and decides to marry the widow's daughter. Again the agricultural landscape does not seem indispensable to Menander's dramatic purposes: Kleainetos's wealth need not have been in land, and a different accident could readily have been contrived with the widow's son at hand to help.

Terence's *Heautontimoroumenos* is avowedly derived from a Menandrian original. What changes Terence made to the play remains a matter for debate, but the rural setting is certainly taken from the original, for, as a fragment shows, Menander's play was set at one or other of the two places called Halai in Attica.[1] The scene in Terence's version may well be in a village; there are, at any rate, three houses in a row on the stage. One of the three belongs to Menedemos, who made money as a soldier in Asia (111–12) and so became owner of a large house and numerous slaves, but sold up everything (except some slaves fit to work in the fields) in order to buy land (140–6) and presumably the house on the stage. We learn that, despite Menedemos's wealth and advancing age, his neighbour Chremes sees him working himself in the fields every day (65–74). There are other casual references to the farmland in the area, for instance that two other neighbours are in dispute about their boundaries (498–501). The rural setting is used for dramatic purposes (e.g. in allowing Chremes to see Menedemos out working), but the main plot is about the sexual affairs of the two men's sons, and again it does not seem essential that the action be located in a rural setting.

From the *Epitrepontes*, the *Georgos*, and the *Heautontimoroumenos* it thus seems that Menander, much more than any other surviving Athenian dramatist, was willing to use Athenian agriculture and the cultivated landscape as material for his plays, even if he had little comment to make on them. There remains

---

[1] On the play generally see the recent edition by Brothers (1988); on the choice between Halai Araphenides on the east coast and Halai Aixonides on the south coast see Brothers on lines 61–4.

to be discussed, of course, the *Dyskolos*, the play in which he makes most use of the countryside.[1]

Osborne, in discussing the question of isolated farms in classical Greece, says the following on the setting of the *Dyskolos*:

> The people of the countryside appear only at the margins of dramatic literature. When they come on stage it is as the messengers and supporting cast in tragedies, and as the butt of jokes and jibes in comedies which distance the real life of the agricultural community. Menander's *Disagreeable Man* [*Dyskolos*] has as its title figure a farmer who is portrayed living on his own up in the heavily contoured landscape near the cave of Pan at Phyle . . . in northern Attica. This farmer is of interest because he has a beautiful daughter. By making his disagreeable man live out on his own in a wild landscape, Menander stresses that he is an unsociable type. In actual fact even this remote part of Attica was peopled: there was a small farming community residing in the village of Phyle, and troops were stationed at the nearby fort controlling the pass towards Boeotia. The glimpse which comedy gives of the countryside is extremely partial.
>
> (Osborne 1987, 19; cf. 1985, 21–2)

Osborne thus lays considerable emphasis on the wildness and remoteness of the setting of the *Dyskolos*, suggesting that Menander has exaggerated them; if correct, his view would allow the argument that the farm in the *Dyskolos* is 'isolated' (in the sense of the aforementioned debate about isolated and nucleated settlement) because it is marginal and remote, set in wild surroundings, and so cannot be representative of any ordinary Attic farmsteads. This emphasis on the wildness and remoteness of Menander's setting can, however, be challenged.

The setting is given very clearly by the prologue and some supplementary references later in the text. In the centre is a shrine of the Nymphs and Pan at Phyle in northern Attica; to one side is the house of the misanthrope Knemon, with his farm adjoining; to the other side, again with an adjoining farm, is the house in which Knemon's estranged wife lives with Gorgias, her son by her first marriage.

In theory it might be supposed that the three buildings on stage – the farms of Knemon and his estranged wife, and between them the shrine of Pan – form part of a nucleated settlement, which would presumably be the principal settlement of the deme of

[1] On the play see the edition by Handley 1965.

Phyle; but there is no reason to think so. Apart from requiring Menander to have moved the site of Pan's shrine (see below) into a nucleated settlement, the supposition also encounters such difficulties as the following. (1) Though explicitly and clearly set in Phyle, the play makes no reference to any nucleated settlement at Phyle, or to the well-known fort there.[1] (2) Pan explains in the prologue (lines 2–4) that the shrine he comes from belongs to the Phylasians (demesmen of Phyle), in terms which would hardly be necessary if the shrine was situated in a nucleated settlement of the demesmen. (3) During the play Sostratos' mother arrives on the scene to conduct a sacrifice to Pan (430–55). When Sostratos earlier (260–4) announces his mother's intention to sacrifice, he mentions that in her habit of daily sacrifice to one deity or another she goes around the entire deme. His words certainly do not suggest that she is on that day sacrificing to a cult situated in or beside a central nucleated settlement of the deme. (4) Knemon has neighbours (32–4); but neighbours in farming communities can live some distance apart, and there is no reason to think their houses are immediately beside his.

The immediate setting of the play has been generally – and surely rightly – interpreted, not as being part of a nucleated settlement, but as having only the three buildings mentioned.

A road runs past, leading in one direction towards the fields of Knemon and Gorgias and beyond; in the other to Cholargos and eventually to Athens (Handley 1965, 22). There is clearly traffic on the road, which crosses the stage and leads on past Knemon's land, for he no longer cultivates the fields beside the road in order to avoid the passers-by (162–5). It has also been noted how often in the play Knemon is badgered by others seeking to borrow one object or another (Millett 1991, 38).

The shrine of Pan mentioned in the play is commonly identified with an archaeological site at a cave near Phyle, shown by the finds to have been a shrine associated with this god. The identification seems inescapable, given that the play opens with Pan himself saying, 'Suppose that the place is Phyle in Attica, and the

---

[1] Whitehead 1986, 341, assembles and discusses the references to the deme of Phyle and its demesmen in the play; Osborne 1985, 193, gives references to finds of surface sherds which may indicate nucleated settlement within the deme of Phyle.

shrine of the nymphs from which I'm coming forward belongs to the Phylasians and those who can farm the rocks here – a very evident shrine' (lines 1–4).

The cave (which I have not visited) in which the archaeological material has been found is small and relatively inaccessible,[1] though reports differ on the difficulty of reaching it. The *Blue Guide* says the site is approached by an 'easy scramble' down a slope from a path (Barber 1988, 231–2). Handley (1965, 25), who was guided to the site by the American archaeologist and expert on Attic topography Eugene Vanderpool, writes that 'one arrives by scrambling precipitously down the mountainside from above, or by a sharp ascent from the torrent-bed below'. At any rate, it is clear that Menander has moved the shrine from a small cave that is awkward to reach, has made it more commodious, and has set it beside two houses and a road. He is at some pains to claim a real location in contemporary Attica for his play, but has adapted the topography to his dramatic purposes, and has done so – significantly – by making the setting less remote and inaccessible.

Knemon's farmhouse is isolated, but not because it is remote. (The composite nature of the invented landscape in which Euripides sets the farmhouse of his *Elektra*, similarly, makes it difficult to argue that that farmhouse is isolated because it is remote and inaccessible.) In addition, Menander is at pains to show Knemon as a farmer (albeit a very disagreeable one) in a farming community. In addition to his estranged wife, he has other neighbours in the area, though he detests them (see the prologue). The wealthy man whose son Sostratos falls in love with Knemon's daughter has a large and prosperous estate not far away (prologue; cf. 774–5). In the play there is a strong insistence on the fact that Knemon and Gorgias are working farmers, and in the hope of influencing Knemon Sostratos, too, has to do his share of digging with Gorgias. The fact that the play is set in a cultivated landscape is made very plain, and there are references to rebuilding a dry-stone wall (376–7) and to moving manure (584–6). The ground is certainly stony, but Knemon's lot, fighting with this

---

[1] Gomme and Sandbach 1973, 135, give archaeological references and describe the cave. There are detailed descriptions of this and the other Attic caves dedicated to the cult of the god Pan, together with the archaeological findings from them, in Deligeorgi-Alexopoulou 1985.

stony soil, is not that of a recluse but is described as that of the typical Attic peasant (604–6). The whole area of Phyle may have seemed out of the way to Athenian city-dwellers, but Menander does not depict Knemon as a man alone in a wild landscape.

It was argued above that Athenian dramatists reshape the landscape radically to suit their dramatic purposes. There is no reason to doubt that Menander does the same. That he should have chosen to construct a landscape not unlike cultivated areas of contemporary Attica need cause no surprise, since his plays generally construct a society not unlike the society of contemporary Athens. His plays were not documentaries, and discordances between Menandrian society and actual Athenian society are well known: girls in his plays, for instance, receive dowries much more lavish than those actually attested (see e.g. Handley 1965, 278–9), and we need not believe that Athenian society contained as many recovered foundlings as do the plays. Yet Menandrian society *is* contemporary Athenian society – distorted but not unrecognizable – and the Menandrian landscape is presumably a comparable distortion of contemporary Attica. This is the more likely because the landscape of the *Dyskolos* is not a unique invention to serve the purposes of that play alone, but belongs along with the references to agricultural landscape in Menander's other plays.

Conclusions

Menander has constructed a dramatic landscape in which we find the isolated farm of Knemon, and also that of Gorgias. While not a precisely accurate depiction of the contemporary agricultural landscape in Attica, Menander's landscape can be taken as a distorted version of the real contemporary landscape. It follows that the isolated farm, as shown by Menander, is not a pure invention created for dramatic purposes but a reflection, admittedly distorted, of one of the features of the Attic countryside of the late fourth century; moreover, it reflects not remote and marginal terrain, but a cultivated landscape.

These considerations help us to assess the isolated farm in Euripides' *Elektra*. There is no doubt that Euripides chose the farm as a setting for dramatic purposes; but the question remains whether in so doing he invented a setting which for his audience was unknown, or at least rare and marginal, or one that they could readily recognize from their knowledge of the Attic landscape. In Athenian tragedy, and for that matter in Aristophanes also, landscape is ruthlessly subordinated to the playwright's dramatic purposes, and is usually described very summarily; for that reason, most classical drama is not a rich source of evidence on the rural environment in classical times. In the *Elektra*, however, Euripides has gone to some pains to describe in some detail a rural landscape with an isolated farmstead. This landscape is unique in his work, and quite unlike his handling of the countryside in the *Bacchae*. If there were no dramatic parallel we might suppose that the landscape of the *Elektra* is entirely imaginary, invented for the purposes of the play. Yet the peasant farm of the *Elektra* ceases to be unique when set beside the farms of the *Dyskolos*. Menander, unlike earlier Athenian dramatists, uses agricultural themes and settings even when they are not obviously necessary for his dramatic purposes, and his rural landscape appears to be a version, admittedly adapted, of the countryside in his day. Menander's farms therefore make it easier for us to believe that the peasant's farm in the *Elektra*, while certainly introduced and exploited for dramatic purposes, also reflects the countryside of Euripides' day.

If that is so, then Athenian drama, on the fairly rare occasions when it takes more than a passing interest in the agricultural countryside, presents us with examples of that controversial phenomenon, the isolated classical farmstead.

Bibliography

Amouretti, M.-C. (1986), *Le Pain et l'huile dans la Grèce antique* (Paris).

Barber, R. (1988), *Greece* (Blue Guides), 5th edn (London and New York).

Bernand, A. (1985), *La Carte du tragique: la géographie dans la tragédie grecque* (Paris).

Brothers, A. J. (1988), *Terence: The Self-tormentor* (Warminster).

Buxton, R. G. A. (1992), 'Imaginary Greek mountains', *JHS* 112: 1–15.

Chalkia, I. (1986), *Lieux et espaces dans la tragédie d'Euripide: essai d'analyse socio-culturelle* (Thessalonica).

Cropp, M. J. (1988), *Euripides: Electra* (Warminster).

Crouwel, J. H. (1992), *Chariots and Other Wheeled Vehicles in Iron Age Greece* (Amsterdam).

Deligeorgi-Alexopoulou, Ch. (1985), 'Σπήλαια της Αττικής αφιερωμένα στη λατρεία του θεού Πάνα', *Αρχαιολογία*, 15: 45–54.

Donzelli, G. B. (1978), *Studio sull'Elettra di Euripide* (Catania).

Easterling, P. E. (1985), 'Anachronism in Greek tragedy', *JHS* 105: 1–10.

Finley, M. I. (1985), *The Ancient Economy*, 2nd edn (Berkeley and Los Angeles).

Gomme, A. W., and Sandbach, F. H. (1973), *Menander: A Commentary* (Oxford).

Hammond, N. G. L. (1984), 'Speech and parody in Euripides' Electra', *Greek, Roman, and Byzantine Studies*, 25: 373–87.

Handley, E. W. (1965), *The Dyskolos of Menander* (London).

Hodkinson, S. (1988), 'Animal husbandry in the Greek polis', in C. R. Whittaker (ed.), *Pastoral Economies in Classical Antiquity* (Proceedings of the Cambridge Philological Society, supp. 14), 35–74.

Isager, S., and Skydsgaard, J. E. (1992), *Ancient Greek Agriculture: An Introduction* (London and New York).

Jones, J. (1962), *On Aristotle and Greek Tragedy* (London).

Kassel, R., and Austin, C. (1991), *Poetae Comici Graeci*, ii (Berlin).

Krummen, E. (1993), 'Athens and Attica: polis and countryside in Greek tragedy', in Sommerstein *et al.* (eds), 191–217.

Langdon, M. K. (1991), 'The farm in classical Attica', *Classical Journal*, 86: 209–13.

Millett, P. (1991), *Lending and Borrowing in Ancient Athens* (Cambridge).

Osborne, R. (1985), *Demos: The Discovery of Classical Attika* (Cambridge).

—— (1987), *Classical Landscape with Figures: The Ancient Greek City and its Countryside* (London).

Padel, R. (1990), 'Making space speak', in Winkler and Zeitlin (eds), 336–65.

Parry, A. M. (1989), 'Landscape in Greek poetry', in A. M. Parry, *The Language of Achilles and Other Papers* (Oxford and New York), ch. 2 (also published in *Yale Classical Studies*, 15 (1957), 3–29).

Pikoulas, Y. A. (1989), 'Το οδικό δίκτυο της αρχαίας Οινόης (Μερκούρι)', in *Πρακτικά τού Β' Τοπικού Συνεδρίου Αργολικών Σπουδών (Άργος, 30 Μαΐου – 1 Ιουνίου 1986)* (Athens; Πελοποννησιακά, supp. 14), 296–8.

Pritchett, W. K. (1980), *Studies in Ancient Greek Topography*, iii: *Roads* (Berkeley, Los Angeles, and London).

Rieu, E. V. (trans. 1991), *Homer: The Odyssey* (revised by D. C. H. Rieu; London).

Roy, J. (1988), 'Demosthenes 55 as evidence for isolated farmsteads in classical Attica', *Liverpool Classical Monthly*, 13: 57–9.

Saïd, S. (1993), 'Tragic Argos', in Sommerstein *et al.* (eds), 167–89.

Sommerstein, A. H., Halliwell, S., Henderson, J., and Zimmerman, B. (eds 1993), *Tragedy, Comedy, and the Polis* (Bari).

Taplin, O. (1978), *Greek Tragedy in Action* (London).

Whitehead, D. (1986), *The Demes of Attica 508/7–ca. 250 BC* (Princeton).

Winkler, J. J., and Zeitlin, F. I. (eds 1990), *Nothing to Do with Dionysos? Athenian Drama in its Social Context* (Princeton).

Zeitlin, F. I. (1990), 'Thebes: theater of self and society in Athenian drama', in Winkler and Zeitlin (eds), 130–67.

6

Ancient hunting:
from Homer to Polybios

Robin Lane Fox

Society and landscape

In Lampedusa's great Sicilian novel, the Leopard sets out for a
morning's hunting in a landscape which Greek historians still share
on their travels.

> The term 'countryside' implies soil transformed by labour, but the scrub
> clinging to the slopes was still in the very same state of scented tangle
> in which it had been found by Phoenicians, Dorians and Ionians when
> they disembarked in Sicily, that America of antiquity. Don Fabrizio and
> Tumeo . . . saw the same objects, their clothes were soaked with just as
> sticky a sweat, the same indifferent breeze blew steadily from the sea,
> moving myrtles and broom, spreading a smell of thyme. The dogs'
> sudden pauses for thought, their tension waiting for prey were the very
> same as when Artemis was invoked for the chase.
>
> (Lampedusa, trans. Colquhoun 1988, 70)

Lampedusa's intuition was well-grounded. Throughout antiquity,
Sicily remained a sportsman's paradise, despite the vast crops of
grain which were grown in the island's river-plains. Hunting dogs
are shown on the fifth-century coinages of Panormos and Elymian
Segesta in the north-west of the island;[1] in the east around Enna

---

[1] *BMC* (Sicily) 121, 133–6; on Segesta, Kraay 1976, no. 849; Dubourditu
1990, 51–83, esp. 59 and 63–4, with a mythical explanation of the city's
other dog-coins which I doubt.

the fields were said to be so fair that hounds lost the scent in the sweetness of the flowers (Diodorus of Sicily, 5. 3. 2); before Timoleon took over, Plutarch (using Timaios) paints a rhetorical picture of neglected Sicilian cities given over to deer and wild boar so that people went hunting in their suburbs and beside their walls (*Timoleon*, 22. 5). The huge late Roman villas and hunting mosaics which are now known in the eastern end of the island were heirs to a long Sicilian tradition of the chase.

Hunting was a Sicilian speciality, but not, of course, a Sicilian peculiarity. Throughout the ancient world we can find a similar continuity in our textual and visual evidence, from the boar hunts of Homer's Odysseus (19. 394) to the keen hunting men of Augustine's Africa who 'care nothing for bites and broken bones and are content with the roughest food and dirtiest water in order to bring down a boar or a stag' (Augustine, *Sermon* 70. 2). In art, we can watch it from Mycenaean gold to the silver of late Roman grandees, from the Vapheio cup to the large silverware owned by Sevso with its newly published scenes of mythical hunters and late Roman sportsmen among hare, boar, deer, and the captions for Sevso's horse and dog, around AD 400 (Mango 1990; cf. Lavin 1963, 179; Henig 1986, 186 ff.). Modern scholars have given us fine studies of the evolution of hunting techniques, but here I wish to draw the coverts from two different angles.

To suit the theme of this volume, I will begin by putting Greek hunting in a setting: much of it is latent in J. K. Anderson's elegant book, but there is room for other emphases and for aspects he excluded (Anderson 1985; Manns 1889–90; Aymard 1951; Hull 1964). Then I wish to relate the apparent continuity of hunting to changes in its social and political context. A generation of Greek historians has given us a political story, mapping out the Long March to democracy and the Roman road back from it. Meanwhile, antiquarians and iconographers continue to remind us how much the ancients enjoyed in life besides voting and political meetings. We now need to integrate these two traditions of scholarship. In his recent introduction to Paul Veyne's *Bread and Circuses*, Oswyn Murray proposes an arresting set of priorities: 'The history of pleasure ... and such phenomena explains the real preoccupations of mankind; and it is politics, not this sort of history, which is trivial and ephemeral' (Murray 1990, xvii). By contrast, I wish to argue for an interrelationship, not a crude separation.

Aspects of the culture of fun are relevant to the outlook of a political class, and sometimes to their bids for honour and power among their contemporaries (see Beinart 1990, 162, on hunting and modern imperialism). So, too, a history of fun and culture is a shallow history if it is ring-fenced to leave out political change, the setting for changes of meaning and practice in some of its parts. Hunting, a prolonged public activity, is an excellent test case. In his *Augustan Aristocracy* Sir Ronald Syme tells us: 'Under benevolent despotism an aristocracy debarred from useful occupations turns to hunting, racing, gambling.' He sees Augustan Rome in these terms, suggesting a comparison with 'Versailles under Louis Quatorze' (1986, 72). I wish to challenge this model of hunting and politics with evidence from the Greek world, from Homer to Polybios. The evidence is abundant, at least as abundant as our evidence for Greek democracy.

First, we must sort out the setting, the questions of definition and gender, landscape, and the gods. Nowadays the difference between hunting and 'pest control' is keenly disputed between supporters and opponents (Cartmill 1993); in antiquity, the absence of our modern technologies made the distinction less relevant. Philosophers' theories of the origins of human society did emphasize man's need to keep off wild animals: the virtues of this rudimentary pest control are prominent in fragments of Demokritos.[1] In real life, hunting remained the ancients' best way to control a pest: the 'great thing of a boar' in Herodotos' Mysia (Hdt. 1. 36), Antinoüs' lion in Egypt, or the big game, according to Tertullian, which might settle in the basements of town houses in North Africa (*P. Oxy.* 1085; Tert. *Ad martyras*, 6. 1). It would not, however, be hunting if it was always unsought and conducted only in self-defence. Nor did hunting include trapping and snaring, which were usually practised by night and never involved expensive hounds or face-to-face combat. Xenophon (*Kynegetikos* (*The Hunting Man*), 12. 7) and Plato (*Laws*, 824 a–c) insist on the differences, while reminding us how widespread this trapping must have been, even in a culture that did not have a lust for furs (Pollard 1977, 104–6). The Boiotian in Aristophanes' *Acharnians* (line 879) does bring otters, martens, and the enigmatic *piktides* (possibly

---

[1] Procopé 1989, 311–12, on Demokritos, frs 257–9, and Plato, *Protagoras*, 322 b; Porphyry, *On Abstinence from Animal Food*, 1. 10.

badgers) into Attica for sale, but the Greeks never settled on the geographic latitude west from the Caspian Sea where fur towns were to spring up, like early Astorias, in the tenth and eleventh centuries to meet the Mediterranean's new demand (Lombard 1969).

In antiquity, hunting was distinguished by leisure and expense, sometimes against a pest, essentially for the sake of prowess, although Xenophon (*Kyn.* 11. 2) accepts that hunters may put down poisoned bait against big game in rough country and 'poison panthers', but not in the park. Much of the catch was welcome as food, especially in Sparta, and was one of the few sources of meat that was not shared with the gods: hares, the hunter's main prey, were not even animals for religious sacrifices, except occasionally to Aphrodite.[1] Yet hunting, not snaring, was mainly for the better-off, and the class who pursued hares did not rely on them in their diet. According to Alain Schnapp (1989, 59), for the Greeks 'hunting is not only a matter of subsistence but a means of affirming themselves as men among other living beings'. There are other ways of seeing it, above all as a combination of those central Greek concepts *agôn*, *technê*, and *aretê* which was also fun, especially when you took the dogs, a slave, or some old friends into wild scenery. Of course other justifications were offered: Xenophon (*On Horsemanship* (*Peri hippikês*), 8. 10) and others defend their sport as a healthy training for warfare, of which Aristotle, too, classes it as a subdivision (*Politics*, 1256 b 25); the Spartans evidently agreed. Perhaps hunting helped fitness, and certainly it was a source of generals' stratagems throughout antiquity, from Philip II (who hunted enemies with hounds: Polyainos, 4. 2. 16) to Belisarius in the Byzantine wars against Persia in the 540s AD (Procopius, *Wars*, 2. 21. 8). However, Polybios also knew huntsmen who were poor soldiers. There is no reason to derive the Greeks' practice of hunting from a military origin among those elusive *Männerbunde* of pre-polis life. When we first read about it in Homer, it is already the independent sport of individual heroes who are out for fun and prowess.

This combative test of endurance was a male activity only. In Britain we take women who hunt for granted, an important

---

[1] Aristophanes, *Acharnians*, 1112; *Wasps*, 709; *Peace*, 1150, on hares as food; Xen. *Lakedaimonion politeia*, 5. 3; Stengel 1910, 200.

element in Anthony Trollope's novels and in the social and sporting annals of High Leicestershire. In ancient Greece we would never expect to see women riding (except side-saddle on a plodding donkey in a very few archaic figurines: Voyatzis 1992, 259). We never hear of them hunting, except in Roman poets' fantasies of Laconian life. This barrier helps us to appreciate a famous scene in Euripides' *Hippolytos* (line 224; Anderson 1985, 89–91, 129). Phaidra recounts her love-sick fantasy where she will range the woods hunting beside Hippolytos, the lover whom she cannot name. 'Ti kai soi?', the nurse notes: 'Whatever has this to do with you?' Hunting was not a Greek woman's business, the nurse is reminding her.

Away from Greek culture, matters might be slightly different. 'If the Persian king goes out to a hunt', wrote Herakleides of Kyme in the fourth century, 'his concubines go out with him' (Athenaeus, 12. 514 c), no doubt as spectators.[1] In Etruria a few images of Etruscan art show a woman in the context of a hunting scene, but never as a combatant (Camporeale 1984, 99–100; 104; 149; 159; 187). Other barbarians were even more brisk: in Armenia Xenophon and the Ten Thousand failed to capture the son-in-law of a village chieftain because he was away hunting hares, although married only a week before. His bride, naturally, had had to stay at home (Xenophon, *Anabasis* (*Persian Expedition*), 4. 5. 24). Xenophon no doubt envied him. At the end of his *Hunting Man* he concludes: 'All men who have loved hunting have been good men ... and not only men, but women too to whom the goddess Artemis has granted the sport, Atalanta, Prokris, and so forth' (*Kyn.* 13. 18). Significantly, he is referring only to mythical women; in the area of hunting, as elsewhere, Greek myth transgressed social reality.

Women would also have had to contend with the hunters' natural landscape. Patterns of settlement and cultivation gave Greek hunting a different setting from the hunts of medieval Europe or modern Britain. There were none of those days spent in huge tracts of forest that left such a mark on the hunting tales and literature of post-classical Europe (Rooney 1993). Nor were there the specialized grass farms for sheep or cattle that make up the best modern hunting countries: there was no Belvoir or

[1] cf. Quintus Curtius, 8. 9. 28, on Indian kings.

Saddington Vale in Attica or the Argolid. Draught animals and cavalry horses had to be grazed in meadows, but most of the farming in the plains combined temporary fallow, like our 'set-aside', with planted crops (Guiraud 1893, 63–7). More promising ground, we might think, would be hilly and unsettled, whether the maquis of hillsides or the thicker woods and valleys. This contrast is beautifully expressed for us in the *Homeric Hymn to Aphrodite*, between the 'works of man' and 'unallotted, unsettled land', a home for wolves, lions, bears, and insatiable leopards who mated wildly, the poet tells us, when Aphrodite, goddess of love, passed through Asia Minor (122 ff.; 70 ff.). The same contrast between rough 'mountains' and *erga*, the cultivated works of farmers, is important to Xenophon's advice on the sport (*Kyn.* 5. 34).

Once we look more closely, the divisions are not quite so sharp. 'Mountains' have recently been upheld as the Greek hunter's natural territory (Buxton 1992, 4); conversely, 'meadows, fens and water' have been stressed as the site of Xenophon's precepts, rather than 'noble forests' (Rackham 1990, 96–7). However, the exact nature of mountain landscapes varied between thick scrub and genuine wood, and among this variation we must also allow for the varying habits of game. Hares usually avoid woods and prefer scrubby hillsides and mountain slopes, but they also lie in cultivated plains and set-aside. Boar can be found in reed-beds, fens, or level coverts beside open water (Rackham 1983, 283–337), yet they are not merely hunted in these lowland dells and plains: Xenophon also assumes a boar hunt in woods, as we would expect (*Kyn.* 10. 6; 10. 23). We would expect to find deer up in hilly woods, but he reminds us that they could be trapped in plains too (9. 17).

It is wrong, then, to picture Greek hunting only on 'mountains': the possibilities were greater, and we must remember how the 'steep' country varied between scrub and forest (Rackham 1990, 103; Rackham and Moody 1992, 123–33). In more populated areas we should also expect that terrace walls complicated hunting on the upper slopes. No text, however, settles the vexed question of terracing's extent in Greek antiquity (cf. Foxhall in this volume, ch. 3). Xenophon's work on hunting ignores it, and although his treatise *On Horsemanship* refers to the need to jump walls, these walls were presumably on flat ground (3. 7, surely on level ground).

Distinctions between plain and 'hill' varied locally in Greece. In Attica tracts of steep and rough ground, the *eschatiai* of Attic evidence, did break up the cultivated 'works of men'; the *eschatiai* were not necessarily on the polis's boundaries.[1] On the intervening flat farmland, hares could always be chased from Attic corn and meadows, but sport must have become harder as cultivation extended. Apart from the enigmatic tombstone of a Phoenician buried in Attica, there is not a hint of a lion in fourth-century Athenian evidence (Clairmont 1970, 114–15 and pl. 38); a comedy by Nausikrates, meanwhile, aired the opinion that hares could no longer be found in the Attic countryside (Ath. 9. 399 e). For the best sport, huntsmen of the period had to look further afield, to Sicily, to Philip's Macedonia where boar and lions were available,[2] and no doubt to baronial Thessaly. Our most vivid stories of wild game in Thessaly are in Apuleius's *Golden Ass*, but although 'hunting is a fundamental feature of the world in which Apuleius's characters live' (Millar 1981, 73–4), we cannot be sure that this literary setting was quite so fundamental in the Thessaly of the real world. In Boiotia wild boar could be found in rush-beds round lakes and major watercourses (Rackham 1983, 328; 337; Pausanias, 9. 23. 3). In the Peloponnese hunting remained a keen topic of conversation for Spartan kings and a practice for individual Spartiates.[3] Arkadia must have been the sporting equivalent of Scotland, while near Olympia Xenophon and his friends enjoyed hunting boar and stags in the woods and meadows of his estate near Skillous and on the steeper slopes, surely unterraced, of Mount Pholoë. His early days of hare-chasing in Attica must have seemed tame by comparison.

Nevertheless, hunting was not universal in the Greek world, even when conditions might have suited it. Xenophon remarks unexpectedly that 'most men' on inhabited islands were not keen on hunting and that hunters 'rarely' visited deserted islands for sport (*Kyn.* 5. 25). It was not that game was in short supply. We know of 'goat islands', although we know nothing about goat

---

[1] Aeschines, 1. 97–9; Lewis 1973, 210–12; Traill 1982, 165; id. 1986, 48, with bibliography; Goossens 1944, 265–8.

[2] See Briant 1991, for evidence, to my mind (not his) conclusive.

[3] Xen. *Hellenika*, 5. 3. 20; *Lak. pol.* 6. 4; *Agesilaos*, 9. 6; Pipili 1987, 22–4, on archaic Laconian vase scenes which others interpret as 'everyday' life, not mythical hunts.

hunting after the *Odyssey* and the scenes on a few archaic vases, mostly Cretan.[1] During his great polemic against Timaios on the nature of the animals of Corsica, Polybios admits that foxes and wild sheep did live on the island, together with rabbits 'which look like a hare from afar but have a very different taste' (12. 3. 9–10). Xenophon, too, comments on the general abundance of hares on most islands, and connects it with the scarcity of predators, both foxes and mountain eagles. The islanders' indifference to hunting, he implies, was a matter of taste and of a sparse human population. There were also islands 'sacred to the gods' (Delos, presumably, and others) where hunting dogs were forbidden and hares proliferated.

Xenophon's comments are borne out by other evidence. Local Greek myths concern the punishments of hunters for hunting in a sacred landscape: there are many stories of old sacred groves and the rare fauna which sheltered in their sanctuaries (Birge 1982, 228–30). As for unhunted islands, we know of two cases where the game became a pest and hunting was finally begun in order to control it. According to Strabo (3. 2. 6 (144)) rabbits became an agricultural pest in southern Spain, extending to Massilia and some of the islands: they were known as *leberides* or 'peelers', a popular allusion to their toothwork and a word that was indeed traced to the people of Massilia by ancient lexicographers (Lasserre 1966, 189). Between *c.*120 and 80 BC the people of the Balearic Isles had to petition Rome for a new territory because they could no longer cope with their rabbits; the remedy was to breed Libyan ferrets and go ferreting with them, much as we do nowadays when troubled by a warren. Earlier the people of Astypalaia had consulted Apollo himself with a similar problem (Hegesander, in Ath. 9. 400 d). In the reign of Antigonos Gonatas the island was beset with hares; a man from Anaphe had introduced the breed by letting two hares loose on the island, just as an Astypalaian had once let out two partridges. The imports became a plague, like Sitka deer in the modern Scottish highlands, and threatened to drive men out of their homes; Delphic Apollo told them to keep hounds and hunt, and as a result they caught 6,000 hares in one season.

Neither these stories nor any ancient praise of hunting appeal to a 'balance of nature', an idea Greeks never formulated. Instead

[1]   Bremmer 1986, 256; Robert 1949, 161–70; Buchholz *et al.* 1973, 157.

they show men transferring wild species into new habitats – Libyan ferrets, hares, or partridges – and remind us of the constant scope for change in an area's game. They also show that Apollo, founder of the Astypalaian Harriers, was no 'anti', opposed to blood sports. How could he be, when the gods were such a constant presence to hunters in their vicissitudes? Xenophon tells his Hunting Man to vow to share part of the catch with Apollo as well as with Artemis (*Kyn.* 6. 13; 13. 17; cf. Arrian, *Kynegetikos*, 34); we should probably think of a dedication of skins or horns, as various hellenistic epigrams like to imagine for their readers. According to Xenophon, young hunters must try to be 'dear to the gods' because the gods are watching them and delighting in the chase. None was more watchful than Artemis, the only great Greek huntress. As Artemis Agrotera she was honoured by the Spartan army with a sacrifice when in view of the enemy. The army's sacrifice (later copied by the Athenians) probably evoked the killing common to the hunt and war, rather than a belief that hunting had evolved from warfare or that battle was a continuation of hunting by other means.[1] The origin of her epithet Agrotera remains disputed, but Greeks derived it from *agra*, the hunt, and their derivation is the most convincing.

Why was the great patron of this all-male activity a goddess, not a god? Professor Burkert (1983, 81) has tried to explain the fact by the gender and psychology of early hunters. The male hunter's 'long-range objective forces him to abstain from sexual intercourse. When sexual frustration is added to the hunter's aggressivity, it appears to him as though a mysterious female being inhabits the outdoors.' The idea might have appealed to Ovid, but hunters will doubt if Burkert's diagnosis is correct. In the Greek world, males usually hunted in company and had the homosexual option, as vase-painters sometimes remind us. Like the mythical huntresses, Artemis is better understood as another 'transgression' of earthly reality and its boundaries; having mapped out those boundaries, we can now move on to the changes inside them.

---

[1] See Jameson 1991, 209–11, for evidence; I do not share his conclusion.

Homer to Xenophon

I wish to relate changes in this all-male activity, best practised in wild landscape under the gods' approving eyes, to the broad changes in Greek political experience. The most important changes are the coming and going of monarchy, but aristocracy and democracy are also relevant.

The first change is the transition from Mycenaean monarchy to the heroic aristocracies of the Homeric poems. Mycenaean hunting art illustrates hunting in action, against boars, bulls and lions then wild in Greece, while the link between the symbol of the lion and the palace is too well known to need discussion.[1] In Homer, however, monarchy is imagined very differently: the monarch's reality has disappeared from the poet's own world, and the Homeric 'king' often seems more like one of early Greece's aristocratic *basileis*. Apart from Odysseus' hunting of stags for food, hunting does not exercise any of the heroes in the main plot of either epic. Hunting is reserved for flashbacks, the feats of Meleager or the boar hunt of Odysseus, though its main role is in those frequent similes where people confront a lion. In his recent study, Steven Lonsdale has suggested that all Homeric lion similes are based on the same basic idea: a marauding lion who has to be killed in defence of human life and property.[2] Certainly, the similes never show a king engaged in a lion hunt, and where they are precise they usually refer only to herdsmen or shepherds defending or taking revenge. We could hardly be further from Mycenaean imagery of the lion and the lion hunt as a noble sport, or from the fragmentary wall-paintings at Tiryns which are unique in showing female participants.

Outside the Homeric world, we catch a hint of a continuing 'royal' alternative on the Bernardini plates, dated *c*.700 BC and found in Sicily and Italy (Burkert 1992, 104). They have recently been interpreted as scenes from a lost Greek story, represented by a Cypriot workshop: alternatively, they show a story imported into the Mediterranean from the Near East. If so, their scenes of a hunter in his chariot relate to areas of a continuing monarchy

---

[1] See Buchholz *et al.* 1973; Anderson 1985, 10–15; Marinatos 1990, 143–8; Morris 1990, 149–56.
[2] Lonsdale 1990, 39, well reviewed by Griffin 1991.

which was different from the *basileis* of Greece at the time. In Greece, monarchy had long since disappeared, and in its place a world of individual noble hunters and villagers is the one that Homeric hunting reflects. With the passage from monarchy, hunting has changed its scope.

The Homeric epics, therefore, evoke the aristocracies' style of hunting in archaic Greece, not the symbolism of the lion and Mycenaean royalty. Odysseus goes on a boar hunt with hounds, as later nobles also did; a simile in *Iliad* 21 alludes to another such hunter who encounters a female leopard, startled from her thicket to face his barking dogs (*Od.* 19. 418–58; *Il.* 21. 572). We hear much less about hare-hunting, a mainstay of the later Greek chase, but Homer did know it: Odysseus's faithful Argos had been taken 'in days past' by the young men after 'wild goats, deer, and hares'. Hare-hunting also occurs in one simile during the ambush for Dolon, a debated part of the epic (*Od.* 17. 295; *Il.* 10. 361).

During the eighth and seventh centuries BC, the great Assyrian art of the royal lion hunts reminds us vividly what hunting meant in an established monarchy: the king kills the lions before onlookers, including women, even if some of the lions are shooed towards him from prearranged traps (Anderson 1985, 6–10; 63–7). The aristocracies and tyrannies of archaic Greece have left us quite a different hunting 'image': one of individual pursuit, competition and gift-exchange, conforming to key values in their culture of noble 'equals'.

Surprisingly, references to hunting in our literary sources for the early aristocracies are very rare. The hellenistic author of *P. Oxy.* 664, perhaps Herakleides Pontikos, presents a young noble Athenian in the age of Peisistratos as 'surpassing all his contemporaries in horse-breeding, hunting and other such expensive pursuits'. So we think it must have been, but hunting poetry is absent in surviving archaic texts: we have to look ahead to Roman Sparta for traces of what may be an old Spartan hunting dance and hunting song; we have nothing comparable to Wyatt's sonnets; we know of no hunting emblem for a *genos* or its dress, let alone of a badge with the symbolic range of Richard II's white hind. Noble Greek hunters wore no special dress or livery, although the nudity in hunting art cannot be interpreted literally, whatever may have happened on a hot summer's day:

male Greek hunters wore the simple tunic or *chlamys* and did not even use hunting horns.[1]

It is when we look at their archaic vases, not at texts, that some of the gaps in our evidence are corrected. Beginning on Cypriote pottery *c.*900 BC, the imagery of hunting hares, deer and foxes blossoms on the bands of large Attic Geometric kraters, the art of contemporary Attic nobles.[2] It continues on the famous Chigi vase, but from *c.*600 BC onwards most of the group scenes have a mythical, heroic reference, even in Sparta: the Kalydonian boar is a favourite subject. The many hunting heroes of Greek myth, from Aktaion to Orion, no doubt acquired their hunting exploits in this age of story-telling, rather than as 'prehistoric' survivals. How, though, should we connect these images to a social and political context?

If we follow one wing of French scholarship, we can draw close connections between this changing image and changes in the social and political order.[3] Schnapp has emphasized the differences between those vases that show individual hunters and those that show hunters as a group; he has explained the latter by an otherwise unattested institution, a 'corps civique de la chasse', designed, he assumes, to prepare young males for the new discipline of hoplite warfare.[4] If Schnapp is right, the military changes in Greece of the seventh century influenced the very form and place of hunting in civic life. However, there are serious objections to this theory. On to this supposed structure of the archaic city falls the distant shadow of the ephebic corps, although the evidence for a corps of organized ephebes does not begin until the later fourth century. In early Greece, these young *énarques* of the hunt are nowhere attested. There are also acute problems in inferring changes of social structure from variations in the imagery of vases, especially when some of them are vases by such inferior artists, a poor base for theories about significant changes in social practice (Boardman 1991, 99). In my view, the scenes of collective hunting

---

[1]   On songs and dance see Chrimes 1949, 118–30; Ath. 14. 631; on nudity Sansone 1988, 107 ff., is unconvincing.

[2]   Coldstream 1994, 85–94.

[3]   For archaic vases see von Steuben 1968, esp. 42 ff.; 117 ff.; Pipili 1987, 22–4. Social interpretation: Schnapp 1979a; 1989; Schnapp and Schmitt 1982.

[4]   Schnapp 1979a; 1979b; Schnapp and Durand 1989.

represent nothing more formal than groups gathered suddenly for the purpose, just as we find in our one literary description of a hunt in the mid-sixth century. In Croesus' Lydia, Herodotos imagines how a posse of young men, *neaniai logades*, gathered to go out against a 'great thing of a boar' (Hdt. 1. 43; cf. Hom. *Il.* 20. 165–72). There was no formal call-up, but a volunteer band which Atys begged his father to be able to join: 'Whatever will my newly married wife say if I do not go?'

The hunts on archaic vases do not require a new civic institution; their results, however, gained new meaning from distinctive aspects of the culture of this age. Prowess and competition were central to it, and successful hunting was connected with both: in aristocratic Attica, and in the Spartans' 'alternative' peer group of *homoioi*, we can detect its differing roles. In Sparta individual prowess and riches were potentially at odds with the new social order, yet hunting, an outlet for both, was valued as proof of manliness and military fitness. In Xenophon we can see both the tensions and ways of limiting them. Hunting dogs, he claims, were made openly available to any Spartiates who wanted to go off and hunt, and hunters would help each other by caches of supplies. The hunters' catch was consumed in the common messes or *syssitia*, supplementing the awful basic diet (*Lak. pol.* 6. 4; 5. 6). According to Molpis, the cooks would announce the names of the hunter-donors to their fellow messmates (Ath. 4. 141 d). The catch became part of the *epaikla* or 'extras' on the menu, which began to become customary and give scope for richer Spartiates to show off. Hunting, however, helped to preserve the 'model of parity': *hoi polloi* resorted to it to provide *epaikla* and keep up with their less equal superiors, who gave produce off their bigger estates.[1] Reality, perhaps, was not always so nicely balanced.

In Eupatrid Attica, by contrast, there were no such stringent limits on individuality, and we find hunting in a highly competitive personal context. On Attic black-figured vases, beginning in the early sixth century, we find older men bringing animal gifts to young men or boys: foxes (usually dead), living hares (held by the ears), living deer, or even cheetahs on leads (which must be imports into Attica).[2] The amorous, sexual context is sometimes

---

[1] Xen. *Lak. pol.* 5. 6; Sphairos, in Ath. 4. 141 c–d.
[2] Koch-Harnack 1983; Schauenburg 1969; Schnapp 1989, 79.

obvious: literary texts make us aware of the role of competitive giving in homosexual courtship, but only the vases show us the range of animals that were exchanged for the purpose. The hopeful Attic lover would 'say it with hares' or foxes, not bunches of cut flowers. Presumably the hares, deer, and foxes were spoils from a day's hunting; prowess in the field, pursuit, and gift-giving were thus combined in the lover's actions. Did the gifts also play on a shared metaphor, linking the hunt to the pursuit of love, as in a few of our surviving literary texts? The hare, we must remember, was not an animal for sacrifice, except, significantly, to Aphrodite.[1] Occasionally one or both of the partners are shown touching each other up. Nobody, however, suggests what the boys, or their parents, did with the animals afterwards.

This culture of hunting, gift-giving, and erotic pursuit is quite different from anything in the Homeric world, and is arguably the invention of post-Homeric aristocrats whose style developed in the seventh and sixth centuries.[2] After various changes of emphasis these vase scenes almost disappear in Attic iconography, and the practice of hunters' love gifts is not even mentioned by Xenophon, to whose taste it ought to have appealed. The connection between 'saying it with hares' and a particular cultural milieu looks even stronger if we contrast these scenes with hunting in the contemporary Near East. While noble Athenians brought hares and foxes to their boyfriends, Assyrian kings were engaged in preplanned lion hunts, killing big game which was released before an approving audience, including women. The king had the privilege, at least in art, of killing the lion: he poured libations over the lions' dead bodies to thank the gods; the hunts were then immortalized in royal palace sculpture as symbols of their superior, royal prowess (Anderson 1985, 63–4). Nobody would have thought for one moment of sending paws or tails to a boyfriend.

This contrasting Assyrian style would have been at home in ancient Mycenae, but not in Eupatrid Attica. The reason is not simply ecological. Even though lions became marginal or non-

---

[1] Philostratos, *Imagines*, 1. 6; Ziehen 1906, 307–8; Stengel 1910, 200; Goodenough 1958, 85–95, an excellent survey of hares' symbolism.
[2] It lives on in films: (a) heterosexual courtship with a hare, in *Manon des sources*; (b) homosexual, with rabbits, in *Torch Song Trilogy* (which A. D. Nuttall points out to me).

existent in most of Greece, a wild boar could have been an alternative Athenian symbol, or even a stag, like those that were shooed towards the late Duke of Atholl so that he could satisfy baronial honour by shooting them from his chair. Significantly, no tyrant, not even Periander, is said to have staged a wild boar hunt 'by appointment' or to have tried to monopolize the prestige of big game. Here, too, tyrants remained part of the general aristocratic culture which they shared: Polykrates imported better hounds into Samos (Alexis in Ath. 12. 540 d–e), but tyrants did not introduce a new monarchic culture into Greece.

When democracy emerged in Attica in 508 BC, the old aristocratic culture certainly did not vanish. The scenes of hunters riding on horseback happen to dwindle in Attic vase-painting, along with the dead foxes and living hares for young lovers, but we would be quite wrong to infer that hunting was becoming a controversial pastime, better practised in private and not mentioned too often in public. A corrective can be found in Attic drama and literature. In Attic tragedy, hunting was presupposed by myths which the dramatists used, and so its presence in the *Hippolytos*, *Philoktetes*, or *Agamemnon* is unremarkable. However, its imagery is used freely and entwined deeply into the tragedians' language. In the *Oresteia* Agamemnon is hunted, netted, and sacrificed, and then Orestes, the 'hunter' of his own mother, is 'hunted' in turn. In Euripides' *Bacchae* Pentheus begins as a 'hunter' of wild nature but then (at line 848) he himself becomes the prey, while metaphors promptly make the Bacchants into hunters who tear the former hunter in pieces (Neuburg 1987, 159–60). Attic audiences were alert to this language: when the first lyrics in the *Hippolytos* (lines 61–70) invoked Artemis on the hero's return from hunting, Athenians would surely recognize the traditional form of a hunting song, its one surviving echo in our sources.[1]

Hunting stories were also a recognized feature of a proper symposium: Philokleon in *Wasps* 1199–204 is told to relate a manly action of his youth, 'how you once pursued a boar or a hare'.[2] Audiences expected this sort of talk at parties, and were also familiar with hunting metaphors. Plato, admittedly no democrat, describes homosexuality as the 'chase' (*Sophist*, 222 d;

---

[1] E. L. Bowie's suggestion.
[2] I owe this suggestion, too, to E. L. Bowie.

Symposium, 182 e, 203 d), but the image must have been widely familiar because Aischines, too, describes homosexuals as 'hunters' in a speech to a democratic jury (1. 195). Plato also refers to knowledge as a 'wild chase' and to teachers and sophists as 'hunting' for pupils (Classen 1960), an extension of the metaphor that may well have been his own but enjoyed a very long life, from the lives of hellenistic philosophers to biographies of Christian holy men on their pillars. The imagery even extended to Attic sycophants. In 330 Aischines (3. 255) hints to an Attic jury that Demosthenes might bring hunting companions from his younger days to plead for him in court, although he no longer hunted wild game but 'hunted' men of property. Proper hunting, the passage implies, was not objectionable, even in the eyes of a jury of democrats.

None the less, the development of democracy cannot have left hunting unaffected. In the Eupatrid heyday of the seventh century, the young Attic nobleman could have ridden or coursed more or less where he wanted, even allowing for the proportion of public land in Attica: πᾶσα γῆ δι᾽ ὀλίγων ἦν, 'all the land was with the few', as Aristotle imagined it (*Athenaion politeia*, 2. 2), and however we qualify his words a noble's freedom of action on the land was greater before 594 than afterwards (see Foxhall 1992, 155–9, for the fourth century). He was also competing conspicuously with members of his own peer group; but as democracy took root, selfish spending became more controversial and the upper class could no longer take its power for granted while doing what it pleased with most of its time and effort. Unlike horse-racing, hunting was never presented as an action that won glory for the polis. The era of empire led, surely, to an increased Attic population, and in turn the growth must have caused a decline in wild game. The taming of Attica did not suit the hunters, but it did suit the cause of peaceful social relations. Inland, the decline in animals will have reduced the everyday wearing of arms. A wild boar would still need to be taken with spears and javelins, but the everyday hunting of hares called only for clubs, sticks, and nets. Hunting feuds are not attested under the democracy: hoplite Athenians had weapons, but there were probably not the widespread arsenals for rural self-defence which later enabled more than 30,000 members of a rural uprising to arm themselves in Gaul under Roman rule with nothing but hunting-knives and spears

(Tacitus, *Annals*, 3. 43; cf. Apuleius, *Metamorphoses*, 8. 16; 9. 36–8).

The best sources for the change in hunting's context are the works of Xenophon on the topic. They are usually read for their technical knowledge,[1] although he warns strongly against letting hounds chase foxes and has little faith in the wet ground, 'southerly wind and cloudy sky' that are a modern promise of a good day's scent. Among the expertise, however, it is less often emphasized that signs of opposition to the sport show through. He is explicit that there are those who complain that hunting is extravagant and a waste of property and households (*Kyn*. 12. 10 ff.). Such a view is not based on class prejudice, but on moralizing which could have arisen among his social equals; none the less, it would not have been heard in the aristocratic age, except among Pythagoreans.[2] Xenophon complicates his case by endorsing the increasing cost of hunting in style. His hare-hunting presupposes the ownership of trained slaves; the best hounds derive from Crete or India (perhaps through Babylonia); flax for the best nets has to come from Carthage or from Kolchis up on the Black Sea (*Kyn*. 10. 1; 2. 4);[3] according to Pliny (*Historia naturalis*, 19. 10), flax (which needs damp soil) was only at its best in specific places, particularly near Cumae where it could cut through a boar's bristles. Through hunting, these crops gained extra value and marketability; near Cumae, no doubt, they had been introduced by Greek colonists. The gap between the everyday trapper and the proper huntsman had certainly not narrowed in the democratic era. Hunters remained a privileged minority, but the telling fact is that their privileges were not as great as before. Nowadays, Xenophon complains, hunters can no longer run with hounds where they please on cultivated land, whereas trapping and snaring by night are unregulated around centres of settlement. In the past, he claims (*Kyn*. 12. 6–7), an ancient law (*nomos*) had given hunters the right to pursue wherever necessary, while other laws had banned night trapping and created a snare-free zone round the polis. Neither law is known to us otherwise, and both

---

[1] Körte 1918 is wrong to doubt it: Xen. *Kyn*. 6. 3.
[2] Iamblichos, *Life of Pythagoras*, 100; Eudoxos, in Porphyry, *Life of Plotinus*, 7.
[3] Contrast Paus. 5. 5. 2, on excellent flax at Elis and among 'the Hebrews'.

may be the wishful thinking of a keen hunter, but they remind us how changes in the old aristocratic order had cramped hunters' freedom.

Xenophon's essay has been read as a plea for a return to archaic institutions and the elusive 'corps de chasse' for young men in the archaic polis. It is nothing of the sort. Its horizon is individual, addressed to would-be hunters by a keen sportsman who is at home with his contemporaries in the 'landed green belt' of the Peloponnese. His text on horsemanship commended riders to hunt 'where the ground and prey is suitable', but his text on hunting does not once allude to hunting on horseback. Mounted hunters had disappeared from Attic vase-painting, and the two sports were not naturally paired (Xen. *On horsemanship*, 8. 10; Vigneron 1968, 220–34); Euripides (*Hippolytos*, 109–12) reminds us of this fact with a bump when his Hippolytos returns from hunting and only then thinks of taking out the horses in order to exercise them. Elsewhere, practices may have been different, but for Xenophon's text, hunting is essentially hunting on foot. Big-game hunting belongs on the margins of the Greek world or in the Near East. His subject is the young man of good family and upbringing, and he nowhere considers monarchy or the training of a prince.

In the late fifth century there had already been a hint of the future, although Xenophon ignores it. Poulydamas, the winning Olympic wrestler in 408, killed a lion on Mount Olympos, reputedly with his bare hands (Pausanias, 6. 5).[1] It was one of several feats against wild beasts, and so the Persian king invited the champion to his presence. Sporting prowess bridged the two cultures, as Herodotos had already implied: at Susa, Poulydamas was said to have distinguished himself further in combat against several Immortals. The exploit has been recognized in a damaged relief at Olympia, the base, perhaps, of Poulydamas's famous statue at the site. Within twenty-five years of Xenophon's death, the main emphasis of his handbook had been overtaken by a new Poulydamas and his companions: a decisive shift from democracy to monarchy led to an expansion by conquest beyond even Xenophon's experience.

---

[1] See Frazer's note; Robertson 1975, 469 n. 58.

Royal blood sports

Throughout the years of Attic democracy, big game and monarchy had continued to flourish in the wild woods and mountains of the barbarian world and the northern fringe of Greek culture. In Thrace the iconography of the Rider god, slaying scores of beasts in his path, continues to remind us of the rich animal presence in the local forests.[1] In Macedonia evidence begins with silver coin-types of the fifth century; King Archelaos is said to have been murdered out hunting; Philip II was said (by Arrian's sources) to have instituted the corps of royal pages who attended him while out hunting; Herodotos, Pausanias, and Aristotle include Macedonia in the habitat of wild lions, and Xenophon knows that lions could still be hunted around Mount Pangaion, as also in Epeiros.[2] A silver coin of Amyntas III shows on one side a horseman with a spear, and on the other a lion pierced by a broken spear, presumably during a hunt.[3] Hunting also shaped Macedonian manners at table. From the Black Sea westwards, hunters lived on the geographic latitude for great drinking-horns, the real or simulated trophies of wild oxen, stags, and so forth (Jeffery 1976, 37). Philip II is said to have drunk toasts from them; according to Hegesander (*c.*150 BC), a Macedonian could not recline at dinner until he had killed a wild boar without using nets (Hegesander, in Ath. 1. 18 a).

In hellenistic Macedonia we have epigraphic evidence for 'hunt clubs' under the patronage of Herakles Kynagidas, Herakles the Hunter (Hammond and Griffith 1979, 155 n. 4; Edson 1940, 125–7); Polybios (31. 29) also refers to the maintained game parks of the Macedonian kings and their history of careful upkeep before 167 BC. Although modern 'histories' of Macedonia run evidence from later periods into the classical era, we should be wary of assuming that the parks and the hunt clubs existed already in Alexander's early years. The great hunt painting on the façade of the double

[1] Cantacuzene 1932, 103–15; Plut. *Moralia*, 174 d (Kotys's gifts).
[2] Kraay and Hirmer 1966, no. 556; Diod. 14. 37. 6; Arrian, *Anabasis*, 4. 13. 1 (*pace* Hammond 1990, 263–4); Hdt. 7. 125; Paus. 6. 5. 4; Arist. *Historia animalium*, 579 b 6; 606 b 14; Xen. *Kyn.* 11.
[3] Greenwalt 1989, 509, with earlier bibliography; Briant 1991, 238–41, for doubts which I do not share.

royal tomb at Vergina is more to the point.[1] It shows three horsemen and seven young men, and scenes of the hunting of deer, a boar (probably), a bear, and a lion. The hounds fall into two distinct types, one of which grasps the prey and is a noticeably heavy breed (Reilly 1993, 160). A garlanded tree and a tall pillar, topped with decoration, frame the main scenes and led the excavator, Manolis Andronikos, to the view that their hunt is represented in a 'sacred grove'. Xenophon tells us how he and his friends hunted on his 'sacred estate' for Artemis (*An.* 5. 3. 10 ff.), but there are also Greek myths and cautionary tales about hunting indiscriminately in a sacred grove (Birge 1982, 28 and n. 62; 222–30); perhaps the painting shows hunting in the grove of a specifically hunting divinity, or hunting in a royal game park which combines several preys and incidents from real life.[2] The main lion-hunter is mounted, and his features, though damaged, resemble those on portraits assumed to be of Philip II, while the young men should be the young royal pages initiated by Philip II (above). If we accept (as I do) that the tomb is Philip II's, the painting shows a royal Macedonian lion hunt among the pages before Alexander's invasion of Asia.

We can wonder whether Philip's corps of royal pages was inspired by reports of a similar corps in the Persian monarchy; pages, however, are a widespread feature of royalty, and can arise without a specific model. It is much more difficult to accept that lion hunting was only adopted by Alexander after entering Asia and was another part of his assumption of Persian customs.[3] Apart from the Vergina painting, which has to be downdated unconvincingly, the Amyntas coin and the references to local lions ranging from Herodotos to Aristotle tell against this theory. When we have evidence for a practice in two separate societies, historians are always tempted to derive one from the other and give their contact a story (Kienast 1973). The approach is unsubtle, and in this case convergence is the better model.

[1]   Andronikos 1984, 106–19; Tripodi 1991, 143–209, not convincing on the questions of dating, but important for parallels.
[2]   Tripodi (1991, 167; 181; 193) argues for a stock scene derived from satrapal–dynastic art in Asia.
[3]   Briant 1989, 267, argues this, whereas Briant 1991 is rightly more cautious.

Alexander's conquests brought two lion hunting monarchies into a new relationship.

'As for the King's Land, I recognize it as mine', Alexander proclaimed in his edict to Priene (Tod, *GHI* ii. 185, line 11). As in Macedonia, royal land tenure favoured the sport. In his newly conquered Asia Minor, the maintained hunting parks were famous in a system where the land outside city territories had been 'mine', in the sense that the Persian kings taxed it or bestowed it on favoured subjects or governors. Around Kelainai in Phrygia, or by Lake Manyas near the satrapal seat at Daskyleion, we are given glimpses of these mature game parks; the latter example went back to the previous era of the Lydian kings, and still finds a descendant in the bird sanctuary of the Turkish neighbourhood.[1] These reserves must have been tended by a staff of keepers for royalty, satraps, and other top people. In the *Cyropaedia* (*Education of Cyrus*; 1. 3–4) Xenophon plays on the oddness of these parks, at least to his Greek eye which was accustomed to chasing hares in the wild. In one particular flourish, he even implies that their contents were mangy and in poor condition.[2]

Where there were game sanctuaries there were more likely to be lions, panthers, and other predators. However, game parks were only one part of Persian society's sporting facilities. In wild nature, bears, lions, and other big game ranged the mountains and forests from Mysia to Syria and, hard though it is to imagine in our deforested age, skulked in plains from the Orontes to Persepolis and the vicinity of the Oxus.[3] There is no doubt that princes and satraps pitted themselves personally against these beasts: Xenophon (*An.* 1. 9. 4) describes with admiration how Cyrus the Younger had been scarred by a bear-bite. Our best sources are the sculpted funerary art and engraved sealstones which Greek artists worked for Asian patrons (Briant 1991, 220–2, with bibliography). In his essay, Xenophon had warned against letting hounds chase a fox: a recipe for disaster, he felt. On an engraved sealstone we see a Persian alternative: a mounted hunter spears a fox on the run by wielding a long-handled trident from the saddle.

[1] Xen. *An.* 1. 2. 7–9; *Hell.* 4. 1. 15; the same 'paradise' in Strabo, 13. 1. 17 (589), with Akurgal 1956, 20–2.
[2] Schnapp's analysis (1973) is not convincing.
[3] Robert 1978, 437–52, on Mysia; Xen. *An.* 1. 4. 10 (Syria); Briant 1982, 451–6.

This virtuoso act of skewering is matched by the scenes of funerary sculpture for satraps and noblemen in the Persian hierarchy. A stele for a nobleman or satrap in Phrygia shows a boar hunt; the great funerary monuments from Xanthos in Lycia are carved with scenes of the hunting of boar, stags, and bears, while deer, panthers, and lions are shown on the fine cache of satrapal sarcophagi found in the cemetery at Sidon.[1] They show us hunting on horseback, in chariots, and on foot with hounds, spears, and single-headed axes. Scholars have tended to interpret them symbolically, as a heroization of the dead man or as a suggestion that his triumphs in this world have culminated in a triumph over death itself. The scenes tend to be stylized and repetitive, but so does much of the hunting art in other societies without being symbolic. In all the allusions to hunting in Greek literature, the idea of hunting as a triumph over death is not present. In its absence we should be wary of seeing these scenes as anything other than memorials of the dead man's glorious sport and prowess. Even in a funerary context individual details intrude, supporting this simple approach. The Satrap's Sarcophagus is the most obvious album of stylized hunting snapshots: on one panel a fallen stag is being speared while a crouching panther is attacked by two huntsmen, and another huntsman is shown falling from his terrified horse (Kleemann 1958). The fall is a unique survivor in Greek hunting art, and evidently refers to a particular occasion. Perhaps the entire panel commemorates a single hunt when a panther was put up while hunters were bringing down a stag. The Sarcophagus of the Mourning Women, to be dated later in the fourth century BC, commemorated a life of hunting even more intimately: the dead man was laid to rest inside with a dog, presumably a favourite hound.

Hunting was also the sport of kings, although the main sources here are Greek. Unlike the Assyrian kings, Persian rulers are not known to have referred to their hunting prowess in their royal inscriptions or illustrated it in their palace art.[2] The silence, however, is explicable by the general 'timelessness' of their royal

---

[1]   Anderson 1985, 71–5, with bibliography; Demargne 1974, 61–87; Childs and Demargne 1989, pls 115–19, on Lycia.
[2]   Onesikritos, in Strabo, 15. 3. 8 (730) is lying; Stronach 1978, 77; Sancisi-Weerdenburg 1993, 155; contrast the Sassanians, Harper 1978.

imagery, not by any particular reticence about the hunt. We should not draw any conclusions, either, from the scarcity of hunting scenes in the minor arts of the Persians: new finds may fill the gap, although we rely meanwhile on one traditional seal of Darius I (Schmitt 1981) and on the minor arts of provincial notables. It has become axiomatic to study Persian kings only from Persian and Asian evidence (Briant 1991, 220–2), but historians of hunting should trust the Greek evidence for royal hunts of lions and bears. Greek sources tell us of the beginning and ending of a royal monopoly on taking the first shot, the refusal of the drunken Artaxerxes II and his court to hunt personally, and the concubines' exodus with the king on hunting days. Herodotos writes of Darius I twisting his ankle in a fall when out hunting, perhaps in one of the special game parks or 'paradises' (*paradeisoi*) which must have been visited by kings from time to time, and perhaps it was on those occasions that women were onlookers.[1] We hear nothing of prearranged game in traps.

Macedonian and Persian hunting shared one particular practice, distinct from hare-hunting in Greece: participants often rode on horseback (Xen. *Cyr.* 8. 8. 12). This practice (as Xenophon had acknowledged) was an excellent training for cavalry warfare. In a recently found inscription from Macedonia's new territory in Chalkidike, we find the evocative names of villages that had been settled with Macedonians under Philip II (Hammond 1988): Thamiskia, Kamakaia, and Tripoatis, which we might translate as Fox Town, Cavalry Spears, and Supergrass. The settlements lay in the territory of former Greek cities on a belt of rich, well-watered grassland, and the names point to the inhabitants' hunting and riding culture. It is no coincidence that the fine Macedonian and Iranian cavalries had riders from the two best hunting countries of the period.

According to the enigmatic 'Royal Diaries', Alexander would 'hunt birds and foxes' frequently in Asia. In Syria, while he was waiting for the march east to Gaugamela, we have evidence of at least three Macedonian encounters with wild lions, two of which involved Alexander personally: the king, aged twenty-one, was not sparing of his officers despite the imminence of battle (Quintus

---

[1] Ktesias, *Persika*, 40, and Plut. *Mor.* 173 d, with Xen. *Cyr.* 1. 4. 14; 8. 8. 12; Hdt. 3. 129. 1; Herakleides, in Ath. 514 c.

Curtius, 8. 1. 13–17; Plut. *Demetrios*, 27. 3).[1] One lion hunt caused Krateros to vow the famous dedication at Delphi which his son later realized in stone (Plut. *Alex*. 40. 3; Perdrizet 1898, 566–8; Robertson 1965, 80–1); another nearly cost Lysimachos his shoulder, and the third, shown on the 'Alexander Sarcophagus', presented an image of Alexander hunting steadily towards a lion which had sunk its teeth into the horse of an oriental, probably the king of Sidon. It was not that lions were supposed to be killed only by kings (Plut. *Alex*. 40. 4 must not be over-interpreted): in practice a hunt might turn out otherwise, and satraps and nobles always had a chance for prowess by themselves.

All across Asia, local 'paradises' were waiting for the Macedonians' attention; richer, no doubt, after wartime neglect, like Leicestershire's coverts in 1946. Beyond the Oxus, at Bazeira, magnificent sport was enjoyed in a game park equipped with towers and hides for hunters but supposedly 'untouched for four generations' (Quintus Curtius, 8. 1. 11–13). The site has not been located, but the contents had a ferocity that refuted Xenophon's comments on Asian park animals. Alexander himself killed a lion and other beasts, whereupon the Macedonians, according to Curtius (8. 1. 18), decided that thenceforward these heroics were too risky and he must not hunt on foot or without personal companions.[2] Fearless exposure in the front line was a hallmark of Alexander's leadership in battle. Significantly, he practised it in his other theatre of combat, the hunting field; the one reinforced the other.

None of this hunting fits Syme's notion of an outlet adopted by an aristocracy which 'benevolent despotism' has debarred from useful politics. Rather, hunting enhanced the prestige of monarchs and nobles alike, Lysimachos and Krateros no less than Cyrus or Alexander. Both monarchies, especially the Macedonian, rested on personal prowess and hunting was a chance to display it with less of a risk of outright death. It also brought the king and his nobles together, whether or not the concubines watched. In early modern Europe, hunting was later to be valued by nobilities as their chance to consort with the king, away from his palace bureaucrats. In Asia the hunt could have been valued for similar contacts,

---

[1] With Lund 1992, 210–18 and nn. 6–8.
[2] The text is corrupt: I take *scivere gentis suae more* together.

away from scribes and secretaries. No doubt hunting was by royal invitation only, a further source of royal patronage and favour.

Above all there was convergence. The two cultures' sporting practices and passions were reassuringly similar: hunting thus offered a possible bridge between the conquerors and the residents. Alexander did not borrow the practice of lion and big-game hunting from Asia: it was in his blood and his culture already. The Macedonians brought axes with two heads (not one), and according to Plutarch's sources some of the nobles kept hunting-nets 'up to 12 miles long', like the fishing-nets of modern Japanese trawlers.[1] Yet their king (like Persia's) also hunted with pages and expected them to allow him the first shot;[2] 'Indian' hunting-dogs had already been exported westwards (Xen. *Kyn.* 9. 1; Aymard 1951, 244–5); Alexander had a favourite Indian hound, possibly before he visited India (Theopompos, *FGH* 115 F 340; Plut. *Alex.* 61. 3); the gems and seals that Greek craftsmen had made for Iranians already hinted how the sport and imagery of the two cultures could overlap.

In Alexander's era, the 'Alexander Sarcophagus' from Sidon is the best contemporary witness to convergence. V. von Graeve has interpreted its scenes in a programmatic sequence, and the core of the interpretation is convincing (von Graeve 1970, 154 ff.; cf. Grabar 1988 for two hunting cultures). On one side we see Asiatics only, hunting a panther; on another, Macedonians attack Asiatics in a battle scene, presumably at Issos; on another, Macedonians and Asiatics fight side by side against big game, led by the main oriental (the king of Sidon?) against a lion. In one of the gables of the sarcophagus, Macedonians and Asiatics are shown wearing an ethnic mix of armour. In another, one Macedonian commander is being murdered by another, a scene von Graeve interprets more speculatively as the murder of Perdikkas by Ptolemy. In his reading, the sculptural programme runs from conflict to 'concord' and on to 'concord's' breakdown. The orientals hunt alone and fight Macedonians; then they hunt with Macedonians; and then they serve (in the gable) as fellow soldiers in mixed armour, until the murder of Perdikkas breaks up the age of 'concord'. Certainly

---

[1] von Graeve 1970, 100, Xen. *Cyr.* 1. 29, and Robertson 1965, pl. 30. 2 (axes); Plut. *Alex.* 40. 1 (nets).
[2] Arr. *Anab.* 4. 13. 2; Quintus Curtius, 8. 6. 11; Ktesias, *Persika*, 40.

the artist illustrates the role of hunting in bridging the former hostility of Macedonians and orientals. Through it, fellow sportsmen become brother officers, at least in Alexander's eyes. Two of the most notorious myths of modern scholarship thus meet here at an unexpected angle: Sir William Tarn's 'brotherhood of man' and Pierre Vidal-Naquet's 'black hunter'. What occurred under Alexander was a 'brotherhood of hunters', brown not black; the sarcophagus can be read as a witness to it.

His example passed to the Successors' kingdoms, based like his own on personal prowess. From Somalia to Kandahar, Syme's image of hunting as an 'outlet' continued to be inapplicable. Instead, big game was a powerful source of public prestige and continued to be claimed by the Successor kings (Stewart 1993; Lund 1992, 160). On coins, Ptolemy I was shown in an elephant cap, Seleukos in a bull cap; Lysimachos' coins showed a lion's head, alluding to his reported prowess against a lion under Alexander. His insistence on this feat was probably the reason why Krateros' son put up the belated lion monument at Delphi for his father, the other great lion-killer in the years with Alexander. Later kings followed suit: Philip V's exploits and dedications have remained famous, as have the stories of Antiochos IX's addiction to the sport (*Anth. Pal.* 6. 114–16; Diod. 35/36. 34. 1). Their officers and colonists patronized hunting verse: the 'son of Aristonax' at Kandahar made a verse dedication on stone whose fragments probably refer to a wild beast killed by his dog (Fraser 1979, 9–11); in Egypt, poems were composed for the Indian dog, Tauron, of the great finance minister Zeno, whom Tauron had saved from a wild boar; on Cyprus, Nikokles' 'New Paphos' incorporated a shrine to Artemis Agrotera, the huntress.[1] Only outside the Greek monarchies do we find a king who renounced hunting altogether: the Indian King Aśoka, who converted to Buddhism in the 260s and had his renunciation inscribed in Greek on his kingdom's border near the Alexandria at Kandahar; he is the one known 'anti' of importance between Pythagoras in the sixth century BC and Mani in the 240s AD (Schlumberger 1958, 3; Koenen and Römer 1988, 93).

In Renaissance Italy the movements of despots often have to be understood in terms of their 'hunting progress' from one villa

---

[1] Page, *GLP* 109; Fraser 1979, 14 n. 9; Mitford 1960, 202–5.

to the next in the hunting season: late summer would find the duke of Tuscany hunting at Pratolino, while in the New Year he hunted near Pisa (Mignani 1991). If we knew more of the hunting calendar, perhaps we would understand the Seleukids' year rather better. There was, however, a significant limit: no hellenistic king is known to have chased the biggest game on offer. In India Alexander never hunted tigers; Nearchos saw only a tiger-skin, not the animal itself (Arrian, *Indica*, 15. 1). It was Alexander who introduced the elephant into western warfare, yet he avoided the new challenge of hunting elephants, leaving it to professionals. His successors were equally cautious. The tomb-paintings at Marissa show a horseman hunting a leopard (Peters and Thiersch 1905, 23–4; 90–5), but elephants were for hardened experts like Satyros, Demetrios, and Lichas who trapped the biggest and most necessary prey for the royal armies.[1] Unfortunately, the participants have left us no hunting memoirs or textbooks, but we know some of their names from the network of colonies they settled along Egypt's east coast in order to supply the Ptolemies with elephants. None of the names is oriental, although local guides must have helped their search.

Meanwhile, in the hellenistic cities no less than at the Successors' courts, the political order favoured the image of the Grand Hunting Man. Democracy had been tempered, and behind its façade, or in its absence, power was usually concentrated in few hands. Here, too, great acts of prowess were proof of social and political pre-eminence. In old Greece, top Peloponnesians were now free to behave like Xenophons in a much more congenial political climate; hunting was both a distinction and a passion for Polybios, Philopoimen, and their like. According to Polybios (6. 6. 8) the killing of wild animals had helped to cause the origin of ethical concepts: men admired it as a 'fine' action, and kingship developed to reward hunting men.[2] Here and now, this age-old prowess made a king seem less alien in the eyes of potential subjects. In 187/6 Ptolemy Epiphanes reasserted his alliance

[1] Scullard 1974, 126–33, esp. 130–1; Arrian, *Indica*, 13; Bigwood 1993, 537; Desanges 1978; Diod. 3. 25; Strabo, 16. 4. 5 (769); Pliny, *HN* 6. 165.
[2] Polyb. 10. 22. 4 and 31. 29. 8 with Walbank 1972, 33 n. 6; Polyb. 33. 4. 3, with commentary of Walbank 1957–79; Plut. *Philopoimen*, 4 (103); Paus. 8. 49. 3.

with the Achaean league, and Polybios' father was sent to swear the oath. His son tells us how the royal envoy spoke freely to the Greeks of Ptolemy's excellence with hounds and hunting and, as evidence, told how the king had once hit a bull with a javelin while hunting on horseback (Polyb. 22. 3. 5–9).[1] The exploit was supposed to encourage their diplomatic friendship. Xenophon's praises of Cyrus, scarred by that bear-bite, would have sat easily in this culture of prowess.

When the Greek world encountered yet another 'barbarian' culture, hunting was to change again in a new political context. As formerly between Macedonians and Persians, so now between Romans and Greeks hunting helped to establish friendship among like-minded top people. Through hunting Aemilius Paullus widened his Greek contacts, a project taken further by his son, Scipio Aemilianus (Plut. *Aem.* 6. 5; Polyb. 31. 29. 3–9). Aged 27, Scipio was given free run of the royal hunting parks, hounds, and hunting staff of newly conquered Macedonia, where he revelled in coverts that had not been hunted during the past four years of war (Polyb. 31. 29. 1–12). Hunting must have confirmed his friendship with Polybios, with whom he shared favourite books (Polyb. 31. 23. 4); perhaps they shared a copy of Xenophon's writings about hunting. Polybios had also befriended Demetrios prince of Syria, whom he knew through boar hunting (31. 14. 4). Through similar contacts Greek experts taught Romans how to manage game parks and to hunt with packs of hounds: in the 30s BC the word for a game reserve in Italy was still Greek, *thêrotrophion* (Varro, *De re rustica*, 3. 13. 2–3). Like the great hunting cardinals of the Vatican in the sixteenth century, Roman senators and notables then exported the sport to their Italian country estates.

In Rome itself they fitted it into a new context. In 186 BC M. Fulvius Nobilior brought lions and panthers to Rome and displayed them in a hunt before crowds in the circus (the Circus Maximus): Livy mentions this hunt (39. 22), not necessarily because it was the first but because it was connected to an individual's personal games. The donor was a philhellene from an old philhellenic family: had he derived this new type of hunting from the hellenistic world?

---

[1] With Walbank *ad loc.*, doubting if the bull was wild.

So far as our limited evidence goes, he had not. The hellenistic kings are not known to have exploited hunting as a spectator sport: the Seleukids, who ruled Babylonia, are not known to have copied the hunts of Assurbanipal, although his monuments might have caught their attention. Polybios (30. 26) happens to refer to 'hunts' among the exceptional shows that the erratic Antiochos IV put on near Antioch in 166, but nothing associates them with an earlier Near Eastern tradition. Instead, the connection of hunts with the games at a festival had a recent, Roman precedent: was Antiochos imitating a new Roman practice? Arguably, the distinctive political culture at Rome had encouraged the innovation. At Rome, competition among the leading citizens was played out before a populace whose support carried constitutional weight, however limited its actual chances of voting (Millar 1984). In the 180s Fulvius was at the centre of an intense competitive rivalry between different political groups and individuals. Unlike the notables of the Greek cities, great men at Rome could play on foreign prowess, exotic imports, and their own enormous profits in order to bid for popular pre-eminence. Hunting thus entered the arena as part of the political contest.

As a result it took root in the cultural life of great cities under Roman rule and persisted into the early Byzantine era, unopposed by Christian leaders (Cameron 1973, 228–30). In classical Greece young men of good family had scrambled on hillsides in order to drive hares into nets which were maintained by their slaves. In republican Rome, and thence in later cities of the empire, men of ambition paid for big game to be brought to the arena and 'hunted' to death: sometimes by trained 'hunters', at other times by pitting one breed of animal against another. Once again, hunting was not the idle outlet of courtiers under benevolent despotism: it was part of their claim, or 'promise', for civic office and pre-eminence.

Outside the arena, meanwhile, real hunting enjoyed yet another extension under global Roman rule. Trappers for the arena emerged beside the trappers of elephants for armies, and among amateurs the supporting cast improved beyond recognition. From Gaul and Britain came the vastly superior Celtic hounds, while the conquest of North Africa brought greater knowledge of Libyan horses and their extra staying-power. A new hunter's paradise, the hinterland of Spain, was opened up as never to the Greeks. By the second century Arrian could look back on the age of

Xenophon as an inferior forerunner, poorly horsed, poorly dogged, hunting merely into nets, and (in Xenophon's case) taking too much pleasure in the kill. The second Xenophon's sense of progress is evident throughout his writings.[1]

From the early Greek aristocrats to the Roman donors of game shows, upper-class hunters had caused a new value to be set on items in the natural world: without hunting and its nets, would flax have been grown and prized in the special conditions round Cumae? Who would have shipped and traded dogs from Britain or panthers from Africa into Rome? We even find Rome's subjects benefiting from the hunting culture and its demands: in 216, Caracalla remitted Mauretania's arrears of regular tribute in return for a 'one-off' gift of wild 'animals for the heavenly emperor' (*caelestia animalia*) from the region's forests.[2] The emperor's edict on the bronze tablet from Banasa sums up the central themes of this paper, the changing relation between hunting, political power, and profit. Across a thousand years, hunting did add to the sum of economic assets in an economy where that sum was never so large that the contribution of the 'culture of fun' was insignificant. Yet the political connections are the ones I have tried to emphasize here, believing that 'fun' should not be fenced off into separate studies during the ancient phase of history. That phase is distinguished from its successors by its long sequence of social and political changes. Hunting was susceptible to them, acquiring a different range and prominence under aristocracy, democracy, monarchy, and the distinctive republican order at Rome. In early Greece, older men courted younger men by 'saying it with hares'; in republican Rome, great men impressed crowds of social inferiors by 'showing it' with panthers, bears, and leopards. The emperors were their heirs, culminating in one who accepted wild animals in lieu of his subjects' arrears of tax. The model of hunting as an alternative to politics may (or may not) fit the age of Louis XIV, but it does not fit its phases in Greek antiquity. Ancient historians, I have hoped to show, should not follow the modern slogan and 'keep politics out of country sport'.[3]

[1]   Anderson 1985, 107–21; Stadter 1980, 51–9; Arrian, *Kynegetikos*, 23–4.
[2]   Corbier 1977, 211, a brilliant study.
[3]   Compare the role of hunting in the festivals of Roman Sparta (Chrimes 1949, 119–30), a far cry from its role in the social life of free, classical Sparta.

Bibliography

Akurgal, E. (1956), 'Recherches faites à Cyzique et à Ergili', *Anatolia*, 1: 15–24.

Anderson, J. K. (1985), *Hunting in the Ancient Greek World* (Berkeley, Cal.).

Andronikos, M. (1984), *Vergina: The Royal Tombs and the Ancient City* (Athens).

Aymard, J. (1951), *Essai sur les chasses romaines* (Paris).

Beinart, W. (1990), 'Empire, hunting and ecological change in Africa', *Past and Present*, 128: 162–86.

Bérard, C. (ed. 1989), *A City of Images* (Princeton, NJ).

Bigwood, J. M. (1993), 'Aristotle and the elephant again', *AJP* 114: 537–56.

Birge, D. E. (1982), *Sacred Groves in the Ancient Greek World* (Ph.D. thesis, University of California at Berkeley).

Boardman, J. (1991), 'Sixth-century potters and painters', in T. Rasmussen and N. Spivey (eds), *Looking at Greek Vases* (Cambridge), 79–102.

Bremmer, J. (1986), 'A Homeric goat island', *CQ* 80 (n.s. 36): 256–7.

Briant, P. (1982), *Rois, tributs et paysans: études sur les formations tributaires du Moyen-Orient ancien* (Annales littéraires de l'Université de Besançon, 269: Centre de Recherches d'Histoire Ancienne, 43; Paris).

—— (1989), 'Les chasses d'Alexandre', *Ancient Macedonia*, v (1): 267–77.

—— (1991), 'Chasses royales macédoniennes et chasses royales perses', *Dialogues d'histoire ancienne*, 17. 211–56.

Buchholz, H. G., Jöhrens, G., and Maull, I. (1973), 'Jagd und Fischfang', *Archaeologica Homerica*, 2 (Göttingen).

Burkert, W. (1983), *Homo Necans* (Berkeley, Cal.).

—— (1992), *The Orientalizing Revolution* (Harvard).

Buxton, R. G. A. (1992), 'Imaginary Greek mountains', *JHS* 112: 1–15.

Cameron, A. (1973), *Porphyrius the Charioteer* (Oxford).

Camporeale, G. (1984), *La caccia in Etruria* (Rome).

Cantacuzene, G. (1932), 'Une chasse inconnue du cavalier Thrace', *Mélanges G. Glotz*, i (Paris), 103–15.

Cartmill, M. (1993), *A View to a Death in the Morning: Hunting and Nature through History* (Cambridge, Mass.).

Childs, W. A. O., and Demargne, P. (1989), *Le Monument des Néréides: le décor sculpté*, i (Paris).

Chrimes, K. M. T. (1949), *Ancient Sparta* (Manchester).

Clairmont, C. W. (1970), *Gravestone and Epigram* (Mainz).

Classen, J. (1960), *Untersuchungen zur Platonjagdbildern* (Berlin).

Coldstream, J. N. (1994), 'Warriors, chariots, dogs and lions: a new Attic Geometric amphora', *BICS* 39: 85–94.

Corbier, M. (1977), 'Le discours du prince d'après une inscription de Banasa', *Ktema*, 2: 211–32.

Coupel, P., and Demargne, P. (1969), *Fouilles de Xanthos*, iii: *Le Monument des Néréides*, 1–2 (Paris).

Demargne, P. (1974), *Fouilles de Xanthos*, v: *Tombes-maisons, tombes rupestres et sarcophages* (Paris).

Desanges, J. (1978), *Recherches sur l'activité des méditerranéens aux confins de l'Afrique* (Rome).

Dubourditu, A. (1990), 'Le chien de Ségeste', *Kokalos*, 36: 51–84.

Edson, C. F. (1940), 'Macedonica', *Harvard Studies in Classical Philology*, 51: 125–36.

Finley, M. I. (ed. 1973), *Problèmes de la terre en Grèce ancienne* (Paris).

Foxhall, L. (1992), 'The control of the Attic landscape', in Wells (ed.), 155–9.

Fraser, P. M. (1979), 'The son of Aristonax at Kandahar', *Afghan Studies*, 2: 9–21.

Goodenough, E. R. (1958), *Jewish Symbols in the Greco-Roman Period*, viii. 2 (Toronto), 85–94.

Goossens, R. (1944) 'Notes sur quelques papyres littéraires', *Chronique d'Egypte*, 19: 265.

Grabar, O. (1988), 'La place de Qusayr Amrah dans l'art profane du haut moyen âge', *Cahiers archéologiques*, 36: 75–84.

Greenwalt, W. S. (1989), 'The iconographical significance of Amyntas III's mounted hunter stater', *Ancient Macedonia*, v (1): 509–19.

Griffin, J. (1991), review of Lonsdale 1990, *Classical Review*, 105 (n.s. 41): 293–5.

Guiraud, P. (1893), *La Propriété foncière en Grèce jusqu'à la conquête romaine* (Paris).

Hammond, N. G. L. (1988), 'The king and the land in the Macedonian kingdom', *CQ* 80 (n.s. 38): 382–91.

—— (1990), 'Royal pages, personal pages, and boys trained in Macedonian manner during the period of the Temenid monarchy', *Historia*, 39: 261–90.

—— and Griffith, G. T. (1979), *A History of Macedonia*, ii (Oxford).

Harper, P. O. (1978), *The Royal Hunter: Art of the Sassanian Empire* (New York).

Henig, M. (1986), *Roman Gems in Britain*, ii (Oxford).

Hull, D. B. (1964), *Hounds and Hunting in Ancient Greece* (Chicago).

Jameson, M. H. (1991), 'Sacrifice before battle', in V. D. Hanson (ed.), *Hoplites: The Classical Greek Battle Experience* (London), 197–227.

Jeffery, L. H. (1976), *Archaic Greece: The City-states c.700–600 BC* (London).

Kienast, D. (1973), *Philipp von Makedonien und der Reich der Achaimeniden* (Munich).

Kleemann, I. (1958), *Der Satrapensarkophag aus Sidon* (Berlin).

Koch-Harnack, G. (1983), *Knabenliebe und Tiergeschenke* (Berlin).

Koenen, L., and Römer, C. (1988), 'Der kölner Mani Codex', *Papyrologica Coloniensia*, 14 (Cologne).

Körte, G. (1918), 'Zur Xenophons Kynegeticos', *Hermes*, 53: 317–23.

Kraay, C. M. (1976), *Archaic and Classical Greek Coins* (London).

—— and Hirmer, M. (1966), *Greek Coins* (London).

Lampedusa: *see* Tomasi di Lampedusa.

Lasserre, F. (1966), *Strabon: Géographie*, ii (Paris).

Lavin, I. (1963), 'The hunting mosaics of Antioch and their sources', *Dumbarton Oaks Papers*, 17: 179–286.

Lewis, D. M. (1973), 'The Athenian rationes centesimarum', in Finley (ed.), 187–99.

Lombard, M. (1969), 'La chasse et les produits de la chasse dans le monde musulman, viii–xii siècle', *Annales ESC* 24: 572–93.

Lonsdale, S. H. (1990), *Creatures of Speech: Lion, Herding and Hunting Similes in the Iliad* (Beiträge zur Altertumskunde, 5; Stuttgart).

Lund, H. S. (1992), *Lysimachus: A Study in Early Hellenistic Kingship* (London).

Mango, M. M. (1990), *The Sevso Treasure: A Collection from Late Antiquity* (Zurich and London).

Manns, O. (1889–90), *Über die Jagd bei den Griechen* (Cassel).

Marinatos, N. (1990), 'Celebrations of Death and the Symbolism of the Lion Hunt', in R. Hägg and G. C. Nordquist, eds, *Celebrations of Death and Divinity in the Bronze Age Argolid* (Stockholm), 143–8.

Mignani, D. (1991), *The Medicean Villas* (Florence).

Millar, F. G. B. (1981), 'The world of the Golden Ass', *JRS* 71: 63–75.

—— (1984), 'The political character of the classical Roman republic, 200–151 BC', *JRS* 74: 1–19.

Mitford, T. B. (1960), 'Unpublished syllabic inscriptions of the Cyprus Museum', *Opuscula Atheniensia*, 3 (1960), 177–213.

Morris, C. E. (1990), 'In pursuit of the white tusked boar: aspects of hunting in Mycenaean society', in R. Hägg and G. C. Nordquist, eds, *Celebrations of Death and Divinity in the Bronze Age Argolid* (Stockholm).

Murray, O. (1990), introduction to P. Veyne, *Bread and Circuses* (London).

Neuburg, M. (1987), 'Hunter and hunted at Euripides' Bacchae 1020', *Liverpool Classical Monthly*, 12: 159–60.

Perdrizet, P. (1898), 'La Venatio Alexandri à Delphes', *Bulletin de correspondance hellénique*, 22: 566.

Peters, J., and Thiersch, H. (1905), *Painted Tombs in the Necropolis of Marissa* (London).

Pipili, M. (1987), *Laconian Iconography of the Sixth Century BC* (Oxford).

Pollard, J. (1977), *Birds in Greek Life and Myth* (London).

Procopé, J. F. (1989), 'Democritus on politics and the care of the soul', *CQ* 83 (n.s. 39): 307–31.

Rackham, O. (1983), 'Observations on the historical ecology of Boeotia', *BSA* 78: 291–351.

—— (1990), 'Ancient landscapes', in O. Murray and S. Price (eds), *The Greek City: From Homer to Alexander* (Oxford), 85–111.

—— and Moody, J. A. (1992), 'Terraces', in Wells (ed.), 123–33.

Reilly, L. C. (1993), 'The hunting frieze from Vergina', *JHS* 113: 160–2.

Robert, L. (1949), *Hellenica*, vii (Paris).

—— (1978), 'Documents d'Asie Mineure', *Bulletin de correspondance hellénique*, 102: 437–543.

Robertson, C. M. (1965), 'Greek mosaics', *JHS* 85: 72–89.

—— (1975), *A History of Greek Art* (Cambridge).

Rooney, A. (1993), *Hunting in Middle English Literature* (Woodbridge).

Sancisi-Weerdenburg, H. (1993), 'Political concepts in Old Persian inscriptions', in K. Raaflaub (ed.), *Anfänge politischen Denkens in der Antike* (Munich), 145–64.

Sansone, D. (1988), *Greek Athletics and the Genesis of Sport* (California).

Schauenburg, K. (1969), *Jagddarstellungen in den griechischen Vasenmalerei* (Hamburg).

Schlumberger, D. (1958), 'Une inscription bilinguale gréco-araméenne d'Asoka', *Journal asiatique*, 246: 3–48.

Schmitt, R. (1981), *Altpersische Siegelinschriften* (Vienna).

Schnapp, A. (1973), 'Représentation du territoire de guerre et du territoire de chasse dans l'oeuvre de Xénophon', in Finley (ed.), 307–21.

—— (1979a), 'Images et programme: les figurations archaïques de la chasse au sanglier', *Revue archéologique*, 195–218.

—— (1979b), 'Pratiche e immagini di caccia nella Grecia antica', *Dialoghi di archeologia*, 1: 36–59.

—— (1989), 'Eros the hunter', in Bérard (ed.), 71–88.

—— and Durand, J.-L. (1989), 'Sacrificial slaughter and initiatory hunt', in Bérard (ed.), 53–70.

—— and Schmitt, P. (1982), 'Images et société en Grèce ancienne: les représentations de la chasse et du banquet', *Revue archéologique*, 57.

Scullard, H. H. (1974), *The Elephant in the Greek and Roman World* (London).

Stadter, R. E. (1980), *Arrian of Nicomedia* (Chapel Hill, NC).

Stengel, P. (1910), *Opferbräuche der Griechen* (Leipzig).

Stewart, A. (1993), *Faces of Power* (Berkeley and Oxford).

Stronach, D. (1978), *Pasargadae* (Oxford).

Syme, R. (1986), *The Augustan Aristocracy* (Oxford).

Tomasi di Lampedusa, G. (1988), *The Leopard* (trans., by A. Calquhoun, of *Il gattopardo*; revised edn, 1961; repr. 1988, London).

Traill, J. S. (1982), 'An interpretation of six rock-cut inscriptions in the Attic deme of Lamptrai', in *Studies in Attic Epigraphy, History and Topography Presented to Eugene Vanderpool* (Hesperia supp. 19; Princeton), 158–71.

—— (1986), *Demos and Trittys* (Toronto).

Tripodi, B. (1991), 'Il fregio della caccia della tomba reale di Vergina e le cacce funerarie d'oriente', *Dialogues d'histoire ancienne*, 17: 143–209.

Vigneron, P. (1968), *Le Cheval dans l'antiquité gréco-romaine* (Nancy).

von Graeve, V. (1970), *Der Alexandersarkophag und ihre Werkstatt* (Berlin).

von Steuben, H. (1968), *Frühe Sagendarstellungen in Korinth und Athen* (Berlin).

Voyatzis, M. (1992), 'Votive riders seated side-saddle at early Greek sanctuaries', *BSA* 87: 259–79.

Walbank, F. W. (1972), *Polybius* (Berkeley).

—— (1957–79), *A Historical Commentary on Polybius* (Oxford).

Wells, B. (ed. 1992), *Agriculture in Ancient Greece (Proceedings of the 7th International Symposium at the Swedish Institute at Athens)* (Skrifter utgivna av Svenska Institutet i Athen, series in 4to, 42; Stockholm).
Ziehen, L. (1906), *Leges Graecorum sacrae* (Leipzig).

7

Where was the 'wilderness' in Roman times?

Catherine Delano Smith

Wilderness is, of course, largely what people *think* it is (Nash 1981, 6). As a concept it has had a long history. One 'Wilderness' Act (1962, establishing a National Wilderness Preservation System in the USA) defines a wilderness region as one which 'shows no significant ecological disturbance from on-site human activity'. Another stipulates that a wilderness should retain something of 'its primaeval character' (Nash 1981, 5). However defined, the concept of wilderness is a binary one, conveying the notion of a scale between two poles, and thus two extremes. It invokes polarized contrasts and provokes oppositions: wilderness against civilization; the wild against the tame; places of disorder, confusion, and savageness against controlled and orderly places; places usually (but not always) hostile and alien as opposed to pleasant, reassuring places. Above all, wilderness represents nature untamed as opposed to nature tamed.[1]

The notion of 'taming' implies control and an awareness of the events and processes that shape the physical environment. Paradoxically, however, one consequence of humanity's taming of nature, we learn from the environmental record, is 'natural' disaster. The self-destructive tendencies of human action and

---

[1] Referring to 'external' nature or the physical environment: the untamed world around us, that is, not the internal untamed of human thought and action.

human 'control' over nature are far too obvious, their consequences too transparent, for the notion to have anything but
a hollow ring. Too many 'Edens' have been lost, as David
Attenborough (1987) has argued for the Mediterranean. I am
beginning to wonder, however, if there ever was an Eden in
post-glacial Italy. Would there have been time after the end of
the ice age for optimum ecological and living conditions to become
fully established while human activity was also expanding? The
archaeological record can be read this way: given the widespread
distribution of human settlement and land use on the one hand,
and Italy's environmental tendencies on the other, it could be
suggested that the 'wilderness' of the ancients in at least parts of
Italy is more likely to have been not nature untamed but nature
derelict – or nature degraded. That is the thesis explored in this
essay; if the argument seems at times exaggerated, this is because
it is intended to draw attention to the interlocking nature of a
wide variety of factors, not to make a definitive statement about
any one of them.

Environmental problems in Roman Italy: four examples

If we were Romans debating the state of the environment – and
there were certainly some observant contemporaries[1] – we would
find ourselves faced with no shortage of worrying situations. Four
examples of the way the physical outline of Italy was changing
under the very eyes of its inhabitants will serve to indicate the
way things were going (I have described them in detail elsewhere).
One example comes from northern Italy (Liguria), the other three
from the south (Apulia).

As part of the process of conquering and holding the north, the
Romans established, in 177 BC, the colony of Luna (Luni;
discussed in greater detail by Ward-Perkins *et al.* 1986). Strategi-
cally placed at the mouth of the Magra, Luni was to command all
movement along the coast, by land or by sea, between Gaul, Iberia,
and Rome and also inland up the Magra valley to the northern
plain. Other than these political and military factors, however,

---

[1] e.g. Aristotle, *Metaphysics*, 1. 14; Ovid, *Metamorphoses*, 15; Pliny,
Historia naturalis, 2. 207; 3. 16; Strabo, 1. 3. 8 (53).

there was little to recommend the situation and still less the site of the new colony. Its hinterland was almost entirely mountainous, yielding few resources, agricultural or industrial. Luni's sole economic asset was a luxury commodity: the marble of Carrara, whose extraction was the first kind of activity to fall victim in times of political uncertainty. There was virtually no lowland or coastal plain, only a narrow strip of stony Pleistocene foothill deposits half the width of today's plain. The low-lying shore was fringed by marshes and separated from the open sea by a sequence of lagoons, sheltering behind the sandy islands of an offshore barrier that hugged the Versilian shore to the Arno and beyond. As regards its site, too, Luni was curiously (and, as it was to turn out, unhappily) placed. Only half of the new colony had been laid out on the *terra firma* of the Pleistocene shelf; the other half rested on a large sandy spit, protruding from the shore at the seaward end of the then open estuary of the Magra river. One advantage of the spit was that it sheltered the shallow estuarine waters behind it, creating a harbour that may or may not have been the *Portus Lunae* described by Strabo (5. 2. 5 (222)) and alluded to by other classical writers.

But not for all that long. All too soon, early in the first millennium AD, sediments began to accumulate, swept down from the surrounding hills by a host of tiny streams or carried by the Magra to feed its steadily advancing delta. Shallow water turned into marsh; marsh became the dry land. Much of the former estuary is now cultivated and even built on. The Roman colony began to suffer from environmental problems. Excavation in the intra-mural area shows how sands were blown in, or swept in by waves breaking over the southern wall or by lagoon water that flooded the lower part of the town as the sea level rose. Flooding certainly was a domestic hazard: at least one householder in this part of the town had to raise his house floor. Outside the walls, to the north, the expanding area of marsh and standing water may have meant not just a disagreeable environment but even, perhaps, a malarial one. Like most urban centres in Italy at the end of antiquity, late Roman Luni had become a miserable ghost of its former dynamic and architecturally splendid self. However, unlike other towns in north and central Italy, medieval Luni was unable to respond to the new economic stimuli, defeated by its physical disadvantages. By the mid-thirteenth century municipal functions had been transferred elsewhere and Luni was abandoned. By the end of the sixteenth century, the formerly deep indentation was obliterated and the coast had taken on its present smooth outline.

Something very similar was going on in southern Italy. In Apulia there was no town at the mouth of the Candelaro[1] (the biggest of several rivers that drain the great lowland of the Tavoliere), but there was a similarly broad, open estuary, Lago Salso, making a major indentation in the coastline south of the Gargano headland. Indeed, travellers leaving Sipontum for Salapia and places beyond (Bari, Brindisi), and using the route prescribed by government documents such as the Antonine and the Peutinger itineraries, found themselves forced to make a detour inland to reach the lowest crossing-place on the Candelaro. Today Lago Salso is distinctly more wetland than open water. Moreover, just as at Luni, the former indentation has disappeared and the coast sweeps in one continuous curve, south from the foot of the Gargano at Sipontum to the Ofanto river and, beyond that, to the port of Barletta. Travellers can motor along the shore, turning inland only in order to cross the Ofanto next to the Roman bridge. Most of the lagoons that fringed this low-lying coast right up to the nineteenth century have been filled; only the salt-pans of Margherita di Savoia (occupying the southern half of Lago Salpi) and the persistent wetland of Lago Salso remind us of their earlier importance.

Siltation was not a problem confined to late Roman or medieval times. The iron age city of Salapia (Salpi) succumbed in the second half of the last millennium BC. Daunian Salpi, one of eight Daunian city-states on the Tavoliere, was flanked to the north by a small inlet of the main lagoon of Lago Salpi.[2] Intensively farmed countryside, with its scatter of isolated farmsteads, surrounded the ramparted town on the other sides. The inlet is marked on sixteenth-century maps as 'Lago di Marana'. Today it is a featureless area, much of it still too wet for cultivation. In Daunian times,

---

[1] The site of Ergitium, listed immediately after the Candelaro crossing in the itineraries, has not been definitively traced, but the site of the medieval settlement of Versentino, today no more than a farmstead, contains Daunian pottery and could well correspond to ancient Ergitium. See discussion in Delano Smith 1978.

[2] For further details on the environmental history of Salpi see esp. Delano Smith 1978; 1979, esp. part 3.

though, Lago di Marana would have been a small lake or lagoon, with clear water sparkling above pale, chalky white bottom muds, signs of freely circulating and well-aerated water. It was never a deep lake (a couple of metres at most); it would not have taken much to block the narrow channel that connected it with Lago Salpi, and for the shallow depression to be obliterated by in-filling. Interestingly, the onset of the in-filling process seems to have been remarkably sudden. Moreover, to judge from their nature (colour and texture), the earliest layers of silt represent not the muds of *in situ* marsh so much as soils washed off farmland upstream and carried down to Lago di Marana by the two small streams that still feed the depression. However it was, by the penultimate century BC Daunian Salapia was deemed to have become sufficiently 'unhealthy' for the Roman authorities to create a new port city just four Roman miles distant, directly on the shore of the main lagoon.[1] This settlement, also known as Salapia or Salpi, continued well into the middle ages, becoming deserted after the thirteenth century (Delano Smith 1975; di Biase 1985).

The final stage of the story of environmental deterioration in early Roman times is exemplified by a small tributary valley not far inland from Salpi and Sipontum. Taking its name from a former medieval settlement, Torre di Lama, it lies not far from the site of Daunian Arpi and even closer to Passo di Corvo, the largest neolithic site on the plain. Today we find a shallow gully, about one and a half kilometres long, almost hanging over the broad, flat-bottomed valley of the Celone, one of the main tributaries of the Candelaro. In early Daunian times, at the start of the last millennium BC, the gully would have been almost twice as deep, but before the turn of the millennium the grey sediments that now fill it began to be deposited. As in the case of the Marana di Lupara, these sediments represent soil wash from the surrounding, very gently undulating farmland.[2]

---

[1] Vitruvius, *On Architecture*, 1. 4. 12. The disruptions of the second Punic war (218–201 BC) could help account for the lack of municipal attention to silting in the narrow channel connecting Marana di Lupara with the main lagoon. For the effects of the war on the region in general, see Toynbee 1965, ii, esp. 191–221 and, for Apulia, 239–42.

[2] At least one well-marked flood stratum was noted, containing sherds of Daunian pottery. These show little sign of rolling, which would suggest a local provenance. See Delano Smith 1981b; 1983.

Three key relationships

These four examples introduce, albeit briefly, one element of a familiar physical relationship: downstream and coastal deposition. The other element is upstream and inland erosion. While the processes and systems involved are well known to geographers, it may be useful to summarize them here by reference to three key relationships.

First, vegetation degradation leads to erosion. A vegetation climax association is by definition self-perpetuating.[1] Undamaged, its interdependent hierarchy of trees and shrubs (if any) and herbaceous layers should ensure permanent ground cover, all-year-round soil protection even on slopes, and nursery conditions for the young saplings of dominant tree species. Under 'normal' circumstances there would be, in theory at least, relatively little erosion. However, such an idyllic steady state is hardly characteristic of nature, least of all in the lands bordering the Mediterranean. The debate may centre on the relative importance of the reasons (natural or human-induced) for, and chronology of, the damaging factors, but common to all instances is the starting-point of erosion: damage to an effectively protective plant cover (forest or grassland). Whether triggered by geological factors (such as landslips) or human activity (such as felling or over-grazing), the unchecked sequence leads to a progressive reduction in vegetation status, plant density, and plant variety. Eventually a stage is reached when a few low-growing species cling to the ground (often the exposed subsoil), the soil between them being exposed to sun, wind, and rain, and to the unmitigated forces of erosion.

Second, erosion leads to deposition. Soil erosion starts with the impact of each raindrop on ground unprotected by plants or by a litter layer. Each raindrop falls with a force that compacts soil particles (inhibiting further infiltration so that surplus water just sweeps downslope, scouring the soil as it goes), or loosens a particle, or moves a particle (by saltation). Thus all rainwater that cannot immediately be absorbed into the litter layer moves over

[1] It has been suggested that it would take some 30,000 years for one centimetre of soil to be eroded under full beech or oak forest cover: Puglisi 1967, 11.

the surface of the ground, gathering velocity downslope and taking loosened soil particles with it. In due course soil wash becomes concentrated into the runnels, furrows, and gullies which feed the headstreams of the river network. The proportion of each rainfall that runs off rather than sinks in depends not only on the existence or state of the plant litter and underlying soil and bedrock, but also on such factors as the intensity and duration of the rainfall. Saturated ground and hard-baked ground alike promote surface flow. Any movement of soil particles is already erosion. The velocity and swelling volume of a stream in flood is a powerful erosive and transporting agent. Once the storm has peaked, however, or the stream's volume and/or velocity is checked for one reason or another, its carrying capacity is correspondingly reduced. The heaviest (coarse-textured) material is dropped first; boulders, pebbles, and shingle in the middle of a channel testify to relatively short-lived bursts of stream flow or intermittent flood. Finer material is dropped where the current is slowed by friction (as on the inside of bends) or impeded by an obstruction (a fallen tree, bridge piers). Some material is carried by overbank flood on to surrounding fields. The rest eventually arrives in the lowest reaches of the stream system, to be dropped when stream velocity is finally checked by the sea (as bars, spits, delta formations, and so on) or (in the case of the finest material of all, that carried in suspension), under the effect of salinity, as estuarine or offshore muds.

Third, just as there are 'high risk' regions, so there are also 'high risk' periods. By classifying all relevant factors as constants, physical variables, or human variables, and setting out each on a time-scale, periods of heightened (or reduced) erosive risk stand out.[1] Under the heading 'constants' are included such factors as the region's geology (in terms of permeability of individual deposits, for example, or characteristics of stratification, or frequency and severity of tectonic movement), altitude (which affects temperatures and the duration of winter, the leafless season), relief (water runs faster down steep slopes, however short in length), and vegetation (on the premise that, if left absolutely alone, the

---

[1] The adaptation of the geomorphologists' model to include the anthropogenic factor and to identify chronological variations was explored in Delano Smith and Parry (eds 1981).

essential nature of a climax vegetation would not normally alter much). A 'high risk' region is one with a high score for each attribute that heightens the erosion potential. Regions of this nature are commonplace in Italy. They include not only the obvious mountainous regions such as Liguria, and soft-rocked hill regions (with their landslips, *frane*, and badlands, *calenche*) like the Apennines of the peninsula, but even lowland regions like the Tavoliere of Apulia. 'Physical variables' include aspects of physical geography that are naturally unstable or changeable, such as sea level, tectonics, and climate. 'Human variables' are those associated with anthropogenic (human and human-induced) activity, chiefly through settlement and land use. They can either exacerbate a natural tendency towards increased risk, or coun-teract it: thus a period of demographic decline could mean *agri deserti*, vegetation regrowth, and thus less risk from erosion even though a change in the weather meant increased annual rainfall or a series of excessively dry summers.

The Eden that never was

The archaeological context from which most of the direct evidence of either erosion or deposition comes, in Italy as elsewhere, has tended to be Roman or post-Roman in date. The shortage of data on the physical environment in prehistoric times in large measure reflects the inherently episodic nature of environmental processes. Major cycles of erosion in the more distant past have removed (destroyed or displaced) the very sediments upon which we depend for the stratigraphic record of geomorphological history (Brunsden and Thornes 1979). There is thus no reason to assume that landscape change through sedimentation is exclusively Roman or post-Roman.[1] On the contrary, bearing in mind the inherent vulnerability of the Italian land, a mosaic of environmentally 'high

---

[1] As is implied by Vita-Finzi 1969. Vita-Finzi's preoccupation with climate as the explanation of sedimentation in Roman times around the Mediterranean (1969, 101–2, 105–11) seems to have distracted him from questioning the chronological and spatial pattern of that onset, and from seeing its connection with the land-use and settlement histories of partic-ular regions. However, the notion persists: see e.g. McNeill 1992, esp. 70–4.

risk' regions, as well as the precocity of human settlement and agriculture in the southern peninsula, the question must be asked: when did the story of degradation, erosion, and siltation start? For a pointer we return to the Tavoliere of Apulia, the region that welcomed the first farmers in Italy.

Few people, crossing what has seemed to most a dismally featureless plain, would think that such a 'flat' land could be at risk from soil erosion, let alone assessed as a 'high risk' region. Such travellers fail to consider the significance of the many short, but steep, breaks of slope that fragment the plain (valley sides, river terrace bluffs, and marine terrace bluffs). They ignore the consequences of the inherent irregularity of almost every aspect of the region's rainfall: unreliable annual totals, unpredictable seasonal regime, and the frequency of downpours and storms, especially in summer when soils are baked hard and dry and at their most impermeable. They might be surprised to discover not only that this is one of the driest regions of all Italy, but that it lies very close to the subarid/arid (desert) margin.[1] They spare no thought for the unconsolidated nature of the sands, gravels, and weakly cemented conglomerates of marine origin that cover by far the greater part of the plain; or for the plain's characteristic calcrete (a subsoil hardpan of calcium carbonate, also an inheritance from that marine origin of the region's surface geology). Soils are generally shallow on the Tavoliere, covering the hard and impervious surface of the calcrete to a depth of less than a metre. Still less do these passers-by reflect on the Tavoliere's long settlement history or the nature of its traditional land use (dry-farmed grain, livestock, and tilled olive groves) to see this as yet another set of 'high-risk' factors, though they might reflect on those elements in the modern landscape that go back at least to Roman times. That Roman landscape was not necessarily, however, the landscape of the neolithic.

The Tavoliere in the neolithic seems to have been one of the most densely settled regions of prehistoric Europe (Bradford 1949, 60). It also seems to have been home to the earliest farmers. What conditions met those farmers? And what would have been their immediate effect on their surroundings? One of the puzzles of

---

[1] For criteria see Miller 1953, 86. For their application to the Tavoliere see Delano Smith 1978, 58 and fig. 4.

Italian prehistory is the way the Tavoliere – one of the great granaries of Roman and medieval Europe – seems to have been quite deserted throughout the bronze age. There are simply no bronze age sites (except Coppa Nevigata and Marandrea, both on the inner shores of their respective lagoons) or attested artefacts (Whitehouse 1984; 1986). We need to discover what had led to such a dramatic drop in population levels from the end of the neolithic until Daunian times. One approach would be to chronicle systematically all that is known of climatic, vegetation, settlement, and land-use history for each region from the start of the neolithic. The present, albeit tentative, essay is offered as a pointer to the potential value of comparative chronology.

A good deal of interlocking information is available on the prehistoric climate of north-western Europe. Much less is known about conditions in northern and central Italy. Virtually nothing is available specifically for the south. In the absence of a single reliable pollen diagram, we have to totter from surmise to surmise (see Delano Smith, forthcoming). We find, for example, no reason to doubt that the general trend of post-glacial climatic history is not radically different on the Tavoliere from that further north. Thus, it can be suggested that, as in northern Europe, the end of the ice age saw a general increase in temperature which continued until 3500 BC, and that this was followed by a downturn from about 1300 BC to the present (Lamb 1982, 185; Tooley 1978, esp. 131, 136). This means that the date 3500 BC marks a thermal peak, the peak of a period often described as the climatic 'optimum', characterized by greater annual warmth (+1–3° C), greater annual precipitation (compared with today's), and – above all – an all-year-round regime (giving summer and winter rain). The general trend is composed of a series of oscillations that, in northern Europe at least, have been correlated with variations in sea level (Tooley 1978, 184–92). A point to note is that climatic prehistory is no longer described in terms of the botanical divisions established by A. Blytt and R. Sernander (pre-Boreal, Boreal, Atlantic, sub-Boreal, sub-Atlantic).[1] These divisions, based on macro-fossils found in peats, may accurately describe vegetation phases but are no longer held to explain what is now

[1] See Goudie 1981, 56.

believed to be the botanical consequences of anthropogenic activity.

For far too long the Tavoliere has been dismissed as a natural grassland in which trees are unable to grow.[1] Even ignoring the archaeological evidence for tree-cropping (olive groves in the Roman centuriation systems, for instance) and the documentary evidence for woodland and forest on the plain as on the surrounding hills, a quick look around the plain today contradicts such a myth. There is thick valley bottom woodland (Bosco di Incoronata), vigorously regenerating scrub wherever grazing has ceased or is tightly controlled (the Fortore valley at Dragonara, the *Ovile Nazionale*), and dense groves of olives and almonds almost anywhere. The only problem is the calcrete hardpan, but once the hardened top of this has been breached and the young tree planted in a trench or pit, its roots have no difficulty in plunging through the softer deposits underneath to reach ground-water, a planting practice standard in Roman times.[2] Instead, postulate a scenario in which, on the Tavoliere as elsewhere in Italy and most of Europe, vegetation associations of woodland status developed after the ice age in step with the rising temperature gradient. We might expect to find a Tavoliere covered first by shrubby vegetation characteristic of relatively cool conditions (with hazel, perhaps). As temperatures continued to rise, and precipitation to maintain (or reach and maintain) an equable (all-year-round) regime, a mixed vegetation, with some tree species (deciduous and evergreen) such as elm, ash, and in wetter areas alder, would have taken over. This could have been a fully developed – though by no means necessarily dense – woodland association, where tall tree species headed a hierarchy of substrata (tall shrubs, low shrubs, grasses) that was well adapted to the climatic conditions of the thermal 'optimum'. That something like this, corresponding to the botanists' pollen zone 6c, may indeed

---

[1] This myth, repeated in almost every geographical description of the region since then, seems to have started with Deecke 1899 (published in English in 1904). One of its most influential perpetrators was Semple, who describes the Tavoliere as 'a lake-strewn lowland of immature drainage underlain by hard limestone which was *impenetrable to the roots of trees*' (1932, 326: my emphasis).

[2] Columella, *De re rustica*, 5. 9. 7; *On Trees*, 1. 6; 4. 3; Cato, *De re rustica*, 45.

have occurred on the Tavoliere by or at the start of the sixth millennium BC (c.5107 ±120 bc), is hinted at by evidence from Foggia, such as it is.[1]

Settlement on the Tavoliere at the end of the mesolithic, when the environment was still rather post-glacial (chilly, dry), had remained sparse. The first hint of a 'neolithic' way of life comes from soon after 7000 BC (Whitehouse 1984; 1986). This was precisely the moment when climatic conditions would have been beginning to warm up, with vegetation still advancing towards forest status, however open a forest. By about the middle of the seventh millennium BC at the latest, however, we are told by archaeologists that 'all the characteristic traits of the southeast Italian Neolithic are present' (Whitehouse 1984, 1112). Whitehouse is referring here to the middle neolithic of the Tavoliere, by when settlement density was at its peak.[2] This was a period of small, widely scattered nuclei of the hamlet or single homestead type. By the late neolithic, a thousand years later (after the start of the fifth millennium BC), the settlement pattern had altered and the farmers of the Tavoliere were concentrated into a few comparatively large nucleations, akin to villages, such as Passo di Corvo, though whether this change in settlement pattern masks a reduction of total population is hard to tell (Whitehouse 1984; 1986; Tinè ed. 1983; Jones ed. 1987). What is not in doubt is some sort of major demographic decline, evident by the beginning of the third millennium BC. The Tavoliere seems to have remained deserted throughout the bronze age except for some coastal settlements (Delano Smith and Smith 1973). The last millennium (Daunian period) saw something similar to the demographic explosion taking place at the same time in southern Etruria (Potter 1979, 52–92).

[1] Nisbet in Simone 1977–82. Botanical data from the early levels of a late neolithic site at Villa Communale, Foggia, showed deciduous oak in level 7, followed by ash and elm in levels 6 and 4, and some evidence for willow and maple together.

[2] This is also stressed in Whitehouse 1986, 42, where she argues that the south-east Italian neolithic should be regarded as 'a specifically Adriatic adaptation, which had achieved a fully evolved form by the mid-sixth millennium bc' rather than an example of colonization. She continues: 'If this were the case, then future work should reveal transitional mesolithic–neolithic communities before this date.'

It would be easy to conclude that the middle neolithic settlement phase on the Tavoliere positively benefited from, if it was not actually stimulated by, the onset of the climatic optimum and the replacement of pine or hazel by the ecologically richer mixed deciduous woodland.[1] An 'Eden effect' is not hard to envisage, with lush vegetation, rich soil, and a balmy climate: think of gardening in the dappled shade of a warm summer's day, when the storm-clouds have just passed and the sun warms the wet earth and dries the refreshed vegetation, drawing out that heady, earthy, vapour. But is that really what the evidence tells us? What effect on the environment did those first farmers in the early neolithic have? Even more to the point, what about the effect on their environment of the ever-growing numbers of middle neolithic farmers? For if the first farmers of the Tavoliere were clearing pine or hazel scrub, their descendants must have been clearing the deciduous woodland as it was developing. This would mean that the climax vegetation – that on which the stability of the ecological system depended – was being compromised as it grew. Thus it could well be that by the end of the middle neolithic there was relatively little unmodified climax woodland on the Tavoliere, and that associated pedological changes had so altered some aspects of the environment that a point of no return was reached within the neolithic itself.

The degradation model

To appreciate more readily the impact of human settlement on the surrounding vegetation of the Tavoliere, it is useful to think of each homestead or village as the rabbit burrow that inspired the botanists' model of vegetation degradation (fig. 7.1), a burrow surrounded by a sequence of zones of varying degrees of grazing intensity (Tansley 1953, i. 138, after Farrow 1917). Immediately outside the burrow the earth is almost bare from trampling, stamping, and over-nibbling. Further away the turf survives though cropped low. Further away still it is comparatively luxuriant, though the original species have been replaced by others more

[1] On balance the term 'climatic', rather than the 'thermal' currently preferred by north-western ecologists, seems more appropriate for the Tavoliere, where it is rainfall that determines growing conditions. Thermal conditions there are always favourable.

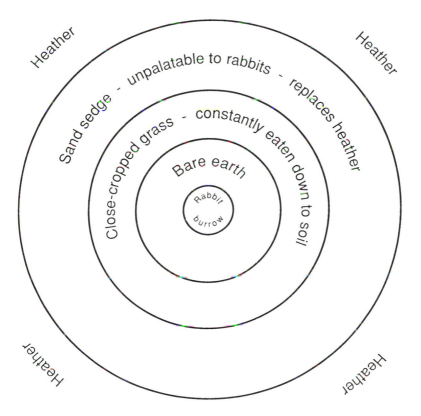

Figure 7.1 The botanical model. A single rabbit burrow is the centripetal focus of vegetation degradation and soil erosion. (Adapted from Tansley's studies of the Brecklands of E. Anglia: Tansley 1953, i. 138. No scale.)

tolerant of the new, rabbit-induced conditions, passing eventually into relatively undisturbed vegetation. Such a model, translated into the land-use zones characteristic of almost any rural settlement anywhere at any time (fig. 7.2), has underpinned much recent thinking in British historical geography on the history of rural landscapes.[1] In the present context the message is clear: each and every site, domestic or other, occupied by man represents not some inert record of mere presence but a potentially pernicious

[1] e.g. Roberts 1977. For one early Mediterranean application see Delano Smith 1972.

cell of active ecological destruction, as likely to endure as to be obliterated by time. This aspect of the model, concerning *affected* territory, has received less attention than have other aspects such as the boundaries of *exploited* territory (as in 'site catchment analysis'). By expanding the model to include not only fields and pastures within an obviously 'exploited' zone, but also the outermost zones – those of the 'waste' of medieval Europe – which supported not only fauna displaced from the exploited territory but also a whole range of occasional village needs, we may gain a more realistic appraisal of the extent of land affected by the inhabitants of each settlement and their livestock. After all, such 'wastes' constituted a vital element of any settlement's territory, allowing too for expansion and further colonization (on wasteland and its uses cf. Forbes in this volume, ch. 4). Even before the metal-using ages, the woods supplied a range of goods. They would

---

Figure 7.2 Land-use zonation around a settlement.

At the centre, vegetation is cleared for the village, the timber being used for buildings, palisades, etc., and much of the space between buildings will now be bare earth. Paths, too, both within the village and beyond, are worn down to bare soil.

Within the arable zone, initial land clearance will have left the stumps of tall trees to rot, while smaller shrubs and all undergrowth will have been cut and (together with the pared herbaceous layer) burnt, exposing a rich and fertile soil. Cultivation, however, involves frequent disturbance of the topsoil in the creation and maintenance of an agriculturally good but ecologically fragile tilth and the replacement of the permanent natural vegetation with periodically harvested crops. This means the soil is seasonally exposed year after year after harvesting, until a new crop is in leaf.

In most of southern Europe farming has traditionally involved extensive methods such as lengthy fallows. For the Tavoliere of Apulia this means that most of the arable land has remained unprotected or inadequately protected for up to six months each year (fallow years excluded) for at least the last 3,000 years. As the newly cleared soil's nitrogen content (and thus fertility) declined rapidly, land was cleared for cultivation (possibly worked on an infield–outfield basis) to maintain the annual level of output. Beyond this, in the grazing zone, the herbaceous cover will have been maintained. However, livestock can be destructive in their feeding. They nibble, break, and trample saplings, browse on the seeds of the dominant tree species (acorns, beech mast), and trample soil structure. They create tracks to the water's edge or through forest and untouched 'waste'. (Scale is not given in the diagram, since the extent of the zones reflects that of the settlement – the human population and livestock numbers.)

have been traversed by people passing to yet other resources, and trampled. They would have been browsed by free-ranging stock (such as swine, which even today are reared in this way in the mountainous districts of southern Europe). From the fourth millennium BC, at least on the Tavoliere, there were also forest-based metal industries and, later still, glass industries.

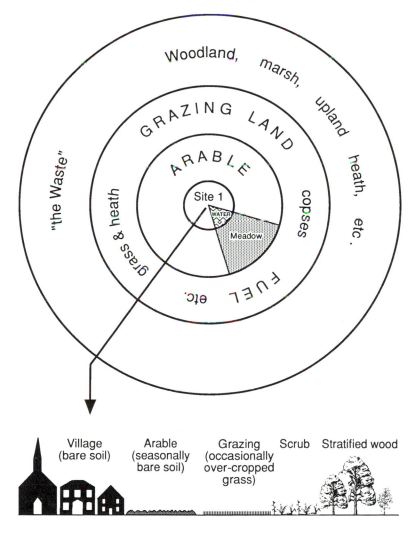

The environmental impact of forest industries

The transition from a stone-using to a metal-using culture by definition implies the development of mining and metal industries. From the Chalcolithic onwards, charcoal-dependent industries tended to be forest industries. In some measure this reflects the distribution of the geologically common raw minerals – various forms of iron; vein minerals such as lead, copper, and tin; silica (sand); and lime – but above all it is a measure of the importance of a fuel supply. Different woods were used in different industries (metal, glass, and pitch, for instance) as well as for domestic use in cooking and heating.[1] Simple economics also underline the advantages of a forest location: the raw materials of these industries (including fuel) are low value and/or bulky and difficult to transport in an unprocessed state. The fact that most of these forest establishments were small in scale and temporary in structure was not accidental.[2] Activities dependent on timber for fuel more regularly moved from site to site in a pattern associated with the coppicing cycle supplying it with fuel. Thus the ecological effect of a single industry is multiplied by the number of stations on its fuel-burning circuit, and computation of the total area affected has to be extended accordingly.

Not all early industries immediately strike one as environmentally unfriendly. Strabo described the Ligurians' retsina production (4. 6. 2 (202); see also Semple 1932, 284). While the pine tree is hardly harmed by resin-tapping, the pitch obtained is useless until distilled – yet another process requiring fuel. Like farmers, hunters, and gatherers, however, no forest worker willingly jeopardizes his own future by being profligate with the resources he depends on; hence the importance of coppicing in

[1] Theophrastos, *History of Plants*, 5. 9, shows how exacting early industrialists were in their demand for fuels producing exactly the required heat and flame. Timber from different species burns in different ways, and so different tree species are targeted according to requirements. The advantage of converting timber to charcoal is that charcoal yields the steady, moderate heat needed, for instance, in metal-smelting and metal-working, as well as in domestic cooking.

[2] The woodcuts in Georgius Agricola's *De re metallica* (1556) are instructive in this respect, as is the drawing of a glass-works illustrating an MS of John de Mandeville's travels (British Library MS Add. 24. 189, fo. 16, Flemish or German, fifteenth century).

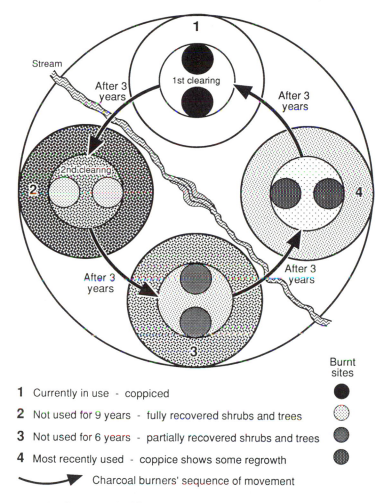

Figure 7.3 The ecological impact of a twelve-year charcoal-burning cycle in a valley.

The impact is not limited to the charcoal-burners' clearing, itself a relatively small area. Immediately after use (site 4) the soil at the site of each burning is darkest, while the vegetation cover, both within the clearing and throughout the coppiced zone, is at its scantiest. The sloping land will remain exposed to soil erosion for several years and, depending on local relief, even areas outside the coppiced zones may be affected by accelerated run-off or down-washed soil. The total area subject to regular disturbance, albeit over an extended period, includes not only the four operative 'cells' but land between them and well beyond them.

order to perpetuate fuel supplies.[1] Notwithstanding such management, though, there is no way vegetation can remain intact. The consequences of charcoal-burning, as outlined for the humid zone of Languedoc, France, may be suggestive (fig. 7.3; Blondel 1941). Trees are felled to make a clearing, two or three burning sites are prepared (sloping land is levelled, disturbing soil and bedrock) before being used for twenty-four hours or longer at a time. The soil beneath, subjected to continuous and intense heat, is sterilized and calcinated; its crumb structure and its organic, and bacterial content are destroyed. What remains is a disturbed, burnt soil containing a good deal of charcoal, whose dark colour greatly exaggerates daytime temperatures. Few species can colonize bare ground under such circumstances. It could take an abandoned site thirty years (so the argument runs) before the

---

Figure 7.4 Where was the 'wilderness'?

The landscape of almost any region in peninsular Italy must have been marked long before Roman times by the more or less successive generations of its prehistoric inhabitants. It is hard to believe that, in such a 'high-risk' environment, neolithic and bronze age settlement had only a negligible or short-term impact. Vegetation needs time to recover in the absence of human or human-induced interference (how much time depends on local climate, relief and geology, soil conditions, vegetation species, etc.), and the effects of human activity around any settlement site will have remained long after its exploited territory was completely abandoned. As demonstrated in the text, some effects of human land use (direct or indirect) are permanent, in which case the environment, once touched by man, never returns to its primeval state.

  Given a certain density and/or longevity of human occupation in any one region (and there are many such regions in peninsular Italy), it may be that there never was an 'Eden' in Italy, only different types of wilderness. In this map, inspired by Potter's remark (1979, 28) that each 'territory ... cannot have been very large ... the main limit is a radius of 5 km of exploited territory', allowance has been made for a zone of disturbance around each 'modest' exploited territory, doubling its area and showing how up to 300 sq km of this part of central Italy (38 per cent) could have been 'affected' by the combined long-term effects of neolithic and bronze age settlement. (Unrealistically, but to underscore the general thesis, it has been assumed that most of these sites – the only ones known to archaeologists – were occupied more or less simultaneously in each period.)

---

[1] For the practice in Roman times, see Cato, *RR* 28. 1; 33. 5; Columella, *RR* 4. 33; Pliny, *HN* 17. 147–9; and Meiggs 1982, 267–9.

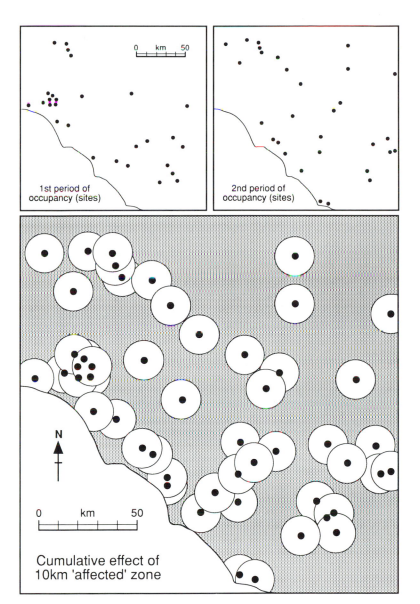

1st period of occupancy (sites)

2nd period of occupancy (sites)

Cumulative effect of 10km 'affected' zone

burnt patch is covered by the taller shrubs. Meanwhile, in a high-risk area, heavy rainfall falls on unprotected ground, scouring the soil on sloping ground and washing it down-slope in the early stages of erosion.

The vegetation mosaic before Rome

Archaeological maps of settlement distribution can tell us much more than just where the 'sites' are. They can be read as summaries of a whole complex of ecological consequences, dynamic and largely predictable. Taking each point as representing a vortex of social and economic activities, it is readily apparent how the cumulative effects of that activity over time can lead to more or less permanent environmental changes (fig. 7.4). For instance, the practice among mesolithic hunters in England of using fire to control the grazing of wild animals as a hunting strategy is held to account for a permanently 'unnaturally' low tree line (Simmons 1975). The bare mountain-tops of so much of the Italian Apennines today may have been equally characteristic of the prehistoric landscape, according to the chronology and scale of human or human-induced activity in the district (see Cruise 1991, and other essays in Maggi *et al.* eds 1991). Once such exposed terrain, with its shallow or regolithic soils, was deforested, vegetation recovery would have been difficult, especially on north-facing slopes and after the end of the thermal optimum. It may be objected that a mountain-top is a special case, an extreme environment where the thresholds of plant tolerance are set by a short growing season due to low temperatures. My concern here is to suggest that there are many quite different types of marginal or 'high-risk' regions around the Mediterranean, and that generalities about deforestation in these lands may need to be more explicitly related to the specific local or regional circumstances on which they are based.

In the case of the Tavoliere of Apulia, for instance, the problem of marginality stems not from low thermal conditions but – especially after the climatic optimum – from aridity.[1] While the climate remained relatively moist, gaining in warmth, and while – above

---

[1] The region lies closer to the subarid/arid border than any other part of Italy except Taranto.

all – the level of population was low (as in the early neolithic), plant growth and vegetation regeneration (of the pine or hazel woods) was assured. Once, however, the number of occupation sites increased, as in the middle neolithic, processes were set in train from which spontaneous vegetation regeneration became increasingly difficult, even before the thermal downturn that marked the end of the 'optimum'. The key factor in the case of the Tavoliere was the calcrete lying below a soil cover that was probably, even then, fairly shallow. Warm rain falling directly on to exposed calcrete sets up a chemical reaction which crystallizes and transforms the upper part of the otherwise friable calcrete into a rock-hard carapace (Duchaufour 1965, 247). Only when this rocky stratum, most common in the central part of the Tavoliere, has been broken can deep-rooted plants prosper; hence the practice of digging olive-pits and vine trenches through the carapace or, in the last few years, of ripping it up altogether (to the great detriment and often total loss of archaeological sites).[1] Otherwise the rocky surface of the calcrete forms an impervious layer, exposed whenever the shallow soil above is scoured by heavy rains.

Population pressure on the vegetation of the Tavoliere during the moist, warm conditions of the middle neolithic cannot but have led to the exposure and transformation of the calcrete, especially in the most densely occupied parts of the plain. Once the equable rainfall regime of the 'climatic optimum' gave way to the marked seasonality characteristic of recent times, the ecological handicap of general aridity and prolonged summer drought could only make matters very much worse, hindering if not checking entirely the regeneration of the mixed deciduous woodland. Thus, already by the latter part of the middle neolithic, a vegetation increasingly composed of drought-tolerant species would have begun to replace those of the deciduous woodland, its more open nature and low status affording ineffective protection from soil erosion.[2] Without the nursery conditions formerly provided by the

---

[1] Up to the 1970s, olives and other tree crops were planted in pits, and vines in trenches, that were akin to those of medieval or Roman date seen so clearly on air photographs.
[2] See Delano Smith 1983, esp. 18–21, where I speculate on the effect of deforestation at the middle neolithic site of Passo di Corvo. (The relevant diagram, p. 20 fig. 7, is incorrectly titled and lacks the key; it is reproduced in Delano Smith, forthcoming.)

undergrowth of the climax association, seedlings and saplings of the dominant species failed to reach maturity.

Conclusion

A region's landscape reflects the essentially episodic nature of both human activity and geomorphological processes over time and space. The vegetation mosaic is a record of its own evolution. Looking at the varied landscapes of Italy today with each region's prehistoric record in mind, all sorts of questions are prompted. Once damaged, did the post-glacial climax woodland ever completely regain its 'primeval' status, either on the Apennine mountain-tops or on the plains of northern Apulia? Indeed, was there ever an extensive 'primeval' deciduous forest associated with the thermal optimum in those regions of particularly early settled agriculture? It may be that not until all the regions of Italy have been examined on their own terms in the light of the Tavoliere's experience will we arrive at a less naïve representation of the prehistoric and protohistoric landscapes of Italy. Other regions have their own combinations of carefully balanced environmental factors. In the Polesine (Ferrara) district of the Po plain, for instance, where settlement chronology is the opposite of that on the Tavoliere (sparse in the neolithic, dense in the bronze age), the key marginal factor is a periodic *excess* of water from river flood or from a high water table. Nevertheless, the twin notions of an environment at risk and of potentially damaging chronological coincidences (as reflected in the comparative graph of human settlement and land use, climatic, and vegetational history) still apply and are well worth exploring.

So where was the 'wilderness' in Roman Italy? Obviously it depends on the region in question; but provocatively I would suggest it was virtually nowhere – if by 'wilderness' is meant primeval as opposed to ancient wood.[1] It seems to me that relatively few of the Roman inhabitants of the 'old' regions of lowland or hill Italy would have encountered true wildwood, a 'wholly

---

[1] The use of terms is ambiguous. Wildwood (= 'primeval') can be distinguished from ancient wood (to which much may have happened). See Rackham 1986, 64 ff.

natural woodland unaffected by Neolithic or later civilization' (Rackham 1986, 443),[1] four or five thousand years after its establishment. Far more common would have been the xerophilous forest (the open holm-oak forest), with its various low-status associations of the modern 'Mediterranean' vegetation that replaced the mixed deciduous oakwood of the 'optimal' climatic phase. An older generation of French botanists gave a classical term to the maquis and garrigue that would have been so common in much of classical Italy (as the contemporary literature testifies), namely *saltus*. For the vast majority of Romans in Italy, the uncultivated *saltus* (as opposed to *silva*) would have offered a quite sufficiently 'wild' landscape to constitute a wilderness. Recovery to woodland status at the end of antiquity, and the nature of the secondary forests of lowland Italy in the early middle ages, however, are another matter.

Bibliography

Attenborough, D. (1987), *The First Eden: The Mediterranean World and Man* (London).

Blondel, R. (1941), 'La végétation forestière de la région de St.-Paul, près de Montpellier', *Mémoire de la Société Vaudoise des Sciences Naturelles*, no. 46, vol. 6.7: 309–82.

Bradford, J. (1949), ' "Buried landscapes" in southern Italy', *Antiquity*, 23 (June): 58–72.

Brunsden, D., and Thornes, J. B. (1979), 'Landscape sensitivity and change', *Transactions of the Institute of British Geographers*, 4: 463–84.

Cruise, G. M. (1991), 'Environmental change and human impact in the upper mountain zone of the Ligurian Apennines: the last 5,000 years', in Maggi *et al.* (eds), 175–95.

Deecke, W. (1899), *Italy* (English edn, 1904; London and New York).

Delano Smith, C. (1972), 'Late neolithic settlement, land use and garrigue in the Montpellier region, France', *Man*, 7: 397–407.

—— (1975), 'Villages désertés dans les Pouilles: le Tavolière', *I paesaggi rurali europei (atti del convegno internazionale, Perugia, 1973)* (Perugia, Diputazione di Storia Patria per l'Umbria), 123–38.

—— (1978), *Daunia Vetus: vita e mutamenti sulle coste del Tavoliere* (Foggia).

—— (1979), *Western Mediterranean Europe: A Historical Geography of Italy, Spain and Southern France since the Neolithic* (London).

—— (1981a), 'Climate or man? The evidence of sediments and early maps

---

[1] Rackham dates the last wildwood in Britain to *c.*4500 BC (1986, xiv).

for the agents of environmental change in the post-medieval period', in Delano Smith and Parry (eds), 88–105.

—— (1981b), 'Valley changes: some observations from recent field and archive work in Italy', in G. Barker and R. Hodges (eds), *Archaeology and Italian Society: Prehistoric, Roman and Medieval Studies* (BAR Int. Ser. 102; Oxford), 239–47.

—— (1983), 'L'ambiente', in Tinè (ed.), 11–21.

—— (1987), 'The neolithic landscape of the Tavoliere, Apulia', in Jones (ed.), 1–26.

—— (forthcoming), 'Consequences of deforestation in a Mediterranean country: Italy', in Thornes (ed.), ch. 10.

—— and Parry, M. J. (eds 1981), *Consequences of Climatic Change* (Nottingham).

—— and Smith, C. A. (1973), 'The bronze age on the Tavoliere, Italy', *Proceedings of the Prehistoric Society*, 39: 454–6.

di Biase, P. (1985), *Puglia medievale e insediamenti scomparsi: la vicenda di Salpi* (Trinitapoli).

Duchaufour, P. (1965), *Précis de pédologie* (Paris).

Farrow, E. P. (1917), 'General effects of rabbits in the vegetation', *Journal of Ecology*, 4: 57–64.

Goudie, A. (1981), *The Human Impact on the Natural Environment* (Oxford).

Jones, G. D. B. (ed. 1987), *Apulia, i: The Neolithic Settlement in the Tavoliere* (Society of Antiquaries Research Report, 44; London).

Lamb, H. H. (1982), *Climate, History and the Modern World* (London and New York).

McNeill, J. R. (1992), *The Mountains of the Mediterranean World: An Environmental History* (Cambridge).

Maggi, R., Nisbett, R., and Barker, G. (eds 1991), *Archeologia della pastorizia nell'Europa meridionale (atti della tavola rotonda internazionale, Chiavari, 22–24 settembre 1989)* (Rivista di studi liguri, 57 (2); Bordighera).

Meiggs, R. (1982), *Trees and Timber in the Ancient Mediterranean World* (Oxford).

Miller, A. A. (1953), *Climatology* (London).

Nash, R. (1981), *Wilderness and the American Mind*, 3rd edn (New Haven and London).

Potter, T. W. (1979), *The Changing Landscape of South Etruria* (London).

Puglisi, S. (1967), 'Criteri per il riordino dei boschi nella provincia di Potenza', *Monte e boschi*, 18 (5): 11–23.

Rackham, O. (1986), *The History of the Countryside* (London).

Roberts, B. K. (1977), *Rural Settlement in Britain* (Folkestone).

Semple, E. C. (1932), *The Geography of the Mediterranean Region and its Relation to Ancient History* (London).

Simmons, I. G. (1975), 'Towards an ecology of mesolithic man in the uplands of Great Britain', *Journal of Archaeological Science*, 2: 1–15.

Simone, L. (1977–82), 'Il villaggio neolitico della villa comunale di Foggia', *Origini: preistoria e protostoria delle civiltà antiche*, 9: 129–81.

Tansley, A. G. (1953), *The British Isles and their Vegetation*, i–ii (Cambridge).

Thornes, J. B. (ed., forthcoming), *Deforestation in the Mediterranean* (London).

Tinè, S. (ed. 1983), *Passo di corvo e la civiltà neolitica del Tavoliere* (Genoa).

Tooley, M. J. (1978), *Sea-level Changes in North-western England during the Flandrian Stage* (Oxford).

Toynbee, A. J. (1965), *Hannibal's Legacy: The Hannibalic War's Effects on Roman Life*, i–ii (London).

Vita-Finzi, C. (1969), *The Mediterranean Valleys: Geological Changes in Historical Time* (Cambridge).

Ward-Perkins, B., Mills, N., Gadd, D., and Delano Smith, C. (1986), 'Luni and the Ager Lunensis: the rise and fall of a Roman town and its territory', *PBSR* 54 (n.s. 41): 81–146.

Whitehouse, R. D. (1984), 'Social organisation in the neolithic of south-east Italy', in W. H. Waldren, R. Chapman, J. Lewthwaite, and R.-C. Kennard (eds 1984), *The Deya Conference: Early Settlement in the Western Mediterranean Islands and the Peripheral Areas* (BAR Int. Ser. 229), 1109–136.

—— (1986), 'Siticulosa Apulia revisited', *Antiquity*, 60: 36–44.

8

Rome and the management of water: environment, culture and power[1]

Nicholas Purcell

The Romans' reputation for hydraulic engineering and the place of the control of water in their culture are indices of the dependence of the power élite on intensification of primary production in the most favoured environmental niches.

When is geomorphology not geomorphology?

Answer: when it is mythical. Land-forms are as much part of the *mythos* of self-construction and self-explanation as are ancestors. Rome was founded by a shepherd, the son of a god, a twin returned from a malign fate; it was also founded in a wilderness, and the wilderness was *wet*.

It is obviously misleading to translate the terminology of the Hippocratic corpus into the language of modern medicine. It is equally unhelpful, if we are to understand the conceptual geography of the ancient world, to superimpose on the landscape the argot of modern scientific landscape description and its implications. The temptation is always intense where contemporary technical terms are actually derived from ancient words; but it must be resisted. Ancient rivers dive underground to re-emerge on the other side of the sea; that the geomorphologist's rivers do

---

[1] My thanks to the audience at Nottingham, and to the editors.

not do this is irrelevant to our assessment of ancient ideas about rivers.

The geomorphologist's wetland is very wet; it has to be, to have survived to the 1990s for description and analysis. Exposure to sea-water or river-flooding, sufficiently frequently for saturation, waterlogging, to occur for a substantial part of an average year, is usually part of the definition. For an understanding of ancient cultural responses, we shall need somewhat different criteria.

The Greeks and Romans did not set about classifying land-forms. They used a great variety of labels for environmental phenomena that were of interest to them, but they foreshadowed very modern approaches in being interested especially in process and dynamic change, and in those phenomena in particular with which human behaviour interacted, and especially those where the processual dynamism itself was directly attributable to human activity. The legacy of descriptive geomorphology, on the other hand, at least in the hands of amateurs, does justice neither to those land-forms in the Mediterranean climatic zone that experience radical mutation according to the distribution of the very variable precipitation characteristic of the zone, nor to the complexity of human responses to, and anthropogenic modification of, the processes by which they change.

Thus even the great expert on ancient wetlands, Giusto Traina, who has done more than anyone else in recent years to illustrate the importance and complexity of ancient attitudes to wetland environments, has been seduced by geomorphological orthodoxy into adopting an insufficiently ambitious standpoint. His subtle analyses take for granted the uncomplicated existence, behind ancient notices of the Greek terms *helos* and *leimôn*, or the Latin *palus* and *pratum*, of wetlands in the modern geographical sense (see now Traina 1990, with earlier bibliography of which the most important is Traina 1988).[1] These concepts are, however, so different from ours in boundaries and definition that we might not recognize the original referred to by the sources if we found

[1]   cf. also Traina 1983, 21: 'il problema archeologico delle Valli grande Veronesi consiste proprio nel ricercare l'interdipendenza fra gli stimoli esercitati dall'ambiente a gli stimoli forniti dai modelli culturali, e le loro conseguenze sul rapporto fra l'uomo e il territorio.' But there is a symbiotic union of humanity and territory which is obscured by the dichotomy Traina sets out to bridge.

ourselves in it. The response of the Romans to so important an environmental a resource as the wetland cannot be understood within our geomorphological categories. Worse, a static and classificatory approach misses the opportunity to engage with the important fact that the ancient writers themselves are aware of the mutability of these environments and of the ever-shifting patterns of human relation to them. In the case of the wetland we have the chance to see at work attitudes to the control of water in the environment which, taken as a whole, form a theme in Roman self-awareness; that is my excuse for using wetlands as the way in to a much wider-ranging discussion extending to lakes, springs, and even to some extent the sea, but most of all to rivers.

This discussion will be ecological in the simple sense that it will be concerned with the distinctive ways in which the Romans conceptualized the world around them and their interaction with it; and in the more intricate sense that this interaction may, perhaps, be seen as a more complicated element in Roman history than in a simple and static picture of environmental constraints as a backdrop to events and secular developments.

Our world is docketed by science: we only feel at home when we have classified things in a terminology that binds the object into the explanatory system that guarantees the order of the whole natural world – an explanatory system, of course, that revolves round human observation. In the undoubted absence of any such all-embracing exegetic system in antiquity, what logic did the Greeks and Romans bring to their relationship to the natural world?

(1) *Different theories of change.* In the first place, the dispositions of nature were not taken to be subject to change in the way that we are so familiar with in a post-Darwinian age. It is sometimes even asserted that, just as the historical imagination of the ancients found no problem in attributing identical reactions and responses to statesmen in the archaic Greek period and the Antonine age, so other sorts of change were not admitted either, to the detriment of technology and the concept of progress. This view (for which see e.g. Sallares 1991, 38) may be too extreme, but it is certainly the case that the *normality* of change, which forms so important a part of our view of these things, is not a feature of ancient thought (see also Trautmann 1992).

(2) *Different views of the role of humanity*. Second, ancient definitions of environmental phenomena were no less anthropocentric than ours. When we talk of 'the environment', although the high-minded sense in which 'environment' is an ecological term for the location of the experience of any organism may feature to some extent, most people most of the time use the word to mean the human environment. In antiquity, too, types of environment are defined by the characteristic human response to them, above all in agricultural terms. Plough-land, vine-land, wetland, meadow, mountain pasture, forest, and so on are all terms of this sort. Rivers, lakes, pools, shoals, harbours, and the like are also primarily human-related in their purpose: the ancients did not bother to define oxbow lakes, moraines, deltas, or fault-lines.

(3) *A different relationship between people and nature*. Not very surprising, perhaps; but the lack of a separation between the domains of natural description and human experience, to which science has accustomed us, makes it possible for the two to cross-fertilize in the ancient world in ways that are unfamiliar to us. Residents of Leicester who regard themselves as dwellers in the clay vale that lies in front of an oölite scarp are probably untypical, but in antiquity learned perceptions of the nature of landscape were not disjoined from ordinary experience in this fashion; the geographical determinism that is so important a theme of Herodotos, with all its ramifications in later thought, is an important case in point. That, in turn, may give us a different perspective on the question of theorics of change.

The ancients did contemplate certain forms of mutability in the human domain, even if they were not changes in the moral or social bases of human experience, and we should expect there to be analogies between that recognition and their descriptions of the natural world. I shall be arguing that that is just what we do find. The greatest changes that ancient thought allowed in the human domain are changes in the fortunes of empires and the geography of power; and those changes are, likewise, the ones that ancient thought allowed in the domain of nature.

Campus 1: urbanizing the productive wetland

Rome, in Strabo's famous description, was the only city actually
sited on the Tiber. It paid the price in its vulnerability to floods
(5. 3. 7 (234)). The Augustan geographer also stresses a related
feature: Rome has two *pedia* (5. 3. 8 (236)). The Greek term
pedion, Latin *campus*, is a very complex term semantically, and
the *campi* of Rome have a very important place in the construction of the city's site as a part of its past. A *campus*, moreover,
is *wet*.

The principal *campus* is, of course, that famous place whose
name is often translated as 'the field of Mars'. 'Field' is a classic
example of the vague canonical translations that obscure ancient
semantic reality. *Campus*, like its late Greek derivative κάμπος,
is often used of valley-bottom land, and it is its level character
that is the principal definer; but land of this kind is usually also
well-watered, if there is any water to be had at all. Sure enough,
in the centre of the Campus Martius the Romans remembered a
swamp, the Palus Caprae, fed by a stream called Petronia.[1] Other
low-lying tracts formed expanses of *prata* or water-meadows, like
the Prata Flaminia on the curve of the Tiber below the Capitol,
or the Prata Quinctia of the opposite bank.

All these areas were the subject of revealing stories. They were,
most importantly, places of private estates that were now public.
The Campus Martius itself had been the *temenos* of the Tarquins,
though the stories disagreed about how that had come about.
When the kings were expelled, however, the grain (*far*: emmer,
Triticum dicoccum, which gave the story a properly archaic feel)
from their land was harvested by cutting away stalk and head
together and jettisoned in a symbolic gesture; it became the Tiber
island (Livy, 2. 5, *desectam cum stramento segetem*; Dionysios of
Halikarnassos, 5. 13).[2] The structural connection of land use and
landscape could hardly be clearer. There were variants: some held
that the Campus had always been dedicated to Mars, but that the
custom had grown up of assigning tiny lots of it to great men,

---

[1] Similar depressions on the other bank were called Codeta after the
horsetails that grew there; one formed the site of Julius Caesar's
Naumachia, just as the ornamental *stagnum* of Agrippa took the place
of the Palus Caprae. On this see now Muzzioli 1992, 189–208.
[2] For emmer as an evocation of a distant past see Spurr 1986, 11.

including the kings; whence the estate of the Tarquins (Servius on Virgil, *Aeneid*, 9. 272).[1] But the central ingredient is the explanation of the Roman institution of *ager publicus*, the state-owned land that was to make so striking a contribution to Roman history, and whose distinctiveness in ancient Mediterranean terms has recently been stressed. Here the aetiology works interestingly *e contrario*, explaining the common ownership as a reaction against the Homeric-style private lots (see Donlan 1989), in the best environmental niches, that were predicated of the Tarquins (on the importance of *ager publicus* see Cornell 1989, 327). The historical status of the Campus Martius guaranteed the tradition and the institution: the land itself was at that point consecrated to Mars and was not then encroached on until the time of Sulla (Orosius, 5. 18. 27; Livy, 4. 22. 7). Part of it became the Villa Publica (first constructed in 435 BC for the purposes of the census), which was by the second century anyway *publica* in a sense that was ideologically meaningful, since its restoration was paired with that of the Atrium Libertatis. Moreover, an early association between the place, the institution, and the military duties of the citizen is also clearly visible.

Alongside the Campus proper, however, lay the meadows. Functionally, their contribution had been the rearing and training of horses, a familiar use of ancient Mediterranean wetlands. Traditional festivals, and the location here of a racetrack (the Trigarium) and, until well into the imperial period, of the stables of the circus factions, were the monument of this memory (Dion. Hal. 5. 13. 2).[2] Their mythistory was still more complex. There was the Campus Tiberinus, gift to the Roman people of the Vestal Virgin Gaia Taracia, gratefully received to the extent that she was rewarded with cult alongside that of the river-god. Again, even if the lady is not to be identified – as there are some hints that she should be – with the Vestal Tarquinia, bringing us back into the nexus of royal grain stories, or with the infamous Tarpeia, eponym

---

[1] This seems likely to be aetiological of the practice of state burial, as practised in the late republic on the model of Athens: cf. Strabo, 5. 3. 8 (236), cited above; Purcell 1987. Though Horatius (of bridge fame) was given a lot of public corn-land as an honour, we are not specifically told that this was in the Campus Martius.

[2] Dionysios says the Campus was voted as exercise ground and ἵπποις λείμονα.

of the nearby crag, we are clearly seeing here some sort of evocation of the connection between the river and the meadow-lands (Pliny, *Historia naturalis*, 34. 25; Aulus Gellius, 7. 7. 4; Plutarch, *Poplicola* 8. 4). The property theme returns in the even stranger parallel tale of the prostitute Acca Larentia, who gave the Roman people four of the estates that she had acquired with her takings: the Ager Semurius, the Ager Lintirius, the Ager Solinius and – with more than a whiff of Gaia Taracia – the Ager Turax. The real existence of these obscure toponyms is established by a swipe in one of Cicero's *Philippics* (6. 14) against a plan to assign lots on the Ager Semurius to military tribunes: 'They are not yet allotting the Campus Martius', he says, conscious of the irony involved in the alienation of these particular tracts of public land with their ancient aetiologies.[1] These four estates are most probably to be sought in the various bends of the Tiber above and below Rome, in positions analogous to the Campus Martius itself.

Similar stories concerned the other bank. Here were the Prata Quinctia, four *iugera* said to have drawn their name from Cincinnatus, whose hut and tiny citizen lot had been here; in the imperial period, in a way that is all too reminiscent of modern urbanization, the developers called a new street in this area the Vicus Racilianus, after Cincinnatus' wife Racilia (Livy, 3. 26. 9).[2] The Prata Mucia were Scaevola's reward for his exploits in the war with Lars Porsenna (Livy, 2. 13).[3] Two further aetiologies, then: the modest expectations of the virtuous senator, and the soldier's reward in land.

Finally, the liminal nature of the site should be stressed. The alien territory of Etruria in Roman conceptions started directly on the other side of the river, and the river bank in both directions was the setting for important rituals that concerned the boundaries of space and time. North and south lay the shrines of the Dea Dia and of Anna Perenna, both reached by boat on the occasion of their highly popular festivals; in the centre of the bend of the river in the Campus Martius lay the strange sanctuary of

---

[1] The antiquarian account is already in Cato: Macrobius, 1. 10. 16.

[2] cf. *CIL* vi. 975, 'collegium iuvenum Racillanensium', *Rendiconti della Pontificia Accademia di Archeologia*, 4 (1925–6), 394–5. Here it is plausible to suggest an Augustan origin for the compital cult of the Lares of that *vicus*, with appropriate antiquarian trappings.

[3] Also Festus; Dion. Hal. 5. 35 (λείμονες Μούκιοι).

the Tarentum, central to the rites of the Saecular Games by which the diuturnity of Rome was guaranteed, and linked in story (if not in tectonic likelihood) to the world of the subterranean fires – a final ingredient in the bizarrerie of the landscape on Rome's doorstep (LaRocca 1984). That rite may have begun in the fourth century, a period of innovation in these ways of thinking to which I shall return.

The landscape in the immediate environs of Rome thus offered some unusual opportunities for the making of symbolic statements. These can be traced in the fragmentary record of the middle republic. The programme of the populist politician Gaius Flaminius in the late third century, though very hard to discern, clearly had a special importance. The building of the spectacularly straight course of the Via Flaminia direct from the Mulvian bridge to the Arx of the Capitol showed a nice sense of the possibilities of the landscape: it is hard not to connect it with the laying out of the quarter of the Circus Flaminius as a place for the preparation of triumphs. The relationship of this work to the name Prata Flaminia is not clear, but the whole constituted a highly significant intervention in the planning of the parts of the plain nearest to the city.

The *triumphatores* of the golden age of Roman imperialism chose this area as the setting for their *monumenta*, in preference to the suburb outside the Porta Capena which had been popular before, culminating in the monuments of Pompey (on the change see Purcell 1987). Caesar had the most spectacular plan: starting at the Pons Mulvius, like Flaminius, he intended to canalize the Tiber and to transfer the functions of the Campus Martius to the Campus Vaticanus on the other side, using the Campus Martius for his plan *de urbe augenda*, 'concerning the enlargement of the city' (Cicero, *Ad Atticum*, 13. 33a).[1] The plain was, despite the flood problem, the obvious direction for the expansion of the city, as happened in practice a century later when the space around the Augustan monuments filled up with the *insulae* that became the core of early medieval Rome (Quilici 1983).[2] A difficult passage in Strabo (5. 3. 8 (236)) comments on how the river, the

[1] No. 329 Shackleton Bailey; cf. *Att.* 13. 20 (no. 328 SB).
[2] cf. L. Quilici, *Notizie degli scavi*, 40–1 (1986–7) and 44 (1990), 175–416, for the S. Paolo alla Regola remains.

monuments, and the surrounding hills were conceived of by the Augustan period as forming a unified scenographic effect. This was achieved by the combination of the munificent projects of Augustus and his family with the private but lavish architecture of villas and *horti* ('suburban estates'), as the super-rich of the late republic attempted to make the Tiber rival the splendours of the Nile.

Caesar's plan was never fully carried out, despite having caused planning blight while the dictator lived; but the development of the *campi* of the other bank did take place, though piecemeal, under the early emperors. Augustus' Naumachia and Nemus Caesarum in Transtiberim were projects of considerable importance, and were followed by the expansion of imperial facilities under Gaius and Nero in the Campus Vaticanus (for the name see Cic. *Att.* 13. 33. 4). Many of these plans, like Caesar's, involved direct manipulation of the water-channels and the creation of new conduits or pools, like the lake and Euripus with which Agrippa embellished his baths, where none had been before.[1] Embanking and bridging the river itself took pride of place: Agrippa completed his work with a bridge on which a device to measure the height of the Tiber floods recalled the Nilometers of Egypt. Fronto[2] quotes the rhetor Gallicanus' extravagant praise for a – presumably imperial – project for the embankment of the Tiber. It is unnecessary to set out the full details of this second phase of the monumentalization of the river and its flood-plain here; the point to establish is that the hearth and home of the Romans had the closest symbiosis with the river and its valley.[3]

The comparison of Tiber and Nile is highly significant. Pliny the Elder has an extraordinary passage on the Tiber that needs attention here:

> Below the Clanius of Arezzo it is increased by forty-two rivers. The two largest are the Nar and the Anio, the latter being navigable itself, and enclosing Latium from the rear. Nor should we omit, for that

---

[1]   Euripi also in the Circus: first in 58 BC according to Pliny, *HN* 8. 87.
[2]   *Ad Marcum Caesarem de orationibus* (p. 155 Naber), 11 (Loeb vol. ii, pp. 110–11); cf. LeGall 1953, 117–19.
[3]   *Pace* Traina 1988, 93, on the frequency of great cities in marshlands, it is worth stressing how singular was Rome's use of this sort of landscape.

matter, the waters accumulated from so many springs and brought down to the city of Rome. As a result it is accessible to ships of the largest size from the Italian sea, and is the tranquillest purveyor of the produce of the whole globe; and more than the rivers of all other lands put together is the setting and the embellishment of villas (*accolitur aspiciturque villis*). Nor is any other river allowed to get away with less, since it is embanked on both sides; and it bears this willingly, although prone to frequent and sudden swells. In fact, flooding is nowhere more common than in the city itself. No, it is thought of as a prophet rather than a warning, and its increase is seen as a matter of religious awe rather than danger.

(*HN* 3. 54–5)[1]

This typical Plinian set piece, with its convoluted negative comparisons, would have read hollowly enough to the inhabitants of one of the houses whose foundations had been eroded by the flooding of the low-lying parts of Rome; but it introduces an important theme. Roman attitudes to water concern the power of water in the landscape in general. That power is at once visual and economic, as in Pliny's remarks about the villas of the Tiber banks, and a sign of the forces of nature that humanity shows its excellence in controlling. It is also a power that transcends locality, making great rivers comparable with one another but also bringing into play in the capital forces which emanate from quite outside its region.

To sum up: Rome was a good city in a difficult place. The Romans constructed their place in the world through a picture of their relationship to the environment that involved constant struggle against very considerable odds. This can be seen in the pastoral tradition of the foundation, in the exaggeration of the wooded wilderness where the city later arose, and in the persistent harping on the relative unproductiveness of the soil in the area; but most of all in the Tiber, their blessing and their curse, ambiguous from mouth to source. These are all facets of the tradition that are more or less well known; my purpose is to show what an important place water has in that phenomenon.

[1] cf. LeGall 1953, 42–3, on the Tiber and the unique site of Rome.

Campus 2: exploiting a marginal resource

Another vital part of the nexus of watery associations out of which
Rome was constructed lies down the river, behind the coast: the
Campus Salinarum Ostiensium (Lanciani 1888; Giovannini 1985).
The Tiber tied this Campus closely to the city: as important as
any road, it featured in the picture the Romans of the Augustan
age formed of the circumstances of the early city, and for Dionysios of Halicarnassus (3. 44. 1) the fortification of the Janiculum
was designed to protect traders sailing down the Tiber from the
raids of Etruscan bandits. The meadows and marshes of this
Campus were less tightly sealed from the Tyrrhenian by chains of
coastal dunes than their more recent counterparts, and punctu-
ated by lagoons and channels other than the main course of the
Tiber, whose mouth was then more obviously deltaic in character
(as the plural *ostia* suggests); the zone (like other Mediterranean
wetlands) offered easy communications around the area. There
was an interesting and curious symbiosis between the city and the
marshes which went beyond the functional connection provided
by the river route: it was symbolized in the use of the latter as
the appropriate repository for the *disiecta membra* of the former
– in the aftermath of the Great Fire the rubble of the burned
buildings was taken to the Ostian marshes (it is important to see
this as more than simply thrifty utilitarianism), and the ruins of
the Capitolium were likewise deposited in marshland by order of
the haruspices after its destruction in the civil war (Tacitus, *Annals*,
15. 43. 4; *Histories*, 4. 53. 2; see Traina 1990, 43, for the significance of these acts). In the once marshy Velabrum below the
Capitoline hill, the first harbour district of Rome itself formed a
kind of extension of this region towards the city, from which port
facilities expanded down the river-banks; this was the location of
the urban salt-warehouses, *salinae*, oddly known by the same name
as the salt-pans of the coastal wetland that gave its name to the
Ostian Campus (Livy, 24. 47. 15; Frontinus, *On Aqueducts*, 1. 5).

The saltworks were located in the shallows of the landward
edge of the marshes, where the water could be easily ponded
and exposed to evaporation in the summer heat. Their importance
to the Roman economy by the third century BC was considerable: production has recently been estimated as 20,000 tonnes
per annum, which at contemporary prices would have been of

equivalent market value to annual grain rations for 30,000–40,000 people (Giovannini 1985). The great contribution of salt is to render perishable products more durable, giving it an important symbiotic role with all kinds of animal husbandry, for which wetlands were also important in other ways. They are an excellent example of the multiple usefulness of landscapes that at first sight appear marginal. But one of the most interesting features is the emphasis they receive in the antiquarian and historical tradition.

Taken from Veii by Romulus in one version, they were more generally ascribed to King Ancus Marcius, who is also said to have founded the *colonia* at Ostia and to have distributed a *congiarium* ('handout') of six *modii* of salt to the *plebs* (Dion. Hal. 2. 55; Pliny, *HN* 31. 89). The Tiber route was reinforced by the land route leading inland along the valleys of the Fosso Galeria and Tiber, in the latter case eventually becoming what the Romans knew as the Via Salaria. Pliny the Elder, our source for the salty associations of the king, also tells us of the antiquity of the Via Salaria, and of the early payments in kind to soldiers from which the term *salarium* derived. The stories are aetiological, like those we met in the Campi of the immediate vicinity of the city: they postulate wide links for the early city across the landscape of a dimly imagined protohistorical world; they are not particularly likely to be historically accurate, though the salt story has a certain plausibility, but they are very revealing about historical attitudes to the environment.[1]

The phenomena of which these stories assert the primordial origin are a striking parallel for the institutions of allotment and public ownership, the fiscal system whose developed state we see in Cicero's summary of the interests threatened by Mithridates: 'those very large households of slaves which they [the *publicani*] keep in the salt-pans, in the estates, in the harbours and the prisons' (*De lege Manilia*, 16).[2] Various accounts have been given of the origin of this fiscal system. The problems of military supply in the Punic wars no doubt promoted new attitudes to fiscality

---

[1] On the early landscape of the Tiber mouth see Purcell, forthcoming; also Fischer-Hansen 1990; Segre 1990.

[2] 'cum publicani familias maximas quas in salinis, quas in agris, quas in portibus atque in custodiis magno periculo se habere arbitrantur'.

and logistics, and many of the best new opportunities were consequences of penal measures taken against the disloyal; the Sila forest is a prominent case.[1] A tradition assigns Phoenician origins to some of these practices, and it has been suggested that – especially in Spain – the victorious Romans were able to adapt many of the more lucrative practices of their enemies in landscape exploitation (Kolendo 1970). But there are older precedents else-where: Alexander, for instance, had assigned wetlands to his father's foundation of Philippi (*SEG* xxxiv. 664b of 335 BC).[2] And we should perhaps take more seriously the Romans' own percep-tion of the antiquity of their own opportunistic exploitation of the wetlands at the Tiber mouth.

It is striking that when, in the first half of the second century, we begin to hear much more about the exploitation of the resources of the Roman people and the letting of public contracts, the locations of which we hear are very reminiscent of the Tiber valley environments. Campania had a special place. Control of the exceptional fertility of the Ager Campanus and adjoining tracts was the most obvious feature, though there are problems concerning the piecemeal and gradual nature of Roman policy in this regard. But the other parts of the productive environment were not neglected: the contract for the fishing of Lake Profit, which was let first by the censors because of the good omen, is symbolic (this area not available before Hannibal), as is the subse-quent intensification of the profit that was to be had by the addition of the famous oysters to the already lucrative lagunar fisheries of the lake (Festus, 108 L).[3] The extraction of salt and pitch at Minturnae, another coastal site where the life of luxury, of trade, and of state enterprise overlapped, may be cited as a parallel (see *AE* 1934, no. 254, for the *salinatores* there). An attitude towards the productive landscape as a whole is to be discerned here, which took the form also of a conscious partitioning of the territory, first by denying the remaining inhabitants access to the sea, next by

---

[1] See Livy, 28. 45. 13–21, on fir from public forests (205 BC). For confis-cation of Sila cf. Meiggs 1982, 462–6.

[2] cf. Philip's drainage projects in this area, which were noted for having changed the climate: Theophrastos, *History of Plants*, 5. 14. 6; Pliny, *HN* 17. 30.

[3] 'lacus Lucrinus in vectigalibus publicis primus locatur fruendus, ominis boni gratia'.

the foundation of coastal colonies which in two cases bore the names of the rivers that gave access to the interior through the coastal marshes and their forests, and finally through the assignation of large tracts in a centuriation scheme (see Frederiksen 1984, 264–75, for the details). The extension of the structures of exploitation to the provinces is a phenomenon to which I shall return, but we may note here in passing the vigour with which the saltworks of Asia were managed.[1]

We cannot help noticing that there are some important precedents. The mythistory or history of the Tiber Campi, Ancus or Gaius Flaminius, provides one set; the dimly visible activities of Manius Curius Dentatus in the third century in the notable wetland environment of Rosea, the central lowland of Sabinum, are another (Coccia and Mattingly 1992). But the most interesting precursor for the policy of conceptualizing, dividing, and managing landscape is the tribal territories of Rome in the fourth century BC, which we may take as a prototype for a cultural attitude to the environment subsequently to be seen in all Roman urban and landscape policy.

The wetland and the Roman town

The control of water became a routine part of the administrative repertoire of the Roman town. Juvenal imagined the acquisitive, opportunistic entrepreneurs of the corrupt city taking on the drying out of areas stricken with flood-water, one of the typical mundane contracts that symbolize urban squalor and demeaning greed (*Satires*, 3. 32), alongside the building of culverts and harbours, funerals, and the sale of slaves. His negative tone at once gives the lie to the image of the Romans with which we have become so familiar since the nineteenth century: precociously civilized in their ability to administration and engineering, and possessed of a unique utilitarian genius.

The consequences of the characteristic hydrological problems of the Mediterranean needed to be faced in any built environment. The winter rain and its run-off are terribly damaging: if the site has high relief the potential for erosion is great; if it is low-

---

[1] Cic. *Leg. Man.* 16, cited above; Hiller 1906, no. 111. 135; no. 117. 48.

lying the problem is flooding and the resulting structural and sanitary problems. But the winter rainfall is often required for summer use and retained through the architecture of the cistern.[1] Much of the architecture of Mediterranean towns that had become standard by the Roman period served to meet these problems. The *cloacae* that were the glory of Rome and a common feature of Roman city foundations were not primarily designed for sanitation: they were culverts for ground-water or storm drains (see especially Pliny, *HN* 36. 104–8; Strab. 5. 3. 8 (235); Dion. Hal. 3. 67. 5). Their theory is as potent as that of the nineteenth-century sewer movement which sanitized the cities of the first world (Goubert 1986), but quite different in quality: they stood for the removal of the city from the free-draining heights to the fertile but more inundatable lowland. The ordinariness of aqueducts has a similar nuance, reflecting the standard equipping of a town with the spring-water of the mountains which it has lost through its transference to the plain.[2] The ecological structure that tied Hellenic urbanism to the hydrology of limestone landscapes, in which the catchment of suitable water resources for maintaining a large nucleated population through the year was ensured by the local lithology, has recently been brilliantly elucidated; the Roman city was shaped by the ecological givens, too, despite some architectural emancipation from the determinism of nature (Crouch 1993). The management of this supply is therefore, in imitation of the capital, a standard part of the essentially euergetistic 'administration' of the Roman town (Corbier 1984).[3]

The hydraulic achievements of Roman cities were routine consequences of a set of choices that were of vastly more importance to Romans than the show of technical expertise or bureaucratic acumen, both of which they regarded with some suspicion;

---

[1] Note in this context Fronto, *Ad Marcum Caesarem*, 1. 3 (5 Naber) contrasting the fruits of reason – pyramids, aqueducts, and cisterns (*receptacula*) – with their natural equivalents: mountains, streams, and springs.
[2] I hope to argue elsewhere that the process by which the availability of healing or sacred waters in the environment came to punctuate the space of Italy and the provincial empire with watering-places or 'spas' was related to this development.
[3] For the provision of artificial *campi*, imitating the architectural transformation of the Campi of the capital, see Devijver and van Wonterghem 1981.

control of water in the environment was an aspect of that wider mastery of productive nature which was on show wherever new settlements of Romans were made. The history of the republican land allotments and colonial foundations from the fourth century had made Roman cities *campus* cities, 'cities of the plain'. The arrangements we admire are mere adjuncts of a strategy that is far more impressive in its ambition – and its greed. As the myths of the early history of the Tiber flood-plain clearly stated, the purpose of making a wide lowland landscape – the recipient of the resources of all that lay around it, from mountain springs to coastal swamp – available to the new town, the new simulacrum of Rome, was the parcelling up of the environment and its assignation to the citizens for their profit.[1] Centuriation often, like the original takeover of the *temenos* (sacred enclosure) of the Tarquins, involved the extension of land at the disposal of the Roman people into areas that had been exploited differently before, and often involved drainage and reclamation works; hence the proud labelling of some of the first areas to receive the attention of the Roman *agrimensor* from the streams and marshes that had now been reduced to submission, like the tribes Oufentina or Pomptina.

The allotment and management of the land through centuriation was impressive in its demonstration of control over the landscape, but it had the effect of highlighting the marginal areas of forest or marsh which could not easily be parcelled up, and which were often assigned to the community itself on the same principle. The *subsiciva* of the centuriation projects should not be regarded as wastelands, as the controversies over their ownership in the early empire show.[2] They constituted an economic resource even if they were uncultivated, through the regimes of gathering, hunting, browsing, rough grazing, and fishing. But their true potential lay in the possibility of improvement. The allocation to the city of the wetland or flood-plain or forest was also an invitation to improve and to maximize the control of the domain of the Roman people, that collectivity of *coloniae* and *municipia*, over

---

[1] See Delano Smith 1986, 130–41, and ch. 7 in the present volume, for the extreme case of selection of a wetland site, the *colonia* of Luni.

[2] See esp. *CIL* ix. 5420 with Hyginus, *De generibus controversiarum*, 133. 9–13 Lachmann; Frontinus, *De controversiis*, 53–4.

the landscape, since the marginal lands could be used, if watery, for improved pasture or for market gardening or for wet vineyard. There are several notable instances of wetlands whose revenues, no doubt very considerable in some cases, were assigned to a nearby Roman community; the principle at work is the anchoring of a new Roman city in the productive landscape, in just the same way as the tradition described Rome itself. Wetlands were positive, an asset.[1]

In making the most of such assets, the resources of the benefactors of the community, from inside or out, could be expected to be mobilized. The founder or the patron might provide major works like an aqueduct, or an intervention like Hadrian's at Koroneia, but the citizens were expected to do likewise. 'All that you see, passer-by, around the spring, had been disgusting swamp and sluggish water' (it had, like the *subsiciva* in so many cases, been the source of many a legal wrangle). The equestrian owner – we are just outside the walls of Parma – left the 35 *iugera* of market gardens that were the result of this reclamation scheme to provide revenue for a festival in his honour.[2] The principle was rapidly extended to other communities under Roman guidance, in the style of the British élites in Tacitus' *Agricola*. Indeed, spectacular testimony to the normality of such interventions has come in the last few years from the coastal wetlands of even the most distant periphery of the empire: the remarkable discoveries at Wentlooge east of Cardiff (in the territory of either the cantonal capital of Venta or the legionary fortress whose name was taken from the river Isca) have started to reveal a *campus*, improved through the provision of a (probably extensive) network of ditches, whose pasture was deployed for a number of forms of animal-rearing, including that

---

[1] Nemausus: Pliny, *HN* 9. 29. Kalydon: Strabo, 10. 2. 21 (460). Ephesos: Strab. 14. 1. 26 (642). See Traina 1983, 92–5, for positive attitudes to *paludes*.

[2] *AE* 1960, no. 249, from *Notizie degli scavi*, 1957, 264–6; cf. Traina 1983, 123: 'C. Praeconius P. f. Ventilius Magnus eques Romanus hortulorum haec iugera xxxv ita ut reditus eorum in cenis ibe [*sic*] consumerentur sodalibus suis quique ab eis supstituerentur in perpetuom legavit. Livia Benigna cum eo est seu fuit eadem uxor et nutrix. haec quaecumque vides hospes vicinia fontis [ante]hac foeda palus tardaque lympha fuit [ ] magnus litis rixasque perossus [in]diciumque sibi [ ].'

of horses (Allen and Fulford 1986; Allen *et al.* 1994, esp. 206–10). The involvement of private resources in tandem with those of the community or outside benefactors is the place at which this part of the analysis abuts the next, the world of the élite villa. Villas, too, were about the opportunistic improvement of the landscape for profit.[1]

The villa system in Roman Italy can be seen as a cultural complex comparable in its importance and pervasiveness to the milieu of towns and governmental expectations that was our subject in the previous section. The problems of definition attendant upon attempts to define villas in simple economic or architectural terms may be bypassed by a more holistic examination of the cultural context of investment in rural estates (cf. Purcell 1995). My aim here is to show how both the economic and the cultural dimensions of the themes of water in the landscape and its management are, in fact, spectacularly reflected in Roman villa practice.

The Roman villa might stand in the heart of a well-drained, much-divided arable landscape, but the emphasis in its economic logic on the diversity of productive strategy made it adapted to settings that at first sight seem less favourable; once again we need to nuance our categories of land-form. In the *villa maritima*, for instance, the picturesque or romantic desolation of the seashore is only a limited part of the story. The coastal strip, especially where a sandy beach separates the sea from a coastal wetland, is a prime location for the varied and opportunistic exploitation of the environment. The *villae* of the coast of west-central Italy are not town houses transposed into the wilds for the sake of solitude, but centres for the management of the unique resources of the uncultivated environment, where the fowler, the hunter, and the fisherman reinforced the shepherd and the husbandman in doing the productive work.[2] The villa improved on and replicated the productive surroundings: the aviary was an advance on wild-fowling, the game reserve on the chase; the pools of the marshes

[1] Squatriti 1992, 5: 'Rather than a concern with health, a concern with agricultural productivity seems to be behind the Roman hatred of marshes.'

[2] cf. Varro, *De re rustica*, 3. 3. 4; Pliny the Younger, *Letters*, 2. 17. 28, for the normal expectations of the coastal proprietor. In Purcell 1995, I attempt to put this in a wider context.

were the model and the base for the practice of pisciculture for which the villa was famous. Carrying out the improvements gives the proprietor a range of opportunities for displaying technical virtuosity and power over nature, all in the interests of profit, with port facilities and with fishponds, culverts, sluices, and water-lifting arrangements.[1] *Pastio villatica*, that urbane oxymoron, was a gesture to the watery environment; but that also had its equivalents of more normal production. The best-watered and deepest alluvial soils lent themselves to the most prestigious forms of cereal cultivation, such as the intensive cultivation of *alica* (Spurr 1986, 12). Viticulture in one prestigious form was also characteristic of the wetland, as with the vulnerable coastal marshes where grew the grapes from which Caecuban wine was made.[2] Wetlands, when improved (with hard and conspicuous labour), yielded rich winter pasture for the villa.[3] Hence the agricultural appeal of inland wetlands like the basins of Reate or the Fucine lake. So Pliny's Tuscan villa enjoys water-meadows and access to the Tiber (*Letters*, 5. 6. 10–12, stressing access to the Tiber and emphasizing that the meadows have an abundance of water but no swamp); so Quintus Cicero is told that the builders of his new villa near Arpinum reckon that they can supply it with a decent acreage of irrigated meadow (Cicero, *Ad Quintum fratrem*, 3. 1 = no. 21 SB). The intensive exploitation of those parts of the dense kaleidoscope of Mediterranean microecologies that were best suited to such production was a basic strategy of élite power in the whole region. The association of the wetland with the special interests of the wealthy who could afford to exploit it, and in particular improve it, intensifying the management of the environment, is once again a very ancient tradition, going back to the holdings of the Homeric heroes but reflected in estate practice of the Mediterranean at many other epochs (Donlan 1989, 139–43).

The games villa owners played with underground conduits and fountains and ponds were not just whimsies, but allusions to the

---

[1] The examples are found together in a typical coastal location, where rocks abut a wetland coast, at the Portus Cosanus: McCann 1987.
[2] Tchernia 1986, s.v. 'Cécube'; Traina 1988, 83–4; 104. The tradition goes back to the Homeric vine-ground of *Odyssey*, 1. 193.
[3] See Gasperini 1989, 73–5, for improved *pratum* in a valley bottom near Falerii, in a rock-cut inscription.

control of water as it had gone on since Romulus built his city in the water-meadows. Rome was a place that had grown big on turning the unproductive bits of nature into wealth, and that was the pattern to be reduplicated in her cities and in every villa of a magnate with means enough to have a go. The villa is part of the landscape of production whose origins we traced in the early Roman tradition. It is a landscape categorized by the productive opportunities, the *campi* and the water sources. It was a distinctive feature of the Roman system that the property and political power of the élite formed an integrated – though not necessarily stable – system with the political rights and agricultural independence of the rest of the citizen community. Villa-centred improvements and centuriation schemes should be seen in tandem; for the villa landscape, although we see it at its clearest in the great complexes of the very rich, formed a continuum with the agricultural experience of the settler on a centuriated lot. Land division, in Roman practice, was founded on the systematic intensification of production, aimed at a market in widely distributed and relatively highly priced commodities, or at least at cash crops rather than a basically subsistence regime. Rome did not divide the Ager Falernus, reputedly the most productive terrain in Italy, to provide annual sustenance for a subsistence peasantry.

Nature as enemy: environmental improvement

A late third-century milestone from Spain records the repair of a road that had been notorious for its rocks and vulnerable to the incursions of river water: it had been levelled, the soil pacified, and the hostile river thoroughly tamed (*CIL* ii. 4911: *solo pacato et perdomito averso flumine*).[1] Narses, restoring the bridge where the Via Nomentana crossed the Anio, used language that blends with this confident pagan tradition the prophetic thunders of the Vulgate Isaiah (*CIL* vi. 1199). Rome staked its diuturnity and the image of its divinely sanctioned imperial destiny on the arts of

---

[1] Improved as *AE* 1960, no. 158: 'viam ad fa[ ] rupibus famosam iam fluvialibus aquis perviam [ ] complanari solo pacato et perdomito averso flumine inundatione solitis'.

environmental control that had been implicated in its experience
of nature from the first settlements on the Seven Hills, even in
an age when the nature of the sanctioning deities was changing
and the power itself was more precarious than ever. The fame of
the Roman boast of overcoming the limitations of nature was such
that it can be seen to have had a disastrous effect in providing
Rome's imperialistic heirs in the age of European colonialism
with a repertoire of attitudes which have been the source of environmental degradation worthy of the political oppression that
accompanied it, for instance in the central lake basin of Mexico
(Musset 1991). Our survey of the watery landscape of the neighbourhood of Rome itself has provided numerous examples of the
developed state of this cultural phenomenon, and it is worth
returning to the *regio Romana* to examine a further important
aspect of the relationship between water and power (for the theme
in general see Kleiner 1991).

We are all more or less familiar with the hydrological cycle;
but there are still important ambiguities as to the identity of the
waters at various points within it. Which bits are mine, in what
sense? Where did they come from and where do they go, and
at what point do they become alienated from me? Which bits
may I name? Such questions are culturally important and variable,
and it needs only a moment's reflection to perceive that we are
here in an area in which the views of the Greeks and Romans
are remote from the scientific consensus of today. It would be
interesting to reflect on the implications of the differences in
more detail, but here I have space only to stress that the idea of
mobility in water, the concept of some sort of a cycle, however
contrary to actuality, was a vital ingredient of the perception.
Water, that potent and vital element, was by definition a thing
from elsewhere, going elsewhere, of which your experience, unless
you took steps to prolong it, was a fleeting encounter with the
alien (on the ambiguities of water see Bruun 1992; Dunbabin
1989).

It has long been noted that the ancient toponymy of the site of
Rome is dominated by the names of springs and watercourses
(not to mention the flood-plain names already discussed): evocations of a pre-urban state, to be compared with the equally dense
tradition on the sacred groves and woods of the city, reflections
of that great explanatory force which, I have argued, the city's

environment possessed.[1] In the naming and claiming of its own groundwater Rome was hardly unique. In a similarly parochial spirit the first subdivisions of the *populus Romanus*, the tribes (*tribus*), were named after parts of the city; the other seventeen in existence before the fall of Veii drew their names from Roman *gentes* or from the names of communities subsumed into the Roman polity.[2]

In the early fourth century BC – if the date is credible – a revolution took place. In 387 four new *tribus* were all named after the hydrological landscape: the Aniensis after that principal affluent of the Tiber, the Anio (Aniene); the Sabatina after Lake Bracciano; and the other two, Stellatina and Tromentina, in the tradition of those mysterious *campi* and *agri*, after a Campus Stellatinus in the territory of Capena (therefore in the Tiber flood-plain) and an otherwise unknown Campus Tromentus (for which a similar interpretation seems likely). These names proclaim a transformation in cognitive geography, and a new approach to the incorporation of territory that was to remain familiar throughout the Roman period.[3] The Romans of the early fourth century here began to deploy a way of thinking about the world that was characteristic of the Greek 'colonies' (*apoikiai*), where river names were prominent ways of transferring the topography of home to the new setting overseas, as with Sybaris or Siris, both named after Achaean streams (Lepore 1977; see Coarelli 1988 for the Italian situation; also now Peretti 1994). In turn, this is probably to be seen against the background of the importance of rivers in the early geographic consciousness of Greek culture. It is already found in Hesiod; and in places like the Black Sea, where cities like Borysthenes, Tyras, and Tanaïs took their names from the rivers that provided their *raison d'être*, it seems to have been a natural and much-used way of

---

[1] The management of the water sources of the site is a further interesting subject, and one neglected because of the greater glamour of the aqueduct system. The mysterious *fontani* are relevant here.

[2] See Thomsen 1980, 128 ff., against the view that all the early tribes except Clustumina were named from *gentes*; probably rightly. The community names would be that one and Camilia, Galeria, Lemonia, Pollia, Pupinia, and Voltinia. Cf. Taylor 1960.

[3] Festus (464 L) is explicit that it is not after the hills, but after the lake, that the tribe is named.

making sense of an alien world. Developing the *mentalité* in their Italian and finally in their provincial practice, the Romans, one cannot but notice, were heavily involved in the process by which the name of a wetland at the mouth of the Kaÿstros (Caÿster) river was gradually extended until it became the name of a continent![1] We do not need to dwell on the importance of Padus, Rhenus, or Baetis to Roman administrative geography. Faced with the mysteries of the Celtic north-west, they regularly adopted the names of local rivers as the names of their bases or the cities that followed them; in this they were of course following their own domestic practice, and were also locating their remoter activities in a map of the world which, ever since the days of the Greeks overseas, had had a privileged place for rivers. The cartographic cachet you gained from reaching the Rhine, the Danube, or the Elbe was to be had in smaller doses when you were posted to Deva, Derventio, or Isca – even if your administrators' convenience meant there was a certain ambiguity as to which of the many homonyms was actually intended.[2] I have explored elsewhere some of the role of the significant river or confluence in guiding the pattern of roads and city foundations; here what we need to stress is the underlying reasons why the hydrological landscape lent itself to this geographical and administrative project (Purcell 1990).

Physical control of the natural watercourse, or, better, the artificial creation of one *ex novo*, was a natural adjunct of this conceptualization of space and its onomastics. In the same book as his remarks about salt, Pliny attributes the first plan for an Aqua Marcia to king Ancus Marcius (*HN* 31. 41). The grandeur of the aqueducts and their role in the landscape were tempting things to retroject to the age of origins from the fourth-century realities: the rest of the source tradition is clear that Rome's first aqueduct was the Aqua Appia at the end of the fourth century, which made a similar statement to the more famous Via Appia

---

[1] See Strabo, 14.1.45 (650), for the meadow Asios and the heroön of Kaÿstrios and Asios near the river mouth.
[2] Coles 1994 now provides some interesting thoughts on the environmental context of river onomastics in these areas, helping to close the circle we started with attention to the relationship between watercourses and whole geographical settings.

about the binding to Rome of its territory.[1] The name of the Aqua Anio, the monument of that other great conqueror, wetland drainer, land-divider, and road-builder Manius Curius Dentatus, reflects the closeness of the link between aqueduct and natural river (also apparent in the passages of Pliny and Fronto cited above, p. 188–9 and n. 1, p. 194 respectively). The Roman tradition of canal-building in hostile (in one sense or the other) environments – Marius and the Rhône, Drusus and the Rhine–Meuse, Trajan and the Danube – belongs in this context; but the modification of the waterways of Italy remained, as with Caesar's plans for the Tiber or Nero's for the ship-canal from Campania to Ostia, the acme of prestige.[2]

The cultural manipulation of the relationship with water which characterizes so much of the villa landscape manifested many of the same associations. Roman villas often displayed a keen sense of cultural topography. Choices of site and region were often informed by an awareness of the historical, religious, and legendary associations of a place. The falls of the Anio at Tibur were not just a beautiful place but offered a setting rich in cultural links concerning the mythical period of origins, the picturesque Republican past, and the grandeur of the present. The effect depended, as it did in a different way for the *hortus* estates of the inner suburbs, on maintaining the tension between the proximity of the city and remoteness from it. At places like Tusculum or Tivoli, though well out of Rome, you could still see the city in the distance, while the villas on the hills were in turn visible from the city (Häuber 1990; Purcell 1987).

To this rarefied landscape effect, water had a vital contribution to make: directly through the basic problem of conceptualizing a mobile element in a wide environment, and indirectly through the

---

[1] Serbat 1972 *ad loc.* (the Budé editor), on the basis of Frontinus, and on the argument that the link with Ancus is a piece of fiction on behalf of the *gens Marcia*, excises it from Pliny's text, quite gratuitously. It is poor method to believe in the salt trade of archaic Rome but to reject this testimony to what it was possible to believe.

[2] The display of the human resource through the control of labour for such projects was also important; as in the inscriptions of the project of Marcus Ulpius Traianus at Antioch, stressing the control of the Orontes (van Berchem 1983), or the embankments of the Adige (Keppie 1983, 199).

complex cultural and legendary associations connected with each watery land-form. Thus, at Tivoli, the aqueducts that carried the river of the waterfall provided a very strong sense of the intangible immediacy of the metropolis, an umbilical connectivity in illustration of which we may cite Nero's dangerous swim in the catchment of the Aqua Marcia, still further up the Anio valley. His very untypical piece of landscaping at Subiaco, with its dam and winding lake, emphasized the mountain setting in which invisible Rome was many landscape zones away; and yet this was the source of the water that kept his people healthy – and which proved a source of dangerous illness to the would-be master of all these environmental evocations (Tacitus, *Annals*, 14. 22). It must indeed have felt odd, as you filled your pitcher at the cool faucet in the Subura, to think that Caesar was frolicking in the pond at the other end.

Nowhere were such associations denser than in the Alban hills. The site of Alba, looking north across the Campagna to Rome, was central to the foundation cycle itself. The landscape was crowded with cultic and historical links, chief of which was the cult of Jupiter Latiaris, still celebrated annually at the Feriae Latinae. Beneath the Mons Albanus the landscape centred on the twin lakes of Nemi and Albano, especially the latter. The best of the villas were actually on the site of Alba Longa; the *nymphaea* on the waterfront carefully framed the view of the Mons Albanus.[1] The lake was not just a pretty place, however: it offered a set of statements about hydrological control which are most instructive for our theme. The great *emissarium*, built in a heavily rusticated display of solidity, is the key monument. *Emissaria* are found in other villa contexts, too, particularly in Campania, as at the villa complex of Pausilypon; they went with the impossibilist architecture of artificial landscape so beloved of very wealthy Romans, alongside waterworks of many other kinds. Here the *emissarium* had an important story to tell: the portentous connection between the letting out of the waters of the lake and the conquest of Veii. No story in early Roman history makes clearer – and in a fourth-century context, too – the closeness of the association of thought between hydraulic and political power.

---

[1] See Lavagne 1988, 385–6, on the 'Doric' *nymphaeum*; ibid., 589–94 on the 'Ninfeo Bergantino'.

The antecedents of the story, whether in the drainage heroes of the Greek poleis – Herakles, Danaos, Kadmos[1] – or in the architecture of the *cuniculus* on which agricultural intensification on the tufas of west-central Italy always depended, concern us less than the obvious progeny: the romance of drainage as represented by Curius Dentatus' project in the Reate basin; the work of Appius Claudius, Cornelius Cethegus, and their successors in the Pomptine marshes; and, above all, the epic saga of the Fucine lake.

In imperial projects of this sort, it is important to stress that what was achieved was not the wholesale transformation of modern *bonifica*, but a patchwork of various improvements, for different productive purposes and many different *possessores*, of complex environments (as stressed by the excellent account of Leveau 1993). The grandeur of the rhetoric of the conquest of nature was therefore inseparable from the long tradition of capital-intensive modification of the more manipulable bits of the Mediterranean landscape. The great works of the emperor Hadrian in the Kopaïs basin of Boiotia (Fossey 1979; Knauss 1987) are the direct heirs of the palace-sponsored drainage works of the Mycenaean period. This way of thinking was around at the time of the creation of the four landscape-named tribes in 387: in good time for the further development of the first roads, aqueducts, and land divisions later in the century, and at the same time as the deployment of the water of the Alban lake to irrigate the fertile plain below Aricia to the west. It was integral to the genesis of the whole phenomenon of Roman imperialism.

Empire versus nature: who won?

A soldier of the third cohort of the praetorian guard in the late second century AD, called Artemidoros, had an enemy. Before setting out, as he hoped, for his own homeland, the enemy cursed Artemidoros. In the course of a fairly comprehensive curse he included the place of their current abode, Rome and Italy: 'batten

---

[1] These may be connected with the real achievements of improved internal drainage in landlocked limestone basins that we associate with the Mycenaean period.

on the land of Ytaly' (*sic*), he adjures the infernal spirits, 'and silt up completely the *ostia* of the Romans'.[1]

The Romans had refined the rhetoric of control over the land-scape to express their power in the world, and it was inevitable that they should be vulnerable to attack on the same terms. Subversive texts, like the Apocalypse of St John, concerned themselves with the economic symbolism of Roman power, and it is interesting to see the repertoire including flood damage likewise; nor is it surprising to find that the difficulties of the Tiber delta were used in the same way.[2] The case is instructive: the antithetic structure is so universal an ancient habit of mind that these complementary pairs of commonplaces must always be assessed in tandem. It was natural for opponents of Rome to exploit the imperial rhetoric by invoking natural, and especially watery, disaster. The Romans themselves were capable of reversing the polarity of the rhetoric of environmental control, as we see in Tacitus' figure of Calgacus (*Agricola*, 31). Equally, they naturally came to express the political crises of late antiquity in the language of losing the battle against the wilderness. It is usually wiser, when faced with these antitheses, not to be predisposed to one pole rather than the other. We are used to discounting eulogies of the felicity of the dominion of Rome, like Cicero's in the *De natura deorum* (2. 99) or Tertullian's famous *ubique populus* passage; but the laments that are their counterpart may be equally factitious.[3] It would be incautious, for instance, to use the various testimonies to damage by flood and alluviation uncritically, as proof of the onset of a historically significant phase of malignant alluviation of

---

[1] Guarducci 1951: κατασχέτε τὴν Ὑταλικὴν γῆν, ἐχθεινοίετε τὰς Ῥωμαίων πύλασς (*sic*).

[2] For Sibylline oracles and texts such as the prophecy of Vegoia, see Heurgon 1959. *Dirae*, 76–8: 'praecipitent altis fumantes montibus imbres / et late teneant diffuso gurgite campos / qui dominis infesta minantes stagna relinquant' ('May frothing deluges of rain pour down from the mountains, take over the whole expanse of plain with spreading flood, and portend misfortune for the proprietor as they leave behind them lakes').

[3] Tert. *De testimonio animae*, 30. 4: 'omnia iam pervia, omnia nota, omnia negotiosa; solitudines famosas retro fundi amoenissimi oblitteraverunt, silvas arva domuerunt, fera pecore fugaverant; harenae seruntur, paludes eliquantur; tantae urbes quantae non casae quondam'. Note also the classic scepticism about the Antonine plague of Gilliam 1961.

the sort that used to be associated with Vita-Finzi's Younger Fill.[1] Accepting this inversion of an imperial rhetoric at face value has sometimes distorted pictures of the late antique collapse.[2] But this chapter has not argued that the rhetoric of environmental power is essentially a fantasy, to be discounted by the historian interested in a real world.

In the precarious climatic circumstances of the Mediterranean lands, the management of ambient water was essential for survival in each locality from day to day. Hydrological power-rhetoric was therefore deeply rooted in a microenvironmental context. In a response to the argument about the malign influence of ancient theory on the environmental policies of the Conquistadors in the basin of Mexico, it has rightly been stressed that there was a local logic to projects such as the drainage of the Fucine lake, and that the imperatives of opportunistic production, by that period for a relatively wide market, must be given their due weight in explaining the ideology of the project (Leveau 1993). It is my aim in this chapter, however, to have showed that there was no incompatibility between the most grandiose imperial applications of the language of control over nature and the theory of local environmental improvement for survival or profit; rather, there was the closest of links between the two. As it happens, a parallel may be drawn from another part of the New World.

What we can reconstruct of the *mentalités* of the Inca empire suggests a preoccupation with hydrological control which was expressed in cultural terms even more complex than those of the Roman tradition: eschatological, cosmogonical, and deeply ritualistic, they were also fascinatingly implicated in the formation of the cohesive structures that made possible the formation and maintenance of the Inca polity at its greatest extent. An analysis of the relationship puts it like this:

> aquatic dependency on an uncontrolled periphery made the regional politics of the Andes susceptible to, even complicit in, grandiose imperial projects like that of the Inca. In this way agrarian ritual helped

---

[1] See Vita-Finzi 1969; Bintliff 1992, with his earlier bibliography, but taking a somewhat more moderate position; cf. now Zangger 1992; 1993.
[2] See Hendy 1985, 58–68, for the tradition in the Byzantine period, sensitive but inclining somewhat to a catastrophic analysis.

generate the massive military and administrative project that was the Inca state.

(Gose 1993, 482)

Our examination of the watery topography of the environs of Rome, and the ancient traditions about it, revealed just such an 'uncontrolled periphery' in the formative period of the Roman state. The Tiber, spectacularly, implicated the sole city on its course in dependence on places and environments it did not – at first – control. But in a less obvious way, the sensible local management of Mediterranean hydrology always involves that uncontrolled periphery, and the interdependence of political ambition beyond the locality with the pursuit of optimum production within it is therefore a given of many Mediterranean landscapes. It is not surprising, in that case, that for Rome as for the Inca state, for all the huge differences of detail, the cultural manifestations of hydrological control should have been one of the primary ideological tools available for overcoming the huge obstacles to a politically and administratively – as well as economically – inclusive, supra-regional polity.

The Romans were habituated to hydraulic insecurity. Demographic circumstances were unfavourable; the world was wide; opportunities were numerous. When an imperial ideology encouraged settlers to move to the Wentlooge Level, or town councils to look after the dredging of harbours, or individuals to build ornamental and lucrative villas or take on the draining of swamps, it was in the nature of things for some of these initiatives to fail or be abandoned. The abandonment of managed countrysides, and the collapse of villas, is only a reflection of business as usual in the shifting occupancy of the ancient landscape; as the Romans knew well, it was symptomatic of the changing fortunes of imperial states and their ruling élites.[1]

Most scholars currently believe in a good deal of stability and continuity in ecological conditions in the Mediterranean. The view has been established with difficulty, because it seems to be essentially at odds with the central instabilities of our view of human history. The difficulty appears more than ever well founded, since the embeddedness of human activity in the historical ecology of

[1] In Purcell 1995 I explore the opportunistic attitudes to the intensification of production that underlie this phenomenon.

the Mediterranean seems more and more complex. Anthropogenic process has shaped the land-forms; symbiosis with humans has totally transformed the plant and animal ecologies. This recognition demands that we place side by side the routine behaviour of our species in its pursuit of survival in the landscape with the most grandiose and culturally complex of its attitudes and ambitions with regard to the world of nature. The result will be to reject the trivializing of routine production inherent in most minimalist descriptions of pre-modern primary production, and to enable us to trace with more sensitivity the processes by which the impact of human activity on ecology has varied through time both quantitatively and qualitatively; variations so wild, in some instances, as to make quite untenable present-centred – or otherwise teleoscopic – visions of the past.

> When capitalism is conjoined to industrialism, as it has been in the European societies, the outcome is the initiation of massively important series of alterations in the relationship between human beings and the natural world. . . . Modern urbanism forms a created environment . . . the obsolescence of city-walls is both symbolic of and substantially implicated in the emergence of that new administrative space that is the nation-state.
>
> (Giddens 1985, 146–7)

The world I have been describing was neither capitalist nor industrialist: but it is characterized by just the kind of change in the relationship between humanity and the natural world that this passage describes. For a while it even experienced the obsolescence of city walls. Our job is not just to see why that happened again in the eighteenth century, but to ask why it came about in the Roman period; and what went wrong. Giddens's remarks, privileging as they do the early modern period, derive from an all too familiar, unreconstructedly unilinear view of history. The value of the human investment in landscape management, as the financial advertisements say, 'can go down as well as up'. This mutability makes history more demanding and more rewarding, and it is fascinatingly prominent in the ancient Mediterranean world. As ancient historians or archaeologists, one of our prime tasks is to demonstrate the feebleness of all approaches to our period that see it as society's kindergarten. I hope to have shown something of how un-childish the Romans were; and who can be so optimistic about the adulthood of the 1990s?

Bibliography

Allen, J. R. L., and Fulford, M. G. (1986), 'The Wentlooge level: a Romano-British saltmarsh reclamation in southeast Wales', *Britannia*, 17: 91–117.

—— , —— , and Rippon, S. J. (1994), 'The settlement and drainage of the Wentlooge Level, Gwent: excavation and survey at Rumney Great Wharf 1992', *Britannia*, 25: 175–211.

Bintliff, J. (1992), 'Erosion in the Mediterranean lands: a reconsideration of pattern process and methodology', in M. Bell and J. Boardman (eds), *Past and Present Soil Erosion: Archaeological and Geographical Perspectives* (Oxford), 125–32.

Bruun, C. (1992), 'Water as a cruel element in the Roman world', in T. Viljamaa, A. Timonen, and C. Krötzl (eds), *Crudelitas: The Politics of Cruelty in the Ancient and Medieval World* (Krems), 74–80.

Coarelli, F. (1988), 'I santuari, il fiume, gli empori', *Storia di Roma*, i: *Roma in Italia* (Torino), 127–51.

Coccia, S., and Mattingly, D. J. (1992), 'Settlement history, environment, and human exploitation of an intermontane basin in the central Apennines: the Rieti survey 1988–1991, part I', *PBSR* 60 (n.s. 47): 213–89.

Coles, B. J. (1994), 'Trisantona rivers: a landscape approach to the interpretation of river-names', *OJA* 13: 295–311.

Corbier, M. (1984), 'De Volsinii à Sestinum: cura aquae et évergétisme municipal de l'eau en Italie', *Revue des études latines*, 62: 236–74.

Cornell, T. C. (1989), 'The recovery of Rome', in F. W. Walbank, A. E. Astin, M. W. Frederiksen, and R. M. Ogilvie (eds), *The Cambridge Ancient History*, vii. 2, 2nd edn: *The Rise of Rome to 220 BC* (Cambridge), ch. 7 (pp. 309–50).

Crouch, D. (1993), *Water Management in Ancient Greek Cities* (New York).

Delano Smith, C. (1986), 'Changing environment and Roman landscape', in B. Ward-Perkins, N. Mills, D. Gadd, and C. Delano Smith, 'Luni and the Ager Lunensis: the rise and fall of a Roman town and its territory', *PBSR* 54 (n.s. 41): 81–146, at pp. 123–41.

Devijver, H., and van Wonterghem, F. (1981), 'Il campus nell'impianto urbanistico delle città romane: testimonianze epigrafiche e resti archeologiche', *Acta archaeologica Lovaniensia*, 20: 33–68.

Donlan, W. (1989), 'Homeric temenos and the land economy of the dark age', *Museum Helveticum*, 46: 119–45.

Dunbabin, K. (1989), 'Baiarum grata voluptas: pleasures and dangers of the baths', *PBSR* 44 (n.s. 31): 6–46.

Fischer-Hansen, T. (1990), *Scavi di Ficana*, i (Rome).

Fossey, J. M. (1979), 'The cities of the Kopais in the Roman period', *Aufstieg und Niedergang der römischen Welt*, ii. 7. 1, pp. 549–91.

Frederiksen, M. W. (1984), *Campania*, ed. N. Purcell (London).

Gasperini, L. (1989), *Iscrizioni rupestre nel Lazio* (Rome).

Giddens, A. (1985), *The Nation-state and Violence* (Cambridge and Oxford).

Gilliam, J. F. (1961), 'The plague under Marcus Aurelius', *AJP* 82: 225–51.
Giovannini, A. (1985), 'Le sel et la fortune de Rome', *Athenaeum*, 63: 373–87.
Gose, P. (1993), 'Segmentary state formation and the ritual control of water under the Incas', *Comparative Studies in Society and History*, 35: 480–514.
Goubert, J.-P. (1986), *The Conquest of Water: The Advent of Health in the Industrial Age* (Oxford).
Guarducci, M. (1951), 'L'Italia e Roma in una "tabella defixionis" greca recentamente scoperta', *Bullettino della Commissione Archeologica Comunale di Roma*, 74: 57–70.
Häuber, C. (1990), 'Zur Topographie der Horti Maecenatis und der Horti Lamiani auf dem Esquilin in Rom', *Kölner Jahrbuch*, 23: 11–107.
Hendy, M. (1985), *Studies in the Byzantine Monetary Economy* (Cambridge).
Heurgon, J. (1959), 'The date of Vegoia's prophecy', *JRS* 49: 41–5.
Hiller von Gaertringen, F. (1906), *Inschriften von Priene* (Berlin).
Keppie, L. (1983), *Colonisation and Veteran Settlement in Italy, 47–14 BC* (London).
Kleiner, F. S. (1991), 'The trophy on the bridge and the Roman triumph over nature', *Antiquité classique*, 60: 182–92.
Knauss, J. (1987), 'Munich Kopais expedition, topographical surveys of October 1986 and May 1987: progress report', *Teiresias*, 17: 1–5.
Kolendo, J. (1970), 'L'influence de Carthage sur la civilisation matérielle de Rome', *Archaeologia*, 31: 8–22.
Lanciani, R. (1888), 'Il "Campus Salinarum Romanarum"', *Bullettino della Commissione Archeologica Comunale di Roma*, 16: 83–91.
LaRocca, E. (1984), *La riva a Mezzaluna* (Rome).
Lavagne, H. (1988), *Operosa antra* (Rome).
LeGall, J. (1953), *Le Tibre, fleuve de Rome, dans l'antiquité* (Paris).
Lepore, E. (1977), 'Fiumi e città nella colonizzazione greca di Occidente, con speciale riguarda alla Magna Grecia', in P.-M. Duval and E. Frézouls (eds), *Thèmes de recherche sur les villes antiques de l'occident* (Strasburg), 267–72.
Leveau, P. (1993), 'Mentalité économique et grands travaux hydrauliques: le drainage du lac Fucin aux origines d'un modèle', *Annales ESC* 48: 3–16.
McCann, A. M. (1987), *The Roman Port and Fishery of Cosa* (Princeton).
Meiggs, R. (1982), *Trees and Timber in the Ancient Mediterranean World* (Oxford).
Musset, A. (1991), 'De Tlaloc à Hippocrate: l'eau et l'organisation de l'espace dans le bassin de Mexico (XVIe–XVIIIe siècle)', *Annales ESC* 46: 261–98.
Muzzioli, M. P. (1992), 'La topografia della IX regione di Roma', *PBSR* 60 (n.s. 47): 179–211.
Peretti, A. (1994), *Dall'Eridano di Esiodo al retrone Vicentino: studio su un idronimo erratico* (Pisa).

212   *Nicholas Purcell*

Purcell, N. (1987), 'Tomb and suburb', in H. von Hesberg and P. Zanker (eds), *Römische Gräberstrassen* (Munich), 25–41.

—— (1990), 'The creation of provincial landscape: the example of Cisalpine Gaul', in T. F. C. Blagg and M. Millett (eds), *The Early Roman Empire in the West* (Oxford), 6–29.

—— (1995), 'The Roman villa and the landscape of production', in T. J. Cornell and K. Lomas (eds), *Urban Society in Roman Italy* (London), 151–79.

—— (forthcoming), 'Discovering a Roman resort coast: the Litus Laurentinum', in A. Claridge and G. Lauro (eds), *Castelporziano, iii* (Rome).

Quilici, L. (1983), 'Il Campo Marzio occidentale', *Città e architettura nella Roma imperiale* (*Analecta Romana Instituti Danici*, supp. 10; Odense), 59–85.

Rackham, O. (1983), 'Observations on the historical ecology of Boeotia', *BSA* 78: 291–351.

Sallares, R. (1991), *The Ecology of the Ancient Greek World* (London).

Segre, A. G. (1990), 'Considerazioni sul Tevere e sul Aniene nel quaternario', in *Il Tevere e le altre vie d'acqua del Lazio antico* (Archeologia Laziale, vii. 2 = Quaderni del Centro di Studi per l'Archeologia Etrusco-Italica, i. 12), 9–22.

Serbat, G. (1972), *Pline l'Ancien, livre 31* (Paris).

Spurr, S. (1986), *Arable Cultivation in Roman Italy* (London).

Squatriti, P. (1992), 'Marshes and mentalities in early medieval Ravenna', *Viator*, 23: 1–16.

Taylor, L. R. (1960), *The Voting Districts of the Roman Republic* (Rome).

Tchernia, A. (1986), *Le Vin de l'Italie romaine: essai d'histoire économique d'après les amphores* (Rome).

Thomsen, R. (1980), *King Servius Tullius: A Historical Synthesis* (Gyldendal).

Traina, G. (1983), *Le valli grandi Veronesi in età romana* (Pisa).

—— (1988), *Paludi e bonifiche del mondo antico* (Rome).

—— (1990), *Ambiente e paesaggi di Roma antica* (Rome).

Trautmann, T. R. (1992), 'The revolution in ethnological time', *Man*, 27: 379–97.

van Berchem, D. (1983) 'Une inscription flavienne du Musée d'Antioche', *Museum Helveticum*, 40: 186–96.

Vita-Finzi, C. (1969), *The Mediterranean Valleys: Geological Changes in Historical Time* (Cambridge).

Wiseman, T. P. (1987), 'Roman Republican road-building', in T. P. Wiseman, *Roman Studies* (Liverpool), 126–56.

Zangger, E. (1992), *The Flood from Heaven: Deciphering the Atlantis Legend* (London).

—— (1993), *The Geoarchaeology of the Argolid* (Berlin).

9

First fruit? The olive in the Roman world

David J. Mattingly

Introduction

It is still the case that many people in north-western Europe rarely encounter the olive outside the context of cocktail parties or pizza toppings, while the words 'olive oil' may call to mind first and foremost the eponymous girlfriend of Popeye. By and large we are still olive green and oil ignorant, geographically divorced as we are from the chief area of cultivation of the olive. Of the approximately 800 million olive trees worldwide, 98 per cent are located in the Mediterranean lands (De Beir 1980, 311–12). There the olive is perhaps a little too well known, to the extent that it is sometimes taken for granted.

The argument of this paper is that the significance of the olive has been consistently undervalued, overlooked, and under-estimated in studies of the Roman world.[1] Scholars specializing in other areas of Roman agriculture might question the priority hinted at by my title, but I have taken my lead from Columella, that most enthusiastic viticulturalist, and his well-known endorsement of the olive as 'first among all the trees' (*De re rustica*, 5. 8. 1: *olea quae prima omnium arborum est*).

---

[1] White 1970 is typical in giving greater attention to viticulture (pp. 229–46) and cereals (pp. 173–89) than to olives (pp. 225–7).

Conversely, I do not wish to present olive oil as some sort of wondrous elixir which allowed the Romans to defeat all comers, in the manner of Asterix the Gaul with his magic potion. Nevertheless, the multi-practicality of the olive, its oil, and its by-products gave it a very special place in the economy and society of the ancient Mediterranean.

There are four sections to this chapter, which will attempt to present a review of the varied and rich evidence relating to ancient oleoculture and its effects. First, I discuss some essential characteristics of the olive tree; second, its products and their various uses. The third section deals with some of the archaeological evidence relating to olive cultivation and to oil production and trade; attention is focused particularly on questions of scale. The final section tries to draw out some of the potential implications of this line of approach for our understanding of the ancient world and its ecology.

The olive tree and its cultivation

First a note of caution must be expressed about the nature of the olive. It is not one tree growing in one homogeneous zone, but many slightly different varieties (cultivars) of a single species cultivated in a wide range of Mediterranean and arid-zone environments (Amouretti 1986, 41–6; J. M. Renfrew 1973, 132–4). The immense differences in regional cultivars, planting densities, and strategies for cultivation pose serious obstacles to comparing data from different regions: every region must be assessed on its own merits, and my estimates from North African case studies, for instance, should not be expected to be compatible with information on oleoculture on the north side of the Mediterranean (figs 9.1 and 9.2).

The cultivated olive tree (*Olea europaea* L. *sativa*) is the archetypal tree of Mediterranean lands. Its geographical spread closely correlates with the defined limits of the Mediterranean climatic zone (fig. 9.3).[1] The chief weakness of the olive is that it cannot tolerate extreme cold (average annual temperatures of between

---

[1]   Amouretti 1986, 17–18, 20–2, 31; Brun 1986, 21–6; cf. also Forbes and Foxhall 1978; Isager and Skydsgaard 1992; Loussert and Brousse 1978; Sallares 1991.

Figure 9.1 Extensive orchard of widely spaced olive trees (near Sfax, Tunisia, 1987).

16 and 22 °C are needed), and this has imposed limits on its northward spread into continental Europe and on the height at which it is cultivated in the mountains bordering the Mediterranean (Amouretti and Comet 1985, 14). In Greece and Italy the upper limits may be as low as 500–700 m, but in the milder winters of the North African Maghreb the olive can be cultivated well above 1,000 m.[1] At the other climatic extreme, the olive is susceptible to damage from prolonged and fierce drought. However, with 150 mm of rainfall being considered the minimum average level for cultivation to be viable, it is considerably more drought-resistant than most cereals and vines. It is also adaptable to a very wide range of soil types, and can thrive even on poor-quality land. There is clear evidence that at certain times olive cultivation has extended beyond the currently observed geographical limits: for instance, a

[1] Brun 1986, 22; Marcaccini 1973, 31–49; Morizot 1993, 177–240; Pagnol 1975, 23–4, 63.

Figure 9.2 Dense olive grove (Sparta, Greece, 1984).

surprising distance into the pre-desert margins of the Roman world.[1]

Cultivation of the olive seems to have spread by stages from the east Mediterranean westwards, from the late Chalcolithic or early bronze age onwards.[2] Scientific opinion is still divided on the precise historical relationship between the cultivated species, *Olea europaea* L. *sativa*, and its wild counterpart L. *Oleaster*, there being no consensus as to whether the former developed from the latter or the latter is a degenerated hybrid of the cultivated plant (Amouretti 1986, 41–4; Turrill 1951). It is certain, however, that the cultivated species must be descended from the stock of a wild species that was improved through cultivation by people, even if we cannot be certain of its relationship with the present-day wild olive. There are good reasons to believe, however, that the grafting of cultivated with wild stock did much to produce

---

[1]   Evenari *et al.* 1971; Mattingly 1985, 38–43; van der Veen 1985.
[2]   Amouretti 1986, 41–5; Borowski 1987, 117–18; Ucko and Dimbleby eds 1969; Zohary and Spiegel-Roy 1975.

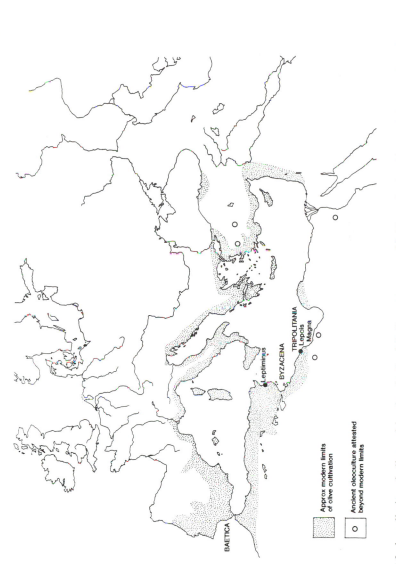

Figure 9.3 Modern limits of olive cultivation in the Mediterranean world. Note the locations of the principal Roman oil-exporting regions of the W. Mediterranean: Baetica, Byzacena, and Tripolitania.

regionally diverse types. Since the olive is naturally suited to the Mediterranean and seems to have existed over a wide area in its pre-cultivated phase, it is likely that it was an improved technology of cultivation that was gradually transmitted westwards, rather than the olive tree itself.[1] In any event, a major role in the expansion of oleoculture in the west must be assigned to Greek and Phoenician colonists, and perhaps also to the Etruscans during the first half of the first millennium BC.[2] By the time the Mediterranean was unified as a Roman empire, olive culture was well established. The evidence I shall present, however, suggests that there was a significant rise in the *scale* of oil production between, say, 200 BC and AD 200.

What are the characteristics that most distinguish the olive tree? First, perhaps, its extreme longevity must be recognized. In ideal conditions, and if carefully tended, olive trees can survive for many centuries, exceptionally for millennia. Some of the largest trees surviving today probably originated within the Roman period (Antolini 1986, 8). Even in cases where the trunk and branches have been killed by disease, old age, fire, or frost damage, new suckers will rise up from the root bowl to rejuvenate the tree. The remarkable capacity of the olive tree for survival and reincarnation has given rise to its reputation for immortality. The synchronized regeneration of Athens and her sacred olive tree after the Persian sack of 480 BC (Herodotos, 8. 55) is perhaps the best-known historical instance of the psychological importance to a community of this peculiar quality. Furthermore, not only is the olive long-lived, but as an evergreen tree its appearance through the seasons and through the years is relatively constant. This undoubtedly enhances its sacred and spiritual importance to Mediterranean peoples. To this day, in the Catholic heartlands of southern Italy, one can see sprigs of olive leaves from the Palm Sunday rites kept in houses for the rest of the year as good-luck charms.

Olive trees are almost never grown from seed: propagation is normally by cuttings, slips, or grafts, with the result that, under

---

[1] Borowski 1987, 117–26, summarizes the Old Testament and Jewish literary evidence for early oleoculture in the Levant. Runnels and Hansen 1986 have challenged the view that there had been a major expansion of oleoculture into the Aegean world by the early bronze age.

[2] Barker 1988, 781–3; Boardman 1977; Vallet 1962.

traditional conditions of cultivation, regional variants are developed through experimental grafting, and once a cultivar has proved well matched to a particular environment, cloning of the existing stock is the general rule.[1] Here again we see an ageless aspect of the olive tree: some cultivars surviving today in remote regions are quite possibly clones of Roman trees, even where no certain trees of that age survive. One consequence of the regional diversity of cultivars in traditional oleoculture is that the size and fruiting potential of olive trees vary considerably from area to area. This is nowadays less apparent than it once was, since modern changes in olive farming are leading to a replacement of many of the regional varieties by a small number of versatile cultivars that can be relied upon to perform adequately in a range of climates and soil conditions.[2]

The traditional associations between the olive and peace reflect the necessity for political and socio-economic conditions to be favourable before a major investment of time and money will be made in new olive groves. It is commonly asserted that a new olive tree will take up to twenty years to bear significant fruit. Certainly it is true that the olive is a long-term investment, with the labour input in the initial years far higher than for a mature tree; but trees grown from cuttings are capable of producing some fruit within five to eight years, and in good conditions the quantity may be quite substantial. The potential problems of the period spent waiting for the olives to come into full production can be reduced by the inter-planting of other, quicker-bearing fruit-trees or by inter-cultivating cereal crops.[3]

The vegetative cycle of the olive tree has significance for an understanding of its place in traditional Mediterranean agriculture. The blossom appears in late spring on the previous year's new-grown wood, a characteristic which in part explains the inherent tendency of olive trees towards biennial fruiting (Amouretti and Comet 1985, 66–7; Forbes 1992, 90–3). Although

---

[1] Amouretti 1986, 58–62; Brun 1986, 27–8; Ceccolini and Bruni 1983, 20–4; Giorgini 1982, 33–50; Loussert and Brousse 1978, 128 f.; Pansiot and Rebour 1961.

[2] Ceccolini and Bruni 1983, 15–19; Pagnol 1975, 29–40.

[3] Amouretti 1986, 59; Brun 1986, 31; Loussert and Brousse 1978, 444; cf. Braconi 1979, 46 (for yields of over 20 kg of olives per tree in modern intensive orchards after only six years).

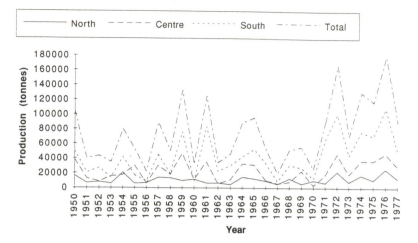

Figure 9.4 Annual Tunisian olive oil output 1950–77, showing the differential performance of orchards in the north, centre, and south of the country. Note the wide deviation between peak and low yields and the periodic disruption of the biennial pattern of fruiting. (Data from Labaied 1981; *Olivae tunisienne.*)

this biennial pattern can be ameliorated to some extent through pruning regimes, the olive is notorious for the unevenness of its fruit production.[1] But the fruiting pattern is not simply one of 'on' and 'off' years: in many regions the pattern is further complicated by other factors, such as climate, that can trigger consecutive poor harvests or, more rarely, consecutive good ones. Analysis of harvest data from the three main olive-growing regions of Tunisia shows a frequent lack of conformity or synchronization in peak and trough years, and an overall complex pattern of 'on' and 'off' years (fig. 9.4). Although during the period 1950–77 about half the years saw poor harvests and the other half good ones, this did not follow a strict biennial sequence and there was considerable variation in production levels between the three regions.[2]

---

[1]   Columella, *RR* 5. 9. 11; Baldini and Scaramuzzi 1981, 119–41 (on the importance of pruning regimes); Ceccolini and Bruni 1983, 8; Pansiot and Rebour 1961, 144 f.
[2]   Labaied 1981; Mattingly 1994; *Olivae tunisienne.*

Figure 9.5 The olive harvest (near Sousse, Tunisia, December 1987).

The olive harvest occurs in the late autumn for green olives, across the winter months for the mature black olives, and is a major event in the agricultural calendar (fig. 9.5). Harvesting olives is very labour-intensive, whatever method is employed: hand-stripping, gathering from the ground, or beating.[1] However, olive groves require comparatively little maintenance for much of the rest of the year, once established, and since the harvest does not clash with those of, for instance, cereals and vines it is possible to 'specialize' in oleoculture while also cultivating a wider range of crops. The classic depiction of Mediterranean agriculture as being founded upon the triad of cereals, vines, and olives reflects in large measure the fact that these crops complement each other so perfectly in the agricultural calendar.[2]

[1] Amouretti 1986, 73–5, and Brun 1986, 36–8, gather the relevant ancient sources.
[2] C. Renfrew and Wagstaff 1982, 106–33 (on traditional polyculture on Melos). Epigraphic evidence (Kehoe 1988) and iconographic material (Dunbabin 1978, pls 36–45) demonstrate its importance in Africa.

The olive, then, is a tree that thrives in the Mediterranean milieu and is comparatively easy to propagate and cultivate, though liable to a high measure of unpredictability in its yield. Yet, despite its pan-Mediterranean distribution, olive orchards have not been uniform in time and space: tree size, tree spacing, and cultivation strategy (monocultivation or inter-cultivation) are crucial variables. Analysis of past practice in any given area must start with an understanding of more recent oleoculture in that locality. The modern evidence must thus be read with care. Oleoculture has not been immutable: in some areas the level of production and the extent of cultivation have oscillated widely above and below modern levels (Forbes 1992; 1993; Mattingly 1994). But, similarly, ancient sources must be used cautiously: what Cato wrote of Campania in the second century BC cannot be automatically held to be applicable to Africa in the second century AD.

The products of the olive

The chief methods of preserving food in the ancient world were salting, drying, smoking, and pickling or conserving using brine, wine, vinegar, honey, or oil. Most foodstuffs were therefore eaten almost exclusively in season, with comparatively small quantities preserved for later use and a great imbalance resulting between, say, summer and winter diets. The picture of the traditional Mediterranean diet comprising bread, olives and olive oil, and wine is truest for the winter months and reflects the suitability of these products for short-term storage.[1] It should be noted that, while comparatively large quantities of grain and wine may be needed to meet nutritional and social needs, the olive and olive oil are economically packaged foodstuffs (Guthrie 1975, 503–32, tables).

Relatively simple treatments exist for rendering the bitter and inedible green olive picked from the tree into a delicious and nutritional food, and black olives are even simpler to treat. Conserved in brine, green or black (that is, ripe) olives will have been the basis for many simple winter meals (Amouretti 1986, 177–9; Brun 1986, 39–42). Olives are rich in calories, essential fats (lipids), and

---

[1]   Brothwell and Brothwell 1969, 153–7; Gallant 1991, 62–7.

vitamins, with significant traces of important minerals. Calcium occurs at higher levels than in other vegetables, meat, or fish. The full nutritional value of 100 grams of olives is equivalent to that of 1.5 litres of milk (Pagnol 1975, 77).

What is far harder for us to appreciate is the likely consumption level of olive oil in antiquity. A common misconception is to regard it simply as a fatty cooking medium comparable to our vegetable oils, butter, margarine, or animal fats. But olive oil is a food of extraordinary nutritional value, and unlike other sources of fat it is 100 per cent digestible. It contains little protein, but 100 grams (3.4 oz) will yield 900–90 calories, all essential edible fats and fatty acids (lipids), and significant levels of vitamins A and E. In comparison, the calorific value of wine is slight, a full 70 centilitre bottle being equivalent to a mere 4 centilitres of oil. In studies of traditional Cretan diets, olive oil has been found to provide 25–40 per cent of total calorie intake (Raulin 1869, 244). Documentary evidence of Byzantine monastic diets shows olive-oil consumption supplying at least 80 per cent of the annual intake of necessary fats and 12 per cent of calories, while making up a mere 2 per cent of the total weight of food consumed.[1] These figures demonstrate both the likely importance and the utility of olive oil in the subsistence diet. Recent research has also demonstrated that olive oil is possibly the safest natural way of incorporating essential fats in the diet without a significant risk of cardiovascular problems.[2]

Traditional Mediterranean diets, then, have made much of this wonderful commodity. It is used primarily as an ingredient and a flavouring rather than as a cooking medium (that is, for deep frying). The quantities consumed are far higher than we might imagine, remote as we are in time and space from authentic Mediterranean peasant cuisine.[3] Anthropological studies, however, provide good reasons for arguing that average annual consumption in the Roman world could have been in the range of 20–50 litres per capita.[4]

[1] Dembinska 1985: data from tables i–ix, pp. 455–62.
[2] Grande Covian *et al.* 1984, 6–10; *The Independent*, 9 Feb. 1988, p. 15.
[3] cf. the Roman gourmet Apicius and the modern classic of Mediterranean cookery, Gray 1986. See also Dolamore 1988.
[4] Forbes and Foxhall 1978, 46, though cf. now Gallant 1991, 60–112.

Yet this is not the whole story by any means, for olive oil has many uses that are even less appreciated today. The principal form of domestic illumination in the Roman world was the oil-lamp, and even if individual households were assiduous in conserving fuel it is clear that temples, baths, and rich houses must have consumed vast quantities (Amouretti 1986, 190). My own experiments with a Roman oil-lamp suggest that 1 litre of oil might provide *c*.134 hours of light for a single-nozzled lamp. As an order-of-magnitude guide, therefore, if every inhabitant lit a lamp for just an hour a day throughout the year, a town with a population of 10,000 would consume over 27,000 litres of lamp oil in a year. Rome, with a population of one million, would need nearly 3 million litres of oil for lighting. I do not mean to imply that these figures are valid estimates of actual use, only to demonstrate that the consumption of lamp oil in the Roman world may have been considerable.

Olive oil served as a moisturizing oil for skin, as the principal cleansing agent in the baths, as the component for the first bars of soap, and as a massage oil. It was also the essential base for the vast majority of ancient perfumes and cosmetics.[1] There are vivid paintings from Pompeii and Herculaneum illustrating special presses used in the extraction of fine olive oils for the perfume industry and the sale of the finished product to elegant customers (Mattingly 1990). Once again, the scale of such usage can easily be underestimated. Some enigmatic comments by Pliny (*Historia naturalis*, 15. 8), speaking of the olive oils of Campania in southern Italy, should alert us to the possibilities: he attributes the fame of the oils of Venafrum first to their suitability for use in perfumes, and only second to their fine taste. In another passage (18. 111) he suggests that Campanian perfume production, centred on Capua, rivals in scale the total olive-oil production of many other regions. The significance of the comparison between perfume production and olive-oil output is only obvious when it is appreciated that olive oil was the major liquid component of the perfumes. If subsistence, lighting, and bathing needs were as high as I have implied, then the quantity of Campanian olive oil devoted to use in making perfumes must have been extraordinary.

[1] Amouretti 1986, 183–9; Amouretti and Comet 1985, 41–5; Brun 1986, 55–6.

There are, in addition, numerous medicinal uses for olive oil, some attested directly for the Roman period in the literary sources, others recorded as being prevalent in medieval times and possibly of long tradition. Whatever the precise medicinal value of olive oil – and it does appear to have a number of positive physiological properties – the important thing is that it was perceived as beneficial and, being readily available, was widely employed. Lesser uses that are attested include the treatment of textiles and wool, and basic lubricating functions.[1]

The by-products of olive oil were also extraordinarily practical. The solid residue left after pressing out the oil was used as fuel, animal feed, or fertilizer. The sticky, black, liquid residue (*amurca*) was variously employed as fertilizer, insecticide, mothproofer, wood-preserver, waterproofer, skin-curer, lubricant, and a cure-all tonic for animals.[2]

When we consider in this manner the uses of olives, olive oil, and their various by-products, it becomes clearer why the olive has been such an important element of the Mediterranean economy.[3] The suitability of oil to a wide range of subsistence needs – from food to lighting, from soap to medicine – has made olive cultivation a sensible investment from the standpoint of self-sufficiency. But it must be clear, equally, that with a growing urban population in many parts of the Roman empire, and because of the various areas of life which depended on oil, it was a product with enormous potential for marketability. One further characteristic of olive oil must be mentioned here. It has a relatively short shelf-life, being at its best in the year after production and increasingly liable to go rancid after more than two to three years. We should presume a sharp and steady depreciation in the value of olive oil after about twelve months in storage, and this will have been a major disincentive to speculative hoarding for longer periods of oil stocks in bulk. Coupled with its propensity for drastically unequal harvests, this may have been a further stimulus to the production and movement of surplus oil. At first sight it is

[1] Amouretti 1986, 189–92; Amouretti and Comet 1985, 37–40, 45–9; Brun 1986, 55–6.
[2] Cato, *RR* 91 f.; Columella, *RR* 1. 6; 2. 14; 6. 4; Pliny, *HN* 15. 33–4; Amouretti 1986, 192–4; 1993; Brun 1986, 56–8.
[3] For a long historical perspective see Amouretti and Brun eds 1993; and *L'Huile*.

ironic that olive oil should have been widely traded, given the ubiquity of the olive around the Mediterranean.[1] But when it is appreciated that regional production will have tended to follow an irregular pattern of gluts and shortfalls, and that it was inadvisable to hold large stocks of oil for more than a year or two against potential future shortages, it should be clear that there will almost always have been a need for oil imports somewhere, and a surplus for disposal somewhere else. The natural unpredictability and quirkiness of the olive harvest may have been an indirect stimulus for the development of inter-regional trade.

The archaeology of the ancient olive

There are many strands of archaeological evidence pertaining to the olive: palaeobotanical data, traces of ancient orchards, olive mills and presses, amphorae used to transport oil (with valuable epigraphic detail stamped or painted on the vessels in some cases), and a rich iconography of the olive in ancient art.[2] Moreover, recent developments in archaeology, notably the growth in field survey, provide new opportunities for evaluating the importance of oleoculture in the ancient landscape. A few examples will demonstrate the potential significance of the material at our disposal.

A detailed excavation of an ancient olive orchard was carried out inadvertently by an Italian prehistorian excavating the neolithic village of Passo di Corvo in Apulia (Tinè 1983, 43–5). His initial trenches within two neolithic ditched enclosures appeared to have located massive rectangular hall-like buildings. The picture became more complicated for him when he excavated the area in between his enclosures and found evidence for further rectangular structures. It was only after several further seasons of painstaking work that he was obliged to admit that he had been

[1] cf. Finley 1985, 133: 'Greek (and Roman) cities were also large consumers of olive oil. Given this latter fact and the ubiquity of the olive tree, where were the external markets for the export of this commodity ...?'

[2] Amouretti 1986; Amouretti and Comet 1985; Amouretti and Brun eds 1993; Brun 1986; Heltzer and Eitam eds 1987; Frankel et al. 1994; Leveau et al. 1993.

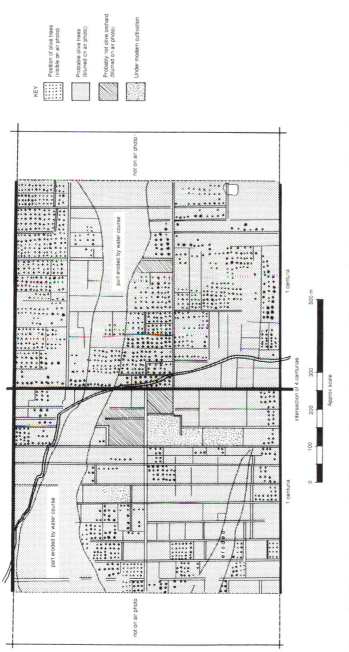

KEY

Position of olive trees (visible on air photo)

Probable olive trees (blurred on air photo)

Probably not olive orchard (blurred on air photo)

Under modern cultivation

not on air photo

part eroded by water course

1 centuria

intersection of 4 centuriae

1 centuria

part eroded by water course

1 centuria

not on air photo

Approx scale

0   100   200   300   500 m

Figure 9.6 Plot of an extensive Roman olive orchard, revealed on an air photograph by differential crop growth over and around the ancient tree-pits. The photograph (from Saumagne 1929) shows the major part of two Roman *centuriae* of land (c.100 ha).

excavating the planting-pits, dug on a regular grid, of a Roman olive orchard that overlay the neolithic site. The well-known archive of wartime air photographs of Apulia compiled by the late John Bradford includes many examples of crop marks revealing such tree-pits for Roman orchards and trenches for vineyards.[1]

Parallels exist in Tunisia, where high-altitude vertical air photographs taken by the French after the last war have revealed a wealth of detail about Roman land survey or centuriation systems.[2] In parts of the Sahel, the main olive-oil-producing region of Tunisia, the fossilized Roman landscape was recorded in great detail (fig. 9.6). A plethora of tiny dots within the rectilinear, centuriated fields on the photographs once again reveals the presence of tree-pits for ancient orchards. On many photographs these orchards, which we may presume to have been predominantly for olives, cover over 60 per cent of the ground area. The regularity of the orchards shows that they were created from nursery propagation of stock, rather than from the grafting of cultivated cuttings on to existing wild olive trees. It is clearly hazardous to extrapolate a pattern for the whole of the ancient Sahel from a geographically restricted part of it, but we can at least admit that the extraordinary concentration of olive groves fits rather well with what we know about African dominance of oil exports in the later empire.

A major body of evidence is, of course, furnished by the remains of olive mills and presses. Roman writers provide literary testimony on the arrangement and functioning of this equipment.[3] Naturally there were changes over time and a degree of regional variation, which make straight comparison between individual archaeological finds and a specific text rather hazardous. The pungent and greasy process of making olive oil is essentially a three-stage operation (Amouretti 1986, 153–7; Brun 1986, 42–55). First olives are pulped, either in a mill or by some other method.

[1] Bradford 1949, pls 2–5; 1957, pls 25–8; cf. Jones 1980.
[2] Bradford 1957, 200–5; Despois 1955, 106–13; Peyras 1975, 188, 213; Saumagne 1929; 1952; Trousset 1977, 199.
[3] Cato, *RR* 18–19 (see also *RR* 3, 5, 10, 12–13, 21–3); Columella, *RR* 12. 52. 3–6; Hero, *Mechanica.* 3. 13; 3. 15; 3. 19–20; Palladius, 1. 20; 12. 17; Pliny, *HN* 18. 317. The best commentaries are Amouretti 1986, 153–75; Brun 1986, 59–136, 236–47; Drachman 1932; 1963; Cotton 1979, 63–6. White 1975, 225–33, and 1984, 67–72, are now seriously outdated.

Second, the resultant paste is put in baskets and placed under a press, which may be one of several different types. When pressure is applied, oil and lees run out of the press into vats or other suitable containers. The third stage consists of the separation of the oil from the lees and other residual matter. This can be done quite easily since the oil floats on top of the lees and can be skimmed off.

Roman olive mills took various forms, the *trapetum* and the *mola olearia* being the two predominant types.[1] Contrary to the literary tradition, there is no good evidence that these mills could successfully separate olive stones from the pulp without crushing the stones: they are basic crushers, designed to pulp both flesh and nut and to produce a well-mixed paste for the press. Modern research stresses the important role played by the sharp fragments of crushed shell in facilitating the free flow of oil from the paste during pressing.[2] Most Roman mills appear to have been turned by human rather than animal power; this is probably a reflection of the relatively slow pressing procedure used (commonly taking up to twenty-four hours), which allowed milling of the olives to be carried out, in numerous small loads and at a steady rate, alongside the press.

There were two basic forms of press in the ancient world. Although the direct screw press was employed to some extent in the Roman period, by far the more popular form was the lever press in its various manifestations (fig. 9.7).[3] It takes up a good deal more space than the direct screw types, but its enduring popularity may have had much to do with its potentially far higher processing capacity. Its principal element was a great timber beam, pivoted at one end in a wall or between timber or stone uprights (*arbores*, 'trees'). The baskets of pulped olives were placed under the press beam and the free end drawn downwards, either by the operation of a windlass system or by a screw mechanism.[4] In

[1] Ben Baaziz 1991; Brun 1986, 68–80; Drachman 1932, 8–44; Foxhall 1993; Frankel *et al.* 1994, 28–35.
[2] Amouretti 1981; Frezzotti and Manni 1956, 49–50; Mattingly 1988d, 156.
[3] Brun 1986, 81–132 (esp. 85–6, 124–5, 132); Frankel *et al.* 1994, 35–77.
[4] Mattingly 1988c, 188–90; Mattingly and Hitchner 1993, esp. 439–41; Rossiter 1981.

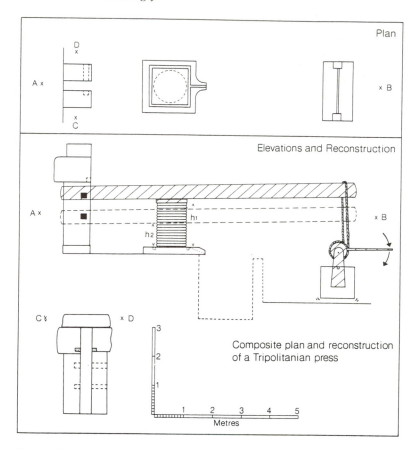

Figure 9.7 The standard form of lever press in use in Roman Africa (after Mattingly 1988c).

many presses the windlass or screw was mounted on a counter-weight block which could be lifted clear of the floor to provide a steady pressure. Presses of the same basic type are still in use in some remote corners of the Mediterranean, such as southern Tunisia (figs 9.7–9.9).[1]

Archaeological evidence for Roman olive presses may take several forms. In areas where the *arbores* were fashioned in stone,

---

[1] Akerraz and Lenoir 1982; Amouretti *et al.* 1984; Callot 1984; Camps-Fabrer 1953; Cresswell 1965; Louis 1969; Mattingly 1993.

Figure 9.8 Baskets of pulped olives under pressure below the beam of a lever press still in use in 1987. (Douiret, S. Tunisia.)

Figure 9.9 The author manipulating the windlass to raise the counter-weight block off the ground. (Douiret, S. Tunisia.)

Figure 9.10 The stone uprights (*arbores*) of Roman olive presses can constitute highly visible monuments in parts of N. Africa. This example is near Kasserine.

these tend to be the most distinctive trace (figs 9.7 and 9.10). In northern Libya their striking similarity to megalithic monuments such as the Stonehenge trilithons led some early investigators into highly fanciful interpretations of their possible religious or ritual use (Cowper 1897; cf. Mattingly 1988c). Other elements that commonly survive are the press-beds on which the baskets of pulped olives were piled, the counterweight blocks for windlass or screw mechanisms, and the settling-vats (Mattingly 1988b–c; Oates 1953).

I have attempted to posit production capacities for a number of well-preserved North African olive presses, using empirical evidence from detailed measurements of the press components. On the basis of its size and the capacity of the associated vats, the small press from a site called el-Amud, in the Libyan pre-desert margins, probably had a maximum annual capacity of about 2,000–3,000 litres.[1] On the other hand, the larger presses common

---

[1] Mattingly 1985, 41–2; Mattingly and Hitchner 1993, 456–8; Mattingly and Zenati 1984, 16–18.

to the oil-exporting areas can be seen to have had a far higher maximum annual output, in the region of 10,000 litres (cf. fig. 9.7). This estimate for the peak productivity of the largest presses is now widely accepted.[1] The existence of these monster presses, with stone uprights standing 3 m tall and a beam of 9 m and more in length, is persuasive evidence for production being geared in many cases to far more than mere domestic requirements. Ten thousand litres could provide for 500 people at a 20 litres per capita subsistence requirement, and 200 people at 50 litres per capita.

Evidence of a complementary kind is provided by the identification of olive presses by field survey projects.[2] For some parts of the Mediterranean it is now becoming possible to make some general observations about the development and comparative scale of olive-oil production.[3] These studies provide extremely crude estimates of numbers of presses (and contemporaneity of operation is a problem), but the inherent bias in such figures is undoubtedly towards underestimation because of the larger problems of survivability and visibility of the evidence. Let us consider briefly two examples that touch on the special nature of oleoculture in Roman Africa.

The high steppe region of central Tunisia contains some of the best-preserved evidence for rural settlement patterns and olive press distribution.[4] The reasons for the fine preservation of the evidence are comparatively straightforward: this part of Tunisia has always been somewhat marginal climatically, and since the final decline of the Roman period agrarian regime, sometime in the medieval period, land use has been far from intensive until the creation of modern artesian wells. Thousands of ancient sites were recorded on the high steppe as a result of the early twentieth-century map-making activity of the French Brigades Topographiques. The quality of the original records was very variable: only a few of the observers had an eye for detail or an

---

[1] Mattingly 1988b, 38; 1988c, 191–3; 1993, 483–93; 1994; Mattingly and Hitchner 1993, 446–60.
[2] Leveau 1984; Ponsich 1974–89; Tchalenko 1953–8.
[3] Brun 1986; 1993; Callot 1984; Eitam 1987; Frankel 1987; Mattingly 1988a.
[4] Hitchner 1988; 1989; 1993; Hitchner and Mattingly 1991; Hitchner *et al.* 1990; Mattingly and Hitchner 1993.

interest in noting down specific information about, for example, the existence and number of olive presses at a site. More recent work around Sbeitla and Kasserine has greatly amplified the picture. The density of olive presses this work reveals is extraordinary for such a marginal zone. The minimum figure is 350 presses in 1,500 sq km (one press every 4 sq km; Mattingly 1988a, 46–8). In reality, wherever more detailed survey has been done the density is rather higher, implying very considerable specialization in oleoculture in the zone. There is currently no evidence to suggest a significantly different climate in antiquity, though environmental changes do seem to have occurred as a result of human mismanagement of the land. We must conclude, therefore, that the remarkable development of this area for oleoculture in the Roman period was achieved in the face of its marginality rather than because of its suitability.

The total survey of an area of just 3.5 sq km of the landscape near Kasserine has produced startling results (fig. 9.11; Hitchner *et al.* 1990, 231–47 and fig. 17). No fewer than ten olive presses are attested within this very restricted area, eight of them located in two virtually adjacent, apparently contemporary, and purpose-built oileries whose joint productive capacity can be estimated at somewhere between 40,000 and 80,000 litres for optimum years. The best agricultural land in this zone is actually the alluvium of the dry river beds (wadis), and the olive orchard necessary to feed these presses must have extended beyond the limits of the area surveyed. The many small farms and farmsteads represented here, and known to have been broadly contemporary with the oileries, must therefore have been encompassed within the organizational structure centred on the oileries. This would appear to be an extensive estate, set up on somewhat unpromising land and geared to produce a very substantial quantity of olive oil.[1]

Production in all but the very worst years must have been well in excess of the subsistence needs of the likely inhabitants of the estate situated here. This agricultural development seems to have reached its peak in the third to fifth centuries AD – theoretically a time of general economic decline in the Roman world. Massive capital investment was required for planting orchards and for building farms and press-ranges (which, in the case of the oileries

---

[1] Hitchner 1989, 400–2; 1993, 502–4; Hitchner *et al.* 1990, 148–55.

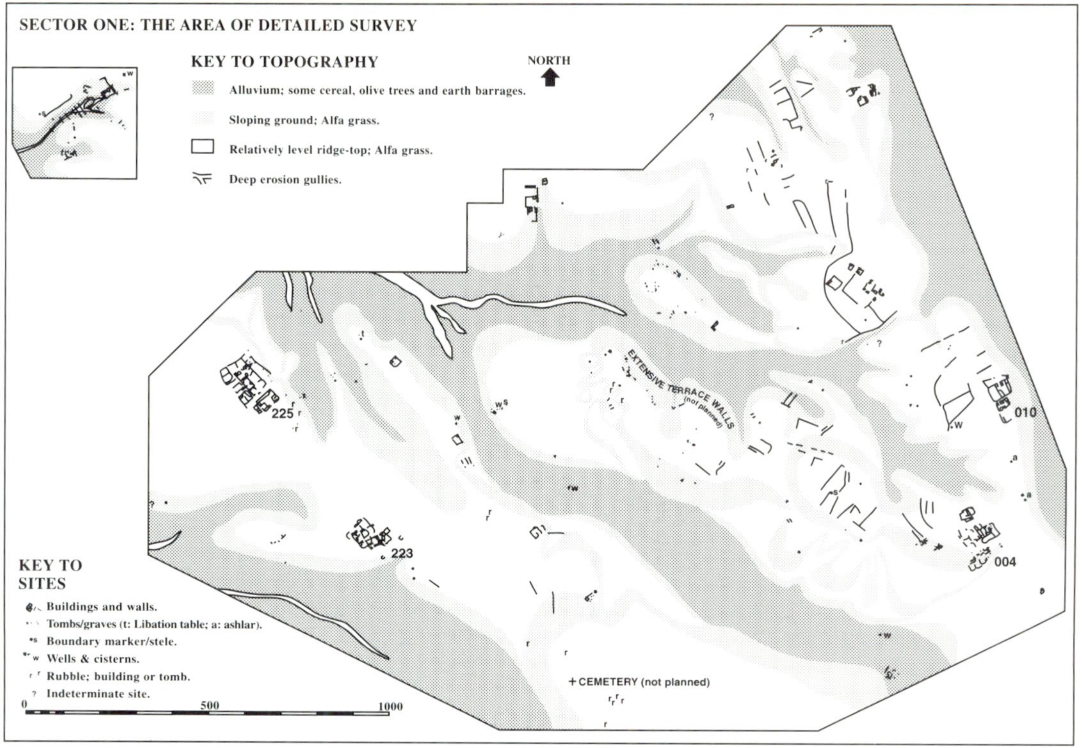
SECTOR ONE: THE AREA OF DETAILED SURVEY
KEY TO TOPOGRAPHY
NORTH
Alluvium; some cereal, olive trees and earth barrages.
Sloping ground; Alfa grass.
Relatively level ridge-top; Alfa grass.
Deep erosion gullies.
EXTENSIVE TERRACE WALLS
(not planned)
225
223
010
004
+CEMETERY (not planned)
KEY TO
SITES
Buildings and walls.
Tombs/graves (t: Libation table; a: ashlar).
Boundary marker/stele.
Wells & cisterns.
Rubble; building or tomb.
Indeterminate site.
0
500
1000

Figure 9.11 Detailed survey of *c.*3.5 sq km of the high steppe near Kasserine, Tunisia, revealing a very dense pattern of rural settlement focused around two major oileries (sites 223; 225). Sites 004 and 010 also possessed olive presses. (After Hitchner *et al.* 1990.)

at least, look like pattern-book designs). It is not too fanciful to describe what seems to have happened here as an 'oil boom'. Yet it must be reiterated that the high steppe was not an obvious place to locate such surplus capacity, given its marginality and its distance from the coast. The aerial photographic evidence already referred to has demonstrated that the Sahel was, in all probability, massively exploited for oleoculture. The extension of specialized culture of the olive and high capital investment deep into the interior of the country must indicate the strength of demand for olive oil. It may also indicate a gradual decline in yields from orchards created earlier, nearer to the coast. There are parallels in the fate of olive yields from orchards replanted in the early decades of this century, with initial outstanding yields progressively declining. Near Sfax, for instance, average yields are now only half what they were in the 1930s (Poncet 1962, 396; cf. Mattingly 1994). Intensive oleoculture, especially in marginal zones, is demanding, and Nature can fight back. Indeed, we must accept the possibility that in some regions the Roman-period increase in olive cultivation may have contributed to ecological stress.

My second African example is from western Libya (ancient Tripolitania), where we shall compare production of the prime agricultural lands with that of the pre-desert zone to the south.[1] Even in the better agricultural zone we are dealing with very low rainfall (much of the country is on the wrong side of the 150 mm rainfall isohyet, commonly taken as the limit for successful oleoculture). Nevertheless the towns of Tripolitania, notably Lepcis Magna, were oil exporters, though on a smaller scale overall than what was ultimately achieved by the towns of the Tunisian littoral; and the wealth generated by even a small percentage of the Mediterranean oil trade is likely to have been far from negligible. It is now clear that the *territoria* of the Tripolitanian cities were unusually large; that of Lepcis can be estimated at 3,000–5,000 sq km (up to 2,000 sq miles). The presses of this area were commonly massive and constructed in multiple units (oileries), the largest containing ten or more presses in a single building. Both these factors accord well with an orientation towards export production. It is conceivable that the annual oil production of the territory of

---

[1] Mattingly 1985; 1987; 1988a–c; 1989; 1993; 1995; Mattingly and Hitchner 1993; 1995.

Lepcis was commonly above 1 million litres (*c.*1,000 tonnes), topping 10 million litres in peak years (Mattingly 1988b, 38).

By contrast, survey in the extremely marginal pre-desert zone to the south reveals a slightly different picture (Mattingly 1985, 38–43; 1990, 143–7). Rainfall here drops below the minimum levels assumed necessary for cereal, vine, and olive cultivation, and conditions are altogether far worse than on the Tunisian high steppe. None the less, using a simple but ingenious system of floodwater management, the ancient farmers were able to cultivate all these crops in the wadi-beds, as is clear from funerary reliefs, archaeological evidence of field systems and olive presses, palaeobotanical remains, and the surviving area of wadi agriculture (with magnificent olive trees) at Beni Ulid. The total of over sixty presses known from this area is quite remarkable, and though they are generally smaller than those of the territories of the towns to the north, and all occur as single or twin presses rather than in oilery-type installations, it may be suspected that some slight surplus capacity existed. The ornate tombs which the wadi farmers were able to buy in from specialist constructors certainly testify that there were some fiscal rewards for the hard and somewhat precarious agriculture.

The provision of expensive presses, whether in the prime exporting areas or in the marginal fringes of the Roman world, is unlikely to indicate purely domestic production. In view of the expense of such equipment it seems reasonable to suppose that the scale and number of the presses were predicated on a strategy of maximizing yield in the bumper crop years, rather than being calculated in relation to some average figure that bore little relation to the year-by-year variations in fruit yield. In poor harvest years, many presses were undoubtedly left idle or operated drastically below potential.

The final category of archaeological evidence to which I wish to allude is that pertaining to trade. The term 'trade', of course, covers a range of activities involving the movement and transfer of goods between people. It is now conventional to recognize at least three potentially distinct mechanisms at work: (a) reciprocity and gift exchange; (b) redistribution; and (c) marketing, which could be by barter, cash purchase, or a combination of the two.[1]

---

[1]   Peacock and Williams 1986, 55–66; C. Renfrew and Bahn 1991, 307–38. See also Greene 1986.

There is clear evidence for all three trading mechanisms in the Roman world.

The habit among the Roman élite of sending each other presents is well documented, and could account for some unique finds of commodities in unusual places.[1] Redistribution by the Roman state was undoubtedly a major influence on trade, most notably through the operation of the *annona* arrangements to feed the people of Rome and the frontier armies.[2] Roman aristocrats also practised redistribution, in moving goods from and between their various estates to support their households and dependants (Whittaker 1985). There is also no lack of information showing the existence of more normal trade and commerce.[3] The problem lies in trying to disentangle these mechanisms in the archaeological evidence, since in practice a single ship could have contained goods relating to all three. A well-off ship-owner or merchant might have contracted to transport a given quantity of goods for the *annona* to Rome, filling up any spare carrying capacity with presents for his contacts in Rome and with as many additional saleable goods as possible. The last could have enjoyed subsidized travel to Rome thanks to the *annona* cargo, and could earn valuable extra hard cash for the shipper.

I have suggested that individual consumption levels of olive oil may have been far higher than hitherto commonly admitted. I believe that 20 litres per capita may be a feasible average across society and across the Mediterranean (Mattingly 1988d, 161). The implications of this, on a Mediterranean population base normally estimated at between 25 and 50 million, are staggering in that they bring 'peak' Roman olive-oil production to at least a quarter or a half of modern levels. But can this hypothesis be sustained? If it is true, one would expect to find evidence for the production and movement of olive oil on a colossal scale. We have seen some production evidence that supports the idea; but what of distribution data? In the last twenty years amphora studies have undergone a revolution, and the evidence is now overwhelmingly

[1] Ausonius, *Epistles*, 25. See Whittaker 1983 for fuller discussion.
[2] Aldrete and Mattingly (forthcoming); Foxhall and Forbes 1982; Manacorda 1977; Rickman 1980; Sirks 1991.
[3] D'Arms 1981, esp. 1–19; D'Arms and Kopff 1980; Giardina 1993, 245–71; Panella 1993; Parker 1992, esp. 16–33; *Producción*, i–ii (various papers).

in favour of a much more active long-distance trade in staples than Moses Finley, for instance, was prepared to admit.[1] Ever since the pioneering excavations by Heinrich Dressel on Monte Testaccio, there has been no real dispute over the scale of imports to Rome itself, though obviously it was a special case. Monte Testaccio is an artificial hill, some 50 m high and 1 km in circumference at the base, located close to the main wharves and warehouses where olive oil supplies for the city of Rome were unloaded (Remesal Rodriguez 1994; Rodriguez-Almeida 1984). Recent calculations by Rodriguez-Almeida suggest that the heap was built up in the course of *c*.250 years and contains the fragments of *c*.53 million oil amphorae, deliberately broken after their contents were transferred into larger storage vessels. Furthermore, he suggests that *c*.33 million further amphorae may have been distributed intact into the city or ended up on other unrecorded dumps. The total 'oil lake' represented by Testaccio (assuming an average amphora capacity of *c*.70 l) would be in the order of 6,000 million litres. The figures seem overwhelming: but then, so was the population of the metropolis. Rome was certainly atypical, but the impact of its consumerism was felt much farther afield.

While many Tunisian and Libyan amphorae have been noted on Testaccio, the majority of the deposit seems to comprise the Dressel type 20 oil amphora from southern Spain. These globular vessels are particularly well studied, largely on account of the rich epigraphic data which they commonly yield in the form of makers' stamps and painted shipping information (*tituli picti*).[2] There is also supporting information of a more conventional epigraphic nature, such as the inscription set up by the *negotiatores olearii ex Baetica* to an ex-prefect of the *annona* who was their patron (*Producción*, i. 27–9; ii. 133–61).

Detailed studies of the olive presses and amphora kiln sites along the river Guadalquivir show that the Dressel 20 amphorae were produced almost exclusively for an export market (fig. 9.12). Olive oil itself, and other pottery, were produced across a much wider area, but it is the river (open to seagoing vessels as far upstream as Seville) that is the key to the distribution of the

[1]   Finley 1985, 133; cf. Parker 1992 (for an exhaustive catalogue of the shipwreck evidence); Peacock and Williams 1986; *Amphores*.
[2]   Keay 1988, 98–104; Peacock and Williams 1986, 9–15; Harris ed. 1993 (esp. article by Remesal Rodriguez); *Producción*, i–ii.

Dressel 20 kilns (Mattingly 1988a; Ponsich 1983). Here, as in Africa, there are clear indications of agricultural specialization in olive-oil production, with a large surplus being exported. A considerable amount of Spanish oil was moved in the context of the state redistributive system (*annona*), as Monte Testaccio testifies. What is less certain is the extent to which Spanish oil enjoyed a free market circulation as well.

When we turn to the growing body of evidence for the distribution of African oil amphorae, their widespread dispersal is most striking. The African amphorae have been recognized comparatively recently, and are far less self-publicizing than the Dressel 20s since they mostly lack stamps and few painted inscriptions have yet been noted;[1] but they turn up in large numbers in almost any place where analyses are being done on western Mediterranean sites. Evidence from one of the exporting cities, Leptiminus in the Sahel, has confirmed the very large-scale and long-running production of olive-oil amphore at a wealthy port site (Dore and Schinke 1992, 120–36). Similarly, the ubiquity of African fine wares (African Red Slip) in the western Mediterranean must reflect massive trade links in other commodities such as oil or grain, rather than an export market for pottery solely on its own merits (Carandini 1970; 1983a; Fentress and Perkins 1988). The evidence I have presented for specialization in olive cultivation in the Tunisian Sahel and high steppe strongly supports the view that African olive oil had access to a remarkably large and lucrative free market. This is now being increasingly corroborated by amphora evidence from some of the reception points in Spain, southern France, Italy, and elsewhere.[2]

Some implications

Olive-oil production, consumption, and trade were on a far larger scale in the ancient world than is generally admitted; there is also evidence for considerable growth in the overall volume of Mediterranean olive production during the Roman period.

---

[1] Keay 1984; Panella 1983; 1986; 1993; Peacock *et al.* 1989; 1990; Peacock and Williams 1986, 153–70.
[2] Keay 1984; Loseby 1992, 171–2, 184–5; Panella 1983, 228–33; 1993.

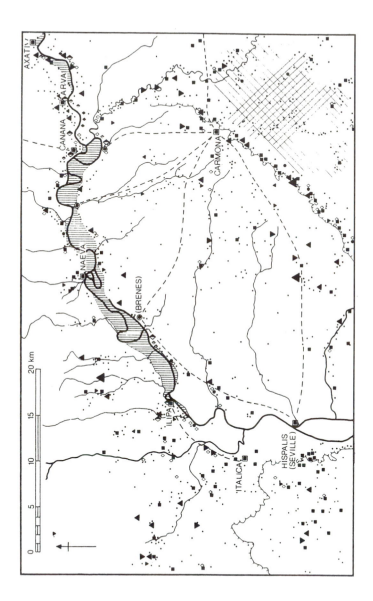

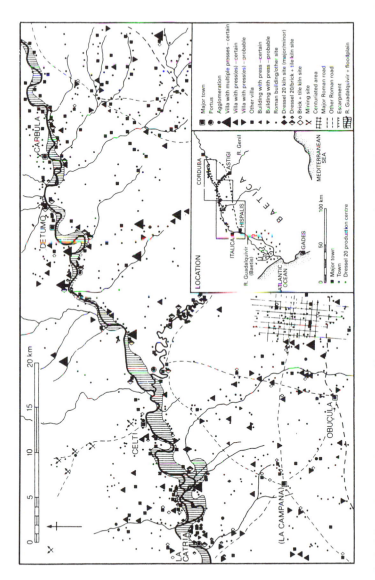

Figure 9.12 Olive oil production and Dressel 20 amphora manufacture in the Guadalquivir valley, Spain. Oleoculture is dispersed throughout the valley, but the production of amphorae for the export trade is concentrated in the vicinity of the navigable rivers and ports (after Mattingly 1988a).

Those are my principal theses. There are important socio-economic implications to be drawn from them. First, one would like to know whether the rise in olive-oil production can be equated with an overall upsurge in Mediterranean population in the early centuries AD, or whether it related more to a progressive rise in the standard of living of the Mediterranean peoples. The answer is probably a bit of both, with increased trade ameliorating the regionalized effects of years with poor production. In general, there was probably more oil available in many local markets, coming from distant as well as local sources. Some was even transported into the non-Mediterranean provinces of the empire (Britain, and the Rhine and Danube provinces). Second, the lives of many millions of the populace of the Roman world were affected by that production and trade: just imagine the countless farmers, harvesters, pressers, transporters by land or river who were involved; the potters and artisans who lived, in part at least, by providing containers, tools, press buildings, and equipment; or the merchants, shippers, shipbuilders, harbour and warehouse workers, retailers, pharmacists, perfumers, lamp-makers, textile workers, and even civil servants who were engaged in the trade. Both in the countryside and in the burgeoning urban centres, people depended on olives and oil not simply for their nutritional requirements, but for the means of earning or paying for their sustenance and meeting their other financial needs.

Acceptance of my understanding of the significance of olive oil in the Roman world also involves embracing a very far from minimalist view of the ancient economy. My model is in no way compatible with Finley's characterization of 'an underdeveloped economy' involving little inter-regional trade (and particularly not in staple foodstuffs) and minimal change or growth.[1] The late Roman *floruit* of the Tunisian high steppe olive lands was exactly the sort of development the minimalist 'school' would like to argue could not have happened.

I also believe that the distribution of wealth and political power in the Roman world may have been disrupted as a long-term consequence of growth in the olive-oil economy. Elite wealth could

---

[1] Finley 1985, esp. 177–207 ('Further Thoughts'). Recently published material on Egypt suggests a much higher degree of economic rationalism may have been present: see Rathbone 1991.

come from many sources, though farming produce and its trade (in whatever sense) was no doubt the most stable and common form. Cereals were an essential commodity, though bulky to transport and store in relation to their value (Rickman 1980; Spurr 1986); the best rewards were doubtless to be had by mild profiteering in years of dearth. Vines could be a spectacular earner – of that Columella leaves us in no doubt – but only the very best wines commanded really high prices, and quality wines were tricky to produce consistently. Wine, more than oil, was susceptible to sudden changes of consumer fashion (Carandini 1983b; Purcell 1985; Tchernia 1986). Olive oil was at least a good rival to its customary stable-mates: because it could produce startling results on lower-grade and even marginal land, it may even have outstripped them in areas where such land predominated (hence in Tunisia, Libya, Greece, and southern Spain).

Oleoculture and oil production can thus be recognized as potentially significant elements in individual aristocratic fortunes in various areas of the Roman world. The families of Trajan and Hadrian, though of Italian extraction, came from the Spanish town of Italica in the Guadalquivir valley, where they surely had major olive-growing estates (Syme 1965). They were accompanied into the upper echelons of Roman society and government in the second century AD by many other families with Spanish connections and landed wealth. Similarly, during the same century there was a steady build-up of Tripolitanian and African members of the senate at Rome, culminating in the creation of the first African *princeps*, Septimius Severus of Lepcis Magna (Birley 1988; Mattingly 1988b). Personal patronage may have played its role in bringing these people into the senate; but without enormous financial resources of their own, provincial aristocrats were unlikely to be taken so far or so fast. The rise to prominence of such a body of African senators is more likely to have been a consequence of their already considerable economic importance, and archaeological evidence now supports the view that the economic centre of the western Mediterranean was shifting to its southern shore in advance of this political development (which may itself, of course, have accelerated the trend). For without the extraordinary and single-minded, long-term development of oleoculture in the *territorium* of Lepcis Magna, that town might have remained undistinguished and Septimius Severus simply a local notable.

Olive oil may not actually have been the kingmaker, but it could be regarded as the prime source of his princely-sized inheritance. Economic developments in the Roman empire could thus have long-term political consequences.

What starts with nature and ecology can be seen to have dramatic effects on socio-economic structures, and it is the inter-digitation of my research on ancient rural settlement, land use, and agricultural technology with studies of the Roman economy and political history that gives wider relevance to this work.[1] I want to conclude by suggesting a series of propositions about Roman oleoculture that highlight its importance to our under-standing of the ancient economy and ecology, which I hope may form a useful basis (as 'performance indicators') for future discus-sions of Roman provincial economic growth or stagnation:

1   During the course of the Roman period there was a dramatic increase in the geographical extent of oleoculture, and in some regions in its scale also.

2   This spread carried the olive into regions before, and since, considered highly marginal for cultivation or oleoculture, involving in some areas a surprising degree of specialization.

3   Some of the expansion in oleoculture was achieved through intensive capital investment in estates, nurseries, and pressing equipment and would seem to have involved a significant degree of risk-taking on the part of both landowners and tenant farmers.

4   Since there is no evidence that the olive was less affected in antiquity by drastically unequal fruiting patterns than it has been down to recent times, the cultivation strategies and rural economies must have been so structured to allow for this.

5   Processing capacity in olive mills is more likely to have been gauged to meet anticipated peak demands in bumper years than some form of (meaningless) average yield or minimum crop.

6   The large scale of olive presses in the key oil-exporting regions indicates a capacity to process in bulk that has not been equalled until the modern era (despite the supposed

---

[1]   The rising importance of such ecological approaches to ancient history is well illustrated by the provocative and stimulating work of Gallant 1991 and Sallares 1991.

technological inferiority of the Roman lever presses in comparison with medieval direct screw presses).

7   The massive investment in oleoculture and processing equipment in the exporting provinces was conditional on the perception of a market for the oil.

8   Long-distance trade in olive oil was an important component of Mediterranean sea traffic, and this involved free trade as well the state's great redistributive mechanisms.

9   Olive-oil production and trade was a significant source of élite wealth in certain regions, notably Baetica, Tripolitania, and Byzacena.

10   The importance of oleoculture varied enormously across the empire, with some areas perhaps never rising above strictly peasant subsistence level; but for the exporting regions, at any rate, it is clear that a primitivist view of the ancient economy simply will not work.

Finally, what did nature matter in all this? The olive boom of the Roman world clearly made important contributions to the way people lived in antiquity, but its impact should not be assumed to have been entirely benign. Nature was variously nurtured, employed, challenged, contradicted, and abused by intensive and large-scale olive farming. Personal and regional fortunes were made on (and then depended upon) an understanding of the potential of the natural ecology and its exploitation. However, there was an ecological price to pay for the economic expansion achieved in some areas of the Roman world. Research is needed to assess the potential environmental debit of intensive olive farming, but it is self-evident that the more marginal soils on to which the olive spread in this period were precisely those most likely to suffer long-term depletion. Thus, natural factors should not be ruled out in our continuing attempts to make sense of the economic, political, and social problems of late antiquity.

Bibliography

Akerraz, A., and Lenoir, M. (1982), 'Les huileries de Volubilis', *Bulletin d'archéologie marocaine*, 14: 69–120.

Aldrete, G. S., and Mattingly, D. J. (forthcoming), 'Feeding the city: the organization, operation and scale of the food supply system for Rome', in D. Potter and D. J. Mattingly (eds), *Life, Death and Entertainment in Ancient Rome* (Ann Arbor, Mich.).

Amouretti, M.-C. (1981), 'Des agronomes latins aux agronomes provençaux: les moulins à huile', *Provence historique*, 124: 83–100.

—— (1986), *Le Pain et l'huile dans la Grèce antique* (Paris).

—— (1993), 'Les sous-produits de la fabrication de l'huile et du vin dans l'antiquité', in Amouretti and Brun (eds), 463–76.

—— and Brun, J.-P. (eds 1993), *La Production du vin et de l'huile en Méditerranée* (Bulletin de correspondance hellénique, supp. 26; Paris).

—— and Comet, G. (1985), *Le Livre de l'olivier* (Aix-en-Provence).

—— Comet, G., Ney, C., and Paillet, J.-C. (1984), 'A propos d'un pressoir à huile: de l'archéologie industrielle à l'histoire', *Mélanges de l'Ecole Française de Rome: antiquités*, 96 (1): 379–421.

Amphores = *Amphores romaines et histoire économique: dix ans de recherches* (Rome, 1989).

Antolini, P. (1986), *Il libro dell'ulivo e dell'olio d'oliva* (Genova).

Baldini, E., and Scaramuzzi, F. (1981), *L'olivo* (Rome).

Barker, G. W. W. (1988), 'The archaeology of the Etruscan countryside', *Antiquity*, 62: 772–85.

—— and Jones, G. D. B. (eds 1984), 'The Unesco Libyan Valleys Survey, vi: investigations of a Romano-Libyan farm, part 1', *Lib. Stud.* 15: 1–45.

Ben Baaziz, S. (1991), 'Les huileries de la Tunisie antique', *Cahiers du Tunisie*, 43 (155–6): 39–64.

Birley, A. R. (1988), *The African Emperor: Septimius Severus* (London).

Boardman, J. (1977), 'The olive in the Mediterranean: its culture and use', in J. Hutchinson (ed.), *The Early History of Agriculture* (Oxford), 187–96.

Borowski, O. (1987), *Agriculture in Iron Age Israel* (Eisenbraums, Wis.).

Braconi, L. (1979), *L'olivicoltura intensiva* (Bologna).

Bradford, J. (1949), '"Buried landscapes" in southern Italy', *Antiquity*, 23 (June): 58–72.

—— (1957), *Ancient Landscapes: Studies in Field Archaeology* (London).

Brothwell, D., and Brothwell, P. (1969), *Food in Antiquity* (London).

Brun, J.-P. (1986), *L'Oléiculture antique en Provence: les huileries du département du Var* (Paris).

—— (1993), 'L'oléiculture et viticulture antiques en Gaule: instruments et installations de production', in Amouretti and Brun (eds), 307–41.

Callot, O. (1984), *Huileries antiques de Syrie du nord* (Paris).

Camps-Fabrer, H. (1953), *L'Olivier et l'huile dans l'Afrique romaine* (Algiers).

Carandini, A. (1970), 'Produzione agricola e produzione ceramica nell'Africa di età imperiale: appunti sull'economia della Zeugitana e della Byzacena', *Studi miscellanei*, 15: 95–119.

—— (1983a), 'Pottery and the African economy', in Garnsey *et al.* (eds), 145–62.

—— (1983b), 'Columella's vineyard and the rationality of the Roman economy', *Opus*, 2 (1): 177–204.

Ceccolini, S., and Bruni, B. (1983), *Note pratiche di olivicoltura* (3rd edn, Bologna).

Cotton, M. (1979), *The Late Republican Villa at Posto, Francolise* (London).

Cowper, H. S. (1897), *The Hill of the Graces: A Record of Investigation among the Trilithons and Megalithic sites of Tripoli* (London).

Cresswell, R. (1965), 'Un pressoir à olives au Liban: essai de technologie comparée', *L'Homme: cahiers d'ethnologie*, 5 (1): 33–66.

D'Arms, J. H. (1981), *Commerce and Social Standing in Ancient Rome* (Cambridge, Mass.).

—— and Kopff, E. C. (1980), *The Seaborne Commerce of Ancient Rome* (Rome).

De Beir, G. (1980), 'Intervention du Conseil Oléicole International', in *Producción*, i. 311–19.

Dembinska, M. (1985), 'Diet: a comparison of food consumption between some eastern and western monasteries in the 4th–12th centuries', *Byzantion*, 55 (2): 431–62.

Despois, J. (1955), *La Tunisie orientale: Sahel et Basse Steppe, étude géographique* (Paris).

Dolamore, A. (1988), *The Essential Olive Oil Companion* (London).

Dore, J., and Schinke, R. (1992), 'First report on the pottery', in N. Ben Lazreg and D. J. Mattingly (eds), *Leptiminus (Lamta), A Roman Port City in Tunisia: Report No. 1* (JRA supp. 4), 115–56.

Drachman, A. G. (1932), *Ancient Olive Mills and Presses* (Copenhagen).

—— (1963), *The Mechanical Technology of Greek and Roman Antiquity* (London).

Dunbabin, K. M. D. (1978), *The Mosaics of Roman Africa* (Oxford).

Eitam, D. (1987), 'Olive oil production during the biblical period', in Heltzer and Eitam (eds), 16–35.

Evenari, M., Shanon, L., and Tadmor, N. (1971), *The Negev: The Challenge of a Desert* (Cambridge, Mass.).

Fentress, E., and Perkins, P. (1988), 'Counting African slip ware', *L'Africa romana*, 5: 205–14.

Finley, M. I. (1985), *The Ancient Economy* (2nd edn, London).

Forbes, H. (1992), 'The ethnoagricultural approach to ancient Greek agriculture: olive cultivation as a case study', in B. Wells (ed.), *Agriculture in Ancient Greece (Proceedings of the 7th International Symposium at the Swedish Institute at Athens)* (Skrifter utgivna av Svenska Institutet i Athen, series in 4to, 42; Stockholm), 87–101.

—— (1993), 'Ethnoarchaeology and the place of the olive in the economy of the southern Argolid', in Amouretti and Brun (eds), 213–26.

—— and Foxhall, L. (1978), ' "The queen of all trees": preliminary notes on the archaeology of the olive', *Expedition*, 21 (1): 37–47.

Foxhall, L. (1993), 'Oil extraction and processing equipment in ancient Greece', in Amouretti and Brun (eds), 183–99.

—— and Forbes, H. (1982), 'Σιτομετϱεία: the role of grain as a staple food in classical history', *Chiron*, 12: 41–90.

Frankel, R. (1987), 'Oil presses in western Galilee and the Judaea: a comparison', in Heltzer and Eitam (eds), 63–80.

——, Avitsur, S., and Ayalon, E. (1994), *History and Technology of Olive Oil in the Holy Land* (Arlington and Tel Aviv).

Frezzotti, G., and Manni, M. (1956), *Olive Oil Processing in Rural Mills* (FAO Agricultural Development Papers, 58; Rome).

Gallant, T. W. (1991), *Risk and Survival in Ancient Greece* (Stanford, Conn.).

Garnsey, P., Hopkins, K., and Whittaker, C. R. (eds 1983), *Trade in the Ancient Economy* (London).

Giardina, A. (ed. 1993), *The Romans* (Chicago).

Giorgini, G. (1982), *Come si coltiva l'olivo* (Milan).

Grande Covian, F., *et al.* (1984), 'Table ronde sur les propriétés de l'huile d'olive et son rôle dans la nutrition humaine', *Olivae*, 3: 6–10.

Gray, P. (1986), *Honey from the Weed: Fasting and Feasting in Tuscany, Catalonia, the Cyclades and Apulia* (London).

Greene, K. (1986), *The Archaeology of the Roman Economy* (London).

Guthrie, H. A. (1975), *Introductory Nutrition* (3rd edn; St Louis, Mo.).

Harris, W. V. (ed. 1993), *The Inscribed Economy* (*JRA* supp. 6).

Heltzer, M., and Eitam, D. (eds 1987), *Olive Oil in Antiquity*, Haifa.

Hitchner, R. B. (1988), 'The Kasserine archaeological survey 1982–1986', *Ant. Afr.* 24: 7–41.

—— (1989), 'The organization of rural settlement in the Cillium–Thelepte region (Kasserine, central Tunisia)', *L'Africa romana*, 6: 387–402.

—— (1993), 'Olive production and the Roman economy: the case of intensive growth', in Amouretti and Brun (eds), 499–508.

—— *et al.* (1990), 'The Kasserine archaeological survey 1987', *Ant. Afr.* 26: 231–60.

—— and Mattingly, D. J. (1991), 'Fruits of empire: the production of olive oil in Roman Africa', *National Geographic Research and Exploration*, 7 (1): 36–55.

Isager, S., and Skydsgaard, J. E. (1992), *Ancient Greek Agriculture: An Introduction* (London and New York).

Jones, G. D. B. (1980), 'Il Tavoliere romano: L'agricoltura romana attraverso l'aerofotografia e lo scavo', *Archeologia classica*, 32: 85–100.

Keay, S. (1984), *Late Roman Amphorae in the Western Mediterranean: A Typology and Economic Study. The Catalan Evidence* (BAR Int. Ser. 196; Oxford).

—— (1988), *Roman Spain* (London).

Kehoe, D. (1988), *The Economics of Agriculture on Roman Imperial Estates in North Africa* (Hypomnemata, 89; Göttingen).

Labaied, L. (1981), *Olivier en Tunisie: étude géographique* (Tunis).

Leveau, P. (1984), *Caesarea de Maurétanie: une ville romaine et ses campagnes* (Rome).

——, Sillières, P., and Vallat, J.-P. (1993), *Campagnes de la Méditerranée romaine: occident* (Paris).

L'Huile = *L'Huile d'olive en Méditerrannée: histoire, anthropologie, économie de l'antiquité à nos jours* (Aix-en-Provence, 1985).

Loseby, S. T. (1992), 'Marseille: a late antique success story?', *JRS* 82: 165–85.

Louis, A. (1969), 'Aux Matmata et dans les Ksar du sud: l'olivier et les hommes', *Cahiers des arts et traditions populaires*, 3: 41–66.

Loussert, R., and Brousse, G. (1978), *L'Olivier* (Paris).

Manacorda, D. (1977), 'Testimonianze sulla produzione e il consumo dell'olio tripolitano nel III secolo', *Dialoghi di archeologia*, 9–10 (1–2): 542–601.

Marcaccini, P. (1973), 'Il limite dell'olivo nella Romagna e in genere nell'Italia continentale', *Rivista geographica italiana*, 80 (1): 28–49; 80 (2): 155–97.

Mattingly, D. J. (1985), 'Olive oil production in Roman Tripolitania', in D. J. Buck and D. J. Mattingly (eds), *Town and Country in Roman Tripolitania: Papers in honour of Olwen Hackett* (BAR Int. Ser. 274; Oxford), 27–46.

—— (1987), 'New perspectives on the agricultural development of Gebel and pre-desert in Roman Tripolitania', *Revue de l'occident musulman et de la Méditerranée*, 41–2: 45–65.

—— (1988a), 'Oil for export: a comparative study of Roman olive oil production in Libya, Spain and Tunisia', *JRA* 1: 33–56.

—— (1988b), 'The olive boom: oil surpluses, wealth and power in Roman Tripolitania', *Lib. Stud.* 19: 21–41.

—— (1988c), 'Megalithic madness and measurement: or how many olives could an olive press press?', *OJA* 7 (2): 177–95.

—— (1988d), 'Olea mediterranea?', *JRA* 1: 153–61.

—— (1989), 'Farmers and frontiers: exploiting and defending the countryside of Roman Tripolitania', *Lib. Stud.* 20: 135–53.

—— (1990), 'Paintings, presses and perfume production at Pompeii', *OJA* 9 (1): 1–90.

—— (1993), 'Maximum figures and maximizing strategies of oil production? Further thoughts on the processing capacity of Roman olive presses', in Amouretti and Brun (eds), 483–98.

—— (1994), 'Regional variation in Roman oleoculture: some problems of comparability', in J. Carlsen, P. Ørsted, and J.-E. Skydsgaard (eds), *Landuse in the Roman Empire* (Analecta Romana Instituti Danici, supp. 22), 91–106.

—— (1995), *Tripolitania* (London).

—— and Hitchner, R. B. (1993), 'Technical specifications for some North African olive presses of Roman date', in Amouretti and Brun (eds), 439–62.

—— and —— (1995), 'Roman Africa: an archaeological review', *JRS* 85: 165–213.

—— and Zenati, M. (1984), 'The excavation of Building Lm 4E: the olive press', in Barker and Jones (eds), 13–18; 21–2.

Morizot, P. (1993), 'L'aures et l'olivier', *Ant. Afr.* 29: 177–240.

Oates, D. (1953), 'The Tripolitanian Gebel: settlement of the Roman period around Gasr ed-Daun', *PBSR* 21: 81–117.

Olivae tunisienne = *L'Olivae tunisienne* (Tunis).

Pagnol, J. (1975), *L'Olivier* (Avignon).

Panella, C. (1983), 'I contenitori oleari presenti ad Ostia in età antonina: analisi tipologica, epigrafica, quantitativa', in *Producción*, ii. 226–61.

—— (1986), 'Le anfore tardoantiche: centri di produzione e mercati preferenziali', in A. Giardina (ed.), *Società romana e impero tardoantico*, iii. 251–84.

—— (1993), 'Merci e scambi nel mediterraneo tardoantico', in A. Carandini, L. Cracco Ruggini, and A. Giardina (eds), *Storia di Roma*, iii. 2, 613–97.

Pansiot, F., and Rebour, J. (1961), *Improvement in Olive Cultivation* (Rome).

Parker, A. J. (1992), *Ancient Shipwrecks of the Mediterranean and Roman Provinces* (BAR Int. Ser. 580; Oxford).

Peacock, D. P. S., Bejaoui, F., and Belazreg, N. (1989), 'Roman amphora production in the Sahel region of Tunisia', in *Amphores*, 179–222.

—— and Williams, D. F. (1986), *Amphorae and the Roman Economy: An Introductory Guide* (Harlow).

——, Benjaoui, F. and Ben Lazreg, N. (1990), 'Roman pottery production in central Tunisia', *JRA* 3: 59–84.

Peyras, J. (1975), 'Le Fundus Aufidianus: étude d'un grand domaine de la région de Mateur (Tunisie de nord)', *Ant. Afr.* 9: 181–222.

Poncet, J. (1962), *La Colonisation et l'agriculture européens en Tunisie depuis 1881* (Paris).

Ponsich, M. (1974–89), *Implantation rurale antique sur le Bas-Guadalquivir*, i–iv (Madrid).

—— (1983), 'Le facteur géographique dans les moyens de transport de l'huile de Bétique', in *Producción*, ii. 101–13.

Producción, i, ii = *Producción y comercio del aceite en la antigüedad*, i (1980); ii (1983) (Madrid).

Purcell, N. (1985), 'Wine and wealth in ancient Italy', *JRS* 75: 1–19.

Rathbone, D. W. (1991), *Economic Rationalism and Rural Society in Third Century AD Egypt: The Heroninos Archive and the Appianus Estate* (Cambridge).

Raulin, V. (1869), *Description physique de l'isle de Crète*, i (Paris).

Remesal Rodriguez, J. (1994), 'Los sellos en anforas Dr 20: nuevos aportaciónes del Testaccio', in *Epigrafia della produzione e della distribuzione* (Collection de l'Ecole Française à Rome, 193; Rome), 93–110.

Renfrew, C., and Bahn, P. (1991), *Archaeology: Theories, Methods and Practice* (London).

—— and Wagstaff, M. (1982), *An Island Polity: The Archaeology of Exploitation in Melos* (Cambridge).

Renfrew, J. M. (1973), *Palaeoethnobotany: The Prehistoric Food Plants of the Near East and Europe* (London).

Rickman, G. (1980), *The Corn Supply of Ancient Rome* (Oxford).

Rodriguez-Almeida, E. (1984), *Il Monte Testaccio: ambiente, storia, materiali* (Rome).

Rossiter, J. J. (1981), 'Wine and oil processing on Roman farms in Italy', *Phoenix*, 35: 345–61.

Runnels, C. N., and Hansen, J. (1986), 'The olive in the prehistoric Aegean: the evidence for domestication in the early bronze age', *OJA* 5 (3): 299–308.

Sallares, R. (1991), *The Ecology of the Ancient Greek World* (London).

Saumagne, C. (1929), 'Les vestiges d'une centuriation romaine à l'est d'El-Djem', *Comptes rendus à l'Académie des Inscriptions*, 307–13.

—— (1952), 'La photographie aériënne au service de l'archéologie', *Comptes rendus à l'Académie des Inscriptions*, 287–301.

Sirks, B. (1991), *Food for Rome: The Legal Structure of the Transportation and Processing of Supplies for Rome and Constantinople* (Amsterdam).

Spurr, M. S. (1986), *Arable Cultivation in Roman Italy* (London).

Syme, R. (1965), 'Hadrian the intellectual', in *Les Empereurs romains d'Espagne*, Paris: 243–53.

Tchalenko, G. (1953–8), *Villages antiques de la Syrie du nord* (Paris).

Tchernia, A. (1986), *Le Vin de l'Italie romaine: essai d'histoire économique d'après les amphores* (Paris).

Tinè, S. (1983), *Passo di Corvo e la civiltà neolitica de Tavoliere* (Genova).

Trousset, P. (1977), 'Nouvelles observations sur la centuriation à l'est d'El Djem', *Ant. Afr.* 11: 175–207.

Turrill, W. B. (1951), 'Wild and cultivated olives', *Kew Bulletin*, no. 3: 437–42.

Ucko, P., and Dimbleby, G. (eds 1969), *The Domestication of Plants and Animals* (Chicago).

Vallet, G. (1962), 'L'introduction de l'olivier en Italie centrale d'après les données de la céramique', in *Hommages à A. Grenier*, iii (Collection Latomus; Brussels), 1554–63.

van der Veen, M. (1985), 'The Unesco Libyan Valleys Survey, x: botanical evidence for ancient farming in the pre-desert', *Lib. Stud.* 16: 15–28.

White, K. D. (1970), *Roman Farming* (London).

—— (1975), *Farm Equipment of the Roman World* (Cambridge).

—— (1984), *Greek and Roman Technology* (London).

Whittaker, C. R. (1983), 'Late Roman trade and traders', in Garnsey *et al.* (eds), 162–80.

—— (1985), 'Trade and the aristocracy in the Roman empire', *Opus*, 4: 49–75.

Zohary, D., and Spiegel-Roy, P. (1975), 'Beginning of fruit growing in the old world', *Science*, 187: 319–27.

10

Barren fields?
Landscapes and settlements in late
Roman and post-Roman Italy

Neil Christie

Introduction

The late Roman period in Italy, as almost anywhere in the Roman world, is generally seen as one of general decay of urban and rural life in the face of the break-up of the state at the hands of hordes of barbarian invaders. Settlement is thought to have returned almost to a murky repetition of pre-Roman modes of upland nucleation, with the classical town–country relationship almost wholly displaced. But how valid is this picture nowadays, in the wake of new archaeological excavations, field surveys, and revised assessments of the documentary sources and of the material impact of the so-called 'barbarians'? For example, was there continuity in 'classical' settlement activity and in rural exploitation beyond Rome's fall? And how far did human control over nature decline as control over society and the economy faltered?

This chapter seeks to offer a guide through the somewhat restricted documentary and archaeological sources for the period from *c.* AD 350 to 650. In the case of the documentary sources, it is valuable to determine the degree to which the late Roman and post-classical authors were aware of changes in settlement, in economy, and in nature, and of steps that needed to be made to counteract such changes – if counteraction was even thought necessary. Through this it should be possible to pinpoint at least some of the mechanisms behind these changes. Against these data can be set the results of archaeology and the level to which field-work corroborates what the texts say. Can a population decline be identified physically? Was there a transition to new settlement forms, and a concomitant decline in human manipulation of the environment?

Death, decay, and demise in late Roman Italy

It can be argued that Roman authors always had a tendency to concentrate on, and perhaps glorify, military matters, and with the late empire this tendency becomes even more pronounced, reflecting the increasing insecurity felt throughout the Roman world (Johnson 1983, 57–66). Other authors, such as Boëthius, began seeking consolation in religion or in philosophy, and still others tried composing poetry in their country estates while shunning the outside world (P. Brown 1971; Roberts 1992). Literary output (of a non-religious nature) was seemingly restricted, at least on the basis of textual survival – the first shadows, it could be claimed, of the impending 'dark ages' (an outmoded but still undeniably useful term). Earlier imperial Roman authors had, of course, touched on nearly all topics, including the countryside, though it is disputed how close to reality the pictures painted by Varro, Columella, or Pliny really are. Some late agricultural writers are known, notably Palladius, but they draw heavily upon the earlier agronomists and therefore tell us little of contemporary note. As time progresses, in fact, the countryside recedes quietly into the distance, becoming merely the scene for romantic poetry, the setting for huge country estates of senators or emperors, or the backdrop to tramping, destructive armies. Certainly the immediate effects of war on innocent peasant populations or on farmland are a frequent means of shocking the late antique reader; but the lasting effects of such conflicts or disasters are only occasionally touched upon and require careful rooting out. Yet, as noted above, relevant sources are scarce: only a limited range of examples can be presented here, but one needs to beware throughout of authors' biases (theirs, and no doubt also to some degree mine) and of the constant desire to exaggerate narratives in terms of numbers, brutality, or misery, whether for poetical and dramatic effect or from diplomatic and political motives.

A suitable starting-point can be made with the words of the poet and senator Claudius Rutilius Namatianus, who composed his half-extant poem *De reditu suo* on the occasion of his journey home to Gaul from his beloved Rome. He writes in around 417, just a few years after Alaric and his Visigoths' brief but destructive tour of the no longer Eternal City, and the tribe's subsequent march to Gaul. In effect Rutilius was travelling from one war-torn land to another, and understandably he was not wholly excited by the prospect. He says:

> Long wars have ruined the fields of my native land; pity takes me from the land that I love. . . . But it is sinful to neglect ruin already compounded by neglect: now is the time, after the fires have cooled, to rebuild, even if we are rebuilding only shepherds' huts.
>
> (1. 28–30)

The shock of Rome's capture still reverberates, but Rutilius still hopes for Rome's renewed glory: 'May misfortune be forgotten; may your wounds close and heal because you have ignored the pain. Surrounded by failure, hope for prosperity: may you be enriched by all your losses' (1. 119–22).

His text, however, does not offer many signs of enrichment from these losses: first he informs his readers that his journey is to be by boat, not just because it is quicker, but more significantly because

> roads can flood, or be littered by landslides and falling rocks; Tuscany and the Aurelian highway have already fallen to the Goths. It is best to trust the sea because the rivers are not bridged and the land has become wild again.
>
> (1. 35–40)

His flowing words present already a striking image of rural decay for what was still the central province of the empire. As his trip progresses, Rutilius speaks of the sites seen or visited *en route*, and drops further hints of Italy's problems: there are various ports, acting as refuges to homeless peasants or terrified Roman citizens; there are abandoned towns like Populonia and rat-infested Cosa, once sizeable and important colonies and trading centres (1. 284–7, 401–12). Rutilius argues that 'We must

Figure 10.1 Map of Italy, showing principal sites mentioned in the text.

not complain if our bodies decay, for we can see that cities also must decay' (1. 412–13).

Yet the pattern is variable, and Rutilius admits to heartily enjoying the fair at Faleria, his lodgings in the nearby groves, and Albinus' fine estates near Volterra; he also duly notes the congested harbour serving Pisa. The poem breaks off abruptly with his view of the white cliffs of Luni on the Ligurian coast, but a further fragment of the text exists describing the town of Albenga, further up the coast, where rebuilding is going on after the destructions wrought by the passage of the Visigoths (Lamboglia 1976–8). Vitality and regeneration are thus evident, at least in some quarters of Italy, but it is difficult to glean how typical this situation may have been (fig. 10.1).

From other sources it is obvious that Italy had suffered badly from barbarian incursions, from military insurrections, and from increasing civil unrest since the mid-third century. This is clearly expressed in the need to fortify, and it cannot be doubted that the emperor Aurelian's fortification of Rome in the 270s sent shock waves throughout Italy and the rest of the empire – this was, after all, a blatant statement of panic and loss of confidence. Not every town fortified itself, or was able to fortify itself: key centres at passes, on pass routes, on road–river cross-roads, and on the coast were modified first. In most cases the work in Italy does not show signs of panic building, in terms of throwing into the wall fabric abundant elements of *spolia* or reused materials. Where spoil is used, it is often rather carefully arranged in wall footings as an almost decorative feature – as is true of many third- and fourth-century circuit walls in Gaul and Britain. A few sites, however, do indicate rougher, more rapid construction using materials taken from buildings demolished along the route of the walls: notably Verona, where an inscription records that in 267 Gallienus ordered the walls to be built in order to counter the specific threat of an Alemannic incursion. By the early fifth century in Italy, unfortified towns are exceptional and for the most part were those whose days were numbered (Johnson 1983, 117–21; 215–20; Christie 1991a). Hence the court poet laureate Claudius Claudianus, in his many praises to Honorius in the late fourth century, speaks of 'the high-walled cities of Italy rejoicing in the blessings of thy presence', and of a countryside protected not just by new army recruits but also 'by so many rivers and fortresses'. The images offered in the *Notitia dignitatum*, an official register of imperial posts compiled over the later fourth and early fifth centuries, likewise show that the term 'city' was now synonymous with fortress, and illustrate barrier walls and other defensive arrangements across the Alps, tied to the command of a *comes Italiae* (*Not. dign. occidentalis*, 24).

The text of the *Notitia dignitatum* (*occ.* 42), and other sources such as Zosimus' *Nea historia*, meanwhile demonstrate the deliberate settlement of federate (that is, allied or conquered) groups of barbarians, in particular Sarmatians, within Italy, primarily across the northern regions. Place-name evidence further attests this settlement in both town and country. But the question here is how far this was a means to aid in military defence, and how far it was intended to repopulate the towns and their territories and revitalize agricultural output. Zosimus, writing in the mid-fifth century but talking of the empire at the death of Theodosius in 395, crudely comments: 'the Roman empire has been gradually diminished and become a home for barbarians, or has been reduced to such a depopulated state that the places where the cities used to be cannot be recognized' (*Nea historia*, 4. 59; cf. 5. 33–4). This was probably fairly true for the frontier provinces, but it is not easy as yet to transfer the picture to the (theoretically) buffered province of Italy. It should be remembered that Italy, as the old home province of the empire, and Rome, as its old capital, were always the goal of the enemy, barbarian and Roman alike. Devastation of towns and their hinterlands is fairly well attested throughout the sources, and does provide a suitable context for depopulation or at least for shifts in population foci. A principal source of data in this respect is the *Codex Theodosianus*, containing laws promulgated between 313 and 438 and also incorporating subsequent laws passed under the emperors Marcian and Valentinian III. Given that these are official statements one might expect a playing down of problems, yet the problems stick out like sore thumbs, and the frequent repetition of laws reveals a high level of desperation on the part of the imperial authorities. In the case of the towns and cities, and of Rome especially, there are constant reprimands against the demolition or robbing of old public buildings, many reduced to a perilous state (*Cod. Theod.* 15. 1. 11–32). Old buildings are to be repaired before new projects are set in hand, with the Heritage Secretary of the day telling the citizens to 'protect the ornamentation of their ancestral municipality' (*Cod. Theod.* 15. 1. 37, promulgated in AD 398). Indirectly, of course, these laws signify urban depopulation and economic decay (see Ward-Perkins 1984).

The image can also be transferred to beyond the towns. Heightened demands for the supply of provisions – the *annona* – for the army were badly affecting the land: rapacious tax demands were making farmers flee, small landowners were tying themselves as tenants to larger landowners, and troopers were pillaging the land for extra rations and illegally billeting themselves on private property. Land became deserted, even in prosperous regions like Campania to the south of Rome. A decree of AD 395 states:

> For the provincials of Campania we remit the taxes of 528,042 *iugera* [1,332 sq km] which appear to be located in deserted and unkempt districts of the said province, according to the report to us of the inspectors and records of the ancient documents.
>
> (*Cod. Theod.* 11. 28. 2)

Warfare prompted further strains on the land, and the emperors were forced to try to ease the pain: for example, in 412 four-fifths of every class of tax payment was 'remitted for Campania, Tuscany, Picenum, Samnium, Apulia, Calabria as well as Bruttium and Lucania ... for five years' (*Cod. Theod.* 11. 28. 7). This was one of the main after-effects of the Visigothic invasions, and it continued to spread ruin: a law of 418 decrees that

> Campania shall have its lands made subject to tax equalization and, with the exception of the tax dues, shall bear only the ninth part of the past amount of payments to the state, since a very heavy tax assessment of former times burdens her territory, and since that assessment, she has been devastated by the incursion of the enemy.
>
> (*Cod. Theod.* 11. 28. 12)

Vandal raids in the 430s and 440s prompted further similar tax remissions throughout western Italy and the islands (*Cod. Theod.*, *nov. Val.* 1. 1–3). The Vandal occupation of Africa from AD 430 deprived Rome of many of its main food supplies, creating numerous food shortages; Sicily became the new supplier, but this area, too, was badly hit by raids. Rome was suffering badly from its over-reliance on external resources, and it is a clear sign of its fatal condition that an agricultural resurgence within Italy itself could not be promoted.

The various wars also needed manpower, but prospective recruits did their utmost to avoid the call-up, mutilating themselves, becoming monks, or deserting; there are also mentions of roving bands of deserters and brigands who then did their best to disrupt the highways in order to fend for themselves (*Cod. Theod.* 7. 13. 4; 7. 18. 10–15; 7. 20. 12). As a factor related to this, it is essential to note that the barbarians or usurpers who pillaged Italy will, of course, have used the same roads the Roman armies would use, since the wealthier towns lay along these highways. On the evidence of milestones, either re-erected ones or new ones claiming road repairs, imperial attention became limited to the major highways, ensuring they were adequate for the troops. After the 370s, however, we lose track of these records, suggestive of a major breakdown in maintenance (see Basso 1986, 223–8). Indeed, a law in the *Codex Theodosianus* of AD 399 states that 'On account of the immense ruin of the highways, it is our will that all persons, with helpful devotion, shall eagerly desire to hasten to the repair of the public roads' (15. 3. 4). Yet, from what Rutilius Namatianus reports less than two decades later, this eager devotion had failed to surface and travel on roads was not something to be recommended.

But to what extent did this all force the late Roman rural population inside the walls of the nearby towns, and was the wasted countryside recolonized by federate barbarians? Do towns show an upsurge of activity to mark the arrival of refugees? Here we must look to the evidence of archaeology for clarification. Of prime value are the results of field surveys, now a rapid and economical means of determining settlement and landscape change in the Mediterranean (Barker and Lloyd eds 1991, 1–17 and *passim*). One of the best known field surveys is that carried out by the British School at Rome between the 1950s and 1970s in the region of South Etruria, north of the city of Rome. The survey comprised fieldwalking, selective excavation, and building surveys, and was designed to sample the full sequence of occupational change from prehistoric into modern times (Potter 1979; Hodges and Whitehouse 1983, 36–43). The basic fact that emerged from the survey was the sizeable and progressive reduction in the number of identifiable Roman-period farm sites throughout the study areas, from the second to the fifth century AD: in the case of the more northerly sector, the Ager Faliscus, 95 sites were occupied in the second century and 67 in the third, diminishing to 31 in the fourth and just 22 in the fifth to sixth centuries (fig. 10.2). To the south the Ager Veientanus, an area in closer reach of

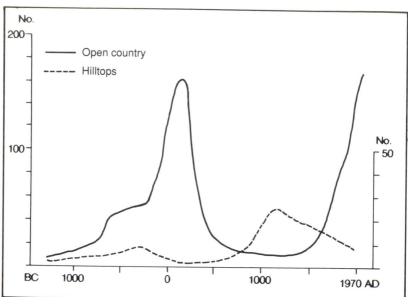

Figure 10.2 Comparative chart illustrating the changing relationship between open, low-lying sites (left-hand scale) and hilltop or defended sites (right-hand scale) between 1000 BC and AD 2000 in the Ager Faliscus region of S. Etruria, central Italy. (After Randsborg 1991, fig. 40.)

Rome and, one would assume, more closely reflective of trends within the city itself, shows a like decline, the nearly 270 sites active around AD 80 being reduced to 91 around AD 350 and then just 39 by the mid-fifth century. In sum, there was an overall fall of around 80 per cent in parts of South Etruria between the first and fifth centuries. A decline in rural exploitation must, even in the case of Rome, point to a lessening in demand from the urban population, caused by reduced numbers. Calculations made on the basis of the food dole in Rome tend to support the hypothesis of decline, with the figure of one million persons in Augustus' day falling by about AD 450 to less than half a million, or even perhaps as low as 250,000 (Hodges and Whitehouse 1983, 48–52).

Against this, however, can be put the fact that Rome was no longer the centre of the civilized universe in the fifth century: the emperors had long since shifted their capital to be closer to the northern frontiers, and from 284 Milan had accommodated the imperial court; in 402 Honorius shifted it to Ravenna to hide among the marshes. Emperors only occasionally visited Rome, and the Eternal City became a virtual, if enormous, museum. Greater wealth was situated in the north, in the Po valley, and fieldwork and excavations by the Lombardy Archaeological Superintendency have revealed over recent years a massive increase in rural activity in the territory of fourth-century Milan, with villages and farms becoming more populous and former road stations like Lomello developing into fortified townships. Work still needs to be done on the territory of Ravenna, to see if a similar rural boom accompanied this city's own elevation to capital status (*Milano*, 233–304; cf. Deichmann 1989).

It has been very tempting, and indeed too tempting for many scholars, to apply the South Etruria data to all of Italy. As new field surveys occur, however, it is clear that the pattern of survival and change is variable. In parts of the north, as noted, there are signs of relative stability, but this is largely dependent on the fortune of the towns around. In the case of Luni on the Ligurian coast, urban prosperity was based heavily on the quarrying and exportation of local white marble, much used in Augustan Rome: excavations here have shown that the fall in demand from the second to the third century hit Luni badly; in the fourth century its port had silted up, and soon afterwards the forum was stripped of its paving. The economy of the hinterland had never really needed to develop, and even in Luni's heyday farms and villas were few and far between, indicating a heavy reliance on imports; but as trade fell away Luni had little agricultural back-up to call upon, making survival even harder (Ward-Perkins *et al.* 1986).

The silting up of the port at Luni indicates a common and significant factor in late Roman times (see Delano Smith, in Ward-Perkins *et al.* 1986, 123–40): an inability – financial and physical – to maintain measures of earlier imperial land protection and water regulation. As this failed, a process of environmental deterioration began, marking a regeneration of earlier marshland, the unchecked flooding of plains, landslides, and so on. This picture is confirmed in survey work in the territory of Piacenza in Emilia, where ecological destabilization is seen to have hastened the decline of the Roman town of Veleia (Dell'Aglio and Marchetti 1991, 166; cf. Cremaschi *et al.* 1994).

To the south, in regions like the Albegna valley in north Etruria, in the hinterland of the old Roman colony of Cosa (desolate by the time of Rutilius, bar the rats), after a first-century BC to first-century AD boom there is a fall-off before villa establishments recover to maintain themselves fairly healthily into the fifth century – but in locations away from the coast, where a re-establishment of marshland may have occurred (Attolini *et al.* 1983). In those southern regions listed most frequently in the *Codex Theodosianus*, the picture is somewhat surprising overall. In some areas progressive decline is apparent: for example, the wine-producing *Ager Falernus* of northern Campania witnessed a decline from 138 first-century AD rural sites to 80 second- or third-century farms, down to 27 by around AD 400; a century later they number just five. Here early urban and rural vitality was closely linked to intensive vine cultivation, and the export trade was badly hit after the first century: coastal towns like Minturnae and Sinuessa declined drastically, their harbours silting up and reverting to swamp, affecting the road also; Suessa Aurunca, meanwhile, less involved in wine production and located inland, did persist into late antiquity, as documented by a number of late inscriptions (Arthur 1991). In the Biferno valley survey in Samnium, a similar decline in rural sites seems apparent from the third century, yet with little evidence for the survival of dispersed Roman settlement after *c*.400 (Barker ed. 1995, 236–40). However, for ancient Lucania (modern Basilicata and western Apulia) the mid-imperial crisis is not so marked; indeed, inland zones again show a healthy resistance to trends elsewhere – though admittedly farm distribution was not in any case that extensive. In late antiquity pig production probably took centre stage in the local Lucanian economy, a hypothesis backed up by the written texts and by excavations at the key villa site of San Giovanni di Ruoti, which have revealed that in the late fifth and early sixth centuries more than 60 per cent of the bone remains on the site were of pigs. It is probable that previously cultivated ground was given up to allow for more intensive pig foraging (Barnish 1987; Small 1991).

An overall decline in rural activity is generally postulated and accepted. So far, however, urban excavations have nowhere revealed evidence for an influx of displaced peasants, suggesting that these were elsewhere or that rural decline does, in fact, reflect an actual decline in population numbers. In this respect it should be remembered that the towns were, after all, the general focus of barbarian assault, the centres most prone to economic privations, plague, tax collectors, and army recruiting officers, and so cannot always have appealed to the worried farmer. Close analysis of urban trends in northern and central Italy from AD 350 duly highlights a decline in patronage from the third century and a consequent decay of public buildings and amenities: robbing of buildings, burials within the urban space and within former public monuments such as amphitheatres and theatres, neglect of aqueducts, and the digging of wells all testify to a deterioration of the urban fabric (Ward-Perkins 1984). The breakdown of the inner machinery of Roman settlement should be taken to reflect broader, external trends of decay, notably failures in land control. Mention has already been made of how nature had begun to reclaim coastal areas, silting up ports and creating marshes and lagoons. Previously important centres in north-east Italy, notably Aquileia, Altino, and Concordia, all named in the *Notitia dignitatum*, begin to lose out to nature in the fifth century, particularly because of flooding of the Via Annia. Excavations reveal a shrinkage of settlement within each of these to the areas around the main churches – similar to what is presumed to have happened at Luni (Schmiedt 1974, 506–36). Thus the towns seem to have been suffering just as much as the farms.

After Rome: Goths, Byzantines, and Longobards

The ailing government of the western Roman empire was too racked with external and internal military pressures to be able to cope with such decay, and succumbed meekly to a revolution among its federate troops in 476. Between 489 and 493 further warfare hit Italy, resulting in the Ostrogothic tribe becoming masters of the peninsula. Little hope, one would assume, for the wretched province of Italy. And yet the Ostrogothic takeover, far from seeing the peninsula slipping into barbarous ways, in fact marked a cultural pick-up, with king Theoderic's strong and long rule stabilizing Italy's position on the economic market, and with various marriage alliances to Germanic neighbours blocking the likelihood of military conflict. With towns back in business, a good degree of building activity is registered – most notably in those frequented by the royal family, notably Verona, Pavia, and Ravenna – and it coincides with a major upturn in rural productivity (Wolfram 1988, 284–9; Lusuardi Siena 1984).

Our principal source for this period, covering *c*.495–535, is the lengthy but invaluable collection of letters by Theoderic's chief minister, Cassiodorus Senator. His ancestral home was in southern Italy, and it is no surprise to find that a good deal of information on this previously much-neglected region suddenly emerges. Cassiodorus proudly highlights the excellent stocks of horse and cattle in the hills of Bruttium, the healthy supply of Lucanian pork to Rome, and the increasing popularity (thanks to his advertising campaign) of Bruttian wine (*Variae*, 8. 31, 33; 11. 39; 12. 12). His tourist board act suggests a happy revitalization of the town–country relationship, in southern Italy at least; for the Squillace district, besides a fine climate, he says that

> residents in the city are not deprived of the fine sight of workers in the field. They look out to their satisfaction on abundant grape harvests; on the threshing-floors, productive work is in their view; the olives, too, display their greenery. No one lacks the pleasures of the countryside who can see all this from the city.
>
> (*Var.* 12. 15)

His comments, in fact, seem to be borne out by villa excavations in the south, notably those at San Giovanni di Ruoti, where major economic prosperity is evident in the late fifth century, extending into the second quarter of the sixth (Small 1991). In Samnium the small villa located beneath the eighth-century monastery at San Vincenzo al Volturno also relates to this period (Hodges 1988) – though admittedly other Roman sites in Samnium, such as San Giacomo or Matrice, show no sign of partaking in this relative boom.

A good indication of rural health is witnessed by Cassiodorus' documentation relating to renewed pressure on arable land. For example, a letter of *c*.510 records the patrician Decius wanting to drain part of the Pontine marshes at Decemnovium, nineteen miles north of Terracina, featuring a stretch of the Via Appia. Decius' workmen have a hard task:

> the marsh ravages ... the neighbourhood like an enemy. ... It is a notorious desolation of the age, which, through long neglect, has formed a kind of marshy sea, and, spreading by its waters a hostile

deluge over cultivated land, has destroyed the kindly arable equally with shaggy woodland. Since it began to be exposed to the marshes, the soil has been robbed of its crops, and nourishes nothing useful beneath the water.

(*Var*. 2. 32; cf. 2. 21)

Decius is starred by the king: his 'old fashioned self-confidence is such that private enterprise has undertaken what the power of the state long shunned'. An inscription verifies that this work was carried out, if with efforts suitably ascribed to Theoderic:

Our lord, the glorious and famous king Theoderic, victorious and triumphant, perpetual Augustus, born for the good of the common-wealth, guardian of liberty and propagator of the Roman name, tamer of the tribes, has restored the route and places of the Via Appia at Decemnovium, that is from Tripontium to Terracina, to the public use and the safety of travellers, by wonderful good fortune and the favour of God.

(*CIL* x. 6850)

This was clearly something to write home about, suggesting that such engineering feats were hard to come by. Decius does in fact get a brief look in, and his labourers are credited with 'leading the waters into the sea through many new channels, and restoring the ground to its all too ancient dryness, unknown to our ances-tors' – though of course the area had been drained under Trajan during his rebuilding of the Via Appia in the early second century.

Technological decline is further hinted at by Cassiodorus' poetic discussion of the glories of Rome's drains, while a fall in popula-tion for the city is clearly noted in the following comments:

The vast extent of the walls bears witness to the throngs of citizens, as do the swollen capacity of the buildings of entertainment, the wonderful size of the baths, and that great number of water-mills which was clearly provided especially for the food supply.

(*Var*. 3. 30–1)

This is not to deny that Rome was still a fairly thriving centre – indeed, tiles were still being produced and lime brought in for repairs to the city walls, while supporters still roared on their teams in the Circus – but some shrinkage of population and economic well-being is evident.

One aspect of Ostrogothic settlement in Italy that has received particular attention recently is that of the tribe's initial installation within the peninsula and their allotment of *tertiae* or thirds (see Goffart 1980; Barnish 1986). The old Roman practice of settling federate barbarians within the empire had been by the process of *hospitalitas*, whereby these groups were billeted on lands, given rights over that land, and in return required to do military service to Rome. In theory this relieved the burden on the native provincials and gave the federates a vested interest in the land and a means of support; for the most part, imperial lands, and *agri deserti* (wasted or abandoned lands) were used. The barbarians did not always settle happily, perhaps in part because of being fobbed off with agriculturally marginal lands, or at least lands needing much hard labour to bring back to fertility. For Italy, the Greek historian Procopius states that first Odoacer in 476 and then Theoderic in 493 made over a third part of the lands to their followers – meaning a third of those lands in which the Goths settled, not a third of all the lands in Italy (Cass. *Var*. 2. 16). As this had a legal precedent, the native landowners had no real say in the matter, especially if confronted with an armed mob of young Ostrogoths in search of new homes. Interestingly, Theoderic wanted to create no real trouble, and in one letter of Cassiodorus (*Var*. 1. 18) the king in fact orders the restoration to Roman owners of properties illegally usurped by Germans since his arrival in Italy. The fairly desperate plight of some of these native farmers in the late empire has already been mentioned: the Gothic takeover in fact gave some relief to aristocratic landowners, since the loss of one-third of their land meant they also lost the obligation to pay tax, services, and recruits on this land. How small to medium landowners fared is less clear, and their fate would of course have been largely dependent on where the Goths wanted to settle.

Even in peacetime Theoderic was thinking ahead to the inevitable war with Byzantium, and defence surfaces as one of his priorities. Although Cassiodorus emphasizes the agricultural output of southern Italy, the strongest area of Ostrogothic settlement lay in the north, within the Padane region, which had always been economically very healthy. Grain depots are recorded in key royal centres such as Pavia and Verona, as well as at Como, Trento, and Tortona (*Var*. 3. 48; 12. 27). In the last two instances

Figure 10.3 Iulium Carnicum–Zuglio, in the Carnic Alps of NE Italy: view from the excavated forum of the Roman town towards the hill of San Pietro, the presumed seat of the early medieval successor to Iulium Carnicum.

the local civilians are even recommended to move their houses up on to the fortified hilltops. While stray finds alone testify to the Gothic presence at Tortona, part of an early sixth-century church has been excavated on top of Dos Trento – suitably called the *Verruca* by Cassiodorus. Life was still going on within the Roman town of Trento on the other side of the river, but clearly new settlement priorities were being established here. Comparable is the situation recognized at Zuglio, Roman Iulium Carnicum in the north-eastern Italian Alps, where excavations in the forum suggest abandonment in the fifth century followed by a shift to the hill of San Pietro (fig. 10.3), where a bishop is attested from as early as AD 480 (*CIL* v. 1858; Mirabella Roberti 1976). In a similar vein, at Verona an upper castle zone is identifiable over the river from the Roman centre, while for Como the island of Comacina may well have become the prime defensive focus (Christie 1991a, 420–6). Some people had already chosen to move to safer ground: Cassiodorus's letters provide an early reference to settlements within the Venetian lagoons, where the locals had their 'homes like sea-birds'. These island sites were slowly replacing decayed mainland seats such as Altino and Concordia. Other northern island or promontory locations like San Giulio d'Orta or Sirmione (on which Catullus had had a villa) were all similar, defence-oriented sites, for the most part already equipped, it should be noted, in the early fifth century. In effect, much as in the early period of Roman republican expansion within Italy, when colonies were planted on strategic hilltop seats – but in contrast with the forceful policy of the later republic and early empire, when the legions were all too dominant – so with late antiquity we find nature coming back into play as a means of defence. Society was again utilizing nature, as opposed to trying to overcome nature.

When war came, following a Byzantine invasion in 535, the south rapidly fell into Byzantine hands; the Goths regrouped in the north, and by and large held out for over twenty years. The historian Procopius, secretary to the Byzantine general Belisarius, provides a chronicle to these Gothic wars (535–54), detailing urban and rural devastation in a war of siege and attrition. Although the scale of warfare was limited in terms of numbers of soldiers involved, this meant that the respective armies were too small to achieve lasting gains; atrocities were occasionally committed, such as the Gothic massacre of all male citizens at Milan, but in general the devastation was cumulative. In one dramatic passage Procopius talks bleakly of rural decline in the region of Picenum in east central Italy:

> Now as time went on and brought again the summer season, the grain was already ripening uncared for in the cornlands, but in no such quantities as formerly – indeed, it was much less. For since it had not been covered in the furrows, either by ploughs or by the hand of man, ... the earth was able to make only a small portion of it take root. And since after that no one reaped it, when it had become fully ripe it fell again to the ground and nothing grew from it thereafter. And this same thing had happened also in Aemilia; and because of this situation the inhabitants left their homes and went to Picenum, thinking that since that country was on the sea, it could not be suffering from absolute lack of food supplies. And the Tuscans ... were attacked by famine for the same cause. ... The natural result of this was that the majority of the people fell victim to all manner of diseases and it was only a few who threw these off and recovered. Indeed it is said that among the Roman farmers in Picenum not less than fifty thousand perished by famine, and a great many more north of the Ionian gulf.
>
> (*De bello Gothico*, 6. 20. 21)

Cassiodorus' letters also extend into the war years, and show the conflict eating into the country, undoing all the good work achieved under Theoderic. But it was not just the enemy armies that were causing the devastation: as he points out in *Var.* 12. 5:

> Now a large army has arrived, known to be assigned to the defence of the state, and is reported to have ravaged the fields of Lucania and Bruttium, and to have lessened the wealth of those regions by enthusiastic robbery

in the name of supplies or taxes in kind, levied for the troops. Crop failures added further woes: for north-east Italy we hear that in 537

> neither wine nor corn nor millet has been produced among them ... the fortunes of the provincials have reached such a state of penury that they can hardly endure the risks of life unless the royal pity should take thought for them with its usual humanity.
>
> (*Var.* 12. 26)

Cassiodorus further recounts that the climate was working against people:

> We have had a winter without storms, spring without mildness, summer without heat. Whence can we now hope for mild weather, when the months that once ripened the crops have been deadly sick under the northern blasts? ... The seasons have changed by failing to change; and what used to be achieved by mingled rains cannot be gained from dryness only. And therefore, from the crops of the past, your prudence is to defeat the future dearth: for such was last year's fortunate abundance that provisions will also suffice for the coming months.
>
> (*Var.* 12. 25)

Climatic fluctuations continue to be attested into the late sixth and seventh centuries. The eighth-century Longobard historian Paul the Deacon, for example, records bouts of widespread winter flooding in the period 589–91 in northern Italy as well as in Rome, and instances of severe drought and famine in subsequent summers (*Historia Langobardorum*, 3. 23). A collation of documentary references relating to such climatic anomalies[1] would support the hypothesis of increased precipitation and a slight but significant temperature drop from around AD 500, which could indeed have led to greater erosion and alluviation in regions such as Italy and Greece at this time (fig. 10.4). For the earlier imperial period the sources suggest that a slightly drier climate was prevalent, in Italy at least. The data, however, are not fully reliable and the effects of climatic change still need more detailed investigation. Indeed, reference to natural disasters by authors such as Paul the Deacon could in many cases be viewed more as an historian's tool for dramatic effect: in Paul's case, for a narrative written 200 years later than the events described (Goffart 1988, 329–431). But short-term fluctuations have always occurred, and it is more likely to be simply the case that human control of the environment had weakened to the extent that whereas in the early imperial period land management, achieved with large financial and manpower resources, had to a large degree countered the swelling of rivers and had, through provision of aqueducts and dams, largely mastered water supply and the immediate effects of land wastage, in the Early Middle Ages the political and economic

---

[1] Randsborg 1991, 23–9; cf. Vita-Finzi 1969; Hodges and Whitehouse 1983, 57–9.

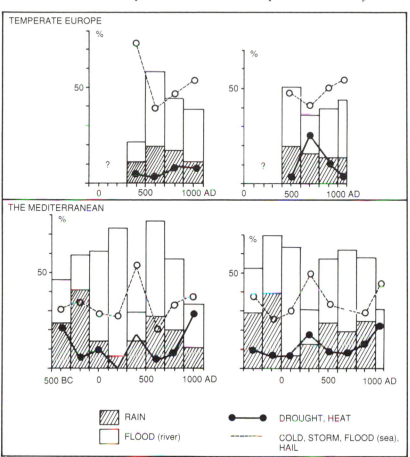

Figure 10.4 Tables depicting fluctuating levels of complaints about rain, floods, drought/heat, and storms/cold recorded in contemporary documentary sources for the regions of (a) temperate Europe, (b) the Mediterranean. (After Randsborg 1991, fig. 10.)

resources for the maintenance or resumption of such control were simply lacking. Likewise economic decay will have meant diminished output and a decay of once marginal lands, giving rise to the erosion of formerly terraced hill-slopes in particular. Even zones of the fertile Po valley, thickly covered with traces of Roman centuriation, reveal clear indications of a re-emergence of marshland and forest cover. War, combined with even slight climatic abnormalities, will therefore have provoked an even more drastic effect on the land.[1]

Lack of land management simultaneously implies lack of sizeable land settlement in this period, with marginal lands swiftly abandoned to nature. As argued above, the documentary sources point largely in this direction. But what about archaeology? How far do field survey data provide clarification in this discussion of rural decline? Certainly it is possible to identify a decline in the number of sites on the basis of datable, imported pottery types, continuing the decline noted since the third or fourth century, but a factor often overlooked is that, as the Roman economy faltered, supplies of such imports tailed off and became too costly for many Italians, particularly middle- to low-ranking farmers. As a result, a lack of dated surface finds does not necessarily mean a lack of people in the countryside: imports were being restricted more and more to the larger towns and coastal centres, with minimal penetration inland. Even forts like Castelseprio in Lombardy, occupied from the early fifth century, obtained precious few imported goods (Brogiolo and Lusuardi Siena 1980). This is not to deny the general trends recognized in field surveys – namely the end of classical open, dispersed settlement in the sixth to seventh centuries, and the subsequent movement to nucleated and upland seats – but merely to state the need for more caution in discussing this transitional phase. Single models cannot be easily applied: variation should be expected regionally, and of course inter-regionally.

Unfortunately, detailed excavations of the latter phases of life at villa sites throughout Italy are few and far between, and too frequently an abandonment is set broadly within the fifth century, giving way to what is generally termed 'squatter activity'. This is true for sites in Britain, too; but here more recent work has begun to reveal the frequency of transition from stone to timber in the early fifth century and from Romano-British to Romano-Saxon, suggesting a greater level of continuity – even if small-scale – than has long been assumed (see Percival 1992 for Gaul). In Italy's case surprisingly few useful examples are available to draw upon, but notable work has been done at the site of Monte Gelato, comprising excavations of a Roman settlement first identified in

---

[1] Brückner 1986; Coltorti and Dal Ri 1985; Cremaschi *et al.* 1994.

the course of the South Etruria survey. The work has revealed a fascinating sequence of change, from a possible Augustan period villa or *vicus*, via a fifth- and sixth-century chapel, to a rebuilding and enlargement of the church in the early ninth century. The excavators identified no actual break in activity, and suggest that a series of timber post-holes identified within rooms, and a corridor to the north of the church, in fact marked a crude pinning up of the dilapidated structure in the seventh or eighth century – though no occupational finds can be ascribed to this phase with any certainty. A few graves presumed to be of this date are, however, present (fig. 10.5), duly indicating that there were people around; but their material traces are otherwise lacking. If close scrutiny alone was able to glean this information from what was a meticulous excavation, one should be very careful in assigning too much certainty to surface scatters alone (King and Potter 1992). A similar sequence of villa decline, intrusion by graves, and church or monastery colonization can perhaps also be recognized at a few other sites, notably Farfa and San Vincenzo al Volturno, signifying the importance of the Church in the maintenance, or more certainly the revival, of rural settlement (see Hodges 1988).

In towns, too, in Italy – but again with an emphasis on Lombardy in the north – indications are finally emerging of timber buildings hiding among the debris of Roman buildings, or traces of a maintenance of certain Roman houses, as well as the re-laying or continued use of the old street surfaces. Churches emerge as the only structurally refined elements in the post-Roman urban landscape, acting as the new focus of patronage and with settlement predominantly gathered around them. Excavations in sites like Verona and Brescia, meanwhile, have revealed open areas, often containing the 'dark earth' so well known to scholars studying late Roman and early medieval towns in Britain (Brogiolo 1985, 1989; Hudson and La Rocca Hudson 1987). Here, then, is an indication of rural activities taking place within the town – strongly contrasting with the small vegetable patches of earlier times – and filling up former occupation zones. There is also the argument that farming was carried out within a much smaller radius outside the townships, the farmers returning home each night to the security of the towns. For this, however, archaeological support is so far inadequate, and there is no ready documentary back-up bar the fact that towns physically persisted

Figure 10.5 Burial 59 at Mola di Monte Gelato. The burial contained the skeletons of two males, one aged 17–25, the other 33–45. A pottery vessel of late sixth- or early seventh-century type lies by the left-hand head. The bones gave a radiocarbon date of 1460 ± BP, calibrated to AD 565–635 (1 σ); BM 2862). Beyond is a tufo sarcophagus. (Photo: T. W. Potter, British Museum.)

as social and economic entities. What the documentation does show for the sixth century onwards, though, is the widespread landowning of the Church: in the case of Ravenna, estates lay as far afield as Sicily, built up from imperial and aristocratic and smaller gifts. Revenue from these lands gives a fairly good indication of the maintenance of farming activity (T. S. Brown 1984, 190–204).

At some point, certainly, there was a movement away from the open plains and away from the exposed roads; for this the Gothic war, followed by the equally destructive Longobard invasion and war with Byzantium, provides a more than adequate context of insecurity and upheaval. The documentary sources give a clear guide in some cases: the letters of Pope Gregory the Great, for instance, at the end of the sixth century, report the evacuation of exposed towns in favour of upland seats like Orvieto or Civita Castellana, and the presence of garrisons and bishoprics on small hilltops like Civitá di Bagnoregio – hardly what a Roman would have classed as a town.[1] In one or two cases, fragments of church furniture such as chancel screens help indicate early medieval activity on these sites, but archaeologically it is not possible yet to pinpoint securely the origins of upland seats like Calcata or Mazzano Romano in the Roman Campagna before the ninth or tenth century (Potter 1979, 155–67). Too frequently they have been occupied throughout the Middle Ages and into modern times, only recently losing out (among other things) to the Italians' need to be close to their cars. Too few excavations have so far been conducted; but those that have been have failed to give a secure link to the immediate post-Roman period.

It was not all upland retreat, however, since some resurgence of open settlement can be located, as in the case of the papal estate of Santa Cornelia, founded fifteen Roman miles north of Rome in the 780s in an area that had once been filled with small to large farms and villas (Christie 1991b, 355–8). Interestingly, although the complex incorporated much material of Roman date, it did not physically overlie a Roman structure; thus there was no immediate continuity here, even if the contemporary *Liber pontificalis* (1. 501–2) implies as much. In terms of land ownership, we also get a clear indication of the role of the Church beyond Rome itself. Noticeably, the foundation of the Santa Cornelia estate coincides neatly with a period of papal dominance in Rome, the termination of the conflict with the Longobards, and the formation of strong political and economic ties with Charlemagne's Carolingian kingdom; so peaceful conditions and economic prosperity gave the prompt. But a new spate of enemy (Arab) incursions into Italy and papal decline in the ninth century soon countered attempts at renewed Roman-style farming, and the

---

[1] e.g. Gregory, *Registrum epistolarum*, 2. 17; 6. 27; 10. 13; Richards 1980, 100–2.

drive towards upland seclusion began once more: this time at an accelerated pace, giving rise to the process known as *incastellamento* (Noyé ed. 1988, 411–535).

Discussion

In discussing the late Roman empire one all too readily thinks of a rapid collapse that overwhelmed all and was perceived as such by all. But this was no modern-day Soviet Union or Yugoslavia with news networks allowing for the instantaneous transmission of events, ideas, and fears. People may well have seen change and been aware of it, but it would rarely have happened overnight, except perhaps in an urban context where siege, starvation, massacre, and plague may have had a rapid impact. Likewise, people who lived through the generally stable and prosperous period of Ostrogothic rule undoubtedly felt the economic upheavals created with the disastrously prolonged war with Byzantium. Indeed, warfare became almost part of normal life by the end of the sixth century, and this forced people and society to adapt accordingly, as reflected most strikingly in the rise of the military over the civil order.

But towns continued to exist, politicians and clergy still wrangled, and armies still guarded frontiers. To feed them, of course, land needed to be farmed. The documentary sources, when explicit, tend to paint a bleak picture of the landscape – barren, cold, and lost to nature – but in land grants, land disputes, and church and monastery foundations enough scattered hints emerge of maintained activity in the countryside involving villages, farms, estates, and shepherds. What modern commentators tend to do is to underestimate the resilience of the peasant, or rather of country-based folk: their livelihood had always lain in the land, and it is wrong to assume an overriding readiness on their part to move up permanently to distant, often inhospitable heights. Yet at the same time their resilience must have been shaken, and a natural response will have been the creation of refuges, periodically employed in times of unrest by such farmers as either a family or even a communal retreat. It is difficult, though, to trace these sites archaeologically except through the rare incidence of generally unstratified late or post-Roman pottery on defended heights.

In the Alpine zones, such as in the former Yugoslavia and in Austria, refuges are identified on the basis of walled upland sites lacking fixed internal features in stone, though often revealing after excavation traces of timber or dry-stone housing (e.g. Hrušica, a fourth-century military base with refuge capabilities: Ulbert ed. 1981; Christie 1995).

Refuges took other forms, too. The recent horrendous conflict within former Yugoslavia has forced families to shelter with their few remaining possessions in caves, a situation which can be closely paralleled in late antiquity by the occupation of many cave sites in Alpine and southern Italy, sometimes extending well into medieval times. As yet, only in a few instances are their origins clear, since secure material traces of cave occupation are not registered until later on in the Early Middle Ages. But, it should be stressed, these sites are only being registered and understood through archaeology.

What the results of excavations, field surveys, and geomorphological analysis are beginning to show is that control over nature undoubtedly suffered as a result of the breakdown of Roman 'open' settlement. There was, overall, a reversion to a virtually pre-Roman mode of exploitation, with a sizeable reduction in the need for production of surplus foodstuffs and goods, a resultant quitting of previously reclaimed land, and the re-emergence of woodland. The likelihood is that reduced control over the landscape led to hillslope erosion, alluviation, silting up of ports, and the renewal of marshland in many coastal zones. This breakdown was clearly under way already in the late empire, as indicated by the evidence from Terracina. It is a problem, however, to determine how far this situation resulted from, on the one hand, over-exploitation of the land, excessive deforestation, or simple bad management or, on the other hand, from social disorders such as increased taxation, depopulation, or insecurity. Combinations of these factors, plus climatic deterioration, must also be considered: it is unlikely that monocausal explanations will be valid even for one region since each was a patchwork of owners, all with their own level of money, resilience, and skill. Geomorphology, in collaboration with archaeology, offers the potential for studying these crucial physical changes in the landscape, although integrated studies are as yet limited and not specifically tied in to examining the period in question.[1] Inevitably, therefore, our picture for the late and post-Roman landscape remains 'dark'. What is clear, however, is that nature had resumed a dominance and that much land had 'become wild again'.

Only with the advent of large monastic land ownership from the eighth and ninth centuries onwards – as in the case of the abbeys of Farfa and San Vincenzo in central Italy – do references reappear to the re-harnessing of water resources, large-scale forest clearance, and the growth of associated village communities. Nature continued to have a strong say in human affairs, however, with hilltops the favoured seats for castles and their attached populations, and with marshland dominating many coastal regions. Thus nature had, for a while at least, begun to get her own back; but a revived economy, a population rise, and the permanence of human resilience all resulted in renewed land pressure and renewed manipulation of the natural resources.

Bibliography

Primary sources

Cassiodorus, *Variae*, in *Monumenta Germaniae historica: auctores antiquissimi*, xii, ed. T. Mommsen (Berlin, 1893–1894); trans. S. J. B. Barnish (Translated Texts for Historians, 12; Liverpool, 1992).

Claudius Claudianus, trans. H. Isbell in *The Last Poets of Imperial Rome* (Penguin Classics; Harmondsworth, 1971).

Codex Theodosianus, ed. T. Mommsen and P. Meyer (Berlin, 1905); trans. C. Pharr, *The Theodosian Code and Novels and the Sirmondian Constitution* (Princeton, NJ, 1952).

Gregory the Great, *Registrum epistolarum*, in *Monumenta Germaniae historica: epistolae*, i and ii, ed. P. Ewald and L. M. Hartmann (Berlin, 1887–99).

Liber pontificalis, ed. L. Duchesne (Paris, 1886–92); trans. R. Davis (Translated Texts for Historians, 5 and 13; Liverpool, 1989 and 1992).

Notitia dignitatum, ed. O. Seeck (Berlin, 1876).

Paul the Deacon, *Historia Langobardorum*, in *Monumenta Germaniae historica: scriptores rerum Langobardicarum et Italicarum, saec. VI–IX*, ed. L. Bethmann and G. Waitz (Hanover, 1878), 12–187; trans. W. Foulke, *The History of the Langobards* (Philadephia, 1907).

---

[1]   But see papers in Frenzel ed. 1994 for Roman-period studies in the Mediterranean.

Procopius, *The Gothic Wars and Secret History*, trans. H. B. Dewing (New York and London, 1914–35); *The Secret History*, trans. G. Williamson (Penguin Classics; Harmondsworth, 1966).

Rutilius Claudius Namatianus, *De reditu suo*, trans. H. Isbell in *The Last Poets of Imperial Rome* (Penguin Classics; Harmondsworth, 1971).

Zosimus, *Nea historia*, trans. J. Buchanan and H. Davies (London, 1967); trans. R. Ridley (Byzantina Australiensia, 2; Canberra, 1982).

Secondary sources

Arthur, P. (1991), 'Territories, wine and wealth: Suessa Aurunca, Sinuessa, Minturnae and the Ager Falernus', in Barker and Lloyd (eds), 153–9.

Attolini, I., Cambi, F., Celuzza, M., Fentress, E., Regoli, E., and Walker, L. (1983), 'Ricognizione archeologica nell'ager Cosanus e nella valle dell'Albegna: rapporto preliminare 1982–1983', *Archeologia medievale*, 10: 439–65.

Barker, G. (ed. 1995), *A Mediterranean Valley: Landscape Archaeology as Annales History in the Biferno Valley* (Leicester).

—— and Lloyd, J. (eds 1991), *Roman Landscapes: Archaeological Survey in the Mediterranean Region* (British School at Rome Archaeological Monographs, 2; London).

Barnish, S. (1986), 'Taxation, land and barbarian settlement in the western empire', *PBSR* 54 (n.s. 41): 170–95.

—— (1987), 'Pigs, plebeians and *potentes*: Rome's economic hinterland, c.350–600 AD', *PBSR* 55 (n.s. 42): 157–85.

Basso, P. (1986), 'I miliari della Venetia romana', *Archeologia Veneta*, 9: 11–228.

Brogiolo, G. P. (1985), 'Le città fra tarda antichità e medioevo', in *Archeologia urbana in Lombardia* (Milan), 48–56.

—— (1989), 'Brescia: building transformations in a Lombard city', in K. Randsborg (ed.), *The Birth of Europe: Archaeology and Social Development in the First Millennium AD* (Analecta Romana Instituti Danici, supp. 16; Rome), 156–65.

—— and Lusuardi Siena, S. (1980), 'Nuove indagini a Castelseprio', *Atti del VI Congresso Internazionale di Studi sull'Alto Medioevo: Longobardi e Lombardia. Aspetti di civiltà Longobarda* (Spoleto), 475–99.

Brown, P. (1971), *The World of Late Antiquity* (London).

Brown, T. S. (1984), *Gentlemen and Officers: Imperial Administration and Aristocratic Power in Byzantine Italy, AD 554–800* (London).

Brückner, H. (1986), 'Man's impact on the evolution of the physical environment in the Mediterranean region in historical times', *Geo-journal*, 13 (1): 7–17.

Christie, N. (1989), 'The archaeology of Byzantine Italy: a synthesis of recent research', *Journal of Mediterranean Archaeology*, 2 (2): 249–93.

—— (1991a), 'The Alps as a frontier, AD 168–774', *Journal of Roman Archaeology*, 4: 410–30.

—— (1991b), *Three South Etrurian Churches: Santa Cornelia, Santa Rufina, and San Liberato* (British School at Rome Archaeological Monographs, 4; London).

—— (1995), 'Late antique cavemen in Italy', in N. Christie (ed.), *Settlement and Economy, 1500 BC–AD 1500 (Papers of the 5th Conference of Italian Archaeology)* (Oxbow Monographs, 41; Oxford), 311–16.

Coltorti, M., and Dal Ri, L. (1985), 'The human impact of the landscape: some examples from the Adige valley', in C. Malone and S. Stoddart (eds), *Papers in Italian Archaeology*, iv. 1 (BAR Int. Ser. 243; Oxford), 105–34.

Cracco Ruggini, L. (1961), *Economia e società nell'Italia annonaria* (Milan).

Cremaschi, M., Marchetti, M., and Ravazzi, C. (1994), 'Geomorphological evidence for land surfaces cleared from forest in the central Po plain (northern Italy) during the Roman period', in Frenzel (ed.), 119–32.

Deichmann, F. W. (1989), *Ravenna: Hauptstadt des spätantiken Abendlandes*, ii: *Kommentar*, 3: *Geschichte, Topographie, Kunst und Kultur* (Stuttgart).

Dell'Aglio, P. L., and Marchetti, G. (1991), 'Settlement patterns and agrarian structures of the Roman period in the territory of Piacenza', in Barker and Lloyd (eds), 160–8.

Drinkwater, J., and Elton, H. (eds 1992), *Fifth Century Gaul: A Crisis of Identity?* (Cambridge).

Frenzel, B. (ed. 1994), *Evaluation of Land Surfaces Cleared from Forests in the Mediterranean Region during the Time of the Roman Empire* (Paläoklimaforschung, 10, special issue: ESF Project 'European Palaeoclimate and Man', 5; Mainz, Strasburg, Stuttgart, Jena, and New York).

Goffart, W. (1980), *Barbarians and Romans: Techniques of Accommodation* (Princeton, NJ).

—— (1988), *The Narrators of Barbarian History, AD 550–800: Jordanes, Gregory of Tours, Bede, and Paul the Deacon* (Princeton).

Hodges, R. (1988), 'The San Vincenzo project: preliminary review of the excavations and survey at San Vincenzo al Volturno and in its terra', in Noyé (ed.), 421–31.

—— and Hobley, B. (eds 1988), *The Rebirth of Towns in the West* (Council for British Archaeology, Research Reports, 68; London).

—— and Whitehouse, D. B. (1983), *Mohammed, Charlemagne, and the Origins of Europe* (London).

Hudson, P., and La Rocca Hudson, C. (1987), 'Riflessi della migrazione longobarda sull'insediamento rurale e urbano in Italia settentrionale', in R. Francovich (ed.), *Archeologia e storia del medioevo italiano* (Rome), 29–47.

Johnson, S. (1983), *Late Roman Fortifications* (London).

King, A., and Potter, T. W. (1992), 'Mola di Monte Gelato in the early middle ages: an interim report on the excavations 1986–9', in E.

Herring, R. Whitehouse, and J. Wilkins (eds), *Papers of the Fourth Conference of Italian Archaeology: New Developments*, ii (London), 165–76.

Lamboglia, N. (1976–8), 'Albenga e i nuovi frammenti di Rutilio Namaziano', *Rivista Ingauna e Intemelia*, 31: 32–8.

Lusuardi Siena, S. (1984), 'Sulle tracce della presenza gota in Italia: il contributo delle fonti archeologiche', in *Magistra barbaritas: i barbari in Italia* (Milan), 509–58.

Milano = Milano: capitale dell'impero romano, 286–402 d.C., catalogue for exhibition at Palazzo Reale, Milan (Milan, 1990).

Mirabella Roberti, M. (1976), 'Iulium Carnicum, centro romano alpino', *Antichità Altoadriatiche*, 9: 91–101.

Noyé, G. (ed. 1988), *Structures de l'habitat et occupation du sol dans les pays méditerranéens: les méthodes et l'apport de l'archéologie extensive* (Castrum, 2; Rome and Madrid).

Percival, J. (1992), 'The fifth-century villa: new life or death postponed?', in Drinkwater and Elton (eds), 156–64.

Potter, T. W. (1979), *The Changing Landscape of South Etruria* (London).

—— (1987), *Roman Italy* (London).

Randsborg, K. (1991), *The First Millennium AD in Europe and the Mediterranean* (Cambridge).

Richards, J. (1980), *Consul of God: The Life and Times of Gregory the Great* (London).

Roberts, M. (1992), 'Barbarians in Gaul: the response of the poets', in Drinkwater and Elton (eds), 97–106.

Schmiedt, G. (1974), 'Città scomparse e città di nuova formazione in Italia in relazione al sistema di comunicazione', in *Topografia urbana e vita cittadina nell'alto medioevo in occidente: XXI settimana di studio del Centro Italiano di Studi sull'Alto Medioevo*, ii (Spoleto), 503–607.

Small, A. (1991), 'Late Roman rural settlement in Basilicata and western Apulia', in Barker and Lloyd (eds), 204–22.

Ulbert, T. (ed. 1981), *Ad Pirum (Hrušica): spätromische Passbefestigung in den julischen Alpen* (Münchner Beiträge zur Vor- und Frühgeschichte, 31; Munich).

Vita-Finzi, C. (1969), *The Mediterranean Valleys: Geological Changes in Historical Time* (Cambridge).

Ward-Perkins, B. (1984), *From Classical Antiquity to the Middle Ages: Urban Public Building in Northern and Central Italy, AD 350–850* (Oxford).

——, Mills, N., Gadd, D., and Delano Smith, C. (1986), 'Luni and the Ager Lunensis: the rise and fall of a Roman town and its territory', *PBSR* 54 (n.s. 41): 81–146.

Wolfram, H. (1988), *History of the Goths* (Berkeley and Los Angeles).

11

Nature and views of her landscapes in Pliny the Elder

Mary Beagon

Landscapes in Pliny? On initial consideration the possibility is unlikely. His frenetic lifestyle can have left little time for gazing at the view. This impression is compounded by the *Historia naturalis*. Here the author states clearly his belief that nature's artistry is nowhere more spectacularly manifest than in her smallest and least regarded creations (11. 1–4).[1] Thus he pledges himself to examine every detail of the natural world; and the result is an itemization of the various components of nature rather than an overview of their wider context. It is his zeal in performing his task, holding even the common housefly up for the close inspection of his readers, that ensures that Pliny has his vision fixed at close range. Seldom does he step back to admire a wider vista, unless the subject under consideration is itself on a large scale. Trees, rivers, and mountains are thus the individual components of nature which most frequently figure in the context of their wider environment. Yet, overall, these three features do offer a reasonable number of what may be termed landscape portrayals, and the passages examined in the course of this paper will, for the most part, be focused on them. The comparative wealth of references to such 'parts of nature' in isolation is also of considerable value in assessing Pliny's reaction to the wider view. The whole

---

[1] References in this chapter are to the *Historia naturalis* (*HN*) unless otherwise indicated.

picture, as it were, emerges when both types of observation are placed against the backdrop of Pliny's philosophical concept of the natural world.

This concept is an amalgamation of ideas derived from various philosophical schools, the sort of eclecticism that was not unusual in a Roman of his class and age. The main thrust of the whole has a Stoic flavour,[1] but Pliny was not a Stoic: he was not interested in the finer points of any doctrine. He was a practical man with no pretensions to intellectual rigour for its own sake. He sees nature as the world around him, both as a whole and as its separate components. The perishable, mechanistic world of the atomists is specifically rejected (2. 2–4), and great emphasis is placed throughout the *Historia naturalis* on the concepts of teleology and of a providential deity. Nature for Pliny is divine; this is usually expressed in pantheistic terms, a divine spirit permeating every part of the universe (e.g. 2. 208). However, she is often depicted almost as an anthropomorphic deity bestowing her gifts on man, who is her highest and most favoured creation (7. 1). Pliny's view of nature may also be coloured by the increasing preoccupation of the Stoics of his time with human issues – ethics – rather than physics or theories of knowledge. At all events, the *Historia naturalis* is concerned as much with nature's relationship with man as with her physical attributes. For Pliny, as stated earlier, nature is not just the world but the world around him, and indeed around every human being; nature is Life, as he says in his preface (13).

Pliny will also have been aware of a specific aspect of nature as life in practical terms. Life for the Roman élite, himself included, was to a great extent lived in luxury dwellings whose siting and construction involved a complex attitude to their natural surroundings.[2] These ranged from villas positioned so as to embrace particular natural views, to the manipulation of nature in the creation of parks and gardens, and even to the wholesale upheaval of the natural landscape, for example in complex water management schemes like that of Lucullus (see below, pp. 292–3). On other occasions nature might be conquered more subtly by

[1] See, in more detail, Beagon 1992, ch. 1.
[2] See esp. Purcell 1987, 187–203. Attitudes could vary depending on the location of the villa (ibid., 203–4).

human ingenuity, with buildings adapted to suit the requirements of a difficult but picturesque site (D'Arms 1969, 129–31).

For Pliny, then, intellectual and practical life in nature intermingle, a symbiosis enhanced by the very practicality of his philosophy.

All of this is important if we are to appreciate the landscapes Pliny describes and the attitudes towards them which may be implied. It therefore seems logical to start with those landscapes in Pliny which clearly reflect the idea of nature as inhabited by man. The kind of scenery that most appealed to Greeks and Romans was that of an essentially civilized nature (Purcell 1987, 200; 203). Wildness, ruggedness, solitude, and any extreme of temperature or terrain were eschewed in favour of gentle aspects, temperate climes, and a countryside that was pleasant and easy on the senses rather than bold, spectacular, or challenging. The Latin word *amoenus* summed it up (D'Arms 1969, 45–8; 126–33; Beagon 1992, 194–5), to the extent that the *locus amoenus* became a literary cliché in poetry and rhetorical exercises. Pliny himself obligingly provides a list of landscapes regarded as pleasant, when acknowledging the Augustan painter who

> first introduced the most attractive fashion of painting walls with pictures of country houses and porticoes and landscape gardens, groves, woods, hills, fish-ponds, canals, rivers, coasts . . . together with people going for a walk or sailing in a boat, or on land visiting country houses . . . and also people fishing, hunting, fowling or gathering the vintage.
>
> (35. 116)

Here he conveniently summarizes the widely documented landscape preferences of the Roman aristocracy in general. Their homes were often sited in the vicinity of the sea, hills, or rivers with a view to the *amoenitas* both of the panorama and of future outings by foot, litter, or boat.[1]

Descriptions of scenery as *amoenus* occur often in Pliny, especially when he is mentioning rivers or lakes. The cooling properties of inland waters, together with those of the shading trees which

---

[1] Cic. *Ad Atticum*, 14. 13. 1; *Pro Caelio*, 35; other examples in D'Arms 1969, 13; 51–2; 134. On *HN* 35. 116 see Ling 1977, 1–16; Leach 1988, 272–6.

often grew in their vicinity, had an obvious appeal for Pliny and other writers who were familiar with hot Mediterranean summers. They built their villas to take advantage of them, as, for example, did Pliny's nephew at Tifernum, who enthuses on the lushness of the surrounding countryside, irrigated by streams 'which never run dry' (Pliny the Younger, *Letters*, 5. 6. 11). These natural features were *amoena* both in themselves and as part of their wider landscape setting. In addition, this setting's *amoenitas* was itself enhanced by the insertion of a villa complex (D'Arms 1969, 47): all the natural leafiness and moisture was copied by human means, throughout the villa and gardens, by fountains, pools, and the judicious planting of trees. Among these, plane-trees predominated, a species whose *raison d'être* was its shade-giving properties in summer (12. 11)[1] and which heads the elder Pliny's own catalogue of trees (books 12–16) despite its non-indigenous origins.

I must at this point summarize a discussion on the qualities of rivers in Pliny which I have set out at greater length elsewhere. A number of passages in the *Historia naturalis* contain conventional descriptions of the pleasantness of lakes or rivers, in the manner just outlined (e.g. 3. 20, *amoeno stagno*; 5. 88, *amoenis stagnis*; Beagon 1992, 194–200). Pliny also has an eye for the utilitarian aspect of landscape: when he is not referring to a river as *amoenus*, he often describes it in terms of its function as a means of transport and communication, as being *navigabilis* (3. 21; 3. 147; 5. 5). Praising inland waters and other natural features for their pleasantness or usefulness was part of the orator's stock-in-trade when discoursing on the praises of a city, as Menander Rhetor recommends (349. 25). Both epithets are not normally applied to the same feature: Seneca (*De beneficiis*, 4. 5. 3) talks of 'these rivers' which surround the fields with pleasant (*amoenissimis*) curves, as opposed to 'those rivers' which, with their wide and navigable (*navigabili*) course offer a route to trade. The younger Pliny praises the landscape generally at Tifernum for its *amoenitas*, but the Tiber specifically for its seasonal navigability (*Letters*, 5. 6. 12). This may have something to do with one

---

[1] In winter, though, their deciduous nature was desirable as it allowed more light to penetrate. Thus Pliny condemns the importation of an evergreen plane as being a perversely unnatural and rather pointless luxury (12. 12).

of the traditional derivations of *amoenus* recorded by Servius (on *Aeneid*, 5. 734; 6. 638), tracing it from *amunus*, 'giving nothing' or 'unproductive'. This would make it, in one sense, the antithesis of *navigabilis* with its connotations of trade and commerce; however, it was more usual to identify *amoenus* with the general productivity of a nature that was friendly, and thus pleasant, to man (it is often connected with such words as *fructuosus, fecundus*, and *dives*). In addition, the frequent use of the epithet *saluber*, 'healthy', in conjunction with *amoenus* when describing water tends to blur the distinction between pleasure and utility. Thus Tacitus (*Histories*, 1. 67) describes a spa settlement and its mineral waters, Velleius Paterculus (2. 81. 2) a grand new aqueduct promised by Octavian to Capua; negatively, Cicero comments on the lack of both qualities in the area of the Pomptine marshes (*Orator ad M. Brutum*, 2. 290). Indeed, Pliny generally tends to identify rather than contrast the aesthetic with the utilitarian aspect of rivers and other features. His aesthetic appreciation is actually increased if the object in question has a utilitarian aspect, as can be seen in his remarks on man-made splendour in the form of public buildings (36. 5–6; 11–12; 121: Beagon 1992, 195–6).[1] The description of the river Jordan and its surrounding countryside is a good example: 'It is a pleasant (*amoenus*) stream . . . wandering about . . . and putting itself at the service of the people who dwell on its banks' (5. 71). The river Tiber (3. 54), 'a most tranquil trafficker in the produce of the earth', has 'perhaps more villas on its banks than all the other rivers in the world', a description which clearly implies that it was widely regarded as a pleasant as well as useful landscape.

In the context of the present discussion, it is worthwhile examining more of the Jordan description. Pliny goes on to make a specific contrast between the gentle appeal of the Jordan, with its productive cooperation with man, and the Dead Sea into which it runs. The latter is a harsh and forbidding landscape, described tersely as *lacus dirus . . . aquis . . . pestilentibus*. *Dirus* is also used to describe portentous occurrences that go against the usual rules of nature, such as the screech owl's appearance in daylight

---

[1] *Clarus* (3. 147) and *magnificus* (5. 5) are paired with *navigabilis* in some river descriptions, suggesting perhaps that a utilitarian appreciation of their size triggers an aesthetic one.

(10. 35). Significantly, the same word is applied to the creature's natural habitat: 'deserts and places which are not merely unfrequented but terrifying (*dira*) and inaccessible'. By using this word to describe certain landscapes, Pliny suggests that they are not in keeping with the cosier views of nature with which he and his compatriots tended to identify and which they actively sought out, thus perhaps coming to regard them as the norm and therefore even as 'natural'. We shall return to such landscapes later. Not only is the Dead Sea aesthetically unappealing, it is also unproductive – except of bitumen, in any case a notoriously intractable natural product separable only by menstrual fluid, as Pliny (7. 65; 28. 80) and, according to Tacitus (*Hist*. 5. 6. 24), many other writers tell us. Finally, its pestilential waters repel rather than invite man's interest, in contrast to the Jordan's user-friendly stream.

However, it is not just natural landscape in a form palatable and useful to man which engages Pliny's interest: often the landscape is worthy of his attention because it has been further adorned by the works of man. Again, this was not a point of view peculiar to Pliny, and it has been explored as a wider phenomenon in an illuminating article by Nicholas Purcell (1987, 187–203, esp. 191, 194–6). Thus the river Guadalquivir is described by Pliny not only as 'gliding gently in a pleasant basin' (*alveo amoeno*), but also as passing by towns on both banks (3. 9). The river Rion (6. 13) in the Black Sea area is also picked out in his normally terse gazetteer because of the large numbers of towns on its banks and the numerous bridges crossing over it. Towns can merit mention as being beautiful in themselves (6. 93), while, says Pliny, if all Italy's fine buildings were brought together in one spot, 'another world' would be created (36. 101), a phrase indicative of the importance he attaches to man's as well as nature's contribution to the world already around him. Once again, it is Pliny's description of the Jordan and its environs that illustrates this facet particularly well. After describing the loss of the Jordan's stream in the pestilential waters of the Dead Sea, he continues by describing its widening into the sea of Gennesareth to the north, nearer its source, as a sort of compensation for its loss further downstream to the south. Gennesareth is described not as a 'pleasant lake' but as a lake 'skirted by pleasant towns', *amoenis circumsaeptum oppidis*: that is, its characterizing beauty lies not in its natural advantages but in those added to it by man. *Amoenus* in this context expresses quite literally a civilized pleasantness. This was, again, a widely held preference, and is reflected, for example, in the prominence of man's buildings and activities in Pliny's list of typical subjects for landscape paintings on walls (quoted above).

The river Tiber and its landscape offer an excellent example of the complete integration of the natural scenery with the human exploitation of it. The peaceful waters are thronged with man's mercantile vessels, while the banks are crowded with his dwellings. 'And no other river', adds Pliny, 'is more circumscribed and shut in on either side; yet of itself it offers no resistance, though it is subject to frequent sudden floods'; the latter are, according to Pliny, a pointer to religious observance rather than a sign of natural savagery against man, the river's tamer and exploiter (3. 54–5).

The flooding of rivers, it should be noted, is often given a utilitarian interpretation by Pliny: the rich alluvial deposits increase the fertility of the surrounding countryside for man to farm (e.g. 3. 117–18). In book 18, chapter 167, the Nile is actually said to 'play the part of a farmer' by its periodic floodings. It goes almost without saying that any landscape with the potential to provide rich rewards for the farmer is deemed worthy of mention by Pliny. Thus in his *laudes Italiae* his native land is praised, among other things, for her temperate fertility, while Campania is singled out for her *felix ac beata amoenitas, . . . gaudentis opus . . . naturae* (3. 40). The products of this felicitous area are enumerated in detail in 3. 60–2. Compare also the 'dewy hills' of the Sabines (3. 108) and the fabled land of the Hyperboreans, *regio aprica felici temperie* ('a sunny region with a delightful climate'; 4. 89).

Finally, when discussing the upper reaches of the Nile (5. 51–3), Pliny describes it as disdaining to flow through arid deserts, instead going underground to emerge in a lake in Mauretania Caesariensis where it seems to make a survey of the communities of mankind (*hominum coetus veluti circumspicit*). It then continues its underground flow 'until it has once more become aware of man's proximity', whereupon it leaps out in a fountain. This description is of course reminiscent of the well-known legend of the river Alpheüs' journey under the sea to spring forth in the fountain

Arethusa in Sicily.[1] Here the close link in Pliny between man and the kind of pleasant scenery which man enjoys and finds useful is taken a step further. Not only does man seek out and colonize the *locus amoenus et utilis*: here the landscape itself actively seeks out man and his dwellings, spurning the setting of the desert, which is harsh and inimical to the human race. Elsewhere Pliny can portray the land of Italy as 'rushing out into the sea, as it were, to help man' in his pursuit of trade and commerce (3. 41). Such imagery has a light touch (Beagon 1992, 189),[2] but none the less bears witness to the domination of Pliny's world-view by the interests of the human race. The natural scenery is not only enhanced by man's works: it can even be portrayed as literally forming itself to comply with man's interests. Nature here adds to the man-made landscape rather than man adding to nature's. Her action is large-scale and deliberate. The image is thus essentially different from, though it may have been inspired by, the random self-sowing of wild trees and other plants in a man-dominated environment. There are many instances in the *Historia naturalis* of nature appearing by happy chance in an essentially human environment. Most are on too small a scale (e.g. self-sown wild herbs in the human garden)[3] to be called landscapes. It is, however, interesting to note Pliny's description of a slightly larger-scale invasion by nature of the urban environment, since it occurs at the heart of Rome, in the middle of the Forum. Around the Lacus Curtius, besides the olive deliberately planted for the sake of its shade, there lived in Pliny's time a self-sown fig and a self-sown vine (15. 78).

Some of Pliny's stories suggest that a wholly natural landscape could actually be defined in terms of human edifices. One well-known passage describes the reaction of the governor Licinius Mucianus upon encountering a huge hollow plane tree in Lycia next to the pleasantness (*amoenitas*) of a cool spring. He turned it first into an impromptu dining-room for his retinue, then followed this up by using it as a bedroom, 'receiving more delight from the agreeable sound of rain dropping through the foliage

[1] Pindar, *Nemean Odes*, 1. 1; Ibykos, *PMG* 323; Servius on Virgil, *Eclogue* 10. 4.
[2] cf. Beagon 1992, 167–8, for the humanized vine which likes to have a stretch occasionally (17. 209–10).
[3] They raise interesting questions about the wild–cultivated divide: Beagon 1992, 87–8.

than gleaming marble, painted decorations, or gilded panelling could have afforded' (12. 9). The emperor Caligula, too, was inspired by 'the natural flooring of a single plane tree' to build himself a tree-house (12. 10). The context of both stories strongly suggests that spontaneous reaction, rather than considered ingenuity, on the part of the viewers led them to see the natural in terms of the man-made edifice. We need not, I think, suppose that Mucianus was short of a conventional dwelling for the night and was forced to look to his own resourcefulness.[1]

Man's impositions on the works of nature are not always harmonious; sometimes his improvements and refinements are nothing less than meddlesome folly or a presumptuous overestimation of his own capabilities in competition with nature's. Dyeing natural tortoiseshell for the sake of luxury (9. 139), and creating complex medical compounds out of simple natural products already in themselves perfectly efficacious as cures (29. 25), are but two of a number of examples in Pliny (Beagon 1992, 45; 77). On the whole, however, these examples of a discordant relationship with nature receive less emphasis than the more positive side of the relationship. Discord with regard to human reworking of the landscape is even less frequent in Pliny. The mining and quarrying for precious minerals which he roundly condemns (33. 1–3; Beagon 1992, 41–2; 100 n. 16)[2] should, of course, be mentioned. Here condemnation is as much for the moral damage which his own greed does to man as for the physical damage it does to nature (though I shall return to this point at the end of the chapter). Once again this comparative infrequency is partly due to his focus on individual elements of nature rather than on whole vistas. The passage in 9. 170 on Lucullus's channel cut through the mountain to the sea to provide sea-water for his fishponds does offer itself for comparison with the well-known expostulations of other Latin writers on such landscape upheavals.[3] However, there is nothing

---

[1] Not all Romans appreciated this blurring of distinctions between the human and the natural environment: witness the triumvir Lepidus' silencing of the dawn chorus, just outside his rustic bedroom window, by means of a snake painted on parchment (35. 121).

[2] cf. on the morality issue Citroni Marchetti 1982; 1992; Sallmann 1986; Wallace-Hadrill 1990.

[3] Horace, *Odes*, 2. 15. 2–4; 3. 24. 3–4; Seneca, *Controversiae*, 2. 1. 13; cf. Purcell 1987, 190–4.

in the *Historia naturalis* to be compared with Strabo's description of the Cappadocian king Ariarathes, who created a whole new landscape to act as a private regal playground by damming a river and flooding a nearby plain to create 'a sea-like lake, where, shutting off certain islands like the Cyclades from the outside world, he passed his time there in boyish pursuits' – until, that is, the dam broke and he was forced to pay a fine to the enraged communities whose houses and fields were swept away in the ensuing deluge (Strabo, 12. 2. 8 (538–9)). Returning to Lucullus, however, it should be noted that Pliny's main concern seems to be rather for the cost of the project – it cost more than a villa – than for its perversion of the natural order. One imagines that he would have made much mileage out of the luxurious frivolity of Ariarathes' motives and the damage he subsequently caused to a cultivated human landscape, and would not simply have concentrated on the unnatural upheaval involved.

However, there is a significant instance in the *Historia naturalis* of man's actions having a deleterious effect on the natural landscape. Human warfare can, it seems, not so much pervert the natural landscape as completely obliterate it. Pliny mentions the campaigning in Ethiopia by the Roman army under Petronius in the time of Augustus, and lists the towns that were captured (6. 182). 'Nevertheless', he insists, 'it was not the arms of Rome that made the country a desert' (*solitudo*), a reversal of the sentiment well known to us from Tacitus (*Agricola*, 30. 6):[1] it was, in fact, worn out over a long period by a series of wars with Egypt. Laying waste the enemy's towns and fields is designed to deprive them of the means of survival; that is, of life itself, the life that Pliny identifies as being synonymous with nature in the sentence from his preface quoted earlier. Elsewhere he condemns man's aggression towards man as supremely unnatural: no other animal fights with its own species (7. 5).[2] Ultimately this is a

[1] Ogilvie and Richmond 1967, *ad loc.*, quote Curtius, 9. 2. 24.
[2] Warfare as unnatural devastation of man and his life-supporting landscape also find expression in poetry. For Lucretius large-scale warfare, as well as threatening the inner peace advocated by Epicurus, is unnatural in the sense that it is an irony of civilization: far more men are killed in pitched battle than in the savage days of primitive man fighting with wild animals for survival (*De rerum natura*, 5. 999; see Segal 1990, 188). Warfare as agrarian devastation was, of course, a preoccupation of the

self-destructive trait that runs counter to the basic urge of all parts of nature towards survival and procreation.

The attendant devastation by man of a productive, fertile natural landscape, his own life-support system, both reflects and emphasizes his unnatural madness. His nurse and mother, the Earth, is destroyed. *Solitudines* in Pliny consist of barren wastelands dominated by one of the more ambiguous elements: fire scorching the barren sands, or corrosive salt sea-water. They are in one sense quite literally voids, since there is little or nothing in them that is living (except monstrosities: see below), nothing supportive of life and therefore of nature herself, according to Pliny's usual definition of her. It is, therefore, not surprising that another of the characteristics of the *solitudo* in Pliny is aural as well as visual: an uncanny silence, for example at 5. 6, where in daytime on Mount Atlas 'everything is silent, with a terrifying silence like that of the desert'. Nero's Golden Palace, according to Tacitus, included some designer *solitudines*: the ultimate paradox of nature, it might seem (Tac. *Ann.* 15. 42; Purcell 1987, 198–9). As mentioned earlier, such large-scale landscape upheavals do not normally come within Pliny's scope. However, he is consistently hostile to the emperor, whose behaviour he portrays as essentially unnatural, and in this instance he has perhaps missed a unique opportunity to let the *contra naturam* rhetoric run riot (Beagon 1992, 17–8, 83).

The very fact that deserts exist at all contradicts Pliny's man-centred image of nature. He therefore plays them down, generally consigning them to the remotest and most inaccessible areas or to the very fringes of the world. We can contrast this attitude with that of Lucretius, an Epicurean who did not accept the man-centred Stoic view of the universe. In one of his best-known passages (*De rerum natura*, 5. 195–209) he takes the opposite tack to Pliny, arguing against the teleological position precisely by stressing the proportion of the world that is devoted to deserts or to areas similarly inhospitable to man.

To return to the positive side of the man–nature relationship with regard to landscape: it can be argued that a particular vista

poets generally. Virgil in particular was aware of the potential clash between the Roman ideologies of agriculture and of warfare, especially when the latter was manifest as particularly unnatural, civil, warfare (*Georgics*, 1. 491–7; 506–8; cf. *Aen.* 7. 635–6).

appealed to Roman sensibilities not simply because it was productive or because it was aesthetically soothing. To be either, it also needed to be comprehensible. Too much wildness might not appeal to human rationality and its sense of order. Both these qualities, rationality and order, are important ingredients of Pliny's concept of nature. He has adopted the Stoic idea of nature as a conscious intelligence, an artist producing order and harmony in the world, which itself has its precursors in Platonic and earlier Greek thought.[1] Moreover, ancient philosophical systems generally claimed to offer comprehensive explanations of the origins, nature, and purpose of the universe. It has often been observed that this tendency is itself indicative of a psychological need to feel in control of, and at ease with, an explicable world and not to stand in awe and fear of the unfathomable.

The rational order of the world is seen even in its basic shape: Pliny takes pains to point out that the world is a perfect sphere (2. 5) and to play on the double meanings of the Greek term *kosmos* (universe) as 'ornament', and of the Latin *mundus* (world) as 'elegance' and 'neatness' (2. 8). Nature as artist produces many masterpieces: the myriad colours of flowers, the various shapes of sea-shells, the minute intricacies of insects. The artistry of her larger-scale canvases evokes some significant imagery, which once again connects the works of nature with the works of man. Nature is, in several passages, depicted not simply as an artist but actually as a gardener,[2] the epitome of the human controller of the natural landscape (compare the description of the Nile as farmer: 18. 167, mentioned earlier). For example:

> The Indian fig-tree is self-propagating, as it spreads its branches to an enormous width and the bottom ones bend down to earth so heavily that in a year's time they take root, and produce for themselves a fresh offspring planted in a circle round the parent tree like the work of an ornamental gardener (*opere topiario*).
>
> (12. 22)

It provides a shady bower for the shepherds, and an attractive prospect when viewed from below or from a distance; both effects

---

[1] Cic. *De natura deorum*, 2. 81–167; Beagon 1992, 32 and n. 15 (Diogenes of Apollonia; Anaxagoras; Plato, *Timaeus*; Cic. *ND* 1. 18; 2. 57; and others).
[2] For other natural 'garden' features, see Beagon 1992, 85.

are deliberately striven for by the human gardener,[1] but are here produced spontaneously in the natural landscape. The mountain Nymphaeus in Pthiotis is described as 'once being most noteworthy for the ornamental gardening of nature' (4. 29). The beech grove near Tusculum sacred to Diana has foliage 'which has the appearance of having been trimmed by art' (*velut arte tonsili coma*, 16. 242).

So far we have looked at landscapes with which the Roman psyche felt at home. With the exception of the odd pocket or fringe of desert, nature has been gentle, harmonious, rational, and even tidy. But in Pliny there are other, darker, less friendly landscapes. Nature sometimes seems savage and unapproachable. In the form of volcanoes such as Mount Etna she savagely threatens the earth with fire (*saevit exustionem terris denuntians*, 2. 236). The language of strife and discord frequently appears. The sun and moon 'retaliate on each other', each taking light from the other, in the various types of eclipses (2. 47). In the world's atmosphere the upper and lower airstreams clash, producing thunder, storms, and whirlwinds; 'from [this clash] come most of men's misfortunes and the warfare between the elements of nature' (2. 102–3). The sea encroaches on the land, and even steals away some areas entirely; Pliny refers (2. 204) to the legend of Atlantis in Plato's *Timaeus*. Part of the world to the far north 'lies under the condemnation of nature and is plunged in dense darkness' (4. 88). In one passage he abandons, if only briefly, his normally upbeat picture of a natural world revolving around man's needs: instead he comes close to Lucretius' pessimistic estimation of the extent of *solitudines*, when he talks of the mere pinpoint (*punctus*) that is earth after the seas, lakes, mountains, forests, and *solitudines* have been subtracted from the world (2. 174). Elsewhere he says he does not wish to dwell on nature's crimes (*scelera*), listing earthquakes and any phenomena which have led to the mere tombs of cities (*busta urbium*, 2. 206) surviving.

Such passages as these present a nature that is savage, discordant, irrational, and remote from, or even opposed to, human interests. This is not the predominant view in the *Historia naturalis*, yet such sentiments should not be glibly dismissed as illogical

---

[1] See the younger Pliny's Tuscan villa: *Letters*, 5. 6. 32. For the importance of views generally, see Purcell 1987, 194–7.

intrusions from a different tradition of thought. There is no reason why Pliny should not consciously attribute to his supreme being, *natura*, a complex, multifaceted personality. Below the tranquil surface runs a sinister undercurrent: *scelera naturae* are rare but real, a streak of regal, divine, cruel unpredictability.[1]

It should perhaps be added at this point that much of the perceived discord in nature does not jar on her relations with man; nor does it compromise her overall harmony. Nature compensates for the sea's inroads into land by interposing mountains as barriers (4. 22). The sun and moon, as we saw (2. 47), are mutually obstructive of the other's light. Even the water which appears to dominate the other elements – swamping the land, quenching fire, and covering the air with a blanket of clouds – ultimately restores the balance of nature by falling to the ground again as life-engendering rain (31. 1–3). Nature balances the land lost by earthquakes by throwing up islands out of the sea (2. 202). This kind of discord is neither destructive nor irrational, but ultimately holds the universe together by a tension and balance of comple-mentary elements (e.g. 2. 11; 2. 166); an idea that has a long pedigree in ancient philosophical thought.[2]

Pliny, indeed, rarely if ever suggests that there is anything irra-tional about the working of nature (the only clear example is in his passage on the alleged properties of goat's blood, 37. 60). The balance which nature must achieve is a subtle one. The earth is more unstable in some areas than in others: Pliny mentions places where the earth trembles when trodden on, and the phenomenon of floating islands (2. 202). He says that nature created mountains like the Alps to hold the earth together and to curb the restless elements (36. 1); 'these alone of her creations were not for man', he adds. It was 'almost portentous' for Hannibal and the Gauls to have managed to cross them. The comment adds to the impres-sion that landscapes in which the more elemental of natural forces are to be seen at work are remote from, if not actually dangerous to, the concerns of man. This is nature at her most impersonal.

Yet even here the apparent divorce of man from the natural landscape is by no means complete. Almost in the same breath, Pliny goes on to say that these selfsame mountains were also

[1] Cruel nature: Beagon 1992, 37–9; 151–2; 159–60.
[2] cf. *SVF* ii. 547–73, and the tradition of Aristotle's *Meteorologika*.

created to act as the boundaries of nations (36. 2). In 12. 5 the Alps are described as a barrier designed to imprison the Gauls; in book 3. 31 as a protection to the Roman empire. Indeed, it was as boundaries of nations, rather than as *solitudines naturae* untouchable by man, that the Romans of Pliny's era tended to see mountains. By this time they were well used to crossing these buttresses of the earth in pursuit of Rome's interests. Pliny himself sees fit to commemorate the Roman conquest of the Alpine peoples by quoting the inscription on the arch of Nicaea (3. 136). His own military and administrative career must have familiarized him with transalpine routes.

Again, the clash between the elemental forces of the river Euphrates and Mount Taurus (cf. Beagon 1992, 199–200) is depicted in Pliny as a landscape of dramatic strife, a running battle being fought between the two which favours first one element and then the other (5. 83 ff.). However, this *dimicatio naturae*, as Pliny terms it, is a battle in which the contestants are portrayed in almost human terms, while its drama evokes the atmosphere of the amphitheatre, where fights were deliberately staged as human entertainment. Indeed, Pliny often portrays nature as deliberately staging *spectacula* in the form of duels between one kind of animal and another (Beagon 1992, 151–2). As with the strife of the elements, these duels, though on a smaller scale, serve to uphold the balance of nature: thus the crocodile has more than one natural enemy because it is so great a pest (8. 91). At other times, however, Pliny offers no such justification, and instead portrays nature as putting on the contest in human fashion simply to amuse herself: the enmity between the snake and the elephant is arranged by nature for no other reason than to provide herself with a spectacle involving a pair of contestants (8. 34). Pliny, then, often chooses to look at the strife and upheaval in the natural landscape from a human standpoint and even in human terms, using human points of reference.

As to the purpose of such upheavals, Pliny recognizes the principle of world cohesion and survival which arises from the tensions and balance of the elements; an impersonal law of physics that is remote from the particular interests of the human race. Yet he also portrays even the elemental balance as affecting these interests to a certain extent. Some of the elements are closer to man's interests than others. Land, for instance, is very much man's own element in the *Historia naturalis*, with Pliny often expatiating on the theme of Earth as nurse and mother to the human race (especially 2. 154–9). Earth's rather ambiguous relationship with the encroaching Ocean is therefore of direct interest to man. However, the tension is to a large extent dissipated by the increasing confidence and expertise gained by man in seafaring,[1] enabling him to exercise a certain amount of control over the more troublesome element, just as he does over the bleaker elements of dry land, the mountains mentioned earlier. To a certain degree, man in the *Historia naturalis* is inhabiting the seascape in his ships as he inhabits and adorns the landscape and its inshore waters with his houses. The emperor Claudius, when celebrating the triumph over Britain which he had described in the Lyon tablet (Smallwood 1967, no. 369, lines 39–40) as a victory over Ocean, sailed out into the Adriatic in a vessel which, according to Pliny, was more like a house than a ship (3. 119).

Finally, the balance of nature, which prevents one element dominating the landscape and causing it to disintegrate into turmoil and chaos, is not invariably achieved by tension between impersonal natural forces. On a smaller scale, man, in one passage (17. 96), plays a direct role: he prevents the earth from being overrun by brambles, 'which would cover everything, were not resistance offered by cultivation, so that it would be possible to imagine that man had been created for the sake of the earth'. An obvious comparison is the famous expression in Cicero (*ND* 2. 99) of the Stoic idea of man as the civilizer of the natural world: men are the gardeners of the earth, keeping it clear of savage beasts and rampant vegetation like Pliny's brambles. Once more, of course, we see the high esteem attached by Romans to a landscape that is cultivated. Indeed, it is perhaps Pliny's enthusiasm for agriculture – the theme, after all, of book 17 and the two subsequent books of the *Historia naturalis* – that leads to the rather unusual emphasis in this passage. Rather than the normal Stoic idea of the earth being created for the sake of man, man is here provided for the sake of a cultivated earth! (Incidentally, by way of contrast, Lucretius, in the passage mentioned earlier, stressing the non-teleological view of nature, sees the brambles as merely

---

[1] For the wider question of man's relations with earth and sea, see Beagon 1992, ch. 5.

another aspect of nature's hostility to man: man must do battle with them to secure the meagre area of earth which is cultivable and not given over to total wilderness.)

In Pliny, then, even the potentially daunting 'wild' landscape is rationalized, viewed from a human perspective, and described in terms drawn from human experience. He acknowledges the existence of landscapes that are inimical and positively dangerous to man, but prefers, as he says in 2. 206 (above, p. 296), to pass over *naturae scelera* and on to *terrae miracula* such as the treasures of the mines, mysterious exhalations from the bowels of the earth, floating islands, and flesh-devouring rocks. A separate study would be needed to do justice to the topic of *miracula naturae* and to examine the complexities of the Roman fascination with them. Within the confines of the present topic, however, discussion will be limited to specific remarks on a clutch of *miracula* in the form of wondrous landscapes. Their linking characteristic is their strangeness, rather than their pleasantness or harshness to Roman eyes, though they may also partake of one or other of these two qualities as well. Perhaps the tendency to look for, and approve, order and rationality in the natural world only served to fuel a fascination with the anomalies that disrupted this tidy and predictable world-view. As oddities they appeal, in any case, to another facet of the Roman mind, indeed of human nature generally: a desire for novelty. Pliny remarks, when discussing the ease with which certain trees may be transplanted to an alien soil, that trees, like humans, may have a nature hungry for novelty and travel (*avida novitatis ac peregrinationis*, 17. 66). Wonders, especially distant wonders, exercise a fascination over the human mind. The following examples all have the tree, or in one case a mysterious lack of trees, as their focal point.

The first is a description of white mangroves on the coast of the Red Sea (12. 37). They are trees of a wondrous nature (*mira natura*); when the tide is out, they may be seen embracing the barren sands with their naked roots like octopuses, eaten away by salt and looking like trunks that have been washed ashore and left high and dry. When the tide rises they are completely covered and appear to be nourished by the harsh water. These trees are fascinating because their existence creates a landscape which defies all the usual expectations of a 'pleasant', tree-dominated vista. The bare roots grasp barren sand rather than bury themselves in fertile soil. They do not shade a pleasant freshwater pool, but are submerged and gnawed away by the salt of brackish sea-water, which somehow also nourishes them. It is a miracle that such a conventional product of earth as the tree should grow in such inhospitable circumstances. The sea is, according to Pliny, in one sense very fertile, but in an unconventional way: her fluidity and instability as an element contrast with the firmness of Earth and produce an excessive and wayward fecundity which tends to breed monstrosities (9. 1–2). The mobile element of fire has a similar propensity to produce monsters in the most distant parts of the sun-scorched country of Ethiopia (6. 187). Towards the extremities of the world, where her vast expanses of brine dominate to the exclusion of man's necessities (land and fresh water), the sea is regarded as a watery equivalent of the desert. Pliny talks of the empty voids of nature beyond Ocean when he mentions Britain (30. 13).[1] The stress on the barren sand, medium of the desert proper, reinforces the impression that the mangrove swamp is a paradox of nature.

Three other strange landscapes are to be found in Germany and around the shores of the North Sea, and it is probable that here Pliny is recounting first-hand experiences from his periods of service with the Roman cavalry in these northern parts. The Hercynian oak forest (16. 6) was considered worthy of comment by a number of writers before and after Pliny, but their descriptions seem for the most part rather pedestrian, stating the density of the forest and the size of the individual trees (Caesar, *De bello Gallico*, 6. 25; Strabo, 7. 1. 5 (292); Mela, 3. 29). In contrast, Pliny has an eye for vivid detail and imaginative description. The forest is admired by him as a primeval landscape, unchanged by time and as old as the world itself. The trees' huge roots burst out of the soil and fight with each other for space, forming archways underneath which squadrons of cavalry may pass. Once again it may be noted that the focus is on their roots, the part of a tree in normal circumstances hidden from view. Their extraordinary size is measured in human terms, the cavalry squadron acting as a unit, but this is rather to emphasize a remoteness from, rather than an affinity with, the human world. Otherwise Pliny's emphasis on the forest's age – 'as old as the world itself'- does more than

---

[1] cf. the elder Seneca, *Suasoriae*, 1. 1–16; Beagon 1992, 185–7.

simply express its status as a marvel, its departure from the natural norm: that is, from the nature with which man is familiar and at home. Here is something more unusual, an implication that certain parts of nature are too old to be dated in terms of human history; that the world may be older than the earliest memories of man, and that man cannot in some respects be the point of reference for all the things around him. This is, in fact, specifically stated in one passage:

> if one thinks of the remote regions of the world and the impenetrable forests, it is possible that some trees have an immeasurable span of life. But of those that *the memory of man preserves* there still live an olive planted by the hand of the elder Scipio Africanus ... and a myrtle in the same place.
>
> (16. 234; emphases added)

One is, of course, reminded of the fact that natural objects believed to be very ancient, among which trees figured prominently, had always elicited awe of the religious, rather than the merely curious, kind.[1] An old oak on the Vatican hill (16. 237) 'was older than the city [of Rome]'. It had an inscription in Etruscan letters 'indicating', according to Pliny, 'that even in those days the tree was regarded as venerable' (*religione ... dignam*). Underneath the olive and myrtle on the elder Africanus' estate was 'a grotto in which a snake is said to keep guard over [his] shade'. The beech grove at Tusculum, whose artistically trimmed foliage has already been mentioned, 'has been held in reverence from early times as sacred to Diana' (16. 242). One of its trees had, however, elicited passionate rather than purely religious feeling from the orator Passienus Crispus, who used 'not merely to lie beneath the tree and pour wine over it, but to kiss and embrace it'.

The next example once again involves trees growing near the sea, in this case around the lakes on the coast of Holland, now the Zuyder Zee (12. 5). The oaks here are often uprooted by winds and waves, complete with a large ball of soil, so that they float balanced in an upright position, their branches resembling a ship's rigging. They have caused panic among ships of the Roman

---

[1] For a catalogue of references to trees as sacred or wonderful, and to other forms of tree citation in Pliny, see Chevallier 1986, 147–72.

fleet at anchor for the night, as they appear to be driven purposely against the bows by the waves, 'thus forcing the ships to engage in a naval battle with trees'. Once again, trees have left their normal environment of the soil and have taken to the water. As with the mangrove swamps, the norms associated with landscapes and seascapes, respectively, have been confused. All this adds to the terror of the human sailors in the dark, confronted by the enemy 'ships' of nature. In an article centred on this and other descriptions of Free Germany in Pliny, Klaus Sallmann suggests there is a paradox of nature involved in the idea of aggressive trees. Trees are normally prime gifts of nature to man (12. 1), and should therefore be friendly towards him (Sallmann 1987, 108–28).

The final landscape of this group is remarkable for its complete lack of trees. Trees, according to Pliny, first produced food for man and were the foster-mothers of his helpless and savage lot (*inopis ac ferae sortis*, 16. 1). Wonder born of experience compels Pliny to ask what quality of life is had by people who survive without such basic gifts of nature. His experience comes once again from his time in the north, in a region not far from the Hercynian forest and the scene of the bizarre naval battle with nature mentioned above. The wretched tribes (*misera gens*) of the Chauci (16. 2) inhabit huts on raised ground or platforms over an area of land which is covered by the sea twice a day. 'They resemble sailors in ships when the water covers the surrounding land, but shipwrecked people when the tide has retired.' Round their huts they catch fish rather than keep herds; they use marsh sedge for their fishing lines and dried mud for their fuel. Their only drink is rainwater collected in tanks. 'And these are the races', he exclaims, 'who, if they are nowadays conquered by the Roman nation, say that they are reduced to slavery! Fortune often spares men as a punishment.'

Pliny's reaction has excited comment on several counts. It is surprising to find him eschewing a *topos* popular in ancient ethnography, the moral superiority of primitive life. This was the line later taken by Tacitus in the *Germania* (ch. 35) when discussing the same tribes. Pliny's contemporary, Seneca (*De providentia*, 14. 4), suggested that Germanic tribes who lived in harsh conditions were not wretched, but were toughened and contented by living thus in accordance with nature and with Stoic thinking on the truly happy existence. Pliny's own Stoic-influenced view of man as a perverter of kindly nature's simple gifts might reasonably have led him also to approve the existence of the Chauci.

However, there was no strict Stoic orthodoxy on the question of primitivism and civilization;[1] even if there had been, Pliny is himself no strict philosopher. Practicality often intervenes to modify theory. Moral criticism of the production of luxury goods, for example, may be tempered by the fact that it is a way of making a living (9. 133, 19. 139; Beagon 1992, 77–8). Man's life in nature should, as far as Pliny is concerned, be a comfortable one. In landscape terms, the more pleasant and useful the natural surroundings the better. Moreover, in Pliny's opinion one of the greatest influences for cultured comfort has been the *pax Romana*, the imperial control which the Chauci have rejected. This *pax* can have a deleterious effect, in that it disseminates luxury and blunts the intellect (14. 1–6). However, it is also assigned a more positive role: owing to 'the greatness of the *pax Romana*' a world-wide commerce in healing plants thrives (27. 2–3). The power of Rome can thus overcome even the deficiencies of nature in particular areas, controlling the ambiguous oceans and shipping nature's gifts from more favoured to less favoured places. The Roman people have become, in Pliny's words, a 'second sun' (27. 3), an alternative 'guiding principle of nature' (2. 13, *principale naturae regimen*). Sallmann suggests that the natural landscape of the Chauci, devoid of nature's gifts and dried more by chill winds than by the sun, could only have benefited from the ministrations of a 'second sun' (Sallmann 1987, 120).[2] Thus it may well be that Pliny is criticizing them for repulsing not servitude but a Roman civilization endorsed by and even identified with nature; an improving influence on their barren landscape. Excessive material

---

[1] Sallmann argues that Pliny's non-acceptance of a 'Stoic' line on the Chauci is so surprising as to suggest that some other, overriding ideology has here come into play. He suggests Roman patriotism: Pliny the Roman soldier is rationalizing away Rome's failure to conquer Free Germania. But, as he himself says at one point (112–15), within Stoic thought there were variations in emphasis on the question of civilization. Posidonius had seen man's progress as a positive use of the reason given him as a survival aid by nature; Seneca, however, contested (*Letters*, 90) that in using his reason to invent unnecessary luxuries man had actually gone against nature.

[2] However, Sallmann fails to mention the less favourable view of the culture brought by *pax Romana* in 14. 1–6.

culture undoubtedly produces a moral servitude: an *embarras de richesse* (*rerum amplitudo*) is said by Pliny to cause men to cultivate the vices of others rather than the good gifts that are their own (14. 5–6). The unnatural lack of gifts to call their own, however, eliminates that possibility for the Chauci. It was a commonplace in the Roman historians[1] for foreign opponents to claim that they were upholding liberty against Roman servitude. For people in the position of the Chauci to make such a claim is absurd. Pliny concedes that they resent the idea of conquest, but pulls no punches about the stupidity of this attitude.

It has also been suggested that Pliny exaggerates the pitiable condition of the Chauci, whom other authors such as Tacitus (*Germ.* 35) and Velleius Paterculus (2. 106) portray as thriving communities; archaeological evidence is cited to show that their settlements were rather more substantial than Pliny makes out (Sallmann 1987, 116). But this is beside the point. As far as Pliny was concerned, what he had seen, even if exaggerated in the telling, was not comfortable enough. He rounds off the description with a stylized epigram on fortune sparing these people from conquest as a punishment. But autopsy surely directed the choice of *topos*.[2] Pliny's reaction to the Chauci is ultimately based on personal experience, not books.

In fact, Pliny's sentiments on the Chauci are in line with the practicality of his philosophy and its bearing on man's life in nature. Roman influence may have its attendant moral and social evils but it can in some cases, paradoxically, provide a less perverted setting than the one presently provided by nature unaided. For the landscape inhabited by the Chauci is a paradox of nature. Like the trees of the Zuyder Zee and the mangroves of the Red Sea, these people are naturally inhabitants of a landscape setting who have been inexplicably thrown into a seascape. Man may, on occasion, hold his own quite well even at sea when he sails forth in his ships; but while the Chauci may intermittently appear to be sailors in their sea-surrounded huts, they cannot

---

[1] e.g. Sallust, *Histories*, 4. fr. 69. 5; Caes. *B. Gall.* 7. 73; Tac. *Ann.* 1. 59; 12. 33; *Hist.* 4. 17; *Agr.* 30. 4; cf. McGushin 1994, 174, on the schools' criticisms of imperialism.

[2] Sallmann 1987, 126–7: the literary Pliny drew on the poetic tradition's use of the historiographical commonplace of Fortune as a power in history (e.g. Virgil, *Aen.* 5. 624; Hor. *Od.* 2. 125 ff.; etc.).

choose to leave this element for their natural land setting when
they wish. The sea, not the Chauci, is in control. It leaves them
at low tide, but leaves them as people who have been worsted by
that element: the shipwrecked, with no hope of rescue.

The whole landscape is a natural wonder because it is so
unusual, a prime example of unnatural nature in two respects.
First, we have here what Pliny normally chooses to portray as an
insignificant part of nature, a *solitudo*, the sort of landscape he
locates only in isolated pockets or on the fringes of nature. Second,
it is actually inhabited by man, whose natural setting is the overwhelming area of the world that is pleasant and useful. *Solitudines*
are normally inaccessible to him, except perhaps where he has
created them himself by force of arms. But warfare could not be
blamed for the Chauci's environment, already in effect a wasteland; the Roman army would in this case bring much-needed
culture to a desert.

Pliny's environmental attitude seems clear enough. The comfortable, civilized, man-inhabited natural landscape is the right and
proper face of nature: 'normal' nature, as we have discussed above.
The modern preservers of nature would be taken aback: for them,
'true' nature is to be found in those areas that Pliny marginal-
izes.[1] In Pliny's time these areas were less marginal than he
chooses to suggest. His lack of interest in a positive crusade against
them may be due less to environmental scruples than to the simple
fact that a sparser human population had no need to look beyond
the resources of its more immediate surroundings. Where such a
human necessity exists, as in the case of the Chauci who are already
situated in such a *solitudo*, Pliny voices approval of a campaign –
even a military campaign – of civilization, rather than a protest
that the wild should be preserved. Sallmann, in the article on Free
Germania already mentioned, argues that the ancients generally
believed that such wildernesses ought to be conquered by man.
He cites Strabo,[2] who records that members of a Cypriot community were offered free land if they cleared it of trees themselves,

---

[1] For Pliny's environmental attitudes see also Schilling 1978, 272–83;
Sallmann 1986, 251–66; Wallace-Hadrill 1990, esp. 86.
[2] Sallmann 1987, 120, cites Strab. 14. 6. 5 (684): 'Eratosthenes says
that in ancient times the plains were thickly overgrown with forests and
therefore were covered with woods and not cultivated. . . . because they

after earlier attempts to eradicate the forest had failed. But it seems to me that Strabo implies such destruction is essential to the viable establishment of a human community in this area, rather than recommending it as a matter of principle. Sallmann suggests Pliny would have liked to see the 'hostile' landscapes of the Hercynian forest and Zuyder Zee conquered, together with the Chauci, in a Roman conquest of Germany. But while Pliny may have felt patriotic, there is no evidence that he wanted the first two treescapes, which unlike the Strabo landscape are unpeopled in his descriptions, civilized for civilization's sake when such a course was unnecessary for human needs. After all, if you believe that nature is there for man's benefit you take and use what man wants, but on the same premiss you can surely ignore what he does not want.

Indeed, it is Pliny's careful evaluation of what man's needs really are, both material and moral, that often leads him to place restrictions on man's activities in nature. Thus he presents a more balanced picture of the relationship between man and nature than his man-centred ideology might lead us to expect.

To start with, man's ingenious mind is not the mark of a super-being with a right to conquer nature. It is the compensation given to a creature with fundamental natural deficiencies of instinct, self-defence, and protection from the elements.[1] It is a tool to enable man to meet his needs in nature. These needs are, of course, interpreted liberally by Pliny to suggest a comfortable existence; on the other hand, he allows no excuse for destructive self-assertion.

In addition, man should work towards the satisfaction of his real needs, but too often lapses into greed, a greed which turns out to be morally and materially ruinous. Witness Pliny on the evils of gold, and of iron weapons: 'how innocent, how blissful, how luxurious, even, would life be, if it coveted nothing from any source but the surface of the earth; nothing, in short, but what lies ready to hand' (33. 3; cf. generally 33. 1–5; 34. 138). There is no need for landscape upheavals, neither the digging of goldmines nor the clearance of remote wildernesses.

could not thus prevail over the growth of the timber, they permitted anyone who wished, or was able, to cut out the timber and keep the land thus cleared as his own property and exempt from taxes.'
[1] For this see *HN* 7. 1–5, a passage in the tradition of writing on the differences between men and animals (Beagon 1992, 69).

Moreover, Pliny praises man's cultivation of nature, but only where man's needs can justify it. The brambles which would 'cover the whole earth' (17. 96, cited above) must be destroyed to allow for agriculture. Man improves nature's trees by grafting, to produce new or better varieties of fruit (17. 58). This does not mean, however, that man should cultivate or urbanize every area of wilderness. This, as suggested earlier, would produce an amount of cultivated nature that lay beyond human requirements. Certainly Pliny, like other moralists, condemned the ownership of over-large tracts of land by rich individuals (Seneca, *Letters*, 88. 10; 89. 20–1; Beagon 1992, 63). In addition, he knew that many of man's most valued natural remedies grew in areas of wasteland or desert. At the beginning of his discussion of healing herbs, he says that 'not even the woods and the wilder face of nature are without medicines, for there is no place where that holy mother of all things did not distribute remedies . . . so that even the very desert supplies drugs' (24. 1). The plants might be harvested and transported round the world as part of that Roman commerce in healing herbs mentioned earlier (27. 3, cited above). Perhaps they were also transplanted into herbal gardens nearer home, of the kind Pliny describes in 25. 9.[1] But to cultivate their habitat, to cut down *silvae* or plough up *horridior naturae facies*, would be to destroy the source of these precious products. It seems, then, that even some *solitudines* are part of nature's divine plan to benefit mankind; but only so long as they remain *solitudines*.

Once more, then, we have reached, by an unlikely route through the bleakest parts of the landscape, the Plinian concept of a nature that revolves around mankind. But it must never be forgotten that for Pliny nature is a deity, whose mistreatment by man amounts to sacrilege. When man digs into earth for hidden riches, the occasional earth tremors that result are 'an expression of the indignation of our holy parent' (33. 2).[2] Nor can the human mind, ingenious though it is, compete with that of divine nature, however

---

[1] Pliny's approval of the transportation of plants to alien environments declines in inverse proportion to the operation's necessity. The less useful and more luxurious their intended use, the more disapproving he is. Thus the importation of healing plants is enthusiastically approved, while that of the evergreen plane (mentioned above) is condemned.

[2] On nature's divinity and its significance see Beagon 1992, ch. 1.

complex the compound medicines (24. 4), however painstaking the attempts to measure the earth (2. 247) or count the stars (2. 87; 95). Nature provides for man, but from a position of authority: the servant is also parent. Pliny uses both *ancilla* and *parens* to describe earth in 2. 154–5. Both premisses might seem very remote from today's environmental thinking; yet the conclusions Pliny draws are not so different as we might expect. As far as the landscape is concerned, he makes it amply clear that man can and should live very comfortably in nature without actually defacing or destroying his surroundings.

Bibliography

Beagon, M. (1992), *Roman Nature: The Thought of Pliny the Elder* (Oxford).

Chevallier, R. (1986), 'Le bois, l'arbre et la forêt chez Pline', *Helmantica*, 37: 147–72.

Citroni Marchetti, S. (1982), 'Iuvare mortalem: l'ideale programmatico della NH di Plinio nei rapporti con il moralismo stoico-diatribico', *Atene e Roma*, 27: 124–48.

—— (1992), *Plinio il Vecchio e la tradizione del moralismo romano* (Pisa).

D'Arms, J. H. (1969), *The Romans in the Bay of Naples* (Cambridge, Mass.).

Leach, E. W. (1988), *The Rhetoric of Space* (Princeton, NJ).

Ling, R. (1977), 'Studius and the beginnings of Roman landscape painting', *JRS* 67: 1–16.

McGushin, P. (1994), *Sallust: The Histories*, ii (Oxford).

Ogilvie, R. M., and Richmond, I. (1967), *Cornelii Taciti de vita Agricolae* (Oxford).

Purcell, N. (1987), 'Town in country and country in town', in E. MacDougall (ed.), *Ancient Roman Villa Gardens* (Dumbarton Oaks, Washington, DC), 187–203.

Sallmann, K. (1986), 'La responsabilité de l'homme face à la nature', *Helmantica*, 37: 251–66.

—— (1987), '"Reserved for eternal punishment": the elder Pliny's view of free Germania, HN 16. 1–6', *AJP* 108: 108–28.

Schilling, R. (1978), 'La place de Pline l'Ancien dans la littérature technique', *Revue de philologie*, 52: 272–83.

Segal, C. P. (1990), *Lucretius on Death and Anxiety* (Princeton, NJ).

Smallwood, E. M. (1967), *Documents of Gaius, Claudius, and Nero* (Cambridge).

Wallace-Hadrill, A. (1990), 'Pliny the Elder and man's unnatural history', *Greece and Rome*, n.s. 37: 80–96.

12

Cosmic sympathies: nature as the expression of divine purpose

Gillian Clark

It seems reasonable to expect that a distinctive and dismissive attitude to the natural world should develop in late antiquity.[1] The dominant philosophy was Platonist, and Platonist philosophers were taught to direct their attention away from the detail of this world because the world around us is the lowest level of being: multiple, changeable, material. Matter has no real being – we can never securely say that it is anything – and Plotinus at least considered the possibility that its non-being is infectious, actively (though not deliberately) evil (*Enneads*, 1. 8; 2. 4: see further Armstrong 1970, 257). But even if, on a more optimistic view, the universe results from the outpouring ('emanation') of the One in creative thought, it is still a mistake to focus the mind on this lowest level. The perception of physical beauty should lead us to reflect on what beauty is and how we are capable of perceiving it, advancing by ever greater abstraction to contemplate the truly beautiful.

> Asking myself why I approved the beauty of bodies, whether heavenly or earthly, and what resource I had for making a consistent judgement on mutable things and saying 'This ought to be so, and that ought not to be so' – asking myself, then, why I made these

---

[1] My thanks to the members of the seminar who discussed the first draft of this paper, and won some of the arguments.

judgements, I discovered the unchanging and true eternity of truth
above my mutable mind.

(Augustine, *Confessions*, 7. 17. 23: *CCL* 27. 107)

Philosophers were interested in physics and metaphysics, in
arguments about change and coming to be, and about the
relationship of the many changing particulars to the unchanging
One. Christian debate about creation 'out of nothing', and about
the relationship of God to change, stimulated the discussion (see
further Sambursky 1962; Sorabji 1983; 1988). But it was concerned
with the principles, not the particulars, of being. Non-Christians
had no religious motive for attending to nature: traditional
Graeco-Roman religion survived the efforts of Christian emperors,
but it would be sheer romanticism to think of 'pagan' philosophers
as reverent worshippers of Naiads and Dryads and Oreads,
profoundly aware of the spirits of water and wood and hill. They
regarded such beliefs as picturesque storytelling, helpful only for
the simple faithful who could not grasp more abstract teaching
about the divine (for the survival of traditional religion see
Trombley 1993). Christian intellectuals were just as likely as non-
Christians to think that the study of the natural world deals in
appearance, not reality (Wallace-Hadrill 1968, 3–9). The important
fact, for them, was that God made the world. They acknowledged
the essential goodness of God's creation, unlike those Gnostics
and Manichaeans who held that the physical world was negative
or evil, but they also believed that the world has fallen: human
sin has affected all of creation, so that the earth now requires
cultivation to produce food instead of thorn-bushes, and animals
that had lived in peace are a danger to humans and to each other.
Some Christians believed that God would some day restore
Paradise on earth, but the central concern of Christian teachers
was the struggle of the individual human being against personal
sin. Christians were 'just passing through', and there was no reason
to encourage attention to this fallen world at the expense of preparation for the next.

These variously other-worldly attitudes can be used as evidence
for the 'progressive devaluation of the cosmos' (Dodds 1965, 37).
The natural world, it can be argued, was interesting only in so far
as nature conveyed something about the purposes of God and
their impact on human souls. This contention has long since been

challenged in terms of the sheer range of material about the natural world which is displayed by Greek patristic writers (Wallace-Hadrill 1968). The material is not itself evidence for careful attention and new research: much of it belongs to the tradition of 'natural wonders', and is derived from reading not from observation (for the tradition see French 1994). But still it is used, not disregarded, and there is something to be learned from the symbolic and moral interpretation of nature in both Christian theological, and non-Christian philosophical, writings.

Transplanting mallow

Late in the third century AD, or perhaps early in the fourth, the philosopher Iamblichos wrote his *On the Pythagorean Life*. He used stories of the legendary sage Pythagoras, and of the lifestyle allegedly followed by his disciples, to inspire his own students for the hard intellectual work and discipline of life which they would need in the study of philosophy. The aim of philosophy, in his Platonist tradition, was to raise the human mind from preoccupation with bodily needs and immediate surroundings to the level at which it can contemplate, or even be united with, the mind of God.

Iamblichos explains that, as part of the discipline, Pythagoras banned some kinds of food. He wanted his committed followers to be vegetarian.

> Other students, whose life was not entirely pure and holy and philosophic, were allowed to eat some animal food, though even they had fixed periods of abstinence. He also forbade them to eat the heart or the brain, and told all Pythagoreans to abstain from these, for these are the governing organs and, as it were, the seats and abodes of thought and life: their nature is that of the divine reason and he declared them sacred. They were not allowed to eat mallow either, because it is the first sign of the sympathy between heavenly and earthly beings, or the blacktail fish, because it belongs to the gods of the underworld, or the *erythrinos* fish for other such reasons.
>
> (*On the Pythagorean Life*, 109; trans. G. Clark 1989, 48)[1]

---

[1] Another annotated translation is now available: Dillon and Herschbell 1991.

Iamblichos does not explain why mallow is 'the first sign of the sympathy between heavenly and earthly beings', nor does he discuss whether this interpretation of the ban on mallow belongs to a later time than Pythagoras. He is not concerned with the complicated history of Pythagorean tradition and the possible social context in which mallow was forbidden, but with philosophical teachings which were not dependent on context. He holds that Plato and Aristotle taught the same as each other; that both expounded the essential truths which were also symbolized in traditional Greek religion; and also (which was not so commonly held) that Pythagoras had conveyed the same truths in profoundly symbolic utterances. So in his *Exhortation to Philosophy* (*Protrepticus*) he offers a symbolic explanation for the ban on mallow:

'Transplant mallow but do not eat it' is a riddling way of saying that such plants turn with the sun, and one should observe this. It also says 'transplant': that is, having inspected the nature of it and its striving towards the sun and sympathy with it, do not be satisfied and rest there, but transport and, so to speak, transplant your thought to other plants and vegetables of the same kind, and to other creatures not of the same kind, and to stones and rivers and simply to all natures; you will find an abundant and manifold and astonishingly rich indication of the unity and harmony [lit. 'breathing together'] of the universe, beginning from the mallow as from a root or starting-point. So do not just refrain from eating it, or from making such observations disappear, but increase and multiply them like one who transplants.

(*Protrepticus*, 38)

So reflection on one plant with a particular characteristic will lead to awareness of the universe as an integrated whole, in which the many distinct 'natures' of plants and animals and natural objects are linked to higher levels of being. Mallow had earlier carried a symbolic charge as an uncultivated food produced by the earth, a gift from the gods (Detienne 1977, 47). Iamblichos exploits its symbolic value within the different system of late Platonist philosophy. He envisages several different levels of being, some closer than others to the One which is the source of all being, but all linked by the bonds of *philia*, friendship or belonging (G. Clark 1989, 29 n. 68).[1] These are manifested (for instance) in the relationship of mallow to the sun. In Greek religious tradition the sun is a

---

[1] For a fuller discussion of Iamblichos' philosophy, see Dillon 1987.

visible divinity, and in Platonist terms it belongs to a higher, more ordered, more permanent level of being. Mallow is perishable, but also heliotropic: something on the lowest level of being moves in sympathy with a much higher level. These 'vertical' links are apparently more important to Iamblichos than the interrelations of different natural kinds in his immediate surroundings.

Iamblichos does not only use plants, or other natural objects, to make a philosophical point. The doctrine of 'cosmic sympathies' justifies the use of particular natural objects in the traditional practice of divination and sacrifice.

> It is better to take the reason [for sacrifice] to be friendship and kinship, a bond which links the craftsmen to what they have made and the begetters to what they have begotten. So when, under the guidance of this common principle, we find a living creature or plant upon the earth which preserves intact and pure the intention of its maker, then through one such we set in motion, in the appropriate way, the cause which made it and which rules over it without losing purity.
>
> (*On the Mysteries*, 5. 9. 209)

The same doctrine explains theurgy. This was an attempt to raise the soul to higher levels of being by the use of ritual and incantation, sometimes using natural objects as a focus.

> Let no one be amazed if we say that some kind of matter is pure and divine, for, since it too comes into being from the father and maker of all, it has its own perfection which is an appropriate receptacle for the gods. . . . The art of theurgy, seeing this, and discovering in these general terms the fitting receptacles for each of the gods according to what is appropriate, often interweaves stones, plants, animals, fragrances, and other such sacred and perfect things which are divine in form, and makes from all these a complete and pure receptacle.
>
> (*Myst.* 5. 23. 233)

Late antique interpreters, like modern scholars, disagreed about theurgy, seeing it (according to religious temperament) as sacramental worship or as an attempt to constrain the gods by magic.[1] The techniques of theurgy and magic were indeed very similar, but Iamblichos insists that the purpose is quite different:

---

[1] On the content and the revaluation of theurgy, see esp. Shaw 1985, 1993; Fowden 1986, 131–4. Further bibliography is in G. Clark 1989, xii n. 4.

the theurgist, helped by the benevolence of the gods, seeks to purify his soul. Hostile critics, such as Iamblichos's older contemporary Porphyry, said that theurgy was *goêteia*, the familiar attempt to manipulate supernatural powers.

Porphyry, too, wrote a life of Pythagoras, as part of a history of philosophy. He takes the trouble to describe in detail some Pythagorean recipes which include mallow, but appears to present them for their practical rather than their symbolic value. As usual in Graeco-Roman recipes for food or medicine, the instructions are sketchy at best, and it is difficult to be sure about some of the ingredients.[1]

> [Pythagoras] ate, for breakfast, honeycomb, or honey; for dinner, bread made from millet or barley, cooked and raw vegetables, rarely meat from sacrificial victims and that not from every part. Most often, when he intended to enter a sanctuary of the gods and spend some time there, he used foods which counter hunger and thirst. The hunger-suppressant was a mixture of poppy seed, sesame, the outer skin of squill carefully washed until it was cleansed of its sap, asphodel heads, mallow leaves, barley and chickpeas; he chopped them all up in equal quantities and moistened them with Hymettos honey. The thirst-quencher was cucumber seed, raisins (he took out the pips), coriander flower, mallow with the seed, purslane, grated cheese, fine wheat-flour and cream, all of which he mixed with island honey. He said that Herakles learnt these from Demeter when he was going to the Libyan desert.
>
> (*Life of Pythagoras*, 34–5)

Porphyry does not discuss the possible magical significance of such ingredients as poppy, squill, and asphodel (see further Scarborough 1991, especially 146–9 on squill). But although he rejected the use of natural objects to influence higher levels of being, in magic or in theurgy, he was prepared to interpret them as symbols of these higher levels. One of Porphyry's minor, but most influential, works is an interpretation of Homer's Cave of the Nymphs on Ithaca (*Odyssey*, 13. 102–12). He starts with the assumption that Homer conveys truths about the soul and the universe in the form of stories, which should be interpreted allegorically (just as Jewish and Christian theologians dealt with the more unpromising sections of the Old Testament). The Cave

---

[1] I am much indebted to Lin Foxhall and Hamish Forbes for a happy evening spent trying to identify some of these items.

of the Nymphs, Porphyry observes, is not fiction: it is mentioned in the work of a leading geographer. But why should Homer trouble to describe a sanctuary, or to invent its peculiar features, unless they have a greater significance? Homer says, for instance, that at the head of the harbour there is an olive-tree with spreading leaves, and near it is a cave:

> This tree does not grow there by chance, as one might suppose, but holds the riddle of the cave. For since the *kosmos* did not come into being at random or by chance, but is the creation of the thought of God and of intelligent nature, there is planted by the image of the *kosmos* – the cave – a symbol of the thought of God, the olive. The plant belongs to Athena, and Athena is thought (*phronêsis*). . . . The olive, being always green, has a particular quality which is most appropriate to the turnings of souls in the *kosmos*; the cave is sacred to these souls. In the summer the white side of the leaves faces upwards, in winter it turns downward . . .
>
> (*On the Cave of the Nymphs*, 32–3)

The examples of Pythagoras' mallow and Homer's olive-tree illustrate a late Platonist approach to the natural world. If a particular plant, or another natural object, can help raise the mind to a higher level of reality by analogy or by the operation of 'cosmic sympathies', so much the better. But the natural world is of value only in so far as it inspires us to abstract from its immediate beauty and order and contemplate higher things. Late Platonism, as one of the leading scholars on the subject put it, 'encourages of itself a contempt for the empirical study of nature' (Lloyd 1970, 276).

There has been some change in scholarly attitudes. Ritual and theurgy, cosmic sympathies and occult influences, used to be dismissed (and sometimes still are) as irrational or superstitious survivals which have nothing to do with serious philosophy. Recent work is prepared to consider theurgy, Hermetism, and even magic as coherent belief systems which can be integrated with more abstract arguments (see, for instance, Shaw 1985; Fowden 1986; Faraone and Obbink eds 1991). But the argument still stands that late antique philosophers were not in general interested in the natural world. The essential fact about human beings, according to Platonist philosophy, is that we can abstract and systematize and understand the underlying principles: we have *logos* so we can grasp *logos*. Humans are distinctively rational, and philosophers argued about just how much *logos* non-human animals had. There is a scale of being: stones have continued existence; plants can take nourishment and grow; animals can move; humans can think and speak; angels or *daimones* are thought unimpeded by body. Humans should aim up the scale.

This is not an argument for indifference towards non-humans. Iamblichos (*On the Pythagorean Life*, 60) presents Pythagoras as able to teach animals, which must therefore be at least receptive of reason.[1] Plutarch in the *Moralia* (959–99) has an impressive assemblage of animal behaviour which appears to show rationality and affection, and Porphyry has a particularly engaging example from his own experience. There was a partridge which not only took the initiative in making friends with him, but made sounds in response to his voice – different, he says, from the sounds that partridges make to each other (*On Abstinence from Animal Food*, 3. 1. 7; see further Sorabji 1993, 84–5). This partridge had at least a wish to communicate by speech and to be associated with humans. Dogs too, especially the small Maltese dog, were thought to show affection and understanding; cats, who also make different sounds when addressing humans, were portrayed only rarely, as fierce little creatures (Toynbee 1973, 87–90; 109–22).[2]

If animals share to some extent in *logos*, and show affection, it becomes difficult to justify the practice of using them for food. Ancient arguments for vegetarianism tend to be anthropocentric: carnal food encourages carnal desires, and drags the would-be philosopher (or Christian ascetic) down the scale of being, because in eating meat a human behaves like the *zôa aloga*, the irrational beasts which hunt their food and are ruled by their immediate desires. Porphyry, in his *On Abstinence from Animal Food*, develops a dilemma. If animals are unlike humans, in that they are red in tooth and claw and make no social contracts, humans should not behave like animals. If animals are like humans, in that they manifest affection and some kinds of reason or responsiveness to reason, it is clearly unjust to kill them for food. It may be necessary to kill in resisting attack, but it is not then necessary to eat the creature. Wild animals have no choice about eating others, but humans do.

---

[1] I am indebted to John Dillon (pers. comm.) for discussion of this difficult passage.
[2] The book is dedicated to a distinguished cat.

Porphyry's arguments for abstinence from meat go much further than the anthropocentric perspective: he draws on a philosophical debate which challenged the assumption that the world was made for rational beings, or indeed for any of the creatures that live in it.[1]

> If it is true that the god made animals for the use of humans, what use are we to make of flies, mosquitoes, bats, beetles, scorpions, vipers? Some are hideous to see, revolting to touch, unbearable to smell, and make terrifying and unpleasant noises, and others are outright fatal to those they meet. As for whales and sharks and other sea-creatures which, as Homer says, 'deep-voiced Amphitrite nourishes in their thousands', why did the Maker not teach us how they are naturally useful? And if people say that not all came into being for us and because of us, the distinction is in any case unclear and confusing, and we still do not escape injustice in attacking and harming those who did not come into being for us, but like us in accordance with nature. Besides, if we define animals in terms of their usefulness to us, would we not have to concede that we came into being for the sake of the most dangerous animals – crocodiles, whales, snakes? They are of absolutely no use to us, but they seize and devour any available humans and use them as food; and thereby do nothing worse than we do, except that need and hunger drive them to this injustice, whereas we slaughter most animals from arrogance, for luxury, or for amusement in theatres and hunts.
>
> (*Abst.* 3. 20. 4–6)[2]

But Porphyry's concern for the non-human, and his readiness to accept that we share this world with other creatures, does not lead him to close study of such creatures. Platonist philosophers need not disregard the natural world: the proper reaction is to admire the divine purpose displayed in all its aspects. The universe may be a falling away from the One, but it is still a *kosmos*, a manifestation of beauty and order. Nevertheless, the details of the *kosmos* are important only as part of a general argument, and a Platonist philosopher is unlikely to engage in the empirical study of nature for its own sake.

---

[1] See Chadwick 1947 and Renehan 1981 for the history of this argument.
[2] For other ancient arguments on vegetarianism, and on the moral status of animals, see S. R. L. Clark 1977; Dombrowski 1984; Sorabji 1993.

Grafting olives

Christian writers of the third and fourth centuries shared the common philosophical culture. Basil and the two Gregories, Ambrose, and Augustine have all been accused of too much regard for Platonism. They use allegory, as Porphyry does for Homer, to expound the hidden meaning of the Hebrew scriptures, and the hidden meaning usually turns out to be very Platonist, conveying messages about spiritual struggle or the relationship of God to the world. But it seems reasonable to expect that their attitude to the natural world would differ from that of a Platonist. The Christian doctrine of creation, which caused so much debate, is that God made heaven and earth. The world is not just a 'falling away' from the unity of the One. It is now a fallen world, because human sin made the earth resistant and some animals hostile, but it is God's creation and must not be devalued. Christian preachers also had to expound the Judaeo-Christian scriptures, most of which assume an agricultural economy, and which frequently use images from the natural world. Celsus in the second century AD charged Christians with anthropocentrism: it may still need saying that these scriptures are not uniquely exploitative of the natural world, and that they can be interpreted either to justify human domination of the non-human or to challenge and restrain it.[1]

Christian preachers could – and often did – allegorize references to nature. But they did not deny the surface meaning of the text, and they had to expound it not only to the educated élite of the lecture-rooms, but to church congregations who were often, if not always, a much wider cross-section of society.[2] Basil gave his sermons on the *hexaêmeron*, the six days of creation,

> in a crowded church to a big audience: he had to adapt to his hearers. Among so many people there were several who understood more advanced arguments, but far more who did not grasp the subtler refinements of thought – uneducated and working men who were

---

[1] These points are briefly documented in Thomas 1983, 22–5; the early 1990s have seen several works on the 'green gospel'. For Celsus, Origen's reply (*Against Celsus*, 4. 74–99) and the history of the dispute, see Chadwick 1947, 36–8.

[2] MacMullen 1989 argues that much Christian preaching assumes an élite audience.

preoccupied with ordinary trades, women who are untrained in such disciplines, young children and the elderly. All these needed the kind of preaching which, through readily understandable and fascinating material on the visible creation and its beauties, would lead them on to knowledge of the Maker of these.

(Gregory of Nyssa, *On the Hexaêmeron* = *PG* xliv. 66a)

But it does not follow that Basil himself engaged in study of the natural world. He offered his congregation material which seems to be derived not from observation, but from the tradition of 'natural wonders' (Wallace-Hadrill 1968, 37–8; French 1994). His sermons on the six days of creation include some suspiciously Herodotean claims about what people have told him.

I shall not abandon examples from the sea, because these things lie before us to be expounded. I have heard from a seafaring man that the sea-urchin, a very small creature and easily despised, often becomes the sailors' teacher about calm and storm. When it foreknows trouble from the winds, it goes under a strong stone and is safely tossed on it as if at anchor, held down by the weight so as not to be easily swept away by the waves. When the sailors see this, they know that violent movement of the winds is to be expected. No astrologer, no Chaldaean, predicting disturbance of the winds from the rising of the stars, has taught the sea-urchin this, but the lord of sea and winds, who has put a clear trace of his own great wisdom in this small creature. Nothing is unforethought, nothing is neglected by God. The unsleeping eye sees all. He is present to all, providing security for each. If God has not left the sea-urchin out of his care, will he not watch over your concerns?

Husbands, love your wives, for even if you are foreign to one another, you have come together for the community of marriage. Let the bond of nature, the yoke imposed by blessing, unite those who are separate. The viper, most dangerous of reptiles, goes to meet and marry the sea-lamprey, and having signified its presence by hissing calls her[1] from the depths for the conjugal embrace. She obeys and is united with the poisonous one. What is the meaning of this? That even if the spouse [male] is harsh and savage in character, his yokemate [female] must bear it, and it is not acceptable on any pretext to pull apart the union. Is he violent? But he is your husband. Drunk? But he is united to you in nature. Harsh and hard to please? But he is a member of your body, indeed the most honoured member.

(*On the Six Days of Creation*, homily 7. 5 = *PG* xxix. 160)

---

[1] In fact both *echidna* and *muraina* are feminine nouns.

The abrupt transition from the sea-urchin's ballast to the toleration of husbands (however poisonous) is Basil's own, and no doubt it woke up the congregation. But the sea-urchin and the lamprey's wedding derive from his reading, and it is (so far) not possible to reclaim them as authentic observation of nature. Admittedly, not all 'natural wonders' can be dismissed as merely tralatitious: would anyone believe that mudskippers exist, if there was only a description by Herodotos? Basil also relates, and Ambrose translates for use in Milan, that the turtle-dove covers her nest with squill leaves because wolves dislike the smell (Ambrose, *Hexaêmeron*, 6. 4. 29 = *CSEL* 32. 1. 223). This sounds most improbable; but it also sounds improbable that the eider-duck should cover her eggs with droppings so as to safeguard them from foxes. But eider-ducks have been filmed covering their eggs with droppings, and foxes, which do eat birds' eggs, do not take eggs covered with droppings; twentieth-century interpretation draws a moral about survival strategies.

It may be possible to rescue some of Basil's other assertions.

> People have already observed that when pines (*pituës*) are cut down or burnt they change into oak-woods. We have also known natural badness cured by the care of farmers, for instance, sharp pomegranates or bitter almonds: when the trunk is bored close to the root, and a wedge of rich pine-wood (*peukê*) is driven through, they change the unpleasantness of the juice to something good to use. So let no one who leads a life of badness condemn himself, knowing that agriculture changes the qualities of plants, and care of the soul in accordance with virtue is capable of overcoming all kinds of illness.
>
> (*On the Six Days of Creation*, homily 5. 7 = *PG* xxix. 109)

The pine-woods that turn into oak-woods can be explained: the roots of holm-oaks, undamaged by fire, have a chance to produce more shoots when the pines are not starving them of light and food. But the tactic for dealing with pomegranates and almonds is not convincing. Basil had perhaps misunderstood (and failed to investigate) some farming technique such as bark-ringing or root-pruning, which might shock an unproductive tree into producing fruit.[1] He came of a landowning family, but landowners do not always know about farming, and there is no way of knowing how any farmers in his congregation reacted. But just as recent research

---

[1] I owe this suggestion to Lin Foxhall.

on herbal medicines has lent credibility to ancient contraceptive techniques, so future research may yet lend Basil some support.[1]

So there is a danger of being too dismissive; but there is a rival danger of interpreting patristic writing with too much sympathy. It is easy enough to find interest in natural diversity, and in particular animal and plant species, but difficult to find anything like the twentieth-century ecological consciousness of human impact on the natural world.

> How is it that the kinds of fish, each keeping to the territory suited to them, do not go on each other's territory but on their own? Is it divided by boundaries? No geometer assigned living-places to them; there are no walls to surround or barriers to divide. What is needful is spontaneously assigned to each. This bay nurtures these kinds of fish, that one others; those which abound in one place are lacking in others. . . . There is a law of nature equally and fairly assigning a way of life to each according to its need. But we are not like that. Why? We move ancient boundaries which our fathers laid down, we cut up the earth wrongly, we join house to house and field to field so as to take something away from our neighbour.
> (*On the Six Days of Creation*, homily 7. 3–4 = *PG* xxix. 156)

Basil may here show some awareness of the 'ecological niche' and of human disruption of natural patterns; but his interest is in the moral point about human greed. Similarly, collections of stories about the desert fathers were popular in the late fourth century, and could have made people aware of alternative human relationships to the land. The monasteries founded by Pachomius were, in effect, successful Egyptian villages which, by relieving farmers of the need to provide for families, were often able to generate a surplus for charity. Individual Christians, in Egypt and elsewhere, chose to lead a life of self-sufficiency, growing only the minimum for survival; some attempted to restore the life of Paradise before the Fall, living off the uncultivated earth in harmony with the wild animals (Elliott 1987). But the ecological aspect should not be over-stressed: these ascetics had gone into the desert to escape the distractions of human society and desires, not to minimize their impact on the environment or to eat low on the food chain – something peasants did in any circumstances

---

[1] For contraceptive medicines see Riddle 1992; his deductions are not always acceptable to chemists.

(Rousselle 1988, ch. 10). The people who read about them were expected to admire their self-sufficiency in loneliness and privation, not in organic farming.

So there remains a question whether patristic writers were concerned with the detailed observation of the natural world, or whether they simply reworked a literary inheritance for a particular kind of edification and, like Platonist philosophers, thought that nature is only a starting-point.

> The man who knows he owns a tree and thanks You for the use of it, although he does not know how many cubits high it is or how widely it spreads, is better than the man who measures it and numbers all its branches, but does not own it and does not know or love its creator.
>
> (Augustine, *Confessions*, 5. 4. 7 = *CCL* 27. 60)

The symbolic value of the olive in Christian preaching supplies a final range of examples, the first from Paul's letter to the Romans:

> If the root is holy, so are the branches. If some of the branches have been broken off and you, being a wild olive, have been grafted among them and have come to share in the richness of the olive-root, do not boast over the branches; if you do boast, [remember that] you are not carrying the root, but the root is carrying you. You will say, 'The branches were broken off so that I should be grafted in.' Right: they were broken off by lack of faith, you are established by faith. Do not be conceited, but be afraid: for if God did not spare the natural branches, God will not spare you. See the goodness and the severity of God! Severity[1] for those who have fallen, the goodness of God for you, if you abide by goodness. You too may be cut out. And they, if they do not abide in their lack of faith, will be grafted in. God can graft them back again. If you were cut from a naturally wild olive, and against nature were grafted into a good olive, how much more will those who belong by nature be grafted into their own olive?
>
> (Rom. 11: 17–24)

Paul uses a sustained metaphor to describe the relationship of Christianity to Judaism. It is a reversal of normal farming practice, which was to graft a shoot from a cultivated olive on to the stock of a wild olive. The reason for doing this is that cultivated olives cannot be propagated from seed: they revert to 'wildness'

---

[1] lit. 'cutting off'.

– that is, they produce no fruit usable by humans, and they grow thorns. Irenaeus uses this fact to make a moral point:

> Just as an olive, neglected and left for some time in uncultivated land, becomes a wild olive bearing fruit after its kind; or, on the other hand, a wild olive which receives attention and is given a graft reverts to the fruitfulness of its former nature, so it is with people.
>
> *(Against Heresies*, 5. 10. 1 = *SC* 263–4)

Grafting wild olive onto cultivated olive would normally be pointless; that is Paul's point, in saying that God has done this remarkable thing. But Clement of Alexandria insists on making botanical sense of Paul's image:

> Now the wild olive is grafted into the richness of the olive and grows like cultivated olives; for that which is implanted makes use of the tree in which it is implanted instead of the earth, and all plants alike grew at the divine command. Thus, although the *kotinos* is a wild olive, it crowns Olympic victors, and the elm, leading the vine up to a height, teaches it to be fruitful. Now we see that wild trees take up more nutriment because they cannot digest it, so wild trees are less able to ripen fruit than cultivated ones, and the cause of their being wild is just this lack of ability to ripen. So the olive in which a graft has been made gets more nutriment from the implantation of the wild olive; and, just as the wild olive becomes accustomed to digest the nutriment, being assimilated to the richness of the olive, so also the philosopher, resembling the wild olive in having much that is undigested, because of his eagerness and ready pursuit and desire for the richness of truth, if he also acquires the divine power through faith, will be implanted in true and cultivated wisdom, just as the wild olive, grafted into the truly beautiful and merciful word, assimilates the nutriment which is supplied and becomes a good olive.
>
> *(Miscellanies (Strômateis)*, 6. 15 = *GCS* 32. 490)

Clement then goes on to describe four recognizable techniques of grafting and to compare them to four different ways of becoming a Christian.

Augustine exploits the same farming practice for a different purpose. The 'difficult question' with which he is dealing is the need for infant baptism: do children inherit sin from their parents, even if those parents are Christians whose sins have been remitted by baptism? In a letter to Pope Sixtus he writes:

> But whatever difficulty there is in this question, it does not prevent the labourers in Christ's field from baptizing infants for the remission

of sins, whether they were born from infidel or believing parents, just as farmers are not prevented from changing wild olives into olives by the care of their grafting, whether they grow from wild olives or from olives. If a countryman is asked to give an answer to the question 'Why, when an olive is one thing and a wild olive another, is it only a wild olive which grows from the seed of either?', he does not abandon his grafting even if he cannot solve that problem; otherwise, while he considers that shoots from the seed of an olive are nothing other than olives, his futile laziness ensures that the whole field becomes scrubland in bitter sterility.[1]

> (*Letters*, 194. 44. 10 = *CSEL* 57. 211)

The olive lends support to an argument: it is only common sense to treat olives like this, so the spiritual analogies become more persuasive. The reminiscence of Paul adds authority. But Augustine, when challenged by Julian of Eclanum, accepted that olive-seed is only an illustration, an example which may help to understand something difficult (*Against Julian*, 6. 6. 15 = *PL* xliv. 831). It is not a message from on high in support of infant baptism.

There is, then, in patristic writing both what looks like practical observation of the natural world and what looks like edifying legend that no one could have checked even if they wanted to. The interest in nature is undoubtedly there, but the concern is anthropocentric and moral. Detailed descriptions of plants and animals are used to show how God's providence designed everything for good. Animal behaviour, and even some characteristics of plants, are used to supply moral examples for humans. The natural world is appropriated for human edification, and humans are not seen as part of an ecology. It is taken for granted that animals are for human use, whether as food or as moral stimulus. Animals may behave better than humans, like the turtle-dove which mourns a lost mate instead of seeking a new partner, but humans are superior to animals because humans have *logos*. The astonishing range of the human mind, and human ingenuity, surpasses all the apparent advantages of animal speed, strength, or skill. Animals cannot tame humans, but humans can tame animals.[2]

This range of attitudes is not peculiar to late antiquity: it can be traced back not just to Pliny, but to Cicero, Aristotle, and

---

[1] For other examples, and discussion, see E. A. Clark 1986, 294.
[2] I discuss these themes in more detail elsewhere: G. Clark, forthcoming.

Theophrastos (Beagon 1992 and in this volume, ch. 11; French 1994). The difference is not between classical and late antique attitudes to nature, but between fourth-century admiration for the diversity and design of the natural world, and late twentieth-century ecological consciousness. One of Dodds's starting-points for the 'progressive devaluation of the cosmos' was awareness of this world as part of a much larger universe (Dodds 1965, 6). This perspective can have different effects. In the eighteenth century, according to Keith Thomas, it combined with increased knowledge of the natural world to challenge the anthropocentric perspective (Thomas 1983, 167). In the late twentieth century it encourages a sense of an uniquely precious and fragile ecosystem, to which humans are the main threat and in which they may well be superseded. In late antiquity it seems to have fostered a conviction that the only really important aspect of this world is the rational human soul which can aspire to reach God.

Late antiquity shows no sign of bad conscience about human domination of the world, with the one exception that some people thought it wrong to eat animals or to enjoy the spectacle of animals being slaughtered at the games.[1] But these people were concerned chiefly for the spiritual threat to humans; or, if they did (as Plutarch and Porphyry certainly did) mind about animals, it was because animals come closest to human experience. The general habit of thought was to admire some animals for their strength or beauty or skill, or even for some aspects of their behaviour, but not to see them as having societies and strategies of their own. Animals not domesticated for human use were envisaged as enemies to each other and to humans.

How far did such attitudes depend on the conditions of life? Perceptions of animal behaviour, of course, depend on what one is looking for, though that in turn can be modified by what happens.[2] The behaviour of flocks and herds must have been closely observed by bored or conscientious herdsmen, but people in general may have known very little about the habits of wild animals except when hunting them or keeping them off the crops

---

[1] For the number and variety of animals slaughtered, and for the representation of games and hunts in art, see Toynbee 1973, 21–31; Brown 1992, 180–211.

[2] cf. Beinart 1990 for diversity of attitudes in the late nineteenth and early twentieth centuries.

and the flocks. It is not possible to document the extent of real danger to humans from wild animals, but perhaps – as with the present-day risk from violent crime – it is the perception that matters more than the statistics. Wild animals that were hunted or displayed in the games had to be seen as savage, whereas now a pride of lions devouring their kill have to be seen as ensuring their own survival in balance with their environment. Even when it was difficult to keep up the supply of 'beasts' for the shows, there was no awareness that the beasts were themselves endangered species.

The struggle to provide food was not a question of perceptions, nor was it a refinement of taste to prefer a cultivated to a natural landscape (Wallace-Hadrill 1968, 90–2). Human impact on the land could be increased by the use of draught animals, and sometimes by the use of wind- or water-power for irrigation, transport, or grinding grain, but most agricultural tools were powered by human muscles. Large-scale and permanent environmental destruction, even by invading armies, was correspondingly difficult to achieve. But without constant maintenance land went out of cultivation, scrubland crept back, irrigation channels were choked up, olives returned to the wild, and people starved in famines. Legislation in the later empire sought to keep people on the land, not to keep them off it. Human greed for food or territory was obviously bad, but it is no wonder that human effort was seen not as polluting the earth, but as making it fruitful and sustaining it.

Bibliography

Armstrong, A. H. (1970), 'Plotinus', in Armstrong (ed.), chs 12–16 (pp. 195–268).

—— (ed. 1970), *The Cambridge History of Later Greek and Early Medieval Philosophy* (corrected reprint of 1967 edn; Cambridge).

Beagon, M. (1992), *Roman Nature: The Thought of Pliny the Elder* (Oxford).

Beinart, W. (1990), 'Empire, hunting and ecological change in southern and central Africa', *Past and Present*, 128: 162–86.

Blumenthal, H. J., and Clark, E. G. (eds 1993), *The Divine Iamblichus* (London).

Brown, S. (1992), 'Death as decoration: scenes from the arena in Roman domestic mosaics', in Richlin (ed.), 180–211.

Chadwick, H. (1947), 'Origen, Celsus and the Stoa', *Journal of Theological Studies*, 48: 34–49.

Clark, E. A. (1986), *Ascetic Piety and Women's Faith* (Lewiston, NY).

Clark, G. (1989), *Iamblichus: On the Pythagorean Life* (Translated Texts for Historians, 8; Liverpool).

—— (forthcoming), 'The Fathers and the animals: the rule of reason?', in A. Linzey (ed.) *Animals on the Agenda*.

Clark, S. R. L. (1977; 2nd edn 1983), *The Moral Status of Animals* (Oxford).

Detienne, M. (1977), *The Gardens of Adonis: Spices in Greek Mythology* (Atlantic Highlands, NJ).

Dillon, J. (1987), 'Iamblichus of Chalcis', *Aufstieg und Niedergang der römischen Welt*, ii. 36 (2), pp. 862–909.

—— and Herschbell, J. (1991), *Iamblichus: On the Pythagorean Way of Life* (Texts and Translations, 29: Graeco-Roman Religion Series, 11; Atlanta, Ga.).

Dodds, E. R. (1965), *Pagan and Christian in an Age of Anxiety* (Cambridge).

Dombrowski, D. A. (1984), *The Philosophy of Vegetarianism* (Amherst, Mass.).

Elliott, A. (1987), *Roads to Paradise: Reading the Lives of the Early Saints* (Hanover, NH).

Faraone, C. A., and Obbink, D. (eds 1991), *Magika Hiera: Ancient Greek Magic and Religion* (Oxford).

Fowden, G. (1986), *The Egyptian Hermes: A Historical Approach to the Late Pagan Mind* (Cambridge).

French, R. (1994), *Ancient Natural History: Histories of Nature* (London).

Lloyd, A. (1970), 'Introduction to later neoplatonism', in Armstrong (ed.), 272–82.

MacMullen, R. (1989), 'The preacher's audience (AD 350–400)', *Journal of Theological Studies*, 40: 503–11.

Renehan, R. (1981), 'The Greek anthropocentric view of man', *Harvard Studies in Classical Philology*, 85: 239–59.

Richlin, A. (ed. 1992), *Pornography and Representation in Greece and Rome* (Oxford).

Riddle, J. (1992), *Contraception and Abortion from the Ancient World to the Renaissance* (Cambridge, Mass.).

Rousselle, A. (1988), *Porneia: On Desire and the Body in Antiquity* (Oxford).

Sambursky, S. (1962), *The Physical World of Late Antiquity* (London).

Scarborough, J. (1991), 'The pharmacology of sacred plants, herbs and roots', in Faraone and Obbink (eds), 138–74.

Shaw, G. (1985), 'Theurgy: rituals of unification in the neoplatonism of Iamblichus', *Traditio*, 41: 1–28.

—— (1993), 'The geometry of grace: a Pythagorean approach to theurgy', in Blumenthal and Clark (eds), 116–37.

Sorabji, R. K. (1983), *Time, Creation and the Continuum* (London).

—— (1988), *Matter, Space and Motion* (London).

—— (1993), *Animal Minds and Human Morals* (London).

Thomas, K. (1983), *Man and the Natural World: Changing Attitudes in England 1500–1800* (London).

Toynbee, J. M. C. (1973), *Animals in Roman Life and Art* (London).

Trombley, F. R. (1993), *Hellenic Religion and Christianization c.370–529*, i–ii (Leiden).

Wallace-Hadrill, D. S. (1968), *The Greek Patristic View of Nature* (Manchester).

Indexes

Compiled by Graham Shipley

1 GENERAL INDEX

Modern scholars are not listed. Ancient authors are listed mainly in
Index 2.
'Pliny' without qualification denotes Pliny the Elder.
LR = late Roman.

2   INDEX OF ANCIENT AUTHORS

References to books, chapters, sections, or lines are in parentheses; page
numbers of this volume are outside parentheses. Abbreviations, if used,
are as specified at the front of the volume. In some entries, **bold** numerals
indicate books or individual orations. An asterisk (*) indicates a quota-
tion, usually an extended extract.

3 INDEX OF INSCRIPTIONS AND PAPYRI